THE FATHERS OF THE CHURCH

MEDIAEVAL CONTINUATION

VOLUME 20

THE FATHERS OF THE CHURCH

MEDIAEVAL CONTINUATION

ST. ALBERT THE GREAT

ON RESURRECTION

Translated by

IRVEN M. RESNICK

and

FRANKLIN T. HARKINS

THE CATHOLIC UNIVERSITY OF AMERICA PRESS
Washington, D.C.

Printed in the United States of America

The paper used in this publication meets the minimum requirements of the American National Standards for Information Science—Permanence of Paper for Printed Library Materials, ANSI Z39.48 - 1984.
∞

Library of Congress Cataloging-in-Publication Data
is available from the Library of Congress.
ISBN 978-0-8132-3307-9

CONTENTS

ABBREVIATIONS

General Abbreviations

CCCA	Corpus Commentariorum Averrois in Aristotelem. Versionum Latinarum.
CCSL	Corpus Christianorum Series Latina
ch.	chapter
col(s).	column(s)
CSEL	Corpus Scriptorum Ecclesiasticorum Latinorum
Ep.	*Epistula*
FOTC	The Fathers of the Church
FOTC MC	The Fathers of the Church, Mediaeval Continuation
Glossa ord.	*Glossa ordinaria (Biblia Latina cum Glossa ordinaria: Facsimile Reprint of the Editio Princeps Adolph Rusch of Strassburg 1480/81)*
Hom.	*homilia*
l(l).	line(s)
LCL	Loeb Classical Library
PG	Patrologia Cursus Completus. Series Graeca. Ed. Migne, 1857–66
PL	Patrologia Cursus Completus. Series Latina. Ed. Migne, 1844–1864
vol(s).	volume(s)
Vulg.	Vulgate

Abbreviations for Authors and Texts

Alb.	Albertus Magnus
Anal. Prior.	*Analytica priora* (ed. Borgnet, vol. 1: 459–809)
De anima	*De anima* (ed. Colon. 7/1: 1–284)
De animal.	*De animalibus* (reference by book, tractate, chapter, and number; Stadler, 1916–20)

De bono	*De bono* (ed. Colon. 28: 1–329)
De caelo et mundo	*De caelo et mundo* (ed. Colon. 5/1: 1–341)
De causis et proc.	*De causis et processu universitatis a prima causa* (ed. Colon. 17/2: 1–348)
De causis propr. elem.	*De causis proprietatum elementorum* (ed. Colon. 5/2: 49–106)
De gen. et corr.	*De generatione et corruptione* (ed. Colon. 5/2: 109–219)
De IV coaequ.	*De IV coaequaevis* (ed. Borgnet, vol. 34: 307–789)
De homine	*De homine* (cited according to *quaestiones* in ed. Borgnet 35, and with page numbers to ed. Colon. 27/2)
De Incarn.	*De Incarnatione* (ed. Colon. 26: 171–235)
De mul. forti	*De muliere forti* (ed. Borgnet, vol. 18: 1–242)
De nat. et orig. an.	*De natura et origine animae* (ed. Colon. 12: 1–46)
De nat. loc.	*De natura loci* (ed. Colon. 5/2: 1–282)
De nutrimento et nutr.	*De nutrimento et nutribili* (ed. Colon. 7/2a: 1–18)
De praedic.	*De praedicamentis* (ed. Colon. 1b)
De res.	*De resurrectione* (ed. Colon. 26: 237–419)
De sacrif. missae	*De sacrificio missae=De mysterio missae* (ed. Borgnet, vol. 38: 1–189)
De sacram.	*De sacramentis* (ed. Colon. 26: 1–170)
De sensu et sens.	*De sensu et sensato* (ed. Colon. 7/2a: 19–137)
De somno et vig.	*De somno et vigilia* (ed. Borgnet, vol. 9: 121–212)
De soph. el.	*De sophisticis elenchis* (ed. Borgnet, vol. 2: 525–713)
De spir. et resp.	*De spiritu et respiratione* (ed. Borgnet, vol. 9: 213–255)
De V univ.	*Super Porphyrium De V universalibus* (ed. Colon. 1a)
Metaph.	*Metaphysica* (ed. Colon. 16/1–2)
Meteora	*Meteora* (ed. Colon. 6/1)
Phys.	*Physica* (ed. Colon. 4/1–2)
Quaestio de sens. corp. glor.	*Quaestio de sensibus corporis gloriosi* (ed. Colon. 25/2: 112–25)
Quaest. super de animal.	*Quaestiones de animalibus* (ed. Colon. 12: 77–361)
QDA	*Questions Concerning Aristotle's "On Animals."* Trans. Irven M. Resnick and Kenneth F. Kitchell, Jr.; Fathers of the Church, Mediaeval Continuation 9. Washington, DC: The Catholic University of America Press, 2008

[I–IV] Sent.	*Super [I–IV] librum Sententiarum* (ed. Borgnet, vols. 25–30)
Summa	*Summa theologiae: Summa de mirabili scientia Dei* (ed. Borgnet, vols. 31–33)
Super Dion. De cael. hier.	*Super Dionysium De caelesti hierarchia* (ed. Colon. 36/1: 1–280)
Super Dion. De div. nom.	*Super Dionysium De divinis nominibus* (ed. Colon. 37/1: 1–450)
Super Dion. De eccle. hier.	*Super Dionysium De ecclesiastica hierarchia* (ed. Colon. 36/2: 1–232)
Super Dion. Epist.	*Super Dionysii Epistulas* (ed. Colon. 37/2: 477–554)
Super Is.	*Super Isaiam* (ed. Colon. 19: 1–632)
Super Jn.	*Super Iohannem* (ed. Borgnet, vol. 24)
Super Job	*Commentarii in Job . . . primum ex V codicibus manuscriptis* (ed. Melchior Weiss, 1904)
Super Joel	*Super Ioel, in Super prophetas minores* (ed. Borgnet, vol. 19: 1–654)
Super Luc.	*Super Lucam* (ed. Borgnet, vols. 22–23)
Super Marc.	*Super Marcum* (ed. Borgnet, vol. 21: 339–809)
Super Matth.	*Super Matthaeum* (ed. Colon. 26)
SZ	*Albertus Magnus "On Animals": A Medieval "Summa Zoologica."* Trans. Kenneth F. Kitchell, Jr., and Irven M. Resnick. Rev. ed. 2 vols. Columbus, OH: Ohio State University Press, 2018
Top.	*Topica* (ed. Borgnet, vol. 2: 233–524)
Alex. Hales	Alexander of Hales
Glossa	*Glossa in quatuor libros sententiarum Petri Lombardi* (4 vols.; Quaracchi: Collegium S. Bonaventurae, 1951–57)
Quaest. de resurr.	*Quaestio de resurrectione* (cited in ed. Colon. 26 from Cod. Paris *Bibliothèque Nationale*, MS 16406)
Summa	*Summa Theologica sive Summa Universae Theologiae* (4 vols.; Quaracchi: Collegium S. Bonaventurae, 1924–48)
Alfred of Sareshel	Alfred of Sareshel
De motu cordis	
Alpetragius	Alpetragius (Al-Bitruji)
De mot. cael.	*De motibus caelorum*

Ambrose	Ambrose of Milan
De virginit.	*De virginitate*
Anselm	Anselm of Canterbury
Cur deus homo	*Cur deus homo*
De casu diab.	*De casu diaboli*
De conc. virg.	*De conceptu virginali et de originali peccati*
De veritate	*De veritate*
Ar.	Aristotle (Line references are to the appropriate Loeb editions whenever possible; note, however, that these are frequently inaccurate and that correlation to the actual Greek text will often be approximate.)
Cat.	*Categoriae*
De anima	*De anima*
De caelo et mundo	*De caelo*
De gen. animal.	*De generatione animalium*
De gen. et. corr.	*De generatione et corruptione*
De hist. animal.	*De historia animalium*
De insomniis	*De insomniis*
De sensu et sens.	*De sensu et sensato*
De somno et vig.	*De somno et vigilia*
Eth. Nic.	*Nicomachean Ethics*
Metaph.	*Metaphysics*
Phys.	*Physics*
Top.	*Topica*
Aug.	Augustine of Hippo
Conf.	*Confessionum libri tredecim*
Contra Faustum Manich.	*Contra Faustum Manichaeum*
Contra serm. Arianorum	*Contra sermonem Arianorum*
De agone Christ.	*De agone Christiano*
De bono conjugali	*De bono conjugali liber unus*
De civ. Dei	*De civitate Dei*
De div. quaest.	*De diversis quaestionibus LXXXIII*
De doc. Christ.	*De doctrina Christiana*
De fide ad Petrum	*De fide ad Petrum* (in fact, by Fulgentius of Ruspe)
De fide et operibus	*De fide et operibus liber unus*

De gen. ad litt.	*De genesi ad litteram libri duodecim*
De lib. arb.	*De libero arbitrio*
De nupt. et conc.	*De nuptiis et concupiscentia*
De praedest.	*De praedestinatione*
De trin.	*De trinitate*
De util. cred.	*De utilitate credendi*
Enarr. in Ps.	*Enarrationes in Psalmos*
Enchir.	*Enchiridion*
Epist.	*Epistulae*
In epist. Pauli Gal.	*Epistolae ad Galatas*
In Joh.	*In Johannis evangelium*
Quaest. Ev.	*Quaestionum Evangeliorum libri duo*
Retract.	*Retractationum libri duo*
Sermo	*Sermo*
Solil.	*Soliloquiorum libri duo*
Averr.	Averroes
Compend. libri Arist. De somno et vig.	*Compendium libri Aristotelis De somno et vigilia*
In Porph.	*In Porphyrii Isagogen*
Metaph.	*Metaphysics*
Avic.	Avicenna
Liber VI Nat.	*Liber sextus Naturalium*
Metaph.	*Metaphysics*
Suff.	*Sufficientia* (= *Kitab al-Šifā*)
Basil	Basil the Great
Hom. 6 De fide	*Homilia de fide*
In hexaem. Hom.	*Homilia in Hexaemeron*
Super Ps.	*Homiliae super Psalmos*
Bede	The Venerable Bede
In Epist. 2 Petr.	*In secundam epistolam Petri*
In Luc.	*In Lucae evangelium expositio*
In Matth.	*In Matthaei evangelium expositio*
Bern.	Bernard of Clairvaux
De consid.	*De consideratione*
De gratia et lib. arb.	*De gratia et de libero arbitrio*
In Cant. serm.	*Sermones super Cantica Canticorum*

Sermo 3 temp. resurr.	*In tempore resurrectionis*
Sermo 10 de diversis	*Sermones de diversis: Sermo 10*
Bernardus Papiensis	Bernardus Papiensis
Summa decretalium	*Summa ordinaria decretalium Gregorii Papae*
Boethius	Anicius Manlius Severinus Boëthius
De cons. phil.	*De consolatione philosophiae*
In Isag. Porph.	*In Isagogen Porphyrii*
Bonaventure	St. Bonaventure (Giovanni di Fidanza)
Coll. In Ioannem	*Collationes in Ioannem*
Opera	*Opera omnia, edita studio et cura pp. Collegii a S. Bonaventura*
[I–IV] Sent.	*In [I–IV] librum Sententiarum*
Burg.	Burgundio
Chalc.	Calcidius
Comm. in Tim.	*Platonis Timaeus interprete Chalcidio cum eiusdem commentario*
Cicero	Marcus Tullius Cicero
De invent.	*De inventione*
Dion.	Pseudo-Dionysius the Areopagite
De cael. hier.	*De caelestia hierarchia*
De div. nom.	*De divinis nominibus*
De eccle. hier.	*De ecclesiastica hierarchia*
ed. Borgnet	*Albertus Magnus.* Opera omnia, ex editione lugdunensi, religiose castigata, et pro auctoritatibus ad fidem vulgatae versionis accuratiorumque patrologiae textuum revocata, auctaque B. Alberti vita ac Bibliographia suorum operum a PP. Quetif et Echard exaratis etiam revisa et locupletata cura et labore A. Borgnet. 38 vols. Paris: L. Vivès, 1890–1899
ed. Colon.	*Sancti Doctoris Ecclesiae Alberti Magni Ordinis Fratrum Praedicatorum episcopi Opera Omnia, ad fidem codicum manuscriptorum edenda apparatu critico notis prolegomenis indicibus instruenda curavit.* Institutum Alberti Magni Coloniense. Ed. Bernhard Geyer, 37.2 [1978]: ed. Wilhelm Kübel. Monasterii Westfalorum: Aschendorff, 1951–
Evang. Nicod.	*Evangelium Nicodemi pars II*
Gilb. Porr.	Gilbert of Poitiers (Gilbertus Porretanus)
De sex princ.	*Liber sex principiorum*

Greg.	Gregory the Great
Dial.	*Dialogorum libri iv*
Hom. in Ev.	*Homiliarum in Evangelia libri duo*
Moral.	*Moralia in Job*
Greg. IX	Gregory IX, Pope
Decretal.	*Decretales*
Haimo of Auxerre	Haimo of Auxerre
In Epist. Pauli	*Expositio in epistolas Pauli*
In Rom.	*In epistolam ad Romanos*
Hil.	Hilary of Poitiers
De synod.	*De synodis*
Honor. August.	Honorius Augustodunensis
Elucid.	*Elucidarium*
Hugh of St. Cher	Hugh of St. Cher
Comm. in hier. cael.	*Commentarius in hierarchia caelesti*
De dotibus resurgentium	*Quaestio de dotibus resurgentium* (cited in ed. Colon. 26 from Leipzig, Universitätsbibliothek MS 573)
Hugh Ripelin of Strassburg	
Compend. theol. veritatis	*Compendium theologicae veritatis* (cited according to the text found in Alb.'s *Opera*, ed. Borgnet 34)
Isaac	Isaac Israeli
De diff.	*Liber de definicionibus*
Isid.	Isidore of Seville
Sent.	*Sententiae*
Jerome	St. Jerome
Epist.	*Epistulae*
In Is.	*In Isaia propheta*
John Chrysos.	John Chrysostom
Hom 56 *in Matth.*	*Homilia* 56: *In Matthaeum*
Hom. 86 *in Joh.*	*Homilia* 86: *In Johannem*
John Damascene	
De fide orth.	*De fide orthodoxa*
Joh. Sarr.	John Sarrazin of Saint-Denis
Comm. super Dion.	Translation of *De divinis nominibus* of Dionysius (text found in Albert, *Super Dionysium De divinis nominibus*, ed. Colon. 37/1)

De cael. hier.	*De caelesti hierarchia* (text found in Albert, *Super Dionysium De caelesti hierarchia,* ed. Colon. 36/1)
Justinian	Emperor Justinian I
Cod.	*Codex Justinianeus*
Dig.	*Digesta seu Pandectae*
Inst.	*Institutiones Justiniani*
M. Victor.	Marius Victorinus
Explan. in Rhet. M. T. Ciceronis	*Explanationes in Ciceronis Rhetoricam*
Origen	Origen of Alexandria
Hom. super Lev.	*In Leviticum homiliae*
Peter Lombard	Peter Lombard
In epist. Pauli	*Commentaria in Epistolas Pauli*
In Ps.	*In Psalmos*
Sent.	*Sententiarum libri quatuor*
Plato	Plato
Tim.	*Timaeus*
Ps. Aug.	Pseudo-Augustine
De assumpt. b. M. v.	*Liber de assumptione beatae Mariae virginis*
De fide contra Manich.	*De fide contra Manichaeos*
De spir. et anima	*De spiritu et anima*
De vera et falsa paenit.	*De vera et falsa poenitentia*
Sermo	*Sermo*
Ps. Bern.	Pseudo-Bernard of Clairvaux
Medit. piissimae	*Meditationes piissimae de cognitione humanae condicionis*
Ps. Clement	Pseudo-Clement
Recogn.	*Recognitiones*
Ps. Guerricus	Pseudo-Guerric of Saint-Quentin
	Super sententias (cited in ed. Colon. 26 from Vat. Lat. MS 691)
Ps. Jerome	Pseudo-Jerome
Epist. 9 (*ad Paul. et Eust.*)	[Paschasius Radbertus] *Epistola ad Paulam et Eustochium*
De assumptione b. M. v.	*De assumptione beatae Mariae virginis*

Ps. Odo Rigaldi	Pseudo-Odo Rigaldi
	Super sententias (cited in ed. Colon. 26 from Brussels Bibl. Royale MS 1542 [11614])
Raymund de Pennafort	
Summa	*Summa de casibus*
Rich. Fishacre	Richard Fishacre
	Super sententias (cited in ed. Colon. 26 from Oxford, Balliol College MS 57)
Richard of St. Victor	Richard of St. Victor
De judiciaria potestate	*De judiciaria potestate in finali et universali judicio*
De potest. lig. et solv.	*De potestate ligandi et solvendi*
Tancredus	Tancredus de Bologna
Thomas Aquinas	St. Thomas Aquinas
ScG	*Summa contra Gentiles*
Sent.	*In libros sententiarum*
ST	*Summa theologiae*
Wm. of Auxerre	William of Auxerre
Summa aurea	Magistri Guillelmi Altissiodorensis *Summa Aurea.* Ed. Jean Ribaillier, 5 volumes (Paris: Editions du Centre National de la Recherche Scientifique / Grottaferrata (Rome): Editiones Collegii S. Bonaventurae ad Claras Aquas, 1980–87)

Abbreviations for Biblical Books

Old Testament

Genesis	Gn	2 Kings	2 Kgs
Exodus	Ex	1 Chronicles	1 Chr
Leviticus	Lv	2 Chronicles	2 Chr
Numbers	Nm	Ezra	Ezr
Deuteronomy	Dt	Nehemiah	Neh
Joshua	Jos	Tobit	Tb
Judges	Jgs	Judith	Jdt
Ruth	Ru	Esther	Est
1 Samuel	1 Sm	1 Maccabees	1 Mc
2 Samuel	2 Sm	2 Maccabees	2 Mc
1 Kings	1 Kgs	Job	Jb

Psalm(s)	Ps(s)	Hosea	Hos
Proverbs	Prv	Joel	Jl
Ecclesiastes	Eccl	Amos	Am
Song of Songs	Song	Obadiah	Ob
Wisdom	Wis	Jonah	Jon
Sirach	Sir	Micah	Mi
Isaiah	Is	Nahum	Na
Jeremiah	Jer	Habakkuk	Hab
Lamentations	Lam	Zephaniah	Zep
Baruch	Bar	Haggai	Hg
Ezekiel	Ezek	Zechariah	Zec
Daniel	Dn	Malachi	Mal

New Testament

Matthew	Mt	1 Timothy	1 Tm
Mark	Mk	2 Timothy	2 Tm
Luke	Lk	Titus	Ti
John	Jn	Philemon	Phlm
Acts of the Apostles	Acts	Hebrews	Heb
Romans	Rom	James	Jas
1 Corinthians	1 Cor	1 Peter	1 Pt
2 Corinthians	2 Cor	2 Peter	2 Pt
Galatians	Gal	1 John	1 Jn
Ephesians	Eph	2 John	2 Jn
Philippians	Phil	3 John	3 Jn
Colossians	Col	Jude	Jude
1 Thessalonians	1 Thes	Revelation	Rv
2 Thessalonians	2 Thes		

SELECT BIBLIOGRAPHY

Primary Sources

Works of Albert the Great

Albertus Magnus De Animalibus Libri XXVI. Edited by Hermann Stadler. Beiträge zur Geschichte der Philosophie des Mittelalters, 15 and 16. Münster: Aschendorfsche Verlagsbuchhandlung, 1916–20.

Albertus Magnus "On Animals": A Medieval "Summa Zoologica." Translated by Kenneth F. Kitchell, Jr., and Irven M. Resnick. Rev. ed. 2 vols. Columbus, OH: Ohio State University Press, 2018.

B. Alberti Magni O. Praed. Commentarii in Iob: Additamentum ad Opera Omnia B. Alberti. Edited by Melchior Weiss. Freiburg: Herder, 1904.

Compilatio de novo spiritu. In *Documenta ecclesiastica Christianae Perfectionis. Studium Spectantia,* pp. 115–25. Edited by Joseph de Guibert. Rome: Apud aedes Universitatis Gregorianae, 1931.

Opera Omnia. Edited by A. Borgnet. 38 vols. Paris: L. Vivès, 1890–99.

Opera Omnia. Edited by Bernhard Geyer (after t. 37/2 [1978]: edited by Wilhelm Kübel). Monasterii Westfalorum: Aschendorff, 1951–

Questions concerning Aristotle's "On Animals." Translated by Irven M. Resnick and Kenneth F. Kitchell, Jr. FOTC MC 9. Washington, DC: The Catholic University of America Press, 2011.

Aristotle

The Categories, On Interpretation, Prior Analytics. Translated by Harold P. Cooke and Hugh Tredennick. LCL 325. London: William Heinemann Ltd, 1973.

Generation of Animals. Translated by A. L. Peck. LCL 366. Cambridge, MA: Harvard University Press, 1942.

The Metaphysics. Translated by John H. McMahon. Buffalo, NY: Prometheus Books, 1991.

Minor Works: On Colours, On Things Heard, Physiognomics, On Plants, On Marvellous Things Heard, Mechanical Problems, On Indivisible Lines, Situations and Names of Winds, On Melissus, Xenophanes, and *Gorgias.* Translated by W. S. Hett. LCL 307. Cambridge, MA: Harvard University Press, 1963.

Nicomachean Ethics. Translated by Terence Irwin, second edition. Indianapolis: Hackett Publishing Company, Inc., 1999.

On Sleep and Dreams. Translated by David Gallop. Warminster, UK: Aris & Phillips Ltd, 1996.

On Sophistical Refutations, On Coming-to-be and Passing-away, On the Cosmos. Translated by E. S. Forster and D. J. Furley. LCL 400. Cambridge, MA: Harvard University Press, 1955.

On the Heavens. Translated by W. K. C. Guthrie. LCL 338. Cambridge, MA: Harvard University Press, 1986.

Physics. Translated by C. D. C. Reeve. Indianapolis: Hackett Publishing Company, Inc., 2018.

Politics. Translated by Ernest Barker and revised by R. F. Stalley. Oxford: Oxford University Press, 1995.

Posterior Analytics, Topica. Edited and translated by Hugh Tredennick and E. S. Forster. LCL 391. Cambridge, MA: Harvard University Press, 1960.

The Works of Aristotle. Translated under the editorship of W. D. Ross. 12 vols. Oxford: Clarendon Press, 1908–1931.

Other Authors and Works

Alfred of Sareshel. *Schrift de motu cordis.* Edited by Clemens Baeumker. Beiträge zur Geschichte der Philosophie des Mittelalters. Münster: Aschendorff, 1923.

Alpetragius (Al-Bitruji). *De motibus caelorum.* Edited by Francis J. Carmody. Berkeley: University of California Press, 1952.

Averroes. *Compendium libri Aristotelis De somno et vigilia.* In *Averrois Cordubensis Compendia Librorum Aristotelis qui Parva naturalia vocantur.* Edited by Emily Ledyard Schields. Cambridge, MA: The Medieval Academy of America, 1949.

———. *Commentum magnum super libro De caelo et mundo Aristotelis.* Latin translation by Michael Scot. Edited by F. J. Carmody and R. Arnzen. 2 vols. Leuven: Peeters, 2003.

———. *In Porphyrii Isagogen.* In *Aristotelis opera cum Averrois commentariis,* vol. 1/1. 12 vols.; Venice, Apud Junctas, 1562–1574; reprint, Frankfurt am Main: Minerva, 1962.

Avicenna. *De congelatione et conglutinatione lapidum: Being sections of the Kitâb al-shifâ'. The Latin and Arabic texts edited with an English translation of the latter and with critical notes.* Edited with notes by E. J. Holmyard and D. C. Mandeville. Paris: Geuthner, 1927.

———. *Liber de philosophia prima sive scientia divina.* Édition critique de la traduction latine médiévale. Edited by Gérard Verbeke and Simone van Riet. 3 vols. Louvain, Leiden: Peeters, Brill, 1977–83.

Bernardus Papiensis. *Summa ordinaria decretalium Gregorii Papae.* Edited by E. A. Laspeyres. Regensburg: G. J. Manz, 1860; reprint, Graz: Akademische Druck-u. Verlagsanstalt, 1956.

Evangelium Nicodemi pars II. Edited by Constantinus de Tischendorf. *Evangelia apocrypha,* 2nd rev. ed. Leipzig: H. Mendelssohn, 1876.

Honorius Augustodunensis. *L'Elucidarium et les Lucidaires*. Edited by Yves Lefèvre. Paris: E. de. Boccard, 1954.

Isaac Israeli. *Liber de definicionibus*. Edited by J. T. Muckle. In *Archives d'histoire doctrinale et litteraire du moyen age* 12 (1937–38): 299–340.

John Damascene. *De fide orthodoxa, versions of Burgundio and Cerbanus*. Edited by Eligius M. Buytaert. St. Bonaventure, NY: The Franciscan Institute, 1955.

Platonis Timaeus interprete Chalcidio cum eiusdem commentario. Edited by Johann Wrobel. Leipzig: B. G. Teubner, 1876.

Raymund de Pennafort. *Summa de paenitentia*. Edited by Xaverio Ochoa and Aloisio Diez. Universa Bibliotheca Iuris. Rome: Commentarium pro religiosis, 1976.

Richard Fishacre. *In [I–IV] librum Sententiarum*. Edited by R. James Long, Alexander Eichinger, Hans Kraml, and Gerhard Leibold. Munich: Bayerische Akademie der Wissenschaften. 2003–2011.

Tancredus de Bologna. *Summa de matrimonio*. Edited by Agathon Wunderlich. Göttingen: Vandenhocke et Ruprecht, 1841.

Secondary Sources

Aertsen, Jan A. "Truth as Transcendental in Thomas Aquinas." *Topoi* 11 (1992): 159–71.

Anzulewicz, Henryk. "The Systematic Theology of Albert the Great." In *A Companion to Albert the Great. Theology, Philosophy, and the Sciences*, edited by Irven M. Resnick, 15–67. Leiden: Brill, 2012.

Bazàn, Bernardo C. "Les questions disputées principalement dans les facultés de théologie." In *Les questions disputées et les questions quodlibétiques dans les facultés de théologie, de droit et de médecine*, edited by Bernardo C. Bazàn, John W. Wipple, Gérard Fransen, and Danielle Jacquart, 13–149. Turnhout: Brepols, 1985.

Beiting, Christopher. "The Nature and Structure of Limbo in the Works of Albertus Magnus." *New Blackfriars* 85 (2004): 492–509.

Canty, Aaron. *Light and Glory: The Transfiguration of Christ in Early Franciscan and Dominican Theology*. Washington, DC: The Catholic University of America Press, 2011.

Cunningham, Stanley B. *Reclaiming Moral Agency: The Moral Philosophy of Albert the Great*. Washington, DC: The Catholic University of America Press, 2008.

Elliott, Dyan. "The Physiology of Rapture and Female Spirituality." In *Medieval Theology and the Natural Body*, edited by Peter Biller and A. J. Minnis, 141–73. Woodbridge, Suffolk: York Medieval Press, 1997.

Fauser, Winfried. *Die Werke des Albertus Magnus in ihrer handschriftlichen Überlieferung, Tiel I: Die echten Werke*. Münster: Aschendorff, 1982.

Führer, Markus. "Albert the Great and Mystical Epistemology." In *A Companion to Albert the Great. Theology, Philosophy, and the Sciences*, edited by Irven M. Resnick, 137–61. Leiden: Brill, 2013.

Gaine, Simon Francis. *Did the Saviour See the Father? Christ, Salvation and the Vision of God*. London: Bloomsbury T&T Clark, 2015.

Gavrilyuk, Paul L., and Sarah Coakley, eds. *The Spiritual Senses: Perceiving God in Western Christianity*. Cambridge: Cambridge University Press, 2014.

Goering, Joseph. "The *De Dotibus* of Robert Grosseteste." *Mediaeval Studies* 44 (1982): 83–109.

Greshake, Gisbert. *Resurrectio mortuorum. Zum theologischen Verständnis der leiblichen Auferstehung.* Darmstadt: Wissenschaftliche Buchgesellschaft, 1986.

Groebner, Valentin. "Complexio/Complexion: Categorizing Individual Natures, 1250–1600." In *The Moral Authority of Nature,* edited by Lorraine Daston and Fernando Vidal, 361–83. Chicago: University of Chicago Press, 2004.

Hall, Thomas S. "Life, Death, and Radical Moisture." *Clio Medica* 6 (1971): 3–23.

Harkins, Franklin T. "Angelic Corporeality: A Case of Metaphysical Manuduction in Albertus Magnus and Thomas Aquinas." In *The Discovery of Being & Thomas Aquinas: Philosophical and Theological Perspectives,* edited by Christopher M. Cullen, SJ, and Franklin T. Harkins, 217–31. Washington, DC: The Catholic University of America Press, 2019.

———. "From the Fiery Heaven to the Fire of Hell: Job in the *Sentences* Commentaries of Albert the Great, Bonaventure, and Thomas Aquinas." In *A Companion to Job in the Middle Ages,* edited by Franklin T. Harkins and Aaron Canty, 129–60. Leiden: Brill, 2017.

———. "Scripture and the Development of Scholastic Theology: Robert of Melun's *Questiones de divina pagina* in Context." In *A Companion to the Abbey of Saint Victor in Paris,* edited by Hugh Feiss and Juliet Mousseau, 244–73. Leiden: Brill, 2018.

Hasselhoff, Görge K. "Maimonides in the Latin Middle Ages: An Introductory Survey." *Jewish Studies Quarterly* 9.1 (2002): 1–20.

Henquinet, F. M. "Les questions inédites d'Alexandre de Halès sur les fins dernières." *Recherches de théologie ancienne et médiévale* 10 (1938): 56–78.

Hergan, Jeffrey P. *St. Albert the Great's Theory of the Beatific Vision.* New York: Peter Lang, 2002.

Hoogland, Mark-Robin. *God, Passion and Power: Thomas Aquinas on Christ Crucified and the Almightiness of God.* Leuven: Peeters, 2003.

Hoye, William J. "Heil und Auferstehung nach Albert dem Grossen." In *Albert der Grosse: Seine Zeit, sein Werk, seine Wirkung. Papers from the 22nd Kölner Mediävistentagung held at the Thomas-Institut, University of Cologne, 3–6 September 1980,* edited by Albert Zimmermann and Gudrun Vuillemin-Diem, 61–77. Berlin: Walter de Gruyter, 1981.

Kuryluk, Ewa. *Veronica and Her Cloth: History, Symbolism, and Structure of a 'True' Image.* Oxford: Blackwell, 1991.

Leget, Carlo. *Living with God: Thomas Aquinas on the Relation between Life on Earth and 'Life' after Death.* Leuven: Peeters, 1997.

McVaugh, Michael. "The 'Humidum Radicale' in Thirteenth-Century Medicine." *Traditio* 30 (1974): 259–83.

Möhle, Hannes, Henryk Anzulewicz, Maria Burger, et al., eds. *Albertus Mag-*

nus und sein System der Wissenschaften. Schlüsseltexte in Übersetzung. Lateinisch-Deutsch. Münster: Aschendorff, 2011.

Mowbray, Donald. "A Community of Sufferers and the Authority of Masters: The Development of the Idea of Limbo by Masters of Theology at the University of Paris (c. 1230–c. 1300)." In *Authority and Community in the Middle Ages,* edited by Donald Mowbray et al., 43–68. Stroud: Sutton, 1999.

———. *Pain and Suffering in Medieval Theology: Academic Debates at the University of Paris in the Thirteenth Century*. Woodbridge: Boydell Press, 2009.

Ohlmeyer, Albert. "Zwei neue Teile der *Summa de creaturis* Alberts des Grossen." *Recherches de théologie ancienne et médiévale* 4 (1932): 392–400.

Reynolds, Philip Lyndon. *Food and the Body. Some Peculiar Questions in High Medieval Theology*. Leiden: Brill, 1999.

Rigo, Caterina. "Zur Redaktionsfrage der Frühschriften des Albertus Magnus." In *Albertus Magnus und die Anfänge der Aristoteles-Rezeption im lateinischen Mittelalter/Albertus Magnus and the Beginnings of the Medieval Reception of Aristotle in the Latin West,* edited by Ludger Honnefelder, Rega Wood, Mechthild Dreyer, and Marc-Aeilko Aris, 325–74. Münster: Aschendorff, 2005.

Rodolfi, Anna. "Présence de Dieu et Lieu des Anges chez Albert le Grand." In *Lieu, Espace, Mouvement: Physique, Métaphysique et Cosmologie (XIIe–XVIe Siècles),* edited by Tiziana Suarez-Nani, Olivier Ribordy, Antonio Petagine, 79–92. Barcelona and Rome: Fédération Internationale des Instituts d'Études Médiévales, 2017.

Schwartz, Yossef. "Persecution and the Art of Translation: Some New Evidence Concerning the Latin Translation of Maimonides' *Guide of the Perplexed*." *Yod. Revue des études hébraïques et juives* 22 (2019): 49–77.

Senner, Walter, OP. *Alberts des Großen Verständnis von Theologie und Philosophie.* Münster: Aschendorff, 2009.

Stump, Eleonore. "Resurrection, Reassembly, and Reconstitution: Aquinas on the Soul." In *Die menschliche Seele. Brachen wir den Dualismus?* edited by Bruno Niederbacher and Edmund Runggaldier, 153–74. Frankfurt: Ontos, 2006.

Walker Bynum, Caroline. "Material Continuity, Personal Survival, and the Resurrection of the Body: A Scholastic Discussion in its Medieval and Modern Contexts." *History of Religions* 30/1 (1990): 51–85.

———. *Fragmentation and Redemption: Essays on Gender and the Human Body in Medieval Religion*. New York: Zone Books, 1992.

———. *The Resurrection of the Body in Western Christianity, 200–1336*. New York: Columbia University Press, 1995.

Weber, Hermann J. *Die Lehre von der Auferstehung der Toten in den Haupttraktaten der scholastischen Theologie. Von Alexander von Hales zu Duns Skotus.* Freiburg: Herder, 1973.

Weijers, Olga. "The various kinds of disputation in the faculties of arts, theology and law." In *Disputatio 1200–1800. Form, Funktion und Wirkung eines Leitmediums universitärer Wissenskultur,* edited by Marion Gindhardt and Ursula Kundert, 21–31. Berlin: De Gruyter, 2010.

———. *La 'disputatio' à la Faculté des arts de Paris (1200–1350 environ): Esquisse d'une typologie.* Turnhout: Brepols, 1995.

Wicki, Nikolaus. *Die Lehre von der himmlischen Seligkeit in der mittelalterlichen Scholastik von Petrus Lombardus bis Thomas von Aquin.* Freiburg: Universitätsverlag, 1954.

Wippel, John. *Metaphysical Themes in St. Thomas Aquinas II.* Washington, DC: The Catholic University of America Press, 2007.

INTRODUCTION

INTRODUCTION

I. *On Resurrection* in Scholastic Context

The ultimate goal of Christian faith and life is the resurrection of the body and the beatific vision of God himself, wherein the blessed will see God as he is.[1] Theological reflection on this supreme mystery of faith can be traced back to 1 Cor 15, which may provide the earliest Christian references to bodily resurrection. Here the Apostle Paul assures the Corinthians that although the human body "is sown an animal body, it will rise a spiritual body," and "the dead will rise again incorruptible, and we will be changed."[2] Paul himself was well aware of the intellectual difficulties posed by the doctrine of bodily resurrection. Indeed, already in 1 Cor 15 he anticipated several basic lines of questioning that would become commonplace among theologians in subsequent centuries: "But someone will say, 'How do the dead rise again?' or 'With what kind of body will they come?'"[3] To be sure, how should one distinguish a natural or animal body from a spiritual body? If a spiritual body is bereft of all the properties and characteristics of matter, moreover, how can a spiritual body preserve personal identity and individuality? How can a body become incorruptible? Where will such a resurrected body be located? And what will be the precise nature of its vision of God?

The efforts of medieval theologians to answer such questions led to troubling philosophical paradoxes following from the conviction that the resurrected or spiritual body will be an "impassible body" or a body constituted from "incorruptible

1. See 1 Jn 3.2.

2. 1 Cor 15.44; 1 Cor 15.52.

3. 1 Cor 15.35.

matter." As Caroline Walker Bynum has shown in her impressive study *The Resurrection of the Body in Western Christianity, 200–1336,* by the thirteenth century the tension produced by such paradoxes demanded increased attention both from orthodox theologians and from Church councils.[4] Thus the Fourth Lateran Council (1215) required all to assent to the proposition that "all will rise with their own individual bodies, that is, the bodies which they now wear."[5] Heated debates at the University of Paris into the 1240s led William of Auvergne, Bishop of Paris, and Odo of Châteauroux, the university chancellor, officially to condemn ten errors on 13 January 1241 (which condemnation was reissued in 1244), including the teaching that the blessed in the resurrected body will not see the divine essence.[6] Similarly, one of the thirteen propositions condemned in 1270 by Parisian bishop Étienne Tempier and a group of conservative theologians espoused the view that God cannot grant immortality or incorruption to a corruptible body; another taught that after death the separated soul cannot suffer from corporeal fire—a view to which Albert the Great responded directly in his *De quindecim problematibus.*[7] In the early 1270s, Parisian theologians defended positions contrary to such condemned propositions by having recourse to orthodox teaching on the resurrection. By 1277, the list of propositions condemned at Paris had grown to 219, and some of these also concerned the resurrection specifically, such as the following: that the resurrected body does not return as numerically one and the same;[8]

4. Caroline Walker Bynum, *The Resurrection of the Body in Western Christianity, 200–1336* (New York: Columbia University Press, 1995), 229–30.

5. "omnes cum suis propriis corporibus resurgent quae nunc gestant …" *Conciliorum Oecumenicorum Decreta,* canon 1, ed. J. Alberigo, J. A. Dossetti, P. P. Joannou, C. Leonardi, P. Prodi, with H. Jedin (Bologna: Istituto per la scienza religiose, 1973), 230–71 (230).

6. See *Chartularium Universitatis Parisiensis,* ed. Heinrich Denifle and Emile Chatelain (Paris: Delalain, 1889), 1:128, p. 170. For a discussion of the various theologians caught up in the Parisian controversy, and Albert's role, see esp. Jeffrey P. Hergan, *St. Albert the Great's Theory of the Beatific Vision* (New York: Peter Lang, 2002).

7. Alb., *De quindecim problematibus,* art. 8 (ed. Colon. 17/1, p. 40, 37ff.). Cf. Alb., *Problemata determinata* q. 27 (ed. Colon. 17/1, p. 58, 27–39).

8. "Quod non contingit corpus corruptum redire idem numero, nec idem

that philosophy ought not concede the resurrection because it cannot be proved by reason; and that God cannot grant everlasting existence to a mutable, corruptible body.

Whereas *On Resurrection* responds to a number of difficult and philosophically sophisticated questions concerning this traditional Christian doctrine, Albert was also aware of heretical or sectarian communities in his own region that cast doubt on resurrection. Albert composed an academic work entitled *Compilatio de novo spiritu,* perhaps written while he was still Bishop of Regensburg (1260–1262), which evaluates and condemns more than one hundred heretical propositions encountered by Dominican inquisitors examining unconventional Christian communities in the Swabian Ries. These communities, which Albert identifies generically as "Brothers of the Free Spirit," were often led by female religious or mystics who promoted a more egalitarian popular spirituality and challenged the theology and authority of the established Church. Pope Boniface VIII condemned them for their heresy and "madness" in the bull *Saepe Sanctam Ecclesiam* from the year 1296. Among the propositions that Albert's *Compilatio* attributes to them are: (1) that Christ was not resurrected; and (2) that there is no future resurrection. These he condemns as "Manichaean" errors.[9]

While earlier theologians may have been satisfied with suggestive metaphors in defense of their understanding of the resurrected body, by the thirteenth century discussions of resurrection had become far more technical—both philosophically and theologically—as Christian thinkers sought to assimilate Aristotelian concepts pertaining to generation and corruption and to the nature of matter and natural bodies. The Aristotelian heritage also demanded consideration of whether the resurrection of the individual's body depends on a supernatural rather than natural cause, because nature only reproduces the

numero resurget." *Chartularium universitatis Parisiensis,* no. 17, ed. Denifle and Chatelain, 1: 544. See also nos. 18 and 25.

9. For the text of his *Compilatio de novo spiritu,* see *Documenta ecclesiastica Christianae perfectionis. Studium Spectantia,* ed. Joseph de Guibert (Rome: Apud aedes Universitatis Gregorianae, 1931), pp. 115–25. For the propositions rejecting the resurrection, see nos. 40 and 48.

species and not the individual. For example, the supplement to Thomas Aquinas's *Summa theologiae* maintains that according to *nature* a body will dissolve to dust. It contains no seminal reason or virtue that directs it to return or resurrect, unlike a plant seed, which contains a power to germinate and to become a mature sheaf similar to that one from which the seed came. It is God's divine power and not nature's, therefore, that restores the body, and God's power will resurrect it as identical in number and species, but distinguished by new, glorified qualities or attributes, which include impassibility.[10]

At the same time, thirteenth-century scholastics paid increased attention to the essential character or nature of the body, turning often to its (Aristotelian) form to explain its enduring identity or structure. They taught that the form will be fully restored at the resurrection, whereas its matter may reveal certain changes. As a result, the resurrected body will be both identical to and different from the one we have now. For example, in the work translated here, *On Resurrection,* Albert the Great notes that we have teeth only in order to chew our food; he asks, then, whether at the resurrection the body will have teeth, since we will no longer consume food. In the same way, will the resurrected body have genitals or intestines, since the functions they perform now will have become superfluous for a resurrected body?[11] Thus these discussions often became vehicles for philosophical inquiry into the nature of personal identity and its relation to matter and form.[12] They investigated, for instance, the relationship of natural accretions to our material state (by metabolizing food and nutrition) to the essential or enduring character of that body, leading to an exploration of the "truth of the human nature" (*veritas humanae naturae*).[13]

Scholastic theologians not only focused their attention on

10. See Aquinas, *ST* Suppl. q. 76 a. 1, q. 78 a. 3, q. 79 a. 1, and qq. 82–85.

11. See Alb., *De res.* tr. 1, q. 6, art. 10; pp. 73–74 below.

12. See Caroline Walker Bynum, "Material Continuity, Personal Survival, and the Resurrection of the Body: A Scholastic Discussion in its Medieval and Modern Contexts," *History of Religions* 30/1 (1990): 51–85.

13. Cf. Alb., *De res.* tr. 1, q. 6, art. 1–9; see also Philip Lyndon Reynolds, *Food and the Body. Some Peculiar Questions in High Medieval Theology* (Leiden: Brill, 1999).

the nature of the resurrected body and its relationship to our present body. They also sought to understand better the *purposes* of the resurrection itself. What does the resurrected body contribute to our understanding and enjoyment of God in the future? How will the gifts or dowries (*dotes*) conferred on the glorified body affect our sense experience and our intellectual apprehension? What will be the relationship of the resurrected or glorified body to natural laws of physics and motion? Will each resurrected body have its own "place"?[14] Will the resurrected body retain every organ of the natural, material body? Thus, will sexual differentiation be visible in the resurrected body? Will that body retain the differences in size and shape that characterized the body here below? Will it reveal defects in nature—a club foot or blindness or other privations or deformities? Will we recognize in their glorified bodies the people we have known here below? And will each body arise having the same age, or will glorified bodies reveal age-related distinctions?

Many theological masters working in Paris in the thirteenth century, including the Dominicans Albert the Great and Thomas Aquinas and the Franciscan Bonaventure of Bagnoregio, engaged these questions in their teaching and writing. Albert's predecessor in the Dominican chair at Paris, Guerric of Saint-Quentin—who may have been one target of the condemnations of 1241—treated some of these issues in his own quodlibets.[15] Albert, in particular, composed a treatise under the title *De resurrectione, On Resurrection.* This treatise was part of Albert's *Summa Parisiensis,* which purportedly arose out of his public disputations at the University of Paris, where he incepted as master in 1245 and remained until 1248. The constituent

14. On the relationship of heavenly bodies to place—both angels and glorified bodies—see, for example, Anna Rodolfi, "Présence de Dieu et Lieu des Anges chez Albert le Grand," in *Lieu, Espace, Mouvement: Physique, Métaphysique et Cosmologie (XIIe–XVIe Siècles),* ed. Tiziana Suarez-Nani, Olivier Ribordy, Antonio Petagine (Barcelona and Rome: Fédération Internationale des Instituts d'Études Médiévales, 2017), 79–92.

15. See Guerric of Saint-Quentin, *Quaestiones de quolibet,* ed. Walter H. Principe and Jonathan Black (Toronto: Pontifical Institute of Mediaeval Studies, 2002), esp. *quodlibet* 6.

parts of Albert's *Summa Parisiensis* are as follows: (1) *De sacramentis;* (2) *De incarnatione;* (3) *De resurrectione;* (4) *De IV Coaequavis;* (5) *De homine;* and (6) *De bono.*

The original six-part *Summa* envisioned by Albert includes the three treatises published together in volume twenty-six of the Cologne edition of Albert's *opera omnia: De sacramentis, De incarnatione,* and *De resurrectione.* In the first of these, *De sacramentis,* Albert examines the seven sacraments. In the second, *De incarnatione,* he explores the necessity of the Incarnation, the Annunciation and birth of Jesus, the hypostatic union of divine and human natures in Christ, the consequences of that union both for Christ himself and for others, and finally the Passion and death of Christ as the goal of that union. *On Resurrection* consists of four tractates, which treat, in turn, resurrection on the part of the head of the mystical body and its members and of the wicked generally (tr. 1), resurrection on the part of Christ alone (tr. 2), resurrection on the part of the wicked alone (tr. 3), and resurrection on the part of the good alone (tr. 4). We will consider the structure of Albert's work in greater detail below. *De IV coaequavis, De homine,* and *De bono* constitute the three remaining parts of the *Summa* as conceived by Albert. *De IV coaequavis* and *De homine* sometimes circulated independently under the title *Summa de creaturis,* whereas the entire collection of six treatises is better known today as the *Summa Parisiensis.*

It may aptly be said that all six parts of the *Summa Parisiensis,* including *De resurrectione,* were "completed" during the period 1242–1245, while Albert was an advanced theology student at Paris but before he became a licensed master and assumed his Dominican chair.[16] Such an affirmation, however, hardly tells the whole story of when *De resurrectione* and these other works were composed. In fact, we have set "completed" in quotation

16. See "Zeittafel," in *Albertus Magnus und sein System der Wissenschaften. Schlüsseltexte in Übersetzung. Lateinisch-Deutsch,* ed. and trans. Hannes Möhle, Henryk Anzulewicz, Maria Burger, et al. (Münster: Aschendorff, 2011), 28–31, at 28. During the same period, Albert produced his commentary on Books I and III of Peter Lombard's *Sentences;* the commentary on Book II was composed c. 1246, after Albert was licensed and assumed his Dominican chair, and the commentary on Book IV would not be completed until 1249.

marks because, as Caterina Rigo has demonstrated, Albert continued to revise a number of these works after producing an initial redaction. This is surely the case for *De resurrectione,* to which Albert subsequently made important revisions that are identified in MS V (Venezia, Bibl. Marciana class. IV cod. 10 [Z.L. 130]) of the apparatus to the Cologne edition. That Albert continued to revise some of the six treatises that together comprise the *Summa* does not change their relative chronology, but it does make dating individual works somewhat more complicated. Whereas twentieth-century scholarship tended to date these works to the period of Albert's residence in Paris, more recent work has argued instead that Albert composed an initial redaction of the first three treatises—*De sacramentis, De incarnatione,* and *De resurrectione*—while still teaching in Germany (c. 1233–1240/42) and therefore before his arrival at Paris,[17] and that Albert may have completed a final redaction of *De resurrectione* only after he returned to Cologne in the summer of 1248 to establish a Dominican *studium generale.*[18] Thus, although it is correct to say that *On Resurrection* is an early composition begun perhaps even before Albert's arrival at Paris, later revisions were made to its original redaction as late as 1248, well after the Parisian condemnation of 13 January 1241.

II. Structure and Significant Themes

On Resurrection is a systematic theological treatise composed entirely in the form of *quaestiones.* The work is devoted to a single

17. For the earlier dating of these works, see esp. Caterina Rigo, "Zur Redaktionsfrage der Frühschriften des Albertus Magnus," in *Albertus Magnus und die Anfänge der Aristoteles-Rezeption im lateinischen Mittelalter/Albertus Magnus and the Beginnings of the Medieval Reception of Aristotle in the Latin West,* ed. Ludger Honnefelder, Rega Wood, Mechthild Dreyer, and Marc-Aeilko Aris (Münster: Aschendorff, 2005), 325–74. Although Rigo argues that Albert likely composed an early redaction of *De resurrectione* between the late 1230s and 1241 (349; 360), Hannes Möhle, Henryk Anzulewicz, Maria Burger, et al. identify *De resurrectione* as having been *completed* between 1242 and 1245. See "Zeittafel," in *Albertus Magnus und sein System der Wissenschaften,* ed. and trans. Möhle, Anzulewicz, Burger, et al., 28–31 (28).

18. See Rigo, "Zur Redaktionsfrage der Frühschriften des Albertus Magnus," 358.

theological topic, though one with many facets and wide-ranging implications in such areas as theological anthropology, Christology, ecclesiology, moral theology, soteriology, and eschatology. *On Resurrection* is divided into four tractates, each consisting of a series of questions arranged according to topic. Albert treats a total of thirty distinct questions. The *quaestio,* as both a pedagogical mode and a literary form, is perhaps the defining feature of medieval scholastic culture.[19] The literary form of the *quaestio,* in the words of Henryk Anzulewicz, "opens with an *utrum*-question that may constitute a thesis, the truth of which ... then need[s] to be proven in the ensuing debate of the *pro* and *contra* arguments, formulated according to the rules of the syllogism."[20] All of Albert's early theological works, in addition to most of his *Sentences* commentary, are composed using the *quaestio* form. Although the topics treated in *On Resurrection* are largely determined by those that Peter Lombard introduces in his *Sentences,* Albert has chosen the particular questions to discuss and in what order, emphasizing some, of course, more than others. The focus of the treatise is clearly eschatological, and Albert demonstrates a particular interest in the beatific vision. With *On Resurrection* Albert contributed to a de-escalation of doctrinal controversy at the University of Paris, to which the condemnation of ten errors promulgated by William of Auvergne and Odo of Châteauroux responded.[21] Here in *De resurrectione* Albert directly addresses some of these condemned errors, including the view that glorified souls will not occupy the empyrean heaven with the angels.[22]

In addition to the condition of glorified souls and bodies in heaven, Albert explores many other interesting and important

19. See Franklin T. Harkins, "Scripture and the Development of Scholastic Theology: Robert of Melun's *Questiones de divina pagina* in Context," in *A Companion to the Abbey of Saint Victor in Paris,* ed. Hugh Feiss and Juliet Mousseau (Leiden: Brill, 2018), 244–73, esp. 244; and Marie-Dominique Chenu, *Nature, Man and Society in the Twelfth Century: Essays on New Theological Perspectives in the Latin West,* ed. and trans. Jerome Taylor and Lester K. Little (Toronto: University of Toronto Press, 1997), 291–92.

20. Henryk Anzulewicz, "The Systematic Theology of Albert the Great," in *A Companion to Albert the Great. Theology, Philosophy, and the Sciences,* ed. Irven M. Resnick (Leiden: Brill, 2012), 15–67, here 29.

21. See *Chartularium Universitatis Parisiensis,* 1:128, p. 170.

22. See *De res.* tr. 2, q. 9, art. 5; pp. 155–57 below.

topics, including the location and punishments of hell, purgatory, and limbo. Significantly, Albert here proves himself a pioneer in the development of the doctrine of limbo, particularly the limbo of infants. Whereas eleventh- and twelfth-century theologians like Anselm of Canterbury and Hugh of St. Victor did not allow for the existence of a middle place between heaven and hell wherein unbaptized children would be punished, Albert appears to have been the first to posit a "limbo of infants" (*limbus puerorum*) as distinct from the "limbo of the holy fathers" (*limbus sanctorum patrum*).[23] Indeed, as Donald Mowbray maintains, "Albert was probably the first master to use the term *limbus* as such and to associate it with unbaptised children."[24] Furthermore, though Mowbray engages the commentary on Book IV of the *Sentences* as the site of Albert's pioneering work in this regard, it is actually here in *On Resurrection*—which, even in its final revisions, antedates the completion of the commentary on *Sentences* IV—that Albert first develops a doctrine of the *limbus puerorum*.[25]

The general structure of *On Resurrection* is as follows:

Tractate 1: On Resurrection on the Part of the Head and Members [of Christ] and the Wicked Generally

- q. 1: Whether there is a future resurrection
- q. 2: What resurrection is
- q. 3: Whether resurrection is natural or miraculous
- q. 4: On the ends (*termini*) of resurrection
- q. 5: On the circumstances surrounding resurrection
- q. 6: On the truth of human nature

23. See Donald Mowbray, *Pain and Suffering in Medieval Theology: Academic Debates at the University of Paris in the Thirteenth Century* (Woodbridge: Boydell Press, 2009), 86–88; and Alb., *De res.* tr. 3, qq. 7–8; pp. 232–38 below.

24. Donald Mowbray, "A Community of Sufferers and the Authority of Masters: The Development of the Idea of Limbo by Masters of Theology at the University of Paris (c. 1230–c. 1300)," in *Authority and Community in the Middle Ages,* ed. Donald Mowbray et al. (Stroud: Sutton, 1999), 43–68, at 48. See also Mowbray, *Pain and Suffering in Medieval Theology,* 86–100, esp. 87. See also Christopher Beiting, "The Nature and Structure of Limbo in the Works of Albertus Magnus," *New Blackfriars* 85 (2004): 492–509.

25. As indicated in Part I above, whereas revisions to *De resurrectione* were made as late as 1248, Albert did not complete his commentary on *Sentences* Book IV until 1249.

Tractate 2: On Resurrection on the Part of the Head Alone

- q. 1: Whether Christ's resurrection is the cause of our resurrection
- q. 2: What causal effect it has on the good and the evil
- q. 3: Whether it is the cause of the resurrection of souls
- q. 4: Why the resurrection of all was not joined to the resurrection of Christ as an effect to a cause
- q. 5: Why the resurrection of souls occurs successively whereas the resurrection of bodies occurs simultaneously
- q. 6: What it is that we all come to in the measure of the age of the fullness of Christ

Concerning Proofs of the Resurrection, or concerning Appearances

- q. 7: Concerning proofs before the Resurrection and before death
- q. 8: Concerning the appearances of Jesus Christ after the Resurrection
- q. 9: On the Ascension
- q. 10: On the return for judgment

Tractate 3: On Resurrection on the Part of the Wicked Alone

- q. 1: On the [bodily] members of the wicked
- q. 2: On the punishments of the wicked in the body
- q. 3: On their punishments in the soul
- q. 4: On the punishments on the part of the conjoined [body and soul]

On the Places of Punishment, where Souls are Afflicted

- q. 5: On hell
- q. 6: On purgatory
- q. 7: On the limbo of infants
- q. 8: On the limbo of the holy fathers
- q. 9: On the places of punishment [treated] all together

Tractate 4: On Resurrection on the Part of the Good Alone

- q. 1: On dowries
- q. 2: On eternal life
- q. 3: On enjoyment in itself
- q. 4: On use
- q. 5: On the spiritual senses

As this outline indicates, Albert moves from a consideration of resurrection in general (tr. 1) to more specific categories of resurrection, namely that of Christ (tr. 2), of the wicked (tr. 3), and of the good (tr. 4). In q. 2 of the opening tractate ("What resurrection is"), Albert draws on John Damascene especially in defining resurrection in general as "the union of a soul and of a body made incorruptible."[26] Such a union of a rational soul and an incorruptible body is, according to Albert, in no way natural to man; rather, it is a supernatural end for the sake of which man exists.[27] In Tractate 2, our Dominican master moves to a treatment of resurrection with respect to the head, Christ himself. Here the focus is on the causality of Christ's resurrection on that of both the evil and the good. Although Albert is clear that not all people will rise to eternal beatitude by the causality of Christ's resurrection, he does affirm that its effect "will exist in all with respect to the attainment of what befits divine justice."[28] Thus, whereas Tractate 2 concerns the *cause* of the general resurrection, the remainder of *De resurrectione* considers the various *effects* of this cause among the wicked (tr. 3) and the good (tr. 4). It is noteworthy that the treatment of Christ's resurrection, constituting Tractate 2, occupies both a pivotal position in and the lion's share of *De resurrectione:* here Albert engages more questions than in any of the other tractates—indeed, fully one-third of all the questions in the treatise—and his treatment is about the same length as that of Tractates 3 and 4 combined.[29]

Toward the end of Tractate 2, and thus at the midpoint of *De resurrectione,* Albert engages three questions that take the reader to the heart of the mystery of resurrection and of faith in it, namely those concerning the proofs or appearances of Christ's rising again. Question 7 asks about proofs before Christ's death and resurrection, particularly the Transfiguration; question 8 inquires into the appearances of Christ after the resurrection;

26. *De res.* tr. 1 q. 2 ad 6; pp. 39–40 below.

27. See *De res.* tr. 1 q. 3 sol.; pp. 42–43 below.

28. *De res.* tr. 2 q. 2; p. 82 below.

29. In the Cologne edition, the Latin text of Tractate 2 fills pp. 257–304, whereas Tractates 3 and 4 occupy pp. 305–54.

and question 9 investigates Christ's Ascension, which Albert understands as "a proof of the glory of those rising again."[30] In Albert's view, the post-resurrection appearances were necessary—according to the necessity of "fittingness"—since Christ's power had been completely hidden under the weakness of the Passion. Thus, the resurrection "would not have been easy to believe unless faith also had been led by the hand [*manuducta fuisset*] by means of the appearances."[31] For both Albert and Thomas Aquinas after him, this notion of manuduction (*manuductio*) describes how human understanding in this life is necessarily "led by the hand," as it were, from sensible effects that are better known to us to supernatural causes that are less known, and indeed less knowable, to us.[32]

Article 6 of q. 8 illustrates well Albert's understanding of both the necessity and the challenges of such epistemological manuduction with respect to the resurrection of the body. Here Albert leads readers through each of the ten post-resurrection appearances of Christ that are recounted at the ends of the Gospels, posing and addressing critical questions concerning each. Three examples should suffice. First, concerning the appearance to Mary Magdalene recounted in Jn 20, Albert asks why she perceived him in the form of a gardener. Our Dominican master responds that although Christ appeared to Mary in his proper form, she failed to recognize him and instead mistook him for a gardener because her reason doubted that Christ could have returned from the dead and because the circumstances of the place led her to believe that the one she saw was a gardener.[33] Second and similarly, on Christ's appearance to the two disciples on the road to Emmaus (Lk 24.13–35), Albert asks, among other questions, why the disciples recognized the Lord in the breaking of the bread rather than in some other sign, and why

30. *De res.* tr. 2 q. 7 pref.; p. 94 below.

31. *De res.* tr. 2 q. 8 a. 1 sol.; p. 110 below.

32. See, e.g., Franklin T. Harkins, "Angelic Corporeality: A Case of Metaphysical Manuduction in Albertus Magnus and Thomas Aquinas," in *The Discovery of Being & Thomas Aquinas: Philosophical and Theological Perspectives,* ed. Christopher M. Cullen, SJ, and Franklin T. Harkins (Washington, DC: The Catholic University of America Press, 2019), 217–31.

33. *De res.* tr. 2 q. 8 a. 6 §1 qu. 3 and ad 3; pp. 130, 131–32 below.

immediately thereafter he vanished from their sight (vv. 30–31). Remarkably, Albert's responses highlight Christ's intention to inculcate faith in the truth of his resurrection among the disciples. Christ had a "particular mode" (*specialis modus*) of breaking the bread, together with a particular blessing, to which his disciples had become accustomed, and so they recognized him in this sacred act more easily.[34] Furthermore, on Albert's reading, Christ suddenly disappeared in order to help his disciples distinguish between faith in resuscitation and faith in resurrection. "For it does not belong to those who have been resuscitated to be made invisible," Albert teaches, "but it does belong to those who rise again."[35] Third and finally, concerning Christ's appearance to the disciples through closed doors when Thomas was not present among them (Jn 20.19–23), Albert asks, *inter alia,* why the Lord entered through closed doors, and why he showed them his hands and side since wounds seem to indicate a deformity in a glorious body. In reply to the first, Albert notes that the spiritual state of a body entering through closed doors reveals the glory of its dowries (*dotes*).[36] The particular dowry of the body that enabled Christ to move through the doors without opening them is subtlety, which Albert treats together with the others—namely luminosity, impassibility, and agility—in tr. 4 q. 1 aa. 13–16. Albert replies to the second of these questions by indicating that the display of Christ's side and hands reveals the identity of nature in the one dying and the one rising again. Furthermore, such wounds neither cause nor indicate a deformity in a glorious body, Albert explains; rather, they attest to a strength that cannot be frustrated by even the worst sufferings and so bear witness to "the glory of the martyr."[37]

III. Sources and Subsequent Influence

De resurrectione is informed and enriched by a wide range of authoritative sources, which can be broadly divided into the

34. *De res.* tr. 2 q. 8 a. 6 §4 qu. 4 and ad 4; pp. 135, 136 below.
35. *De res.* tr. 2 q. 8 a. 6 §4 qu. 5 and ad 5; pp. 135, 136 below.
36. *De res.* tr. 2 q. 8 a. 6 §5 qu. 1 and ad 1; pp. 137, 138 below.
37. *De res.* tr. 2 q. 8 a. 6 §5 qu. 3, ad 1, and ad 3; p. 138 below.

scriptural and theological, on the one hand, and the philosophical, on the other. First, in the course of his investigation Albert turns often both to Sacred Scripture and to earlier Christian theologians. The Gospels and Pauline epistles are particularly determinative for Albert's understanding of resurrection, but certain Old Testament texts also shape his treatment in notable ways. He reads none of these texts, however, apart from the long tradition of Christian commentary, theology, and doctrine accompanying them. The ancient and early-medieval theologians and exegetes on whom Albert draws most often are—in order of frequency of citation—Augustine, John Damascene, Gregory the Great, Pseudo-Dionysius, Bede, John Chrysostom, Hilary of Poitiers, Jerome, Ambrose, Haimo of Auxerre, and Boethius. He engages more recent theological authorities as well, including the *Glossa ordinaria,* Peter Lombard (especially the *Sentences*), Bernard of Clairvaux, Anselm of Canterbury, Hugh and Richard of St. Victor, Alexander of Hales (the *Summa Halensis*), and William of Auxerre.

The second major field of sources from which Albert draws in *De resurrectione* is an ever-expanding philosophical tradition. He not only relies on Aristotelian logic (as found in the *Organon* or *logica nova*), but also turns to Aristotle's natural philosophy—his *Physics, On Heaven and Earth,* and *Metaphysics.* In the decade following the completion of *On Resurrection,* beginning about 1250, Albert began systematically to paraphrase and comment on the *entire* Aristotelian corpus, creating a sort of "teachers' manual" on Aristotelian philosophy as part of his larger project to make Aristotle accessible and intelligible in Latin to his contemporaries. Although he applies Aristotle's theories of motion, time, and change in *De resurrectione,* Albert also relies heavily on the neo-Platonizing works of Pseudo-Dionysius the Areopagite (namely, *On the Divine Names, On the Celestial Hierarchy,* and *On the Ecclesiastical Hierarchy*) as well as Pseudo-Aristotle's *Liber de causis.* Albert began to lecture on the Dionysian corpus after he incepted as master at the University of Paris, probably filling the chair left vacant by the death of Guerric of Saint-Quentin (who died c. 1244). These twin influences reflect Albert's conviction that one cannot be a true philosopher without knowing the philosophies of both Plato and Aristotle. In addition to ancient Greek philosophers and their late-antique interpreters, Albert also turns in *De resurrectione* to their medieval Jewish and Arab commentators—for example, Avicenna, Averroes, and Maimonides—and natural philosophers such as Isaac Israeli, Al-Farabi, and Al-Bitruji.

The complete text of Albert's *De resurrectione* has come down to us in only four manuscripts: (1) Firenze, Biblioteca Nazionale Centrale, Conventi soppressi G. V. 347 f. 52va–68va (XIII); (2) Giessen, Universitätsbibliothek 720 (BG XV 83) f. 48va–117vb (XV: um 1445); (3) Venezia, Bibl. Marciana class. IV cod. 10 (Z.L. 130) f. 219ra–268vb (XV); and (4) Wien Staatsbibliothek lat. 1688 f. 95rb–115vb (XIII/XIV).[38] Although the paucity of extant textual witnesses suggests that *On Resurrection* was likely not a medieval "best-seller," Albert's work was copied, disseminated, and presumably read to some degree throughout Western Europe from the thirteenth through the fifteenth century. Not only do remarks from *De resurrectione* appear in marginal glosses of additional manuscripts, but Albert frequently cites material from *De resurrectione* in his other works, which often circulated more widely. Furthermore, the work's impact extends well beyond these few textual witnesses in part because of its influence on Thomas Aquinas, who studied under Albert both at Paris and at Cologne during the very period when Albert appears to have been revising *De resurrectione.*

In contrast to Albert, Thomas Aquinas never penned a separate treatise on resurrection. Nor did he complete the *Tertia pars* of his *Summa theologiae,* whose third major section was to be a consideration of "the end of immortal life, at which through him [that is, Christ] we arrive by rising again."[39] Nevertheless, Albert's teaching in *On Resurrection* clearly shaped Aquinas's basic understanding of the bodily resurrection in general and of Christ's rising again in particular.[40] The master's influence

38. For further details regarding the manuscripts, see ed. Colon. 26, Prolegomena, pp. XI–XIV; and Winfried Fauser, SJ, *Die Werke des Albertus Magnus in ihrer handschriftlichen Überlieferung, Tiel I: Die echten Werke* (Münster: Aschendorff, 1982), 254–55.

39. Aquinas, *ST* IIIa Prol.

40. On Aquinas on resurrection and Last Things more generally, see Carlo

on his most well-known student in this regard can be seen by briefly considering what both Albert and Aquinas take to be two classes of proofs or demonstrations: (1) proofs for a future bodily resurrection, which Aquinas offers in *Summa contra Gentiles* Bk. IV ch. 79; and (2) proofs or manifestations of Christ's own resurrection, which Aquinas discusses in *Summa theologiae* IIIa q. 55.

First, like Albert in *De resurrectione,* Aquinas begins his treatment of resurrection in *Summa contra Gentiles* IV by asking whether there is a future resurrection, and here, again like Albert, he is particularly concerned to demonstrate that there is indeed a future *bodily* resurrection. As for Albert in *De resurrectione* tr. 1 q. 1, so too for Aquinas scriptural authorities such as 1 Cor 15, Jb 19.25–26 ("I know that my Redeemer lives, and on the last day I will rise up out of the earth ..."), and Jn 5.25 ("The dead will hear the voice of the Son of God, and those who hear will live") figure prominently among his proofs.[41] Furthermore, just as Albert observes that—beyond Scripture—there are philosophical arguments for resurrection, Aquinas teaches that "apparent reason likewise lends support to the future resurrection of the flesh."[42] Additionally, the particular rational proofs that Aquinas sets forth run along the same lines as those of his teacher. His first argument—that the immortal soul must be reunited to the body in the resurrection because it is natural to the human for the soul to be so united and because nothing contrary to nature can obtain forever—appears indebted to Albert's two related arguments that (1) whatever exists in matter exists from form, and that (2) proportionality exists in every nature between the movable and the motive power.[43] Similarly, Aquinas's final philosophical proof here in ch. 79, the argument from divine providence, is virtually identical to an argu-

Leget, *Living with God: Thomas Aquinas on the Relation between Life on Earth and 'Life' after Death* (Leuven: Peeters, 1997); and idem, "Eschatology," in *The Theology of Thomas Aquinas,* ed. Rik Van Nieuwenhove and Joseph Wawrykow (Notre Dame, IN: University of Notre Dame Press, 2005), 365–85.

41. Aquinas, *ScG* IV ch. 79.

42. Aquinas, *ScG* IV ch. 79: "... etiam resurrectionem carnis futuram evidens ratio suffragatur ..."

43. Aquinas, *ScG* IV ch. 79; cf. *De res.* tr. 1 q. 1 (pp. 28–29 below).

ment mounted by Albert, with the help of John Damascene, in tr. 1 q. 1. Because divine providence requires that sinners be punished and the righteous rewarded in both body and soul, and because not all in either group receive what they deserve in this present life, Aquinas concludes: "It is necessary, therefore, to propose the conjoining of the soul to the body a second time, so that the human can be rewarded or punished in body and soul."[44]

Second, when Aquinas considers "the manifestation of the resurrection" of Christ himself in *Summa theologiae* IIIa q. 55, he appears to have learned much from Albert's treatment of the topic in *De resurrectione.* Two related examples should suffice. In a. 5, Aquinas asks whether Christ should have made the truth of his resurrection known "by proofs" (*per argumenta*). Christ ought not to have revealed, and in fact did not reveal, his resurrection by the sort of "argumentative proof" (*probatio argumentativa*) that proceeds from certain rational principles known to the disciples, Aquinas responds; but the Lord did show that he had truly risen, which exceeds the capacity of human reason, "by certain most evident signs" (*per quaedam evidentissima signa*).[45] He revealed these signs for two reasons, according to Aquinas: first, in order to inculcate faith among the disciples, whose hearts were not readily disposed to accept faith in the truth of the resurrection; and second, so that their own testimony might be rendered more efficacious by the signs shown to them.[46]

As a second example, in a. 6 of the same question Aquinas asks whether the proofs that Christ showed forth sufficiently manifested the truth of his resurrection. The corpus explains that these proofs or appearances did indeed show that Christ's resurrection was both true and glorious. By certain proofs Christ showed that the resurrection was true on the part of the body, by others that it was true on the part of the soul reunit-

44. Aquinas, *ScG* IV ch. 79: "Necessarium est igitur ponere iteratam animae ad corpus coniunctionem, ut homo in corpore et anima praemiari et puniri possit."

45. Aquinas, *ST* IIIa q. 55 a. 5 co.

46. Ibid.

ed to the body. He indicated the truth of his resurrection on the part of the body, for example, by showing his disciples the scars of his wounds (Lk 24.39–40), demonstrating that his risen body was identical to the body that he had before.[47] Aquinas follows Albert both in maintaining that such a demonstration of bodily identity was the very purpose of Christ's showing his scars and in addressing the further question of whether these wounds might indicate some deformity in the Lord's resurrected body.[48] Immediately after Christ showed his scars, according to the Lucan account, he requested something to eat and enjoyed a piece of broiled fish and a honeycomb (Lk 24.41–43), a work of the nutritive life which Aquinas takes as evidence that Christ showed the truth of his resurrection on the part of the soul and body reunited.[49] Finally, like Albert before him, Aquinas takes Christ's entering in among the disciples when the doors were closed (Jn 20.19–23) as manifesting the glory of his resurrection, although, in contrast to Albert's treatment of this appearance, he makes no mention here of the dowries (*dotes*) of the glorified body.[50] Aquinas does introduce the bodily dowries in q. 54, on the quality of Christ rising again, but he does so piecemeal and as needed rather than treating them systematically as Albert does in *De resurrectione* tr. 4 q. 1.

These few examples highlight the notable influence that Albert's *On Resurrection* exerted on Aquinas's understanding of bodily resurrection generally and Christ's rising again particularly. Joseph Wawrykow has noted the significance of Aquinas's having given the resurrection of Christ such a distinguished place in his theology by devoting four questions of *Summa theologiae* IIIa to it (qq. 53–56): "In putting Christ's resurrection into such prominence, Aquinas is quite innovative when compared with the teaching found in Peter Lombard's *Sentences*.... The effect is to give in scholastic discourse the resurrection of

47. Ibid.

48. Aquinas addresses the question of potential deformity in q. 54 a. 4, "Whether Christ's body ought to have risen with its scars."

49. Aquinas, *ST* IIIa q. 55 a. 5 co.

50. Ibid.

Christ its due."[51] In light of our foregoing discussion and the translation that follows below, there can be little doubt that Albert's *De resurrectione* shaped how Aquinas came to value Christ's resurrection in his own theological understanding and work. Indeed, Albert produced his treatise *On Resurrection* some two decades before Aquinas began to compose *Summa theologiae* IIIa. Well before Aquinas gave Christ's resurrection such a prominent place in his mature theology, then, Albert had completed *On Resurrection,* thereby ensuring that both Christ's resurrection and bodily resurrection more generally were given their due in scholastic discourse.

On account of its influence on his more well-known student, as well as for its interest in its own right, we have prepared the following translation of the complete text of Albert the Great's *On Resurrection.*

51. Joseph P. Wawrykow, *The Westminster Handbook to Thomas Aquinas* (Louisville, KY: Westminster John Knox, 2005), s.v. "Resurrection of Christ," 126–28, at 128.

ON RESURRECTION

After this,[1] one asks about the resurrection. And first, on the part of the head and the members and the wicked generally. Second, on the part of the head alone; third, on the part of the wicked alone; fourth, on the part of the good alone; fifth, [*one asks*] *about those things that accompany resurrection, that is, judgment and the renewal of the world.*

TRACTATE ONE

ON RESURRECTION ON THE PART OF THE HEAD AND MEMBERS [OF CHRIST] AND THE WICKED GENERALLY

CONCERNING THE first, one asks first whether there is a future resurrection; second, what resurrection is; third, whether it is natural or miraculous; fourth, about the ends (*terminis*) of resurrection, from what and into what there is resurrection; fifth, about the circumstances surrounding resurrection, and this is to inquire how it happens in a moment and in the twinkling of an eye, and what the sound of the trumpet is,[2] and what the blowing four winds,[3] and the like; sixth, [one asks] about the truth of human nature (*veritas humanae naturae*).

Question 1: Whether there is a future resurrection

To the first [question] one objects in this way:

Daniel says in chapter 12, "Many of those who sleep in the

1. That is, after his work entitled *De incarnatione,* which precedes *De resurrectione.*

2. 1 Cor 15.52.

3. Jer 49.36.

dust of the earth will awake, some to eternal life and others to reproach, to see always."[4] Therefore, there will be a resurrection.

Also, Ezekiel 37: "Dry bones, hear the word of the Lord. The Lord God says this to the bones: Behold, I will place spirit within you, and you will live. And I will cause flesh to grow over you, and I will give you nerves, and I will cover you with skin, and I will give you spirit, and you will live, and you will know that I am the Lord."[5]

Also, Job 19: "I know that my Redeemer lives, and on the last day I will rise up out of the earth. And I will be clothed again with my skin, and in my flesh I will see my savior,[6] whom I myself shall see, and my eyes shall behold, and not another."[7]

In addition, there are the theological arguments of the Apostle [Paul] in 1 Cor 15.[8] He supposes three things, namely that a falsehood will not be a support for faith, that confusion will not be a reward for hope, and that a falsehood will not be a support for the preaching of the gospel. And if there is no resurrection, one is led to three inappropriate conclusions: namely that faith is in vain, that preaching is in vain, and that "we are more miserable than all men"[9] with respect to hope's reward.

Likewise, John Damascene, at the end of the first chapter of book four, proves the resurrection by the explication of the Sacred Scripture[10] that [says], "The Lord said to Noah after the flood: 'I will require the blood of your souls from the hand of man, of his brother, and from the hand of all wild beasts.'"[11] How will he require it, unless he will raise the bodies of all those who die?

4. Dn 12.2.

5. Ezek 37.4–6.

6. Note the Vulg. reads *Deum* and not *salvatorem meum*, but at *Super Job* 19.26, Alb. comments on the scriptural words "and in my flesh I will see my God" by adding "as judge, not as one who condemns but as my savior."

7. Jb 19.25–27.

8. 1 Cor 15.13–19.

9. 1 Cor 15.19.

10. John Damascene, *De fide orth.* 4.27 (PG 94: 1221A; ed. Buytaert, p. 379, 33ff.).

11. Gn 9.5.

Also, [the Lord said] to Moses: "I am the God of Abraham, and the God of Isaac, and the God of Jacob." "He is not the God of the dead but of the living."[12]

Again, "Those who are in the graves will hear the voice of the Son of God, and those who hear will live. And those who have done good deeds will go forth into the resurrection of life, whereas those who have done evil will go forth into the resurrection of judgment."[13]

Also, in the same place Damascene proves the resurrection from the works of the Lord,[14] saying: "How will the resurrection of the dead be recognized or believed if the properties indicative of a substance do not define it? But he raised Lazarus to reveal his own deity and to establish belief in both his own resurrection and ours."

At the same time, he proves the resurrection morally from the consideration of justice, saying:[15] "If there is no resurrection, how are we different from irrational creatures? If there is no resurrection, let us be happy like herd animals (*agrifera*) that possess a life without sadness. If there is no resurrection, then neither God nor providence exists, but all things happen by chance. For behold, we see many just men who thirst and suffer injury and become master of nothing obtained in this present life, whereas sinners and the unjust abound in riches and in every delight. And who, knowing this well, will ever believe it to be the work of equitable justice and wise providence? Therefore, there will be a resurrection. For God is just and gives a reward to those who stand with him."[16]

And lest someone say that God will reward souls without the body, by way of a conclusion he objects in this way:[17] "If

12. Mt 22.32; cf. Ex 3.6. Cf. John Damascene, *De fide orth.* 4.27 (PG 94: 1221B; ed. Buytaert, p. 380, 43–45).

13. Cf. Jn 5.25, 28; John Damascene, *De fide orth.* 4.27 (PG 94: 1224A; ed. Buytaert, p. 381, 73–76).

14. John Damascene, *De fide orth.* 4.27 (PG 94: 1224A; ed. Buytaert, p. 382, 82–86).

15. John Damascene, *De fide orth.* 4.27 (PG 94: 1220B–C; ed. Buytaert, p. 378, 16–p. 379, 26).

16. Cf. Heb 11.6; Sir 36.18.

17. John Damascene, *De fide orth.* 4.27 (PG 94: 1220C; ed. Buytaert, p. 379, 27–31).

indeed the soul has fought alone like an athlete in contests of strength, then it will be crowned alone. And if alone it has been ensnared by desires, then it alone will be justly punished. But because they [that is, soul and body] have not had a separate existence and because the soul experiences neither virtue nor wickedness without the body, rightly will both enjoy recompense at the same time."[18]

In like manner, he proves the resurrection from a consideration of the works of [this] world, saying:[19] "If blindness does not permit belief in the Lord's words, then at least believe in [his] works. 'For what you sow will not come to life unless it dies. And what you sow is not the body that will be generated, but a bare kernel, if it should happen so, perhaps of wheat or of some other grain. But God gives to it a body as he has willed.'[20] Consider, then, the seeds buried as if in graves, that is, in furrows. Who is he who establishes the roots, trunk, and leaves, and the most delicate ears of grain? Is it not he who is Creator of the universe, who has fashioned all these things according to his command? In the same way, then, believe that there will be a resurrection of the dead according to divine power and will and intent; in fact, he has power that coincides with his will."

In the same way Gregory's authority also applies, who says in the *Moralia* that if we considered the works of this world, the future resurrection would be more certain to us than that the sun will rise tomorrow.[21]

There are philosophical arguments for this. In fact, Avicenna says that whatever exists in matter exists from form.[22] Since, then, the rational soul is form, it is necessary for something in matter to correspond to what is found in it; but there is an es-

18. John Damascene, *De fide orth.* 4.27 (PG 94: 1220B–C; ed. Buytaert, p. 378, 16–p. 379, 26).

19. John Damascene, *De fide orth.* 4.27 (PG 94: 1225B–C; ed. Buytaert, p. 385, 129–40).

20. 1 Cor 15.36–38.

21. Greg., *Moral.* 14.55.70 (PL 75: 1076C).

22. Avic., *Metaph.*, tr. 2, cap. 3, 1: 92 (fol. 77ra in *Opera*). See *Liber de philosophia prima sive scientia divina,* 1. [livres I–IV]. 2. [livres V–X]. 3. [*Lexiques*]. Édition critique de la traduction latine médiévale par S. Van Riet, introduction doctrinale par G. Verbeke (Louvain, Leiden: Peeters-Brill, 1977, 1980, 1983).

sential permanence found in it that always remains the same in number. Therefore, something in a body that is numerically the same will correspond to this [soul], and this cannot occur unless there is a resurrection. Therefore, there will be a resurrection.

Additionally, the Philosopher says that proportionality exists in every nature between the movable and the motive [power].[23] But the soul is the mover, and the body the movable. Therefore, a proportionality will exist between them with respect to the power of moving. But in the soul the power of moving is permanent, which I will prove; therefore, in the body the power to be moved will be permanent. Proof of the minor premise: soul is related to body with a substantial difference, which is clear from its definition: "Soul is the power of the act of an organic, natural body possessing life."[24] And the same one says that it is related to the body as a mover.[25] And all the philosophers defined it in terms of movement and knowledge.[26] Therefore, it is essential to the soul to be the motive [force] for the body. But nothing loses what is essential to it while its substance remains. Since, then, the soul's substance is permanent, the power in it for moving will be permanent.

If perhaps one should say that this is not inappropriate with respect to the soul, but that with respect to the body a defect occurs owing to corruption, [one may say] to the contrary: Nothing in the works of nature is fruitless and useless.[27] Thus a power for moving actively will not exist in anything unless it has some corresponding power for being moved. And so it is necessary that some power to be moved remain in the body.

Also, every soul is a cause of life.[28] But an effect varies according to the nature of the cause. Since, then, vegetable and sensible [souls] are causes of life that are subject to corruption, in harmony with their nature, so the intellectual soul will be a

23. Ar., *Metaph.* 9.6 (1048a36ff.); cf. Alb., *Metaph.* 9.3.2.
24. Ar., *De anima* 2.1 (412a27–28; 412b5–6). Cf. Alb., *De anima* 2.1.2.
25. Ar., *De anima* 1.4 (408a30–33).
26. Ar., *De anima* 1.2 (404b28–30).
27. Ar., *De caelo et mundo* 1.4 (271a33); Alb., *De caelo et mundo* 1.1.10.
28. Ar., *De anima* 2.4 (415b7–8); cf. Alb., *De anima* 2.2.2.

cause of everlasting life in accord with the property of its substance. And it cannot be such without the body's transformation to another state: therefore, there will be a resurrection.

1. To the contrary: Job 14: "A tree has hope: if it has been cut down, it will sprout again, and its shoots will spring forth. Though its root may grow old in the earth, and its stump may die in the dust, it will bud at the scent of water and put forth a branch, as it did when it was first planted. But man, when he has died and been exposed and consumed, where, I ask, is he?"[29] Here Job seems to compare man's death to the double destruction of a tree, namely: to its being cut down, to which is likened a man's accidental death, such as his killing; and to [its] putrefaction in the ground, to which a [man's] natural death is compared. And he seems to say that, although a tree that has been destroyed in either way will come to life again, man will not be restored to life.

Again, in the same place: "Just as waters recede from the sea and a river wastes away and dries up, so too man, when he sleeps, will not rise again; until heaven is destroyed (*atteratur*), he will not awake again nor rise from his sleep."[30] But it is impossible for heaven to be destroyed; therefore, there is no resurrection of the dead.

If perhaps one should say that heaven will be destroyed, then to the contrary: whatever is destroyed is destroyed by an agent stronger than it. But nothing is stronger than heaven, since it rules over all natural bodies, as Isaac says in the book *On Definitions*.[31] Therefore, it will not be destroyed by anything.

If one should say that God will destroy it, this will contradict blessed Dionysius, who says that God, who is the cause of the essence of things, is not the cause of their destruction.[32]

29. Jb 14.7–10.

30. Jb 14.11–12.

31. Isaac, *De diff.* (ed. Muckle, p. 335, 2; cf. p. 315, 16ff.).

32. Dion., *De div. nom.*, §19–23 (PG 3: 716Cff.); cf. Alb., *Super Dion. De div. nom.* 4, 153–65 (ed. Colon. 37/1, pp. 239–50); Alb., *De nat. et orig. an.*, 2.6 (ed. Colon. 12, p. 26, 65). For a brief consideration of how Bonaventure and Thomas Aquinas also use Jb 14.11–12 as an authority against resurrection, see Franklin T. Harkins, "From the Fiery Heaven to the Fire of Hell: Job in the *Sentences* Commentaries of Albert the Great, Bonaventure, and Thomas Aquinas,"

2. If perhaps one should say that it will be destroyed with respect to motion, but not with respect to substance, [one may say] to the contrary: No local motion that is perpetual with respect to all its causes is ever destroyed; but heaven's motion is such as this, and therefore, etc. Proof of the minor premise: according to all the philosophers, the Prime Mover (*primus motor*) is not movable in another disposition.[33] And faith also supports this, because, as James says, God is unchangeable.[34] Likewise, the first movable body is perpetual and unchangeable, since it does not exist in potency with respect to any body acting upon it, as was proved earlier.[35] Similarly, there are an external and an internal form for perpetual motion. Indeed, the external form is a circle, which has neither beginning nor end. The nature of heaven's body, however, is the internal form, which, according to the Philosopher, is to be rotated in a circle from right to left.[36] Furthermore, the ultimate end and the penultimate end are perpetual. In fact, the ultimate end, as is proved in the second book of *On Heaven and Earth,* imitates something of the Prime Mover's nobility.[37] Moreover, the penultimate end is the uninterrupted succession (*perpetuitas*) that exists in things subject to generation and corruption, as is proved in the second book of *On Generation and Corruption.*[38] And both of these are perpetual; in fact, the matter for things subject to generation is perpetual and incorruptible and unbegotten and cannot exist without some form, and this is why it is always the case that the "corruption of one will be the generation of another."[39] The ultimate end of heaven follows upon this, namely that through motion heaven is a cause, which [cause] is the nobility of the Prime Mover. And in this way the motion of heav-

in *A Companion to Job in the Middle Ages,* ed. Franklin T. Harkins and Aaron Canty (Leiden: Brill, 2017), 129–60, at 151–55.

33. "Disposition," or, perhaps, arrangement or order. Cf. Ar., *Phys.* 2.7 (198b1–3); Alb., *De IV coaequ.*, q. 16, a. 1.

34. Jas 1.17.

35. "the first movable body": i.e., heaven.

36. Ar., *De caelo et mundo* 2.2 (285b16ff.).

37. Ar., *De caelo et mundo* 2.3 (286a3ff.).

38. Ar., *De gen. et corr.* 2.11 (338a15–18); cf. Alb., *De gen. et corr.* 2.3.10.

39. Ar., *Metaph.* 2.2 (994b5–6).

en, with respect to all its causes, is perpetual. Therefore, it will not be destroyed.

3. The solution that some[40] offer does not succeed. They say that heaven's motion exists from God's will and the will is subject to delay,[41] and therefore it can will different things, so that he who wills motion now may will rest later. In fact, according to the Catholic faith God is completely immutable in terms of his will. Therefore, he always wills the same thing, particularly since blessed Dionysius says that he relates to all things in the same manner.[42]

Besides, delay does not pertain to him, since he relates to a thing in one way both when it exists and when it does not, as blessed Augustine says.[43]

Likewise, on *Metaphysics* 11, where the Philosopher compares movers, the Commentator says that the comparison should not be understood according to the everlasting nature of motion, because every perpetual motion moves in such a way that one [movement] does not surpass another but it is understood rather with respect to the force in the movement.[44] Therefore, the motion of heaven will be perpetual.

4. The same thing is proved from an argument based on time. For if time is the measure of motion, while time persists motion will also persist. But time will [always] persist; therefore, so too will motion.

5. That time will persist, however, is proved in this way: Nothing of time is experienced except the now, and the now

40. Cf. Alb., *Phys.* 8.1.1.

41. For this expression, *voluntas est dilatoria,* see also Alb., *III Sent.* d. 1a, art. 5; *De IV coaequ.* tr.1, q.1, art.1 (ed. Borgnet, 34, p.308b and 310a). Cf. Alessandro Ghisalberti, "Gli inizi dell'aristotelismo latino e l'avvio della teologia scolastica," in *Was ist Philosophie im Mittelalter? Akten des X. Internationalen Kongresses für mittelalterliche Philosophie der Société internationale pour l'étude de la philosophie médiévale, 25 bis 30 August 1997 in Erfurt,* ed. Jan A. Aertsen and Andreas Speer (Berlin: Walter de Gruyter, 1998), 281–92, esp. 287.

42. Dion., *De div. nom.* 3§1 (PG 3: 680B); cf. Alb., *Super Dion. De div. nom.* 3, 1–9 (ed. Colon. 37/1, pp. 101–7); Alb., *De nat. et orig. an.* 2.9 (ed. Colon. 12, p. 33, 67–69).

43. Aug., *Epist.* 187, 6.19 (PL 33: 839; CSEL 57, p. 98, 9–10).

44. Averr., *Metaph.* 11 text, comm. 41.

is always the beginning of the future.[45] And whatever is always at its beginning is not at an end. Therefore, time will always persist.

6. Moreover, if it [time] is corrupted, either it is corrupted in time or in the now. If in time, then it is in time and is corrupted in it. Therefore, it is temporal, and there is a time for time. And in this way one continues on to infinity. If in the now, then to the contrary: It does not exist in the now, and therefore it is not corrupted in the now.

7. If one should say that only the now of time is experienced, and the now is corrupted in itself, then to the contrary: It exists in itself, as the Philosopher says.[46] Therefore, it is not corrupted in itself.

Besides, based on the authority of Sacred Scripture, it seems that the resurrection will not be general, because the Psalm says, "The wicked will not rise at the judgment."[47]

8. Also, the Apostle's argument that "it [that is, the body] will not come to life (*vivificatur*) unless first it dies"[48] does not seem valid. In fact, to live (*vivere*) means to generate and something generative generates. Therefore, it [that is, the body] lives. Therefore, it is not dead.

9. Likewise, the Lord's argument, "He is not the God of the dead but of the living,"[49] does not seem valid, because even if bodies do not rise again, they can live with respect to the soul.

Solution: We say that there will be a resurrection.

1. To Job's objection, we say that he means that a man will not be brought back to animal life through a principle that is [its] nature, as a tree is brought back to a life similar to the one it had before, and as a river is restored when the source whence it flows has been restored.

2. To the objection concerning the motion of heaven, we say that heaven is destroyed with respect to motion, and this stems from the efficient cause, and nonetheless the efficient cause it-

45. Cf. Alb., *Phys.* 4.3.7.
46. Ar., *Phys.* 4.12 (221b30–31).
47. Ps 1.5.
48. 1 Cor 15.36.
49. Mt 22.32.

self remains immovable.[50] How this is so should be understood from what is said in *Metaphysics* 11, in the commentary and in the text,[51] namely that divine knowledge (*scientia*) is the cause of being and that by understanding himself [God] understands all things, and his knowledge is neither universal nor particular. We understand from this that he relates in a single way to the many as many, and to the one as one, and to the complex as complex, and to the incomplex as incomplex, and to the temporal as temporal, and to the atemporal as atemporal. And this is so because the first cause is one "exceeding (*eminens*) the properties of those things that have been created," as is said at the beginning of *On Heaven and Earth*.[52] Thus, while he remains the same, he is the cause of heaven's motion as motion, and of rest as rest.

3. And we readily concede that there is no solution that relies on a will subject to delay (*voluntate dilatoria*). And this is what Augustine says in the second book of *On the Trinity*, chapter 5: "Without any time there was in the Word itself the time at which the Word would become flesh and dwell among us.[53] 'When the fullness of time had come, God sent his Son, made of a woman,'[54] that is, made in time, in order that the Word might appear to men as incarnate, such that what existed in the Word itself apart from time would come to be at that time. To be sure, the order of [all] time exists in the eternal wisdom of God without time."[55]

To the objection from Dionysius, that God is equally present to things, one must reply that this is true. But it follows in the text that not all things are equally present to him. In fact, what is in God atemporally is in a creature temporally; and what is in him as one is in a creature as many. And this is why heaven's motion and standing still are not the same and do not exist at the same time, but God is at the same time and in the same way

50. Cf. Alb., *De homine* q.80 a. 1, sol. (ed. Colon. 27/2, pp. 585–86).

51. Averr., *Metaph.* 11, text com. 51; Ar., *Metaph.* 12.9 (1075a10); cf. Alb., *Metaph.* 11.2.33.

52. Ar., *De caelo et mundo* 1.1 (268a15); cf. Alb., *De caelo et mundo* 1.1.2.

53. Cf. Jn 1.14.

54. Gal 4.4.

55. Aug., *De trin.* 2.5.9 (PL 42: 850).

the cause of both, and the shift (*ordo*) of motion to rest, which exists in heaven in accord with temporal succession, exists in God without that succession. And therefore it is clear yet again that there is no delay there, for from eternity he willed for motion to cease at that time.

4. To the next objection one must reply that that time that is a property of heaven's motion will cease.

6. To the objection, moreover, whether [time is corrupted] in itself or in the now, one must reply that it is destroyed *per accidens,* seeing that heaven's motion has been destroyed.[56] And therefore the objection does not hold, whether in itself or in another. Or one may say that time is destroyed in another, namely in eviternity (*aeviternitas*). In fact, time is the measure of all things whatsoever, [but] the eviternal and the eternal are the measure of the same things, though not an equal [measure].[57]

5. To the objection that [time] is always at its beginning, one must reply that this is understood according to the analogy of the motion of which it is the measure, which is circular. A circular motion, however, is always at the beginning and the end. But according to motion's relation to standing still (*status*), what is last now will have the nature of an end and not of a beginning.[58]

7. To the inquiry concerning the now itself, one must reply that it ceases *per accidens,* just like what is moved in the case of local motion. Or one may also say that it ceases in the now of eternity or eviternity.

8. To the objection concerning the Apostle's argument, one must reply that death is the corruption of a life that is numerically the same. The generative [power] in the seed, however, is capable of corrupting the very same seed with respect to its species and of giving life to another in the species. And so it is clear that it dies insofar as it is numerically the same. And the Apostle understands this.

9. To the last objection, one must reply that the Lord placed in souls the power of bringing to life, to which a potency in

56. The responses in the text move from 4 to 6 to 5.

57. Cf. Alb., *De IV coaequ.* q. 6, a. 1 sol.

58. Cf. Alb., *De IV coaequ.* q. 5, a. 2 ad 6.

the body will necessarily correspond; otherwise it [namely, the soul's vivifying power] would be for naught, as has been proved. And in this respect they [bodies] live, and so his own [that is, the Lord's] argument holds.[59]

Question 2. What resurrection is

To the second [question] one proceeds in this way:

The Gloss on Phil 3[60] says that "resurrection is the power and efficacy of the resurrection of Christ."[61]

Likewise, Augustine says, in book eight of *On the Literal Meaning of Genesis*,[62] that resurrection is nothing other than restoration (*restitutio*) to a life the same in all respects.

Likewise, Damascene [says] in the last chapter of the fourth book: "Resurrection is a second rising of what has fallen."[63] And a little later: "Resurrection is the reunion of the soul and the body and a second rising of an animal that has been destroyed and has fallen."

1. According to the first [definition] it seems that Christ did not rise again by means of the same resurrection by which we will rise again, because Christ's resurrection is not the power, etc.

2. According to the second [definition] it seems that the resuscitation of Lazarus was his resurrection, because he was restored to a life the same in all respects.

3. Furthermore, that seems to be false, because at that time life will not be the same in all respects to this life. "For in the resurrection," as the Lord says in the Gospel, "they will neither marry nor be married, but will exist just as the angels of God do."[64]

4. According to the third [definition] it seems that man will not rise again, because man has not fallen, so it seems, but only the body, and man is not [only] the body. And this [follows] es-

59. Cf. Alb., *IV Sent.* d. 43 a. 2.

60. Phil 3.10.

61. Peter Lombard, *In epist. Pauli* Phil 3.10 (PL 192: 245C); cf. *Glossa ord.*

62. Aug., *De gen. ad litt.* 8.16.34 (PL 34: 386; CSEL 28/1, p. 255ff.).

63. John Damascene, *De fide orth.* 4.27 (PG 94: 1220A; ed. E. M. Buytaert, p. 377, 5–6–p. 378, 8–10).

64. Mt 22.30.

pecially on account of Damascene's statement: "The very body that is corrupted and destroyed will rise again." And earlier he said: "How will immortally existing souls rise again?"[65]

5. According to the fourth [definition] it seems again that the Lord's resurrection was not of the same sort (*ratio*) as ours, because his body was not destroyed, as Damascene says in chapter twenty-seven of book three:[66] "The noun *Pthoras,* that is, corruption, indicates two things: for it indicates human passions—hunger, thirst, distress, the piercing of the nails, death, namely the separation of the soul from the body, and such things. According to this meaning, we say that the body of the Lord is *ptharton,* that is, corruptible, for he assumed all of these things voluntarily. *Pthora,* that is, corruption, however, also indicates the body's complete destruction and dissolution into those elements of which it was composed,[67] which many people more often designate and name *diapthora.* The Lord's body did not have this sort of experience, as the prophet David says: 'Because you will not leave my soul in hell, nor will you give your holy one to see *diapthora,*' that is, corruption."[68]

6. In addition, farther down Damascene seems to provide another definition of the Lord's resurrection, saying: "The Lord's resurrection is the union of a soul and of a body made incorruptible."[69]

7. Also, one asks what he means by "second." A second resurrection is said with respect to a first resurrection, but he did not rise previously.

8. Moreover, it seems redundant when he says "has fallen and has been destroyed." Actually, the fall and destruction are the very same thing.

9. Moreover, why does he say "animal" since [in the resurrection] bodies will be spiritual?

65. John Damascene, *De fide orth.* 4.27 (PG 94: 1220A; ed. Buytaert, p. 378, 10–11; p. 377, 6–p. 378, 7).

66. John Damascene, *De fide orth.* 3.28 (PG 94: 1097B–1100A; ed. Buytaert, p. 274, 4–15).

67. Cf. 2 Pt 2.12.

68. Ps 15.10.

69. John Damascene, *De fide orth.* 4.27 (PG 94: 1224C; ed. Buytaert, p. 383, 96–97).

10. In addition, the Philosopher says that if there is something found in common in the definition and in what is defined, it is a part neither of what is defined nor of the definition.[70] But resurrection (*resurrectio*) is found in the definition and in what is defined. And so it seems that all the distinguishing attributes (*differentiae*) express only the character of a preposition (*habitudo praepositionis*) in a composite [term].

Solution:

1. We say that the first of these definitions is specific to our resurrection and indicates a relation to an efficient cause, which, I say, is a cause acting in the same genus with it. But God is the efficient cause of our resurrection [which is] outside the genus, just as the Philosopher also says that "a man and the sun generate a man from matter."[71] And man is the efficient cause in the genus, whereas the sun is outside the genus.

2. To the next [definition] we say that resuscitation (*suscitatio*), properly speaking, is not the same as resurrection. For resurrection, properly speaking, is into an incorruptible body. And the power that [Augustine] calls "restoration" (*restitutio*) can occur in it. In fact, one who rises in this way, such that he will die again, has not been restored perfectly to the life that we lost [in death].

3. To the other [objection][72] one must reply that a similarity is observed in the substantial cause of life, which is the soul, and not in the accidents.

4. To the objection concerning the third definition, one must reply that the power (*potentia*) of the act of union [of body and soul], however, according to which it is act, exists with respect to a determinate part of the union, as is evident. To be sure, to walk is an act of man, and nonetheless the power of walking exists in the feet. Likewise, to rise again belongs to man, yet nonetheless the power (*potentia*) for resurrection exists with respect to the body that has been destroyed.

70. Ar., *Top.* 6.4 (142a34); Boethius, transl. ant. PL 64: 974C; cf. Alb., *Top.* 6.2.2.

71. Ar., *Phys.* 2.2 (194b13); note that *ex materia* is not found in the Greek.

72. Namely, obj. 3 above.

5. To the next [objection],[73] one must reply that we readily concede that none of the four definitions, except perhaps the second, is appropriate to the Lord's resurrection and to our resurrection. Yet if one considers the fall (*casus*) as death (*mors*) only in itself and not in relation to a cause, then the third [definition] too will be shared by them. For in us sin is the cause of death, whereas in Christ it is the will to redeem (*voluntas redemptionis*). But the fourth [definition] is not shared in any way.

7.[74] And to the inquiry concerning the [word] "second," one must reply that it indicates an ordering in relation to the first rising (*erectio*), which exists through nature. For a similarity exists, as was said, in the substantial cause of life that raises the body both in this life and in that one. Yet some say that it indicates an ordering in relation to the first rising (*erectio*) in the state of innocence.[75] But according to this [understanding] a general definition will not exist, because it will not apply to the wicked.

8. To the next [objection] one must reply that the fall (*casus*) refers to the separation of the soul from the body, whereas destruction refers to the dissolution of the body into [its] elements.

10.[76] To the last query, one must reply that rising (*surrectio*) does not indicate the same thing in the definition and in what is defined. For in the one defined it indicates an act in relation to an earlier life, which relation refers to the "object" (*notat li 're'*). In the definition, however, it refers to the act united to the ultimate goal or end. For resurrection (*resurrectio*) is the same as an action upwards, and the "upwards" indicates the goal of resurrection. Since, therefore, an act united to an end is better known than an act simply understood, it is clear that resurrection can rightly be defined by resurrection (*per resurrectionem*).[77]

6. Nonetheless, one must note that what was introduced as

73. Namely, obj. 5 above.

74. Note that a response to 6 follows the response to 10.

75. Cf. Alex. Hales, *Quaest. de resurr.* (Cod. Paris. B.N. 16406, fol. 139vb), cited by Kübel. We have been unable to confirm this reference.

76. There is no response in the text to obj. 9 above.

77. That is, and not by *surrectio*.

a definition of the Lord's resurrection, namely that "resurrection is the union of a soul and of a body made incorruptible," is a definition of resurrection in general and not only of the Lord's resurrection. And that definition is offered in relation to the last act, which exists in resurrection according to nature. For there is first the gathering of ashes, then reintegration, and then the change [of the corruptible body] into incorruption; and afterwards the soul is united to this final body. And although these things do not follow one after another according to time, nonetheless they do follow one after another according to nature.

Question 3. Whether resurrection is natural or miraculous[78]

To the third [question] one proceeds in this way:

1. As Augustine says,[79] a miracle is something that appears beyond the hope and capacity (*facultatem*) of the one who marvels at it. But resurrection is not beyond [a person's] hope and capacity; therefore, etc.

2. In addition, whatever exists for the purpose of any particular act also exists for the purpose of the highest, the middle, and the lowest in that act; for the principle of the best ass, of the worst, and of the one in the middle is the same. Since, therefore, the act for the human species is none other than the best in that act, the principle for it and for act in a simple sense will be the same. But [the principle] for act in a simple sense is nature; therefore, nature will also be [the principle] for the resurrection.

3. Besides, what accords substantially with everything of the same species comes from the same principle as the nature of the species itself. The truth of this proposition stems from the fact that nothing exists in individuals except individuating attributes and a common nature. Since, then, individuating attributes are caused by matter, which is not shared by all individuals, it is necessary that those that are shared arise from a

78. Cf. Alb., *IV Sent.* d. 43 a. 3.
79. Aug., *De util. cred.* 16.34 (PL 42: 90; CSEL 25/1, p. 43, 16–17).

common principle. Since, therefore, man's nature is from natural principles, so too the incorruption found in all men will be from the same [natural] principles.

4. If perhaps one should say that nature is an intrinsic principle and that resurrection will be from an external principle, which is God, and thus it is not natural, then to the contrary: heaven's motion is natural and nonetheless comes from a mover who is neither a body nor a power in a body, as is proved in the book *On the One God* by a certain philosopher, Rabbi Moses [Maimonides].[80]

Moreover, God is a more immediate cause than is nature, because nature, which exists and which is a cause, has nothing except insofar as God operates in it.

5. After this one asks whether it [resurrection] is natural, as some say,[81] because it is the end of nature, just as the Philosopher says at the beginning of the second book of the *Ethics*[82] that we have an innate capacity to acquire the virtues, but their perfection stems from habit. It seems, therefore, since to attain to incorruption is innate to us, that incorruption itself will be natural. The authoritative statements of Damascene cited above demonstrate that we were born for this.

6. In addition, some object in this way:[83] Naaman the Syrian[84] was cleansed in the Jordan, and if God had endowed that water so as to cleanse leprosy in general, then he would have been cleansed naturally. Therefore, by analogy, as it is said in the Psalm[85] that he endowed his voice with a power for raising

80. *On the One God* (*Liber de uno Deo benedicto*) is a partial edition containing the beginning of book two of the Latin text of Maimonides's *Guide for the Perplexed* (i.e., *Dux neutrorum*). See Görge K. Hasselhoff, "Maimonides in the Latin Middle Ages: An Introductory Survey," *Jewish Studies Quarterly* 9.1 (2002): 1–20. The translation of *Liber de uno Deo benedicto* was completed c. 1240. For discussion of the translation and translators, see also Yossef Schwartz, "Persecution and the Art of Translation: Some New Evidence Concerning the Latin Translation of Maimonides' *Guide of the Perplexed*," *Yod. Revue des études hébraïques et juives* 22 (2019): 49–77.

81. Cf. Hugh of St. Cher (fol. 284va).

82. Ar., *Eth. Nic.* 2.1 (1103a23–26).

83. Cf. Ps. Guerricus (fol. 168va).

84. See 2 Kgs 5.1–15.

85. See Ps 67.34.

the dead in general, that voice will be a natural principle causing resurrection.

To the contrary: Chrysostom[86] says that things are miraculous that are caused by the divine will alone in an unmediated way. And Anselm says the same thing.[87] But resurrection is [caused] in an unmediated way by the divine will alone, therefore, etc. The proof of the minor [premise]: Damascene, in the last chapter of the fourth book, [says], "Believe that the future resurrection [will be] by divine power and will and command";[88] therefore, etc.

In addition, if nature exists for the purpose of something whose perfection never is attained, it is necessary that it be frustrated in the best [example of the species] in all of its work. But this is unfitting.

Again, nature acts through intermediate first qualities, which are not the principle of incorruption.

Besides, it does not appear to be natural, as an end (*finis*) is called natural, because every natural end of any efficient [cause] is attained by it in one operation or in several. The truth of this proposition is accepted both in [the realm of] natural things and in ethics. For among natural things the end that is the form is attained by one operation of the efficient [cause], whereas the end that is the continuation of being is attained by many operations. Similarly, in ethics the will attains an orientation to act by one operation, but attains an established habit by many operations. Nature, however, attains the incorruption of resurrection neither by one nor by many operations. Therefore, nature is not related to incorruption itself as to a natural end.

Solution: We say that resurrection is in no way natural. For it is natural neither in the simple sense (*simpliciter*) nor even as an end, insofar as nature is said to be that which acts with respect to an end, as was proved in the last objection. If, however,

86. I.e., John Chrysostom; for the opinion attributed to John Chrysostom, see Alb., *Summa* II q. 31 m. 2 a. 3 obj. 7 (ed. Borgnet 32, p. 347).

87. Anselm, *De conc. Virg.* 11 (PL 158: 446A; ed. Schmitt, 2: 154, 6–7).

88. John Damascene, *De fide orth.* 4.27 (PG 94: 1225C; ed. Buytaert, p. 385, 140).

nature designates a natural object, which man is, then in this way man exists for the sake of resurrection. But "for the sake of" (*propter*) here refers to the end of man's creation and not to [the end of his] nature, for nature is not the principle of creation, and therefore the end of creation is not properly the end of nature.

1. We say, then, that "hope" there designates the expectation of an act from a thing's natural principles, and a miracle is contrary to that hope. And hope is understood in this way in Romans 8, where it is said: "Who against hope believed in hope,"[89] where the Gloss says, "[believed] in the hope of grace against the hope of nature."[90] "Capacity" (*facultas*), however, generally assumes the power of the cognitive and operative potential in the one marveling, because neither by knowing nor acting can this [natural] power account for the miracle.[91] For our knowledge (*cognitio*), as Augustine says in the book *On the Trinity*,[92] can only sufficiently [reach] the proximate causes that the philosophers knew. Likewise, our action can only [reach] a form of art that is imposed upon matter. And for this reason, the one marveling at it neither understands nor produces a miracle, nor does he expect it from the principles of nature.

2. To the next [objection] we say that the species, with respect to [its] parts, arises in an unmediated way from two principles. For the intellect comes from God through creation, just as it is said in book sixteen of *On Animals* that "the intellect alone enters from outside."[93] But the body comes from a principle of nature, which exists in the seed. The incorruption of those who are resurrected, however, does not exist in bodies with respect to corporeal elements, but exists in relation to the incorruptible soul, as was proved above.[94] And for this reason it exists from a principle that is a principle of the soul, and not from a natural principle.

89. Actually, Rom 4.18.

90. Peter Lombard, *In epist. Pauli* Rom 4.18 (PL 191: 1376B–C).

91. This passage seems overly terse.

92. Aug., *De trin.* 3.2.7 (PL 42: 871).

93. Ar., *De gen. animal.* 2.3 (736b27–28); cf. Alb., *De animal.* 16.1.12.67 (*SZ* 2: 1191).

94. See p. 238, 62ff., of the Latin text.

3. Similarly, we say to the next [objection] that that proposition is understood of those in whom the entire nature of the species is derived from one principle. But this is not the case in the nature of man, as was already said.

4. To the next [objection] we say that heaven's motion has a double principle of motion:[95] one is internal, which is heaven's nature, and this is the efficient principle of motion that is united to the movable, just as the principle of downward motion is united to one able to be moved downward; the other is an external principle of motion, and that one moves both as the end and as the efficient [cause] at the same time. "For it moves," as the Philosopher says in the eleventh book of the *Metaphysics*, "just as the object of desire moves" desire.[96] And it is not called a natural motion from the one moving, but from the Prime [Mover].

5. To the next [objection] we say that resurrection is not natural as an end proportionate to an efficient [cause], which nature is, as is shown in the objection; but it is the end of a natural object, according to which the natural object is related to the one who created it, as was said above.

6. To the next [objection] we say: If the Jordan were a principle capable of curing leprosy by a power joined to it by nature, then the cure would be natural; but it does not follow that it is natural for it to cure everyone. And, similarly, although the voice may raise everyone, nonetheless it does not follow that it is a natural principle for raising [everyone]. Besides, it has not yet been shown what that voice is.

Question 4. On the ends (termini) *of resurrection*

To the fourth [question] one proceeds in this way:

1. Augustine says in the fourth book of *On the Trinity* that the resurrection of Christ is the model (*exemplar*) for our resurrection;[97] therefore, [his] end will be the model for [our] end.[98]

95. Alb., *De IV coaequ.* q. 16 a. 1 sol; *De homine* q. 4 a. 3. ad 5 (ed. Colon. 27/2, pp. 41–42).

96. Ar., *Metaph.* 12.7 (1072a26).

97. Aug., *De trin.* 4.3.6 (PL 42: 891).

98. By *terminus* here Albert intends the end from which (*terminus a quo*), as

But he did not rise again from ashes; therefore, neither will we rise again from ashes. Against this is what is said at the beginning of Genesis: "You are earth, and to earth you will return."[99] Now this statement, as Haimo says, pertains to all those who inherit Original Sin from Adam;[100] therefore, it is necessary that we all return to ashes.

2. In addition, after this, one asks about those who will remain. For they appear to be covered over and not to rise again, or the end from which (*terminus a quo*) their resurrection stems is a living and animal body.

3. Similarly, one asks whether the other end [that is, the end to which] is the same in number or different. It seems that it is the same in number, because the numerically identical body and the same soul will exist there; therefore, the union will be numerically identical. But to the contrary: Those things that have a corruptible, changed substance are not restored the same in number, as the Philosopher says at the end of book two of *On Generation and Corruption*.[101]

4. Again, if one assumes that the sensible and vegetative soul are not in the same essence with the rational soul, then the substance of the sensible and vegetative soul will be corruptible, and so they do not appear to be restored the same in number. Since, therefore, they are a human's substantial distinguishing attributes (*differentiae*), it seems that the human will not be numerically identical.

5. If perhaps one should say that there is a false assumption there, one may object otherwise. For it follows that the form's essence, by which a human exists and is said to be human, exists in every human. But the soul is not that form, since soul is not predicated of the one whose form it is;[102] rather, that form

---

opposed to the end to which (*terminus ad quem*), a distinction that he makes clear as the question unfolds.

99. Gn 3.19. The Vulg. reads: "pulvis es et in pulverem reverteris." Augustine, however, records the variant found here. See John Strayer McIntosh, *A Study of Augustine's Versions of Genesis* (Chicago: University of Chicago Press, 1912), 22.

100. Haimo of Auxerre, *In Rom.* 5.10 (PL 117: 405C). Cf. Thomas Aquinas, *IV Sent.* d. 43 a. 4 qla. 2.

101. Ar., *De gen. et corr.* 2.11 (388b14–17).

102. That is, the essential or substantial form should be in the predicate position in a definition. But we do not define a human being as a soul.

is [so] predicated. Since, then, after death a human is not a human, that form has passed into non-being, considering that it is simple and not composed from principles. And so it seems that a human rising again will not have a substantial form, which is the form of the whole, that is the same in number.

6. After this, one asks again why resurrection has an end-from-which (*terminus a quo*) that is exactly the same in all members, both good and bad alike, but does not have an end-to-which (*terminus ad quem*) that is exactly the same.

Solution: We say that the end (*terminus*) of resurrection is derived from death's cause, as Haimo says. This cause is Original Sin. In this, there are two things: first, the absence of the requisite justice on which life in the state of innocence depended. And this [lack of justice] causes death with respect to the separation of the soul from the body. In fact, it is just, as Augustine says, that as the soul deserted its life through injustice, so too there was imposed upon it the necessity of separation from the body, for which it was the very cause of life.[103] Similarly, in Original Sin there is an inclination toward every evil, which inclination is a corruption afflicting the body and a disposition contrary to resurrection. And it is necessary for this [corruption] to be removed by means of the body's putrefaction and reduction to ashes, as Haimo says, so that the Lord's decree, which states, "You are earth, and to earth you will return,"[104] might be unchangeable. Owing to the absence of concupiscence and sin in him, however, there does not exist in the Lord the same end [end-from-which] that exists in our members.

1. And in this way a solution to the first [objection] is apparent. He is indeed the model for us in terms of that which rises again, but not with respect to the entire arrangement of the ends of resurrection.

2. To the next [objection] we say that those who will be found alive again will be reduced to ashes by a fire that will consume the face of the earth; and these ashes will be the end from which (*terminus a quo*) their resurrection proceeds.[105]

103. Aug., *De civ. Dei* 13.5 (PL 41: 387; CSEL 40/1, p. 633, 23–30).
104. Cf. Gn 3.19.
105. Cf. Alb., *III Sent.* d. 23 a. 3 sol. ad diff. Hug. (ad 3).

3. To the next [objection] we say that resurrection will be to one [who is] numerically identical. The Philosopher's authoritative statement is understood to concern the substances of those whose substance is so changed that the relation of matter to this [particular] form remains no more than [its relation] to another form. But this is not the case with the matter of a human, as is clear from the objections above concerning the union of a rational soul to a body.

4. To the next [objection] we say that even if one assumes such a position, still the human will rise the same in number because, as the Philosopher intends, there is one potency for one act, and conversely.[106] Therefore, since in matter there remains a potency the same in number, although with respect to another agent, so too the act will be the same in number. Nor must one concede that the sensible and the vegetative souls will be destroyed entirely (*in toto*), since they remain in a potency that cannot be removed from matter.

5. Similarly, a solution to the following [objection] is apparent. For either that form is only the form of the resurrection, or, if it is something in nature, then it will remain in potency in each of those that are joined together.

6. To the last [objection] we say that we are equal, both good and evil [humans], insofar as we are born "children of wrath,"[107] by which the resurrection's end-from-which (*terminus a quo*) is established. But we are not the same in the merit of the will, through which the resurrection's end-to-which (*terminus ad quem*) is established. Therefore, the resurrection's end-from-which is the same for everyone, but its end-to-which is not.

Question 5. On the circumstances surrounding resurrection[108]

To the fifth [question] one proceeds in this way:

The Apostle says in 1 Thes 4 that "the Lord himself will come down from heaven with commandment, and with the voice of

106. See Ar., *De sensu et sens.* 7 (447b17–19); cf. Alb., *De sensu et sens.* 3.3.
107. Eph 2.3.
108. Cf. Alb., *IV Sent.* d. 43 aa. 4, 6, 14.

an archangel, and with the trumpet of God."[109] And the Gloss says that "'with commandment' is the same as with authority (*imperio*), because he will descend as the Lord who reigns (*imperans*)."[110] "'With the voice of an archangel,'" the Gloss says, means "[with the voice] of his very own archangel or angels, which will cause the dead to rise again."[111] And that voice is also called a trumpet "because it will be clear." Or, according to another gloss,[112] his advent is called a trumpet because it will be clear, both vanquishing the impious and calling the pious to the feast of joys, which were the two uses for trumpets under the Law.

1. With respect to this, one asks why it is necessary that there be three,[113] since authority (*imperium*) with a divine command (*iussu*) should suffice.

2. Also, one raises an objection to the second gloss: namely, God does not seem to be called an archangel, either by nature or by function. And so that gloss that says, "with the voice of his very own archangel," seems to be false.

Likewise, the second gloss, which explains this in terms of a multitude of angels, seems false. For it is certain that it does not speak of an external voice, because the dead do not hear that, but rather of an internal voice, of which it says: "He will give to his voice a voice of power,"[114] "that is, the power of resuscitating the dead."[115] And this is not the voice of angels, because in the Gospel it says that "those who are in the graves will hear the voice of the Son of God,"[116] as was said above.

In addition, as the holy fathers say,[117] angels do not cause the resurrection.

3. Besides, Damascene does not mention any of these when

109. 1 Thes 4.15 (Vulg.).

110. Peter Lombard, *In epist. Pauli* 1 Thes 4.16 (PL 192: 304A).

111. Ibid.

112. Ibid. (PL 192: 304B).

113. Three: i.e., with commandment, with the voice of an archangel, and with the trumpet.

114. Ps 67.34.

115. Peter Lombard, *In Ps.* 67.34 (PL 191: 618CD).

116. Jn 5.28.

117. Cf. Aug., *Contra serm. Arianorum* 13 (PL 42: 693).

he says: "Believe that the future resurrection is by divine power, will, and command. For God has a power that concurs with his will" in the resurrection of the dead.[118]

4. After this, one asks to what these three [realities] that Damascene mentions—namely, power, will, and command—refer.

5. Furthermore, one asks what the last trumpet is. For Gregory says that to sound the [last] trumpet is nothing else than to reveal the Son to the world dreadfully.[119] Opposed to this seems to be the statement of others, which is found in the *Sentences*, that the sound of the trumpet is a certain clear and conspicuous sign indicating the advent of the Lord for judgment.[120]

6. After this again one asks how it will occur "in a moment and in the twinkling of an eye."[121] The Apostle does not mention these two—or even one—without reason.

Moreover, it seems that what he says is impossible, since it seems that the gathering up of ashes, the reintegration of bodies, and their change and reunion with souls cannot happen in the twinkling of an eye.

7. Furthermore, one asks again what the four winds, whence the spirit comes, are, as Ezekiel says, "and it will blow upon the slain, and they will come to life again."[122]

Solution:

1. One must reply to this that authority (*imperium*) is the first cause of resurrection. And to the objection that [divine] authority is sufficient in itself (*per se*), one must reply that this is true insofar as concerns God himself but not insofar as concerns those who rise again, just as [divine] authority is sufficient in itself for bringing [humans] into [a state of] grace and for glorifying [them], but, in order for glory to be joined to us more properly, it is necessary to have a medium, namely habitual grace. And it is the same here: there is no need for the other [circumstances, namely, the voice of the archangel and the

118. John Damascene, *De fide orth.* 4.27 (PG 94: 1225B–C; ed. Buytaert, p. 385, 129–40).

119. Greg., *Moral.* 17.13.54 (PL 76: 37f.).

120. Peter Lombard, *IV Sent.* d. 43 c.2 (p. 996).

121. 1 Cor 15.52.

122. Ezek 37.9.

sound of the trumpet] on God's part, but rather on the part of the others [namely, the humans who will rise again].

2. To the next [objection] we say that, according to blessed Gregory, Christ is the archangel, as the first Gloss states. He is the archangel—that is, the prince of angels—with respect to the function (*officium*) that he exercised when he was sent in the flesh.

To the objection concerning the second gloss, one must reply that the voice according to the gloss designates the efficacy of the angels' ministry in the collection of the ashes, and not [their efficacy] in the resurrection itself.

5. To the query concerning the trumpet, one must reply that the trumpet can refer to either, namely to the Son's revelation to the world, as Gregory says, or to the ministry of the angels, as the other gloss says. And, according to the third explanation, what is called a trumpet will be a clear sign.

3. To the next [objection] one must reply that Damascene does not touch upon causes, except at first efficient causes, and so he does not speak of the ministry of the angels.

4. To the next [objection] one must reply that these three [namely, divine power, will, and command] refer to three realities that are in those who rise again according to the Lord's command. For then there will be a change of a corruptible body into an incorruptible [body], and divine power exists for that purpose, because this is the last and the greatest of the things that occur in the resurrection. Resurrection's goal (*finis*), however, is the beauty of justice in the receipt of rewards among the good and the evil, and will exists for that purpose. There will also be in them the obedience of nature, and command exists for that purpose.

One understands there to be a distinction, however, among a divine operation, that of Christ, and that of the angels, which distinction belongs to the works that pertain to resurrection. Now, the first and least [of these] is the gathering of ashes, and this is an angelic operation. Second and greater is the uniting of [bodily] members into a state of incorruption—not, I say, of impassibility—and that is attributed to Christ the man. Third and greatest is the renewed union of the body with the soul, and for this there is a divine operation.

6. To the objection concerning the moment and the twinkling of an eye one must reply that according to the Gloss they both refer to the very same thing,[123] and one is able to point to the other. Nonetheless, if we wished to distinguish them, we would say that an eye twinkles because of the emission of the [eye's] ray, which, according to Plato,[124] is joined to an external ray for the purpose of observing a luminous visible [object], and this seems to apply to the good. A moment, however, which is a deficient fraction of time, seems to apply to those who will always remain in deficient temporality.

7. To the last [objection] one must reply as Isaac [Israeli] does in the book *On Definitions*,[125] that spirits, which are moved in a body as is light in the world, come together for the fashioning of the human body. Therefore, these spirits, insofar as they are luminous, have the nature of the fifth body;[126] and therefore they are incorruptible, and at the destruction of the human body they return to [their] spheres (*ad circulos*). And these [spirits] are the ones that come from the four winds of heaven[127] and from the four regions of the world through the double motion[128] of the higher heavenly bodies; and because they are vital spirits they bring the dead back to life. Now the principal diurnal motion distinguishes the eastern and western regions, whereas a motion from the back to the front of the oblique orbit, that is, of the zodiac, distinguishes the southern and the northern [regions]. For these two motions are the movements of the firmament and of the planets, which act to preserve the physical constitution of humans.

123. Peter Lombard, *In epist. Pauli* 1 Cor 15.52 (PL 191: 1690C).

124. Plato, *Tim.* 45CD (ed. Wrobel, p. 52).

125. Isaac, *De diff.* (ed. Muckle, p. 318, 18ff.); cf. Alb., *De spir. et resp.* 1.1.4.

126. On the fifth body, see Alb., *De caelo et mundo* 2.3.1; cf. Alb., *De causis propr. elem.* 1.1.1, 2.1.2 (ed. Colon. 5/2, pp. 49–50, 91–92), on the fifth element. For a translation, see Albert the Great's *On the Causes of the Properties of the Elements* (*Liber de causis proprietatum elementorum*), trans. and annotated by Irven M. Resnick, Mediaeval Philosophical Texts in Translation (Milwaukee, WI: Marquette University Press, 2010), 20–21, 101–3.

127. See Jer 49.36.

128. On the double motion, see Alb., *De gen. et corr.* 2.3.4; *Metaph.* 11.2.5.

Question 6. On the truth of human nature[129]

Concerning the sixth [question] one first asks according to which definition of truth should the truth of human nature (*veritas humanae naturae*) be understood; second, since [the word] "true"—and, similarly, "truth"—is said of a thing in many ways, [one asks] according to which meaning truth is understood here; third, whether it is a substance or an accident; fourth, whether it is spiritual or corporeal; fifth, what it is according to its own definition; sixth, whether it applies to the head and to the members according to a single definition (*ratio*); seventh, whether it applies to the good and to the evil according to a single definition; eighth, whether it is one or many for all; ninth, from what, as from matter, it is derived; tenth, what exists in the truth of human nature by way of parts; last, whether the truth of one member is able to pass over into the truth of another member on the day of resurrection.

Art. 1. According to which definition of truth the truth of human nature should be understood[130]

To the first, one proceeds in this way:

Anselm says, "Truth is rectitude that can be perceived by the mind alone,"[131] whereas Augustine [says]: Truth is the essence (*entitas*) of a thing.[132] The Philosopher, at the beginning of the second book of the *Metaphysics* [says]: "Truth is the goal (*finis*) of the speculative intelligence."[133] This same one says, before the end of the third book, that truth is an appropriate affirmation or negation.[134] Likewise, a certain philosopher says that "truth is the adequation of things and the intellect."[135]

129. Alb. refers back to this question in *De homine* q. 11 a. 2 sol. (ed. Colon. 27/2, p. 108).

130. Cf. Alb., *IV Sent.* d. 44 a. 5.

131. Anselm, *De veritate* c. 11 (PL 158: 480A; ed. Schmitt, 1: 191, 19–20).

132. Aug., *Solil.* 2.5.8 (PL 32: 889); cf. Alb., *De bono,* tr. 1. q. 1 a. 8 (ed. Colon. 28, p. 16, 9–10).

133. Ar., *Metaph.* 2.1 (993b20–21).

134. Ar., *Metaph.* 4.8 (1012b8–10); that is, not the third book but the fourth. Cf. Ar., *Metaph.* 6.4 (1027b21ff.); Alb., *Metaph.* 4.4.2 and 6.3.1; *De praedic.* 7.9.

135. Cf. Bonaventure, *I Sent.* d. 40, a. 2, q. 1, *Opera* 1: 707, 5; Alex. Hales, *Summa* I pt. 1 inq. 1 tr. 3 q. 2 mem. 1 cap. 3 IV (ed. Quarrachi, vol. I, p. 142);

And it is evident that the truth of human nature is not understood according to any of those [definitions] that are understood by the Philosopher. For all of those speak either of truth insofar as it is the perfection of the intellect alone, or of the truth of a sign, namely language. When, however, one asks about the truth of human nature, one asks according to matter (*secundum materiam*) and not according to the intellect or language.

1. It seems, similarly, that it also should not be understood according to Anselm's first [definition], because the truth of human nature is sought in the body's matter, and this is not something that can be perceived by the mind alone.

2. Likewise, all rectitude exists with respect to the extremes between which it exists, and the truth of human nature is sought in itself, not in comparison to different extremes.

3. In the same way, it seems that it cannot be understood according to the second [definition]. Indeed, the truth of human nature is sought in matter, but essence (*entitas*) is more from form. For man's essence is from the rational soul.

4. Furthermore, the truth of human nature is what will rise again, and as such that truth will remain after death and putrefaction. Man's essence, however, does not remain after death.

Solution: One must reply that truth here is understood according to both of the first definitions. For the first definition speaks of a thing according to its directedness toward what it is in the First Truth, and that directedness is called rectitude. Therefore, since the truth of human nature exists in order to abide forever, that will be its rectitude, and this can be perceived by the mind alone, not by sense.

1. Therefore, one must reply to the first [objection] that noth-

---

Alb., *De bono* tr. 1 q. 1 a.8 (ed. Colon. 28, p. 15, 43; 62–63). Thomas Aquinas attributes this maxim to Isaac Israeli. See John Wippel, *Metaphysical Themes in St. Thomas Aquinas II* (Washington, DC: The Catholic University of America Press, 2007), 110. For Thomas Aquinas, "adequation" implies conformity and a commensurate relationship between the object and the intellect. Accordingly, cognition is a process of "assimilation" that is completed or perfected when a sign or likeness of the object is known in the knower. For a helpful discussion see Jan A. Aertsen, "Truth as Transcendental in Thomas Aquinas," *Topoi* 11 (1992): 159–71, esp. 163–64.

ing among the parts of matter can be perceived by the mind alone, but among its natural properties there are many that can be perceived by the mind alone.

2. A solution to the second [objection] is apparent from what has already been said, because rectitude is understood within nature and it is understood to abide forever, and accordingly one asks about the truth of human nature.

3. To the objection concerning the second definition, one must reply that the essence (*entitas*) of a thing is spoken of in two ways, namely from existence (*esse*) that comes from form, and from existence that is caused by form in matter. For example, man's existence is from the rational soul, and the existence of a hand or foot is also from the soul. Surely, a hand that has been amputated is not a hand, except equivocally.[136] Similarly, we say with respect to the entire body that the true essence of the human body is that which we can say possesses the true essence of the human body.

4. To the next [objection] one must reply that after death and putrefaction the truth of human nature does not remain according to act, just as man's essence does not, but it remains only in material potency.

Art. 2. According to which meaning truth is understood here

To the second, one proceeds in this way:

"True" is understood of a thing in many ways even according to both of the definitions mentioned above, since these definitions are universal and very general. Now the true is said to be the same as the perfect, according to what is said in the Gospel: "If you remain in my word, truly (*vere*) you will be my disciples."[137] And this is understood in contrast to the imperfect.

Similarly, the true is said to be true absolutely (*simpliciter*), as the true is understood of things capable of demonstration and of things everlasting, which is opposed to what appears [true] according to opinion, such as what is true of probable things.

Similarly the true is said to be what possesses the true exis-

136. Cf. Ar., *De gen. animal.* 1.19 (726b23ff.); *Metaph.* 7.11 (1036b30–35); Alb., *De homine* q. 8 a. 2 ad 5 (ed. Colon. 27/2, p. 96); *De animal.* 15.2.6.104 (*SZ* 2: 1132); *Metaph.* 7.3.9.

137. Jn 8.31.

tence of any nature according to species. And this is opposed to something imaginary (*phantastico*), which has only the appearance of that species, just as a reddish ray appears to be gold.

Also, sometimes the true is said to be what has nothing external intermingled with it, which is opposed to something mixed with an external nature.

And all of these are understood as "true" in reality.

Therefore, one asks, in which way the true or truth should be understood here.

It seems that it is not according to the first [meaning]. To be sure, a body is imperfect before it grows to an appropriate size, and nonetheless it possesses the truth of human nature.

Similarly, it is not understood according to the second meaning, since it [that is, the human body] is not everlasting. And in addition that truth belongs to the nature of the reality in itself and not to [the reality] confined to matter.

In the same manner, it does not seem to accord with the third [meaning] because something will exist in our body that truly has the nature of a part of man according to species, but nevertheless will not rise again. Indeed, not all the flesh that is generated in our body will rise again of necessity, as Augustine says;[138] and yet all the flesh has the true definition (*ratio*) of a part of man.

Likewise, it seems that it does not accord with the last [meaning], because the body of man is based on a mixture and complexion of things external,[139] which are converted to nourishment and humors in it.

Solution: We say that truth is understood here in the last way. And "external" is said [here] not absolutely insofar as the body's species [is concerned], but in relation to the power of

138. Aug., *De civ. Dei* 22.19.1 (PL 41: 780; CSEL 40/2, p. 629, 15–20).

139. "Complexion" refers to the interaction of material elements, qualities, or humors to produce a body's individual composition. A body's composition or complexion is typically identified as hot and dry (choleric), hot and moist (sanguineous), cold and moist (phlegmatic), or cold and dry (melancholic). When the four are equal, the complexion will be temperate or balanced. See Valentin Groebner, "Complexio/Complexion: Categorizing Individual Natures, 1250–1600," in *The Moral Authority of Nature*, ed. Lorraine Daston and Fernando Vidal (Chicago: University of Chicago Press, 2004), 361–83.

enduring forever. Now the truth of human nature is not understood such that it is mixed with absolutely nothing, but such that it is not mixed so as to lose the power of enduring forever.

It could also be said that it is understood in the first way. And the perfect is distinguished in a threefold way, namely: with respect to the species, and in this way every man, whether small or large, is perfect in body; and perfect with respect to size, and in this way not every man is perfect in body; and in a third way perfect is said not according to existence (*esse*), but according to the power to endure forever, and in this way everything animated by a rational soul is perfect.

Art. 3. Whether it is a substance or an accident[140]

To the third, one proceeds in this way:

1. Whatever is not matter or form or a composite is an accident. But the truth of human nature is neither a form nor a composite, which is evident *per se*. Nor does it seem to be matter, because the definition (*ratio*) is the same for one part of matter as for the entire matter, and the entire matter will not rise again. Therefore, the truth of human nature will be neither a part of matter nor matter itself; and so it remains that it is an accident.

2. But to the contrary: An accident is what can be absent [from a thing], and the truth of human nature cannot be absent; therefore, it will not be an accident.

3. Again, if truth is the essence (*entitas*) of a thing, as Augustine says,[141] then the truth of an accident will be an accident, and the truth of a substance will be a substance; therefore, too, the truth of a body will be a body.

Solution: If we wish to speak of truth in the abstract, then the truth of human nature in the body will be the power (*potentia*) of enduring forever. And that will be an accident by nature, but not by predication, just as every inherent property (*proprium*) is an accident, and it cannot be absent because it is not related to the subject as to subject alone, but as to subject

140. See Alb., *IV Sent.* d. 44 a. 10.

141. Aug., *Solil.* 2.5.8 (PL 32: 889); cf. Alb., *De bono*, tr. 1. q. 1 a. 8 (ed. Colon. 28, p. 16, 9–10).

and cause.[142] And this is clear from the fact that the subject always falls under the definition of [its] special property. But if we want to speak of the concrete—that is, of a true [thing]—then that truth will be the substance of a body that is capable of enduring forever, and in this way it will be a substance determined by such a property.

1, 2. And the solution to the first two [objections] is clear from this. For the definition (*ratio*) is not the same for all parts of matter, as was assumed, because not all parts can endure forever, as will become evident below in article nine.

3. To the last [objection] one must reply that if essence (*entitas*) is said to be the existence of a thing through [its] proper nature, then the objection holds. But if essence is understood as determined for existence through a property that is consequent upon nature, then it does not hold. And here it is understood in just this way, as is clear from the things already said in the first article.

Art. 4. Whether it is spiritual or corporeal

To the fourth, one proceeds in this way:

1. Every form that exists in a corruptible body is corrupted when that body is corrupted. If, therefore, the power (*potentia*) for enduring [forever] is a form in a corruptible body, then it will be corrupted when that body is corrupted; and if it is a corporeal form, it is a form existing in a corruptible body. Therefore, if it is a corporeal form, it is a corruptible form. On the basis of this, further [one may say]: No corruptible power is a power for enduring forever, because otherwise contradictories and contraries will be presented as true of the same thing; for the same thing will be corruptible and incorruptible, and corruptible and non-corruptible. Therefore, it remains that that power is not corporeal, but spiritual.

2. In addition, if a human body should be generated in [its] organs but the rational soul is not infused, it will not rise again, because Augustine says that unformed infants will not rise

142. Ar., *Top.* 5.4 (132b18ff.); Boethius, trans. ant. PL 64: 960A; Alb., *Top.* 5.2.4.

again.[143] Therefore, the power of rising again comes from the soul and not from the body. And so it appears that that power according to which the truth of human nature is determined is spiritual and not corporeal.

3. To the contrary: Damascene says that souls will not rise again; and the truth of human nature exists in what will rise again.[144] Therefore, it seems that it is a form existing in the body.

Solution: We say that there is a form existing in the body that is called the truth of human nature. Now, the body itself is a true thing (*verum*), insofar as it is able to endure [forever], and [its] truth (*veritas*) is the power of enduring. Therefore, it is a spiritual form, yet one existing in the body nonetheless.

1. Therefore, one must reply to the first [objection] something that we readily concede, that it [namely, form] is corrupted with respect to act but not with respect to material potency. For this potency does not determine the substance of the body in relation to accidental or natural forms with respect to nature, which exists according to first qualities, from which the human body is composed. For Anselm says in the book *Why the God-Man* that neither corruption nor incorruption is from the truth of human nature, but that there is one substance of corporeal matter that remains beneath corruption and incorruption.[145]

2, 3. One must reply to the other two [objections] that these arguments prove only that it [that is, the truth of human nature] is caused by the soul in the body, not that it is in the soul.

Art. 5. What it is in terms of a proper definition[146]

To the fifth, one proceeds in this way:

One magisterial definition is stated thus: "The truth of human nature is the true nature of a body that has been completed and constituted from official and uniform (*similibus*) mem-

143. Aug., *Enchir.* 85 (PL 40: 272); cf. Peter Lombard, *IV Sent.* d. 44 c. 8 (p. 1005).

144. John Damascene, *De fide orth.* 4.27 (PG 94: 1221A–D; ed. Buytaert, p. 379, 32ff.).

145. Anselm, *Cur deus homo* 2.11 (PL 158: 410CD; ed. Schmitt, 2: 109, 13–15).

146. See Alb., *II Sent.* d. 30 a. 4; *III Sent.* d. 5 a. 9.

bers, having the potential for incorruption from the union with a rational soul."[147]

Likewise, certain others propose this [definition]: "The truth of human nature is the integrity of the human substance, [an integrity] safeguarded by the harmony of the parts, which each one was to have in the time of [his] youth, so long as nature did not err."

But Anselm provides this [definition]: the truth of human nature is what will appear on the day of resurrection.[148]

1. Opposed to the first [definition] is that if the true nature is received from a part of matter, as was proved above, then there are many [parts] of the true nature of the body that will not rise again. And so what constitutes the "true nature of the body" is stated wrongly in the definition.

2. One also asks to what "completed and constituted" refer, since both seem to mean the same thing.

3. Likewise, one asks whether, as the Philosopher says,[149] there is any potential (*potentia*) in matter that cannot be completed by an active power (*potentia*) in nature, since that power that exists for incorruption is in the body, as the definition says, "from the union with a rational soul." It appears that it can be completed by some active natural [power]. Since this is false, it remains that such a power does not exist in a body from the union with the soul. For its union with the soul is natural, and so what is caused by that union will be natural.

4. Opposed to the second [definition] is the fact that no integrity [of the whole] exists in those that never possessed [it] according to parts. But dead infants never possessed the pro-

147. By "completed" [*completi*] here Alb. means "perfected" or "fulfilled." For this and the following definition, see the *Quaestio de veritate humanae naturae* attributed to Alexander of Hales (Cod. Toulouse Bibliothèque de la ville 737, fol. 277va). For Alb., uniform or homogenous members are those in which the part and the whole are identical (e.g., skin, when cut into smaller pieces, remains skin), whereas non-uniform members are composed of other parts, as a hand is composed of skin, nerves, etc.; official members are those that are intended to perform a special task, like hands and feet. Cf. *De animal.* 1.2.13 (*SZ* 1: 49). See *infra,* sol., ad 2.

148. Anselm, *Cur deus homo* 2.11 (PL 158: 410C; ed. Schmitt, 2: 109, 10–11).

149. The Philosopher: see Thomas Aquinas, *II Sent.* d. 30 q. 2 a. 1 sol., where this is attributed to the commentator on the *Phys.* 1 text. comm. 81.

portion (*congruentiam*) of the parts of a thirty-year-old body; therefore, neither the integrity of their substance nor the truth [of human nature] exists in that [proportion].

5. Opposed to the third [definition] is the fact that it does not seem to make evident the truth of human nature.

Solution: One must reply that all these definitions speak of truth so far as it is not cut off from the true (*a vero*).

1. We say to the first [objection], therefore, that the true nature is the true substance of human matter, and although that [definition] is a general one that extends to both the complete and the non-complete and to one having and not-having the potential for incorruption, it is restricted nonetheless by subsequent distinguishing attributes (*differentiae*).

2. To the next [objection] one must reply that perfection in the human body is twofold, namely according to the substantial form, which is the rational soul, and this perfection is properly said to be that which completes; and there is also a perfection in the composition of the organs, and this is implied when it says "constituted from official and uniform members." And "official members" are those that are ordered to [particular] acts, and their parts do not share the same definition (*ratio*) with them, just as an eye exists in order to see, but a part of an eye is not an eye, and likewise a hand exists in order to touch, but a part of a hand is not a hand.[150] "Uniform [members]," however, are those whose parts do share the same definition (*ratio*) with them, such as flesh. For a part of flesh is flesh, and the same is true for a nerve and the mouth and skin and hair and nails.

3. To the next [objection] one must reply that it is not the same for the human body as for other bodies. For other bodies, like the bodies of brute animals, have a form caused by nature; to be sure, the vegetable and sensible souls are caused by a nature that exists in the seed, as the Philosopher says in the book *On Animals*.[151] But the rational soul is the substantial form of the human body that enters from outside by [God] creating

150. See Ps. Aug., *De spir. et anima* 15 (PL 40: 791); Alb., *De anima* 1.1.2.10ff.; 12.1.4.50ff.; *Quaest. super de animal.* 1, q. 3 (ed. Colon. 12, p. 80, 51ff.; *QDA*, p. 20).

151. Ar., *De gen. animal.* 2.3 (736a29ff.); cf. Alb., *De animal.* 16.1.10–11, 56–64 (*SZ* 2: 1184–89).

(*per creantem*), and it does not exist from nature, as the Philosopher says in the same place. And therefore a certain potential that is not completed by nature, but rather by [God] creating, can be caused from the union of the body with the soul.

4. To the objection against the second [definition], one must say that it is true that there is no integrity[152] in those that do not possess it in any way. But infants have a body the size of one thirty years old in terms of power (*virtute*), although not in mass, as Augustine says.[153] And therefore there is integrity in them in terms of power.

5. To the objection concerning the third [definition], one must reply that, as the Philosopher says in the *Topics*,[154] a special property is assigned in order to know a thing. And this is why Anselm identifies the very subject of that power through the act of the potential to endure forever; for to appear at the resurrection is the act of the potential to endure forever.

Art. 6. Whether it applies to the head and to the members according to a single definition (*ratio*)

To the sixth, one proceeds in this way:

1. The substance of the body that is possessed through generation is either the truth of human nature or it is the chief source for [this] truth. But this substance is not possessed by us and by Christ according to a single definition (*ratio*); therefore, the truth is not possessed by us and by Christ according to a single definition (*ratio*). The proof of the second [proposition] is that the substance of the body in us is possessed from the mingling of seeds,[155] but in Christ [it is possessed] by the power of the working of the Holy Spirit.

2. Likewise, if we consider the resurrection, there will not be a single definition (*ratio*) because, whereas his nature will

152. "Integrity," i.e., "completeness."

153. Aug., *De civ. Dei* 22.14 (PL 41: 777; CSEL 40/2, p. 622, 13–15). *Virtute* here means potentially or in terms of capacity.

154. Ar., *Top.* 5.2.4 (130a4–5; 132b18ff.); Boethius, transl. ant. PL 64: 955D; cf. Alb., *Top.* 5.2.2.4.

155. That is, the male and female seeds that share in the formation of the human being. In Jesus, however, the father's semen was replaced by the power of the Holy Spirit.

endure for eternity, [and] ours will also endure, his exists as a cause, [but] ours as caused. Therefore, there is not a single definition (*ratio*) at all.

To the contrary: The Apostle says: "He will reform the body of our lowliness, configured to the body of his glory."[156] If, therefore, glory will have the same definition (*ratio*) as glory, then the [body] that remains incorrupt will also have the same definition as the incorrupt.

Solution: A definition can be assigned in two ways, namely a definition indicating what (*quid*) [something is], and a definition indicating on account of what (*propter quid*) [it exists]. There will be one definition indicating what it is, as is evident from what has already been said in the preceding article. But it is not necessary for there to be one definition indicating on account of what (*propter quid*) [it is].

1. And the first objection, which considers true nature through the efficient cause, proceeds in just this way.

2. And the second [objection], which considers nature in Christ, as it is the cause of the resurrection of others, [proceeds] similarly.

Art. 7. Whether it applies to the good and to the evil according to a single definition (*ratio*)

To the seventh, one proceeds in this way:

1. Augustine says that corruptions will not be removed from the bodies of the damned;[157] but the power (*potentia*) of enduring under corruption and that of enduring under non-corruption is not the same. Therefore, a nature with the power to endure with respect to these two will not have the same definition (*ratio*).

2. In addition, a spiritual body and a non-spiritual body do not have the same nature; therefore, they do not have the same definition (*ratio*) of nature. But the bodies of the damned are non-spiritual, and those of the saints are spiritual, because the saints[158] say that the bodies of the damned will be gross, earthy,

156. Phil 3.21.
157. Aug., *Enchir.* 92 (PL 40: 272).
158. Cf. Peter Lombard, *IV Sent.* d. 43 c.7 (p. 999).

[and] ignoble, but the bodies of the saints will be spiritual, subtle, noble, and shining. Therefore, the same definition (*ratio*) of nature does not seem to obtain for them [both].

To the contrary: The Apostle says that "the trumpet will sound, and the dead will rise again incorruptible, and we will be changed," 1 Cor 15.[159] The Gloss there says that all of the dead will rise incorruptible, but not all will be changed according to the resurrection of glory.[160] Therefore, the same power of incorruption will exist in all the dead.

Solution: One must reply that a definition (*ratio*) can be assigned in many ways. In fact, a definition (*ratio*) can be assigned on behalf of the nature's species, which is really the human nature; and this will be one. And according to this [definition], the truth of human nature (*verum humanae naturae*) is the body's substance, capable of enduring forever based on the substantial form of man. A definition (*ratio*) can also be assigned on behalf of the qualities of nature that are concomitant with the body's substance; and this will not be a definition in the proper sense, nor will it be a single [definition]. And according to this [definition], among the good the truth of human nature will be the body's always-enduring substance that is able to resist, by [its] natural power, whatever acts against it. In the damned, however, the body's substance will endure forever without having the same power.

2. And from this a solution to the second [objection] is apparent.

1. To the first [objection], one must reply that corruption is twofold, just as the Gloss on the same passage in the Apostle distinguishes it,[161] namely: a corruption that destroys the union of the body, such as fever and beheading and death, and this will be removed from all [at the resurrection]; and there is a corruption of the power for resisting the torment that stems from God's judgment, and this will be removed only from the good.

159. 1 Cor 15.52.
160. Peter Lombard, *In epist. Pauli* 1 Cor 15.52 (PL 191: 1690B).
161. Peter Lombard, *In epist. Pauli* 1 Cor 15.52 (PL 191: 1691A).

Art. 8. Whether it [that is, the truth of human nature] is one in all or is many[162]

To the eighth, one proceeds in this way:

1. Augustine says in *On the Literal Meaning of Genesis* 8 that all but Christ were in Abraham's loins in two ways—namely, in terms of bodily substance and in terms of seminal reason.[163] Therefore, by analogy we were all in Adam in terms of bodily substance; and so we were in him [namely, Abraham] through some bodily substance. Therefore, in him there was some bodily substance from which the substance of all was produced; but this [substance] is the truth of human nature, from which the substance of all was produced. Therefore, there is one truth [of human nature] for all men.

2. In addition, that from which a son's substance arises is either derived from the father's substance or not. If it is, then in the same way the father has been derived from his father and so on all the way back to the first [father]. Therefore, we all have been derived from one [father], and we all have been produced from one who has been derived from another. And in this way materially again there is one truth [of human nature] for everyone. If, however, it [that is, the son's substance] is not from the father's substance, then it appears that the son is in no way related to the father.

To the contrary: Matter is not divisible to infinity by means of determinate quantities. But an infinite number [of things] can be generated according to the power of nature, and each one has a determinate quantity of matter. Therefore, all those generated [things] are not produced from one quantity.

Again, either flesh or nerve or bone has been designated in Adam substantially, and so too for the other uniform and non-uniform members, none of which exists in potency to the entire body. Therefore, the derivation [of his descendants] was not produced from any of these [particular members].

Besides, the philosophers say that semen is derived from

162. Cf. Alb., *IV Sent.* d. 44 a. 6; *Summa* II q. 110 m. 1.

163. In fact, the reference is to Aug., *De gen. ad litt.* 10.19–20.34–36 (PL 34: 323f.; CSEL 28/1, pp. 321–24). Cf. Peter Lombard, *III Sent.* d. 3 c. 3 (p. 560).

a superfluity of nutriment.[164] But the nutriment from which someone is generated and [from which he] generates is not materially the same; therefore, substance is not materially the same in everyone.

Solution: We say[165] that the truth [of human nature] is not the same in everyone numerically or materially or formally, but [rather] originally (*originaliter*).[166] By "originally," however, I mean that the food that was received by the first man, which was changed by the nutritive power, was made the subject of the generative power, which is in the seed (*in semine*). And that generative power itself in the first father was multiplied through the matter that was multiplied, as all forms are multiplied only through matter, as is evident to one investigating particular natural forms. The generative power received in the seed, however, produces a fetus (*conceptum*) from what has been derived, and food is again changed into that perfected fetus, and it happens in a manner analogous to [how it happened] in the first [human]. And so it is apparent that the substance of the human body is one by means of a reduction to a single original source, but not by means of some designated matter from which the bodies of all humans are produced. And Augustine alleges that all are in one [human] in terms of bodily substance. Examine the question on the punishment of Christ above to see how Christ and others are there [that is, in one human] differently.[167]

1. We reply, therefore, to the first [objection] that this argument—that we were in him [Adam] in terms of bodily substance, therefore by some [substance]—is not valid. In the premise, by virtue of its determination "in Adam," "bodily substance" is drawn out in order to posit the body's substance in accord with the definition (*ratio*) of the original cause. And this existence (*esse*) is only in the potency of the first efficient [cause] and not

164. Cf. Ar., *De gen. animal.* 1.18 (725a21ff.); Alb., *De animal.* 15.2.5.93 (*SZ* 2: 1127); *Quaest. super de animal.* 15, q. 12ff. (ed. Colon. 12, p. 266ff.; *QDA*, p. 456); *De nutrimento et nutr.* 2.2 (ed. Colon. 7/2, p. 16f.).

165. Cf. Alb., *Quaest. super de animal.* 2, q. 1 (ed. Colon. 12, p. 109, 80ff.; *QDA*, p. 79).

166. That is, in terms of its origin or source.

167. Alb., *De incarn.* 40 (p. 211, 76ff.).

in act, just as when one says, "A creature is a life in the creator,"[168] one draws out the [word] "creature" by means of the determination that follows in order to posit the creature only in a qualified sense (*secundum quid*), namely according to the power of the creating cause. When, however, one says, "therefore, according to some [substance]," the "some" demands "bodily substance" in order to posit it of some particular in a designated act. And so it is clear that the argumentation is not valid.

2. To the other [objection] we say that the seed is from the substance of the father according to proximate potentiality, because the seed is the entire body in potentiality (*potestate*). Therefore, since generation results from it [that is, the father's seed], it is clear that the son is related to the father.

Art. 9. From what, as from matter, it is derived

To the ninth, one proceeds in this way:

1. The Lord says in the Gospel, "Whatever enters the mouth goes into the belly and is cast out through the entrails (*in secessum*)," Mt 15.[169] Therefore, no food passes over into the truth of human nature.

2. Again Bede says in the Gloss on the same passage:[170] "Whatever small amount of very fine humor and liquid food remains after it has been decocted and digested in the veins and limbs is discharged into the entrails (*in secessum*) through the hidden pathways that the Greeks call pores." Therefore, the truth of human nature derives nothing from the nutrimental moisture.

3. Again, the definition (*ratio*) seems to lead to this. In fact, the same definition (*ratio*) exists for every nutriment that is converted into the body's substance. But this [nutriment] increases to a quantity greater than the quantity that is required by nature, and especially if all that is received from food during someone's entire lifetime should exist at the same time. Since, then, all of it does not rise again, it seems that the truth of the human body is not from nutriment.

168. Cf. Aug., *In Joh.* 1.17 (PL 35: 1387).

169. Mt 15.17.

170. Rather, see the *Glossa ord. super Marc.* 7.19; *Summa* II q. 110 m. 2. Alex. Hales, *Glossa* 2. d. 30 (ed. Quar. p. 222ff.).

To the contrary: Augustine says[171] that some things are changed and change, like food, which is changed into the body and changes the body in strength. And in the third book of the *Sentences*[172] and in the Gloss on Phil 2 [it says]:[173] "And in form (*habitu*) he was found as a man."[174] Therefore, food passes over into the truth of human nature. If perhaps it should be said that it is one thing to pass over into the body and something else to pass over into the truth of human nature, then to the contrary: The truth of human nature is caused by the actual union of a corruptible body with an incorruptible soul; but nourishment is made into a body united to an incorruptible soul. Therefore, it [that is, nourishment] has the truth [of human nature].

In addition, the Philosopher says that food nourishes in terms of substance and augments in terms of size.[175] And so it is clear that it is converted into the truth of human nature.

Again, if one food does not have the power to contribute to the truth [of human nature], then no [food] does. But generation results from a superfluity of nutriment, as all the philosophers say. Therefore, none of those [humans] who are generated has the truth of human nature. It is evident that this is false, since all will rise again.

4. Next, one asks about a case that Augustine mentions in the book *On the City of God*,[176] when one [person] is nourished on the flesh of another: in which one, then, will that flesh rise again? And if one should say [that it will rise again] in the first because the other one has received the flesh as something that is shared between them, as it were, let us propose that generation results from that nourishment. Then it is necessary either that the one who has been generated will not rise again, or that that flesh will not be restored to the first one.

And the position, namely the one we specify [here], is made much worse if someone is nourished on living embryos that

171. Aug., *De div. quaest.*, q. 73.1 (PL 40: 84).
172. Peter Lombard, *III Sent.* d. 6 c.6 (p. 580).
173. Phil 2.7; Peter Lombard, *In epist. Pauli* Phil 2.7 (PL 192: 235A).
174. Phil 2.7.
175. Ar., *De anima* 2.4 (416b12–13); cf. Thomas Aquinas, *ST* IIIa q. 77 a. 6 co.
176. Aug., *De civ. Dei* 22.20.2 (PL 41: 782f.; CSEL 40/2, p. 632, 13–p. 633, 3).

have not yet received food and generates [an offspring] from that food.

5. Similarly one asks next about the rule, which Augustine offers,[177] that everything rises again in the one in whom the human part was originally animated.

6. After this, one asks again about the words of the Master in the *Sentences*,[178] saying that no food passes over into the human body, but that matter is multiplied in everyone and with respect to everyone's size, just as the Lord multiplied the five loaves.[179] But this seems to contradict Augustine, who poses many questions concerning in which person the flesh of one man will rise again if another person is nourished by the same [flesh]. These questions are of no value if food does not pass into the truth of human nature.

7. Again, Augustine raises a question concerning the rib from which Eve was formed, namely whether it will rise again in Adam or in Eve.[180] If in Adam, then Eve will not rise again. If in Eve, then since when Eve was formed Adam did not yet possess any nutrimental substance, that rib belonged to the truth of his body. And so not all that belonged to his truth will rise again in him.

Solution: We distinguish a threefold moisture (*humidum*)[181] from which the substance of the human body is derived. The first is seminal moisture,[182] from which arises the first substance of the members, namely the substance of bone and flesh and hands and feet and things of this sort. To be sure, a soul is infused only into an organic body that possesses life in potency, as the Philosopher says.[183] It is necessary, therefore, that the body be proportioned to the soul according to the division of the soul's powers. And so, since nerves are the organ for sensation and flesh is [their] medium, it is necessary that the body,

177. Aug., ibid.; and *Enchir.* 88 (PL 40: 273).
178. Peter Lombard, *II Sent.* d. 30 c. 14, 15 (p. 467f.).
179. Mt 14.15–21.
180. Perhaps a reference to *De civ. Dei* 22.17 (PL 41: 778; CSEL 40/2, p. 625).
181. Alb., *De homine* q. 11 a. 4 sol. (ed. Colon. 27/2, p. 110); *De anima* 2.2.6.
182. Cf. Alb., *De homine* q. 17 a. 1 sol. (ed. Colon. 27/2, p. 126).
183. Ar., *De anima* 2.1 (412a16–21).

which has to be animated by a sensible soul, have nerves and flesh throughout.

Again, the motive power of the soul is called motive because it moves according to progressive motion. Progressive motion, however, is accomplished only by strong organs, and so bones are required in these organs. It is also the same for other organs with respect to other powers.

Likewise, there is another reason (*ratio*) for the same thing.[184] For everything that is generated from contraries and is animated by a sensible soul is conserved in being (*esse*) through nutriment and is led to a requisite size through growth. But nutriment is converted to flesh only in the flesh, and is converted to bone only in bone, and so too for other [parts of the body]. Since, then, the soul has the powers (*potentias*) for these acts and can exercise them only in organs, it is necessary, before it nourishes in act and produces growth, that it have fleshy and bony organs and nerves. These, however, are derived from seminal moisture.

The second moisture is nutrimental moisture, which directs the organs of the body to the requisite size by means of a conversion when [the second moisture] is joined to the first one. This is necessary, however, because the soul has powers not only for acts, but also for acts that are perfected according to its own nature. Therefore, it is necessary that an organ be proportioned not only to the soul's acts in themselves, but also to [its] perfected acts. These organs, however, are not the smaller organs that arise from seminal moisture, but the ones that are completed in strength (*consolidatione*) and size by growth and nutriment. I say "in strength and size," however, because although the Philosopher says that growth is twofold[185]—one that happens by the rarefaction (*per extensionem*) of dense matter into thin [matter],[186] the other that happens by the addition of a magnitude to a pre-existing magnitude—we do not see the first kind in humans. To be sure, the body of a thirty-year-old man is not thinner than an infant's body, but rather it is denser. It remains,

184. Cf. Ar., *De anima* 4 (416a18f.).

185. Ar., *De gen. et corr.* 1.5 (320b30). Alb. seems to contradict Ar., however; see *De gen. et corr.* 1.3.2.5.

186. *in rarum:* in rarefaction?

then, that there is the second [kind of growth in humans]. And this necessarily extends it to a larger quantity by means of a quantity added. But by means of its introduction into what is increased by growth and nourished, the body necessarily becomes thicker and more solid. In this way, then, from nutriment there is an increase and strengthening (*consolidatio*) of the organs, in which the perfected acts of the soul are exercised.

The third moisture is the moisture that alone produces a barrier to the natural heat, lest it consume the body's substance, and through which occurs the restoration of what has been lost in the perfected organs. This is necessary because, since the natural heat is a proper instrument of the soul,[187] through which it influences the body's sense and motion, especially the chief sense,[188] which is touch—for it is that sense that makes an animal an animal[189]—it is necessary that heat exist throughout the whole. Since heat, however, is an active quality, it acts continuously on the natural moisture, consuming it and dividing it into the very substance of the members, in order to be able to introduce the nutriment. This division cannot occur without the loss of some part of the body. This is why a moisture is required that can restore what has been lost in the substance of the organs and is capable of impeding the action of heat, to prevent it from acting upon the natural or radical moisture (which are the same thing).[190] And this moisture is derived from food, but it is increased by nature in an accidental fashion (*per accidens*), as is clear from what has already been said. The first and second moistures, however, are increased through themselves (*per se*), since these are required for the operations that the soul has to perform in the body.

187. Alb., *De homine* q. 12 sol. (ed. Colon. 27/2, pp. 111–12).

188. "Chief sense": see Ar., *De anima* 2.2 (413b3–4); Alb., *De homine* q. 33 a. 1 (ed. Colon. 27/2, pp. 246–47).

189. Alb., *De animal.* 1.1.5.64 (*SZ* 1: 69); *De anima* 2.1.6.

190. On radical moisture, see Alb., *De animal.* 20.1.9.51–52 (*SZ* 2: 1387); Alb., *Quaest. super de animal.* 7, q. 3, 17–19, and 29 (ed. Colon. 12, pp. 171–72, 177–78, 184; *QDA*, pp. 230, 232, 234, 244, 259–61). For radical moisture in thirteenth-century thought, see especially Thomas S. Hall, "Life, Death, and Radical Moisture," *Clio Medica* 6 (1971): 3–23, and Michael McVaugh, "The 'Humidum Radicale' in Thirteenth-Century Medicine," *Traditio* 30 (1974): 259–83.

Concerning the truth of human nature, then, we say that the body's substance is received from the first and second moistures, but the substance is not received from the third, since it is increased by nature in an accidental fashion (*per accidens*), as was said.

1. Therefore, one must reply to the first [objection] that the Lord's statement is true in a literal sense. In fact, "whatever [enters the mouth]" applies to parts according to species, that is, to those that participate in the species, but not to parts according to matter. For when it is said, "Every man breathes," in order for the statement to be true it is not necessary for the eye to breathe, but rather for all who participate in the human species to breathe. Similarly, when one says "whatever enters the mouth," the "whatever" applies to all that is signified under the species of food, and all these things proceed into the entrails through which the impure is cast out, since all of these are impure and require digestion. But nourishment is received from matter that is changed into a species other than that which enters into the mouth.

2. To the objection drawn from Bede, we say that it is to be understood of the substance received from the third moisture.

3. The last [objection] must be solved by doing away with [the notion] that the definition (*ratio*) is the same for every nutriment, because one is increased by nature through itself (*per se*), [and] another in an accidental fashion (*per accidens*), as was already made clear.

4. To what was asked next after this, one must reply with Augustine that that flesh will rise again in the first one.

To the objection concerning nutriment and embryos, one must reply that it is impossible that an embryo, which has the possibility of resurrection, never receive any nutriment. In fact, the seminal substance is brought to the organs' initial size through the menstrual blood's nutriment. Likewise, once it has been granted that generation arises from the first substantial [moisture], it is not necessary that the other not rise again, because it has already been stated that food, with respect to all the species' parts, is cast out through the entrails, although some of the matter remains. In fact, the matter, in accord with its own division, suffices for both, namely for the first one and the second, although it is impossible for there to be no loss (*emissio*) from the whole.

5. To the question about Augustine's rule, one must reply that he intends to suggest a threefold understanding of the body's substance according to what is received from the threefold moisture. Now, the first [substance] is the most valuable of all, since it exists for the existence (*esse*) and substance of the members. The second comes after it, since it exists to perfect the size of the members and strengthen them. The third, however, has only a little value. Therefore, Augustine intends [to say] that if there were some of the most valuable substance in one [person] and of the second substance in another, it will be restored to the first [person]. Nonetheless, there are those who say that it is impossible for someone to be nourished by what belongs to the truth of human nature in someone else.[191] By "to be nourished," however, I mean that the nutriment is converted into the truth of the nature of the one nourished. And as for the reason [that being nourished in this way is impossible], they say that God has given those [creatures] that are inferior to us as nutriment, but not those that are equal. And so the human body ought to be nourished, but not provide nourishment. According to nature, moreover, the vegetable is possible [nourishment] for the sensible [creature], and the sensible for the rational; and so the sensible ought to be nourished by the vegetable, but the rational ought to be nourished by both the vegetable and the sensible.

6. To the question based on the words of the Master in the *Sentences*, one can say that those words have no authority, because according to that [argument] the entire work of nature would be assumed to be a miracle.

If someone wishes to defend it, though, he will say that matter is infinitely divisible through forms, and the matter of a human is infinitely divisible through the form of a human, and so it [that is, human matter] is multiplied as [matter is multiplied] in all things. Or, in this way [let him say] that there is a twofold substance in us, namely a heavenly [substance] in the

191. See Bonaventure, *IV Sent.* d. 44, a. 2, q. 1, *Opera* 4: 911b.

spirits that have movement in the body, as Isaac [Israeli] says, just as light's motion exists in the world.[192] Analogously, they are full of light and are the images of the abstract things on which they are imprinted, which all are properties of heavenly light. Whether they are airy or not according to substance remains to be debated concerning natural things. Therefore, some say that human multiplication happens according to the nature of light, whose nature it is to be multiplied in itself.[193] To the objection that according to this [argument] the work of nature will be a miracle, one must reply that this would be true if only that substance existed in us. But in addition to that one there also exists an elemental [substance], on which nature works by adding and subtracting. But God works on the heavenly [substance] in relation to the resurrection. But we do not approve this solution, because it is not demonstrated according to the thing itself by an authority that has to be believed, and it is even contrary to reason.

7. To the last, one must reply that one [rib] was in Adam, and another was in other humans. For there were some things in Adam's body that were from the truth of his person, and there were other things there inasmuch as he was the source (*principium*) of the entire human nature. We say, then, that that rib was never from the truth of his person, but it was made in him inasmuch as he was the source of human nature through Eve. And for this reason it will rise again in Eve and not in Adam.

Art. 10. What exists in the truth of human nature by way of parts[194]

To the tenth, one proceeds in this way:

Teeth exist to divide food, and they would be superfluous if one did not consume food that requires division; therefore, plants do not have teeth. Since, then, at the resurrection we do

192. See Alb., *De homine* q. 78 sol. (ed. Colon. 27/2, pp. 571–72); *Quaest. super de animal.* 16, q. 8 (ed. Colon. 12, pp. 63ff.; *QDA*, pp. 487–88); *De animal.* 20.1.7.36ff. (*SZ* 2: 1378–81).

193. "Some say": cf. Peter Lombard, *II Sent.* d. 30 c. 15 (p. 467ff.); Alex. Hales, *Summa* II pt. 1 inq. 4 tr. 2 sect. 2 q. 1 tit. 1 mem. 2 cap. 2 art. 2 resp. (ed. Quarrachi, vol. II, pp. 569–70); Alb., *Summa* II q. 110 m. 2 sol. (ed. Borgnet 33, pp. 315–16).

194. Alb., *IV Sent.* d. 44 a. 10.

not have to take in food, it seems that it will not be necessary for us to have teeth.

One raises a similar objection concerning the eyes, from which we derive knowledge of sense objects, because at that time we will know in the Word.

One raises a similar objection concerning the genitals and intestines and concerning respiration and blood and the humors. Actually, we say that the Lord's body has blood, and therefore so too will our [bodies].

Solution: One must reply that the acts of the organs and the ordering of one [part of the body] to another, such as of blood and the humors to man's complexion, are related to a double end (*finis*), namely to the end of an animal body's need, and to the demonstration of the power of that which acts in those organs according to the movement of divine providence, which moves creatures. I say, therefore, that such [parts of the body] will remain in acts that demonstrate power, so that the wisdom of God, which orders one [part] to another as a demonstration of such power, might be praised. And this is what Augustine says, that the genital organs will remain, not because nature will continue to procreate from them or because concupiscence will be aroused, but so that on account of them [divine] wisdom may be praised in various ways.[195] I say the same thing for the humors and intestines: to be sure, each [part of the body] will remain in its ultimate act, that is, the humors remaining in the internal [organs] and the blood in the veins, though not passing into the nature of flesh.

But a possible objection to this, that such things are neither parts of man nor quickened, must be resolved and dispatched by destroying it (*per interemptionem*).[196] For although the soul's power has already been communicated to them, they are not yet uniform or non-uniform members in act; rather they are each of these in potency.

195. Aug., *De civ. Dei* 22.17 (PL 41: 778; CSEL 40/2, p. 625, 16–18).

196. A solution *per interemptionem* occurs when one or more of the premises is destroyed owing to its falsity. See Peter of Spain, *Syncategoreumata. First Critical Edition*, 10.10.3, ed. L. M. de Rijk, trans. Joke Spruyt (Leiden: E. J. Brill, 1992), p. 426; cf. Alb., *De Soph. el.* 3.4; 5.1 (ed. Borgnet 2, 698; 708).

Art. 11. Whether the truth of one member is able to pass over into the truth of another member on the day of the resurrection[197]

To the last, one proceeds in this way:

Not all members are equally restored according to merit; therefore, one acts unjustly toward the eye if its matter is not returned to the eye, but to the foot.

Solution: One must reply, following the Apostle, that all members are equally restored according to merit, because "if one member suffers anything, all the members suffer with it; and if one member rejoices, all the members rejoice with it."[198] For merit belongs to the entire man according to all the members. And for this reason it is not necessary that matter be returned to the same member, as Augustine says in the *Enchiridion*,[199] offering as an example a statue that has been broken: if it should need to be restored from the same bronze, it is not necessary for <the artist> to pour the bronze of the foot into the foot and the bronze of the eye into the eye, but only that, once the bronze has been supplied, he restore the statue to the same size and shape that it had earlier.

197. Cf. Alb., *IV Sent.* d. 44 a. 9.
198. 1 Cor 12.26.
199. Aug., *Enchir.* 89 (PL 40: 273).

TRACTATE TWO

ON RESURRECTION ON THE PART OF THE HEAD ALONE

NEXT, ONE ASKS about the resurrection with respect to the head alone. And because what Christ's resurrection is has already been treated, one asks first whether it is the cause of our resurrection; second, what causal effect it has on those who are good and those who are evil; third, whether it is the cause of the resurrection of souls, and what the resurrection of souls is; fourth, why the resurrection of all was not joined to the resurrection of Christ as an effect to a cause; fifth, why the resurrection of souls occurs successively whereas the resurrection of bodies occurs simultaneously, although they are from one cause; sixth, what it is that we all come to in the measure of the age of the fullness of Christ;[1] seventh, [one asks] about the proofs or appearances of his resurrection; eighth, about his return for judgment and what it means to deliver the kingdom to God the Father.[2]

Question 1. Whether Christ's resurrection is the cause of our resurrection[3]

To the first, one proceeds in this way:

The Apostle says in 1 Cor 15 that if Christ has been resurrected, the dead will rise again.[4] The Gloss on that passage says that Christ's resurrection is the efficient cause of our resurrection.[5]

1. Cf. Eph 4.13.
2. 1 Cor 15.24.
3. Cf. Alb., *IV Sent.* d. 43 a. 5.
4. 1 Cor 15.13.
5. Peter Lombard, *In epist. Pauli* 1 Cor 15.13 (PL 191: 1676D).

Again, on Phil 3[6] the Gloss says, "Our resurrection is the power and efficacy of Christ's resurrection."[7] And it intends to say that in our resurrection the power and efficacy of Christ's resurrection are revealed.

Again, this is proved by reason. Man fell into a double curse on account of the first sin, namely, into the power of Original Sin with respect to the soul, such that it was even necessary for the saints before the coming of Christ to descend into limbo or into hell; and into the power of death with respect to the body. And one of these [curses] was caused by the other. Therefore, whatever is the efficient cause of liberation from the first [curse] will also be the efficient cause of liberation from the second. But Christ is the efficient cause of liberation from the first, which is clear from the fact that none of the fathers, no matter how holy, was able to free himself or others [from Original Sin]. And there is an authority for this in Zec 9: "By the blood of your testament you have set your prisoners free from the pit, in which there was no water."[8] Therefore, Christ will be the cause of liberation from the second [curse]. And it follows that the cause is not imperfect, because "with him there is plentiful redemption."[9] Since, therefore, perfect liberation only exists through the resurrection, he will be the efficient cause of our resurrection.

Again, the Apostle says, 1 Cor 15: "Just as in Adam all die, so also in Christ all will be made alive."[10] Therefore, just as Adam is the cause of death by the death in himself, so too will Christ be the cause of resurrection by the resurrection in himself.

Again, if something is found in which different things participate in various ways, and it exists in one of them *per se* but it exists in the others from another (*ab alio*), the one that exists *per se* will be the cause of the others.[11] This is clear from the fact that in every one of these it exists either through itself or from another, and it is always the case that what exists from another

6. Phil 3.10.
7. Peter Lombard, *In epist. Pauli* Phil 3.10 (PL 192: 245C); cf. *Glossa ord.*
8. Zec 9.11.
9. Ps 129.7.
10. 1 Cor 15.22.
11. Ar., *Metaph.* 2.1 (993b24–25).

has a relation to that which exists through itself. And so it is necessary that what exists through itself has a causal relation to the others. For example, heat exists in fire *per se,* but it exists in other things from fire (*ab igne*). Therefore, since resurrection exists in us and in Christ, and since it exists in us from another (*ab alio*) and in Christ *per se*—because he has the power to lay down his soul and to take it up again[12]—our resurrection will be caused by his resurrection.

1. To the contrary: No merit can go unrewarded. But the ancient fathers merited. Therefore, it was necessary for them to be rewarded. But Augustine says that another way was possible to cure our misery.[13] Therefore, if it was necessary that they be rewarded in resurrection, and if this could have been accomplished otherwise than through the death and resurrection of Christ, then our resurrection will be able to be without the existence of Christ's resurrection. And so it will not be the cause.

2. Again, one objects based on the faith of the ancients, in whom no error lies concealed. Since, then, they believed in the resurrection, of necessity the resurrection will be. But Christ's resurrection was able not to be, as is stated in the aforementioned authority, and so the same [conclusion] is held as earlier.

3. There is a similar argument from prophecy, in which again no error lies concealed, and from the aforementioned authority.

4. Likewise, let us suppose that Christ suffered and was not resurrected at the time when he freed us from Original Sin. Since, therefore, when sin does not exist there is no impediment to our glorification, it seems that our resurrection would exist even if Christ's resurrection were non-existent. And so it [that is, Christ's resurrection] will not be the cause.

5. Again, whenever two things are referred to one thing as to a cause, they will both be caused by that other one. But Christ's resurrection and ours are referred to God the Father as to the efficient cause; therefore, both are caused by him. And so one will not be the cause of the other.[14] A proof of the middle

12. Cf. Jn 10.18.

13. Aug., *De trin.* 13.10.13 (PL 42: 1024).

14. That is, Christ's resurrection will not be the cause of our resurrection.

[premise] is provided by the Apostle in Rom 8: "If the Spirit of him who raised Jesus dwells in us, he who raised Jesus will also give life to our mortal bodies by means of his Spirit that dwells in us."[15]

6. Similarly, "He will give to his voice the voice of power."[16] Therefore, that voice will be the cause of the resurrection of the dead. Since that voice will exist, then, at the end of the world, Christ's resurrection will not be the cause [of our resurrection].

7. Also, the existence (*esse*) of something that is caused follows the cause [immediately]. But our resurrection did not [immediately] follow the resurrection of Christ. Therefore, it was not caused by it.

Solution: We say that an efficient cause is spoken of in many ways. Indeed, nature is an efficient cause, as is will. And will too is spoken of in many ways, namely a will that only commands and a will that produces (*operans*) what occurs, for example, when the will produces something by virtue of which some effect occurs later in others, as [when] a physician provides medicine. Likewise, there is an example in ethics, when by his service someone brings about peace for the entire land that is under him.

We say, therefore, that the will of God the Father is the efficient cause of resurrection as [a will] that only commands, but Christ rising is the cause of this insofar as he effects and produces something in himself (*in se*), by virtue of which that same thing is effected in others, since he himself is the mediator for all and not only for one. And this is what is said in the Gloss on Rom. 5: "On the cross is the suffering of those who have confessed, in the grave is the rest of those who have been absolved, in the resurrection is the life of the just, in the ascension is the progress of the perfected, in the sitting at the right [hand of the Father] is the glory of the blessed. Christ not only demands these things from us in the sacrament of the passion, but even effects them if we choose to imitate [him]."[17]

1. We respond, then, to the first [objection] that the merit of the ancients had an effect by virtue of the merit of Christ and

15. Rom 8.11. Alb.'s quotation departs slightly from the Vulg.

16. Ps 67.34.

17. Peter Lombard, *In epist. Pauli* Rom 5.6 (PL 191: 1403D–E).

of his mysteries (*sacramentorum*), namely of the Incarnation, the Passion, the Resurrection. And therefore it [that is, their merit] was deserving of reward on account of the mysteries of the mediator.

2, 3. To the objection that another mode of liberation was possible, however, we say that it was necessary that there be one [mode] of whatever kind; and because it was predetermined [that it should happen] in this [particular] way, it was necessary that it happen in this way. And so this does not prove that Christ's resurrection is not the cause. And there is an example from the fact that in order for the world to be inhabited, it is necessary that there be daylight at some time or another. But it was possible for the days to obtain light from a heavenly body other than the sun, such as from a light-bearing cloud, as happened at the beginning of the world according to some saints.[18] And nevertheless it does not follow that the sun is not the efficient cause of daylight, because the sun causes daylight from the fact that it is ordained for this. Similarly, the resurrection of Christ is the cause of our resurrection from the fact that it was predetermined for this according to our salvation. From this the solution to the second and third [objections] is evident.

4. To the next [objection] we say that if Christ must be the Redeemer, then it would be an impossible proposition for him to have died and not have been resurrected, because in this way he would have had imperfect power. And a certain gloss on the Psalm—on that passage in the Psalm, "Blessed is he who understands," which says, "Can it be that he who sleeps will not rise again?"[19]—says[20] that redemption would profit no one if there were no resurrection of Christ.

To the objection, however, that it seems to have been caused by the Passion, one must reply that each of Christ's mysteries (*sacramentorum*) is the efficient cause of the whole of salvation, but not in the same way. For there are many [mysteries] pertaining to our salvation, namely release from the debt of Original

18. Peter Lombard, *II Sent.* d. 13 c. 2 (pp. 363–64).

19. Ps 40.2, 9.

20. The gloss is not found in the *Glossa ordinaria.* Cf. Aug., *Enarr. in Ps.* 101 *sermo* 7 (PL 37: 1308).

[Sin] and the punishments accompanying it with respect to the body and with respect to the soul. With respect to the body, the punishment is the necessity of being reduced to ashes; and the body cannot, by its own power, be freed from the necessity of remaining in ashes, but Christ's death released the body from that debt of remaining [in ashes]. But once that debt has been absolved, it is still necessary to confer life on the body, and Christ's resurrection causes that.

5. To the next [objection] we reply that nothing prevents two things from being referred to the first cause as the immediate [cause] and nevertheless for one to be from the other. Indeed, there is a difference between the first cause and proximate natural causes, because the Philosopher says that the first cause is equally present to everything, and so it is not mediated to any particular thing.[21] Nature and the effects of nature, therefore, exist immediately from God, and nevertheless one is the cause of the other, although not by the same mode of causality. Rather, nature is conformed (*conformis*) to what is caused by it, whereas the first cause "stands above the properties of the caused."[22] Likewise, we say here that Christ rising again is this kind of cause, conformed to our resurrection, but God is the cause that stands above the properties of those rising again; and nevertheless both [Christ's resurrection and our resurrection] exist immediately from God.

6. To the next [objection] one must reply that that voice has been discussed above, and the solution is apparent from the things that have been said there.[23]

7. To the next [objection] one must reply that a voluntary cause is a cause together with providence. Providence, however, establishes an order (*ordo*) to an end. And therefore it is not necessary that the effect follow such a cause immediately; rather, it is sufficient that it follow when [that is, at the time that] providence, as it governs the will, has appointed.

21. See Alb., *De causis et proc.*, lib. 2 tr. 4 cap. 13–15 (ed. Colon. 17/2, pp. 166–68).

22. Ar., *De caelo et mundo* 1.1 (268a15); cf. Alb., *De caelo et mundo* 1.1.2; and Alb., *De res.* tr. 1, q. 1 (ed. Colon. 26, p. 241, 19–20).

23. See Alb., *De res.* tr. 1, q. 5 (ed. Colon. 26, p. 247, 19–20).

Therefore, a triple cause can be inferred, namely an immediate unconformed (*inconformis*) cause, and this is the will or the command of God; an immediate cause conformed to providence, and this is Christ rising again insofar as it is this kind [of cause]; and a conformed cause (*causa conformis*) after which the effect follows immediately, and this is the sound of the trumpet, according to what Gregory says, [namely] that to sound the trumpet is nothing other than to reveal the Son, who rose again, to the world dreadfully.

Question 2. What causal effect it has on the good and the evil[24]

To the second [question] one proceeds in this way:

The effect of the passion did not generally avail all; therefore, by analogy, the effect of the resurrection will not exist in all.

To the contrary, the Apostle says in 1 Cor 15, "The dead will rise incorruptible."[25] Therefore, incorruption will exist in all, and they do not cause it themselves; therefore, [incorruption will be caused] by Christ rising again. If one should say that incorruption does not have the same definition (*ratio*) [in the good and the evil], this is not an obstacle, because they differ only in what pertains to the state of glory or to the state of punishment, which are the properties united to incorruption. And so it follows that incorruption will have the same definition (*ratio*) in both.

Again, the corruption of death exists in all by virtue of the first sin. Since, therefore, Christ's gift is more abundant than Adam's transgression, incorruption will exist in all by virtue of the resurrection of Christ.

In reply to the objection to the contrary, we concede that the effect will not exist in all with respect to the attainment of beatitude, but it will exist in all with respect to the attainment of what befits divine justice. To be sure, the highest justice itself will be the basis (*ratio*) for the condemnation of one who "has trampled the Son of God underfoot," as the Apostle says in He-

24. Cf. Alb., *IV Sent.* d. 43 a. 26.
25. 1 Cor 15.52.

brews, "and has considered the blood of the testament by which he was sanctified unclean."[26] And incorruption is caused in the damned by reason of this justice from Christ rising again, so that it might be subject to damnation for eternity.

Question 3. Whether it is the cause of the resurrection of souls

To the third [question] one proceeds in this way:

1. Resurrection, as Anselm says,[27] is the passage of true human nature from corruption to incorruption. But the soul's corruption is twofold, namely the corruption of fault and the corruption of punishment. Therefore, its resurrection will be twofold. But the first [resurrection], which is from fault, is by grace, and not therefore by the resurrection [of Christ].

2. If perhaps one says that grace comes from Christ rising, to the contrary: Damascene says that only what has fallen rises again.[28] But divinity never fell; therefore, it does not rise again. Therefore, Christ rising, as regards his nature, is man. And blessed Bernard says in *On the Song* [*of Songs*] that grace does not come from Christ the man.[29] Therefore, grace, by which the soul will rise from sin, does not come from Christ rising, as regards his nature [as man].

3. Likewise, to the same [objection]: the soul is better than the body. Therefore, what is highest in the soul is better than what is highest in the body. But resurrection is highest in the body, and resurrection is highest in the soul. Since, therefore, a higher good never comes from a good less than itself, the resurrection of the soul will not come from the resurrection of any body whatsoever. Therefore, [the resurrection of the soul is] not from the resurrection of Christ because Christ's resurrection is the resurrection of a body.

To the contrary: the Apostle says, "He was handed over for

26. Heb 10.29.

27. Anselm, *Cur Deus Homo* 2.3 (PL 158: 402A; ed. Schmitt 2: 98, 18–20).

28. John Damascene, *De fide orth.* 4.27 (PG 94: 1220A; ed. E. M. Buytaert, p. 377, 5–6–p. 378, 8–10); see Alb., *De res.* tr. 1, q. 2 (ed. Colon. 26, p. 242, 17).

29. Bern., *In Cant. serm.* 10.8 (PL 183: 822D).

our transgressions and rose again for our justification."[30] Justification, however, is resurrection from fault. Therefore, etc.

4. After this, one asks what the resurrection of the soul is. For it is determined by John in the Apocalypse that there is a first resurrection and a second resurrection, and "blessed and holy is he who participates in the first resurrection, because the second death has no power over him."[31] Since, therefore, the second death is the death of eternal damnation, it seems that the first resurrection is the glorification of the soul. For many are justified over whom the second death later acquires power.

In addition, one asks whether there is one definition (*ratio*) for resurrection in the body and in the soul.

It seems that there is, because the Philosopher says that those things that are said to be "before" and "after" with respect to order are united in one particular thing.[32] Since, therefore, "before" and "after" are said here with respect to order when one speaks of the first resurrection and the second resurrection, it is necessary that they have one definition (*ratio*) in that in which they are ordered, that is, in resurrection.

Similarly, a man is not said to be first with respect to a second ass, but he is more correctly designated a first animal with respect to a second [animal]. And from this it is clear that those that are ordered under the name according to which they are ordered have one definition (*ratio*), just as a man and an ass are ordered under "animal," and Socrates and Plato under "man." Since, therefore, a first resurrection and a second resurrection are spoken of according to the soul and the body, it is necessary that resurrection have the same definition (*ratio*) in them.

But to the contrary: Body and soul do not have the same definition. Therefore, neither will their properties have the same definition, because a property always must be defined by the subject.[33] Therefore, although the glory of resurrection is in both of them, the property of each will not have the same definition in both.

30. Rom 4.25.

31. Rv 20.6.

32. Ar., *Metaph.* 5.11 (1018b26ff.).

33. Ar., *Top.* 5.4 (132b18ff.); Boethius, trans. ant. PL 64: 960A; Alb., *Top.* 5.2.4; see Alb., *De res.* tr. 1, q. 6, art. 1, sol. (ed. Colon. 26, p. 250, 47–48).

Solution:

4. We reply to the last [objection] first, saying that the soul's resurrection is its perfection according to beatitude, contrary to fault and punishment. And if it is ever said that justification is the resurrection, this is said with respect to the restricted definition of the resurrection of the soul.

If, however, this resurrection is considered with respect to essence, as it exists in the soul, then it will not have the same definition as the resurrection of bodies. And the last objection proceeds in this way. But if it is considered in relation to the object and cause of glory, which is God, being (*ens*) all in all,[34] then it does have the same definition. For the glory of bodies is nothing other than participation in the glory of souls according to the power of bodies. And the glory of souls will be God perfectly filling them with the fullness of his very own goodness and truth and perfection (*indeficientia*). And in the Apocalypse John orders these two resurrections, the "first" and the "second," according to this [shared] definition.

And from this the solution to a third [question] that could be asked next is apparent, namely whether the first resurrection is a general resurrection, just like the second resurrection. It is clear that it is not, since the second death will have no power over those rising at the first resurrection. And these are the blessed and the saints, as is said in the text of the Apocalypse—saints as to grace, blessed as to glory.

1. To the first [objection], however, we say that Christ rising again is the cause of the resurrection of souls. But "cause" differs when it is said of God the Father and of God the Christ, because the Father is the First Cause, existing above the properties of what is caused. But Christ is a cause as mediator and Redeemer, whose proper causality is to cause according to the property of the mysteries (*sacramentorum*) of our salvation, as he is conformed (*conformis*) to us in nature. And formally this resurrection by grace and by glory is the same. In fact, nothing prevents there being different causes of the same thing according to different modes of causality, as is said in the second

34. Cf. 1 Cor 15.28.

book of the *Physics*[35] and in the fourth book of the *Metaphysics*.[36]

2. To the next [objection] one must reply that grace does not come from Christ the man, insofar as he is man, but rather it comes from Christ rising again, who is God and man. And if we wish to speak properly, let us say that grace comes from God through Christ according to the conformity of the mysteries (*sacramentorum*), namely of the Incarnation and of others, as has been said above many times.[37]

3. To the third [objection] one must reply on the basis of what has been said previously that Christ's resurrection is not understood as the resurrection of the body alone. For there resurrection is understood in the one rising again, and not in an absolute sense. And in this way the cause is better than what is caused. Nevertheless, that argument is not valid, because good is understood equivocally in that comparison. To be sure, when it is said that the resurrection of the soul is what is highest in the soul, "highest" indicates the definition of the good's end. But when it is said that nothing comes from a good less than itself, "good" indicates the power of the efficient cause. This is clear from the fact that the good of walking, which exists according to an efficient cause, causes health, which is, nonetheless, better than [the good of] walking.

From this a solution to another question that could be asked is evident, [namely] whether the first resurrection is fitting for angels. For it is clear that it is not, because resurrection is only for what has fallen.[38] The fall, however, happens only by means of fault and punishment. But those angels who have been confirmed [in the good] never existed in [a state of] fault and punishment, whereas those who exist in [a state of] fault and punishment will never rise again.

35. Ar., *Phys.* 2.3 (195a4–8).

36. Ar., *Metaph.* 5.2 (1013b4ff.).

37. See Alb., *De res.* tr. 2, q. 1; tr. 2, q. 3 (ed. Colon. 26, p. 259, 50–60, and p. 261, 73–76).

38. See Alb., *De res.* tr. 1, q. 2 (ed. Colon. 26, p. 242, 20–21); John Damascene, *De fide orth.* 2.4 (PG 94: 877C; ed. Buytaert, p. 77, 38–39).

Question 4. Why the resurrection of all was not joined to the resurrection of Christ as an effect to a cause[39]

To the fourth [question] one proceeds in this way:

1. An effect ought to follow a perfect cause; therefore, our resurrection [ought to follow] Christ's resurrection.

2. Again, an effect never precedes its cause. But the resurrection of certain individuals did precede Christ's resurrection, because the Gospel says that when Christ had died, "many bodies of the saints [who had slept] arose again"[40] and "they appeared to many."[41] Some of them are named in the Gospel of Nicodemus.[42]

Solution:

1. One must reply, as above, that Christ as rising is the cause, as the Redeemer and mediator possessing a conformity through his mysteries (*per sacramenta sua*) with what is caused, and acting as cause with providence by establishing in things that are caused a disposition according to the best order. And in this way a solution to the first [objection] is evident.

2. To the second [objection] one must reply that Christ's actual death occasionally weakened faith in the resurrection in the head and in the members, for which reason the Lord was transfigured even before the Passion, as the saints say.[43] And therefore it was necessary for some to rise again immediately at Christ's death, so that some anticipation of the resurrection might remain among the elect. Nor is it unfitting—in a particular case (*secundum quid*), though not generally—for something to precede a cause whose causality exists together with the providence of the caused order. Indeed, just as we said above that all who have been saved from the beginning of the world have had one Redeemer, Christ, and so have been saved by his

39. Cf. Alb., *IV Sent.* d. 43 a. 5 obj. 5.

40. Mt 27.52.

41. Mt 27.53.

42. Cf. *Evang. Nicod.* pt. 2, c. 1 (17), 1–3 (Tischendorf, p. 389f.); Alb., *De res.* tr. 2, q. 7 (ed. Colon. 26, p. 270, 13).

43. See John Chrysos., *Hom* 56 *in Matth.*, 4 (PG 58: 554); Pope Leo, *Sermo* 51.2 (PL 54: 309f.). See Alb., *De res.* tr. 2, q. 7, art. 1, sol. (ed. Colon. 26, p. 265, 47ff.).

power, so too if from the beginning of the world some have been resurrected, Christ rising was the cause of their resurrection, not by means of a resurrection that existed in actuality (*in re*), but through a resurrection that existed in the faith of the fathers.

Question 5. Why the resurrection of souls occurs successively whereas the resurrection of bodies occurs simultaneously

To the fifth [question] one proceeds in this way:

1. The saints' reward is the glory of the body. Similarly, the evildoers' reward is the punishment of their body. Therefore, it ought to be granted immediately after merit.

2. Again, Solomon says in Proverbs: "Hope that is deferred afflicts the soul."[44] Therefore, since the saints hope for resurrection, they are afflicted unless it is granted to them immediately. For this reason, resurrection ought to follow in succession after the death of each individual.

3. Likewise, in the Apocalypse it is said, "Avenge our blood,"[45] and the Gloss there says that this is the voice of the saints longing for resurrection. And so it seems that, since they fervently long for that, they will be afflicted unless it is granted to them.

4. In addition, there seems to be a clear example among those who were resurrected at the time of the Lord's Passion. Indeed, those will not rise with the others. Therefore, resurrection will not occur for all at the same time.

5. Moreover, the same can be proved concerning the others on the basis of a supposition (*per hypothesim*), because the reason (*ratio*) for the resurrection of any man and of every man is the same. But some have risen again apart from the general resurrection. Therefore, any of the others should rise again apart from the general resurrection.

6. To the contrary: In the Epistle to the Hebrews 11 it is said that "not all who have been found to be approved by the testimony of faith have received the promise, since God has provided something better for us, so that they would not be perfected

44. Prv 13.12.
45. Rv 6.10.

without us."[46] The Gloss there says: "For although they received individual garments, they will not receive a double garment until the general resurrection, so that the perfection of all the faithful might occur at the same time."[47] And from this it seems to follow that no one rose again at the time of Christ's Passion.

Again, the bodies of all were formed in matter at the same time. But glorification ought to correspond to creation. Therefore, the glorification of all bodies ought to occur at the same time.

Again, the material principles of the world do not exist for only one body, but for all bodies that are generable and corruptible. Therefore, since there ought to be a correlation (*conformitas*) between the material principles and what arises from those principles with respect to the qualities ordered to generation and corruption, as long as the generation of bodies continues, it is necessary for the active and the passive qualities to exercise control over all matter in generation. But the generation of bodies will continue until reaching the fullness of the number of the elect. Therefore, the control of the active and passive qualities will continue over all matter for that long. But such control exists according to the condition (*status*) of the animal body. Therefore, glorification cannot occur in a part of matter unless the control of such qualities is removed from the whole. And so it is necessary for the resurrection of all to occur at the same time, when the glorification of the world will also occur.

We concede this, saying with Basil that at the end of the world the Lord will divide fire's flame, separating out the light for the noble nature above and pressing the heat down to the foundation below, to the place of the damned.[48] And for this reason the glorification of the whole world with respect to matter will occur at the same time. This will become more apparent below, when the renewal of the world is discussed.

46. Heb 11.39–40.

47. Cf. Peter Lombard, *In epist. Pauli* Heb 11.39–40 (PL 192: 500A). The allusion seems to be to Is 61.7: "therefore, they will receive a double portion in their land, everlasting joy will be theirs." Cf. Dante, *Paradiso* 25.91–92.

48. Basil, *Super Ps.* 28.7, 6 (PG 29: 297A–C); *In hexaem. Hom.* 6.3 (PG 29: 121D); trans. Eustathius Africanus, PG 30: 925B. Cf. Bonaventure, *IV Sent.* d. 43 dub. 3, *Opera* 4: 903b.

1. We say to the first [objection], therefore, that reward is due at a time that is opportune according to the predetermination of the providence of him toward whom there was offense or obedience in merit.

2. To the second [objection] we say that every hope exists with respect to something anticipated in the future. And for this reason the hope of the saints is not deferred, although what is hoped for is deferred.

3. To the next [objection] one must reply that the longing of the saints is for resurrection, but that [longing] is ordered by provident wisdom. And for this reason they are not saddened if they should endure "for a little time, until the number of their brothers should be complete."[49]

4. To the next [objection] one must reply that some arose with the Lord as the cause, as was said above.[50] And for this reason the question is not posed concerning those in whom there existed a special cause.

5. And from this, moreover, a solution to the argument that was made on the basis of a supposition (*ex hypothesi*) is evident, because the reason (*ratio*) [for the resurrection] is not the same for them and for others. If one asks, however, what the reason (*ratio*) is, one must reply that it has to be derived from three [modes] related to the specific character of the promise. And as far as this is concerned, some saints say that Abraham and David and some other patriarchs to whom a promise was specifically made rose again.[51] And it is for this reason that at their deaths they were careful to bury them—like Jacob and Joseph[52]—in that land in which Christ rose again.[53] Another [mode] is that their resurrection was a sign (*argumentum*) for hastening the resurrection of Christ, as an effect to its cause. And this is why Nicodemus says in his Gospel that there are some who were known, whom he names, whose celebrity was not doubted and whose death was not doubted, who rose again, revealing the mystery

49. Cf. Rv 6.11.

50. See Alb., *De res.* tr. 2, q. 4 (ed. Colon. 26, p. 262, 46ff.).

51. Cf. *Evang. Nicod.* pt. 2 c. 8 (24)–11 (27) (ed. Tischendorf, pp. 402–7). Aug., *Epist.* 164, 3.9 (PL 33: 712; CSEL 44: 528f.).

52. Gn 49.29; 50.24.

53. Cf. Alb., *Super Matth.* 27.53.

of Christ's resurrection.[54] Now if they had been unknown, one would not have believed this of them. A third [mode] is from the special link to a body that is to be glorified in Christ, like the body of the blessed Virgin, from which Christ's body was taken. And this is why the resurrection of the blessed Virgin preceded the general resurrection, as Augustine says in the *Sermon on the Blessed Virgin*.[55] And by means of these three modes there is something beyond the general rule in certain [individuals]. And so their resurrection does not happen with the resurrection of others.

6. What is said in the text of and in the Gloss on Hebrews, moreover, is understood of those in whom there is nothing except the general rule of those rising again.

Question 6. What it is that we all come to in the measure of the age of the fullness of Christ[56]

To the sixth [question] one proceeds in this way:

1. Augustine says in the Gloss on Eph 4: "It is not proper to say that at the resurrection the body will receive a size that it did not have earlier, nor that the bodies of those who were larger ought to be reduced to the measure of the Lord's body. For much passes away from these bodies, although not a [single] hair [on the head] will pass away."[57] On this basis one understands that we will not all have the measure of Christ's body.

2. But then one asks about the size that infants will have. For Augustine says in the Gloss on the same passage: "Each one will receive the measure of the body that he had in his youth, even if he died as an old man, or that he would have had if he died earlier [than his youth]. To be sure, that is the age that Christ reached, that is, of a youth about thirty years old."[58]

Now one objects in this way: The truth of human nature is

54. Cf. *Evang. Nicod.* pt. 2, c. 1 (17), 1–3 (Tischendorf, p. 389f.).

55. Ps. Aug., *De assumpt. b. M. v.*, c. 5 (PL 40: 1145).

56. Cf. Eph 4.13; Alb., *IV Sent.* d. 44 a. 1.

57. Peter Lombard, *In epist. Pauli* Eph 4.13 (PL 192: 201C–D). Cf. Aug., *De civ. Dei* 22.15 (PL 41: 777; CSEL 40/2: 623f.). Peter Lombard, *IV Sent.* d. 44 c. 1 (p. 1000).

58. Peter Lombard, *In epist. Pauli* Eph 4.13 (PL 192: 201C).

caused from the union with a rational soul. Therefore, what was never united in act to a rational soul will never rise again. But what will be added to infants, whether through creation or through the addition of other things, was never united [to a rational soul]. Therefore, it never will rise again. If one should say that the matter of infants will be multiplied in itself, this will contradict Augustine, because he says that a quantity of matter, which they possessed in power (*virtute*) although not in mass, will be conferred upon them. But that quantity did not stem from its [matter's] multiplication in itself, since the power of nature could not exist in this [matter], but stemmed from the addition of something external.

3. Furthermore, according to this the restoration of bodies will not have one explanation (*ratio*) for all, and thus the work of resurrection will not correspond to the work of creation and propagation. For all bodies were created in one way, namely according to a material principle, and propagated in one way, because they are from one man.

4. One asks, moreover, how size will be determined, since size will not be uniform and nevertheless it will be according to the measure of the age of the fullness of Christ.

Solution:

1. To the first [objection] one must concede that, with respect to quantity when measuring internally, bodies will not have the same size with respect to length, width, and breadth, as [they may be] three cubits or four cubits; but they will be the same size with respect to quantity externally measuring motion in the augmentative potential at the limit of the body's perfection according to the rule of size and growth. Moreover, this is the measure of thirty years [of age], at which age Christ completed [his] life. For nothing measures motion externally except time.

2. To the objection concerning infants, one must reply with Augustine at the same place in the Gloss and in the *Enchiridion*, that if "anything was lacking, he who made whatever he willed from nothing will supply it, and if anything was grossly over-abundant in a particular part, it will be distributed throughout the whole."[59]

59. Aug., *Enchir.* 90 (PL 40: 274).

3. To the objection that the restoration of bodies will not have the same explanation (*ratio*), it can be said without offense that for infants the explanation is not at all the same as for others. Indeed, others have performed good or evil works in the body, and for this reason it is just for them to be punished or rewarded in the very same matter of the body. But infants have not had [good or evil] works, and this is why the body's matter can be provided to them from another source.

4. To the last [objection] one must reply that the effective power, whose active power is proportioned to a determined expansion and no further, exists in the seed. Likewise, the material potency, proportioned to the active power in the seed, exists in the matter of the seed. For in all natural [things] the power of the mover is proportioned to the power of the movable, and vice versa, as is said in the commentary on the second book of *On Heaven and Earth.*[60] And in both of these the farthest limit of this power with respect to act, but not with respect to potency, is said to be the measure of the age of those rising again. And this is what the Philosopher says in book two of *On the Soul,* that "the nature of all constants is the limit and basis (*ratio*) of size and growth."[61]

If, however, one should ask instead why they are said to rise again at Christ's age rather than at someone else's age, one must reply that human nature existed most truly and most simply in Christ, just as the Philosopher says in book ten of the *Metaphysics* that each thing whatsoever is measured by the smallest and the simplest of its kind.[62] It pertains to each species whatsoever to receive one [individual] in which there exists a proportion of mover to matter and of matter to mover such that one in no way relates to the other unduly. Or, if it does not have matter, there is in it a perfect proportion of potencies to acts and of potencies to essence, just as the Apostle Peter says in a dispute with Simon Magus that from the beginning God appointed an angel above the angels, and a horse above horses, and the man

60. Averr., *De caelo et mundo* 2 text. comm. 36.

61. Ar., *De anima* 2.4 (416a16f.).

62. Ar., *Metaph.* 10.1 (1052b31f.). "Simplest": generally, by "simplest" Alb. implies what is non-composite or has the fewest constitutive parts.

Christ Jesus also above men.[63] And so it follows that in Christ the augmentative potential for act is altogether without error, and therefore is simplest, and in this regard all others are measured by it. For the quantity of the simplest thing is best known, and for this reason others are measured by its quantity, just as a piece of cloth is measured by an ell (*ulna*)[64] because the quantity of an ell is better known, and an ell is measured by a palm because a palm is better known, and a palm by a finger; a finger, however, does not have a measure because its quantity is known *per se,* unless perhaps it is said that a finger is only as large as it is from the tip of one finger to another. And it is the same for liquids with respect to an *urna*[65] and its parts, and for dry goods with respect to a peck and its parts, and for weights with respect to a talent and its parts. And we say the same thing concerning the proportion of the augmentative power to the limit (*terminum*) of growth.

Concerning Proofs of the Resurrection, or concerning Appearances

Four issues are investigated with regard to the seventh [question]. First, one asks about the proofs before the Resurrection and before [Christ's] death; second, about those proofs that were after death but before the Resurrection; third, about those proofs that were after both [Christ's death and Resurrection]; and fourth about the Ascension, which was also a proof of the glory of those rising again.

Question 7. Concerning proofs before the Resurrection and before death

With regard to the first [issue], one asks at the outset whether it was fitting that the resurrection be proven. Second, what that is by which it is proven, namely the Transfiguration. And

63. Ps. Clement, *Recogn.* 1.45 (PG 1: 1233A–B). Cf. Peter Lombard, *In epist. Pauli* 1 Cor 15.24 (PL 191: 1679C).

64. The *ulna* is a quantity of measurement, an ell; but *ulna* also means an elbow.

65. An *urna* is a liquid measure equal to about 2.5 gallons; the word also means an urn or pot.

since "transfiguration" indicates a change (*motum*), third one asks what is its end-from-which (*terminus ex quo*); and fourth, what is its end-to-which (*terminus in quem*); and fifth, whether Christ alone was capable of transfiguration; and sixth and last, [one asks] about the circumstances of the Transfiguration.

Art. 1. Whether it was fitting that the resurrection be proven

To the first, one proceeds in this way:

1. Damascene says that the Resurrection was proven by means of the properties indicative of it—by the resuscitation of Lazarus and of the other dead people whom the Lord resuscitated.[66] Therefore, proof by means of the Transfiguration was superfluous.

2. Precisely the same objection obtains concerning the miracles that occurred at [Christ's] death, such as the splitting of the rocks and the opening of graves.[67] Indeed, if the Resurrection is adequately proven by the Transfiguration, then these [miracles] are superfluous.

The question is reduced to this: to what extent may it be proven by means of various proofs?

3. Besides, it seems that it should not be proven, because "faith has no merit when human reason offers proof from experience," as Gregory says.[68]

Solution:

1. We say that two things require attention with regard to the resurrection, namely the resurrection of the head and the resurrection of the members. Concerning each of these, three [things] are ascertained, namely the potential (*potentia*) for rising again, the act of resurrection, and the state of glory of those rising again. A potential for resurrection of the members is proven by the resuscitation of those who had died. Indeed, from the fact that a dead person is resuscitated, it is shown that a corrupt body still has an ordering (*ordinationem*) toward the soul, in which ordering the potential for rising again is rooted. And Damascene calls this ordering "the properties indicative

66. John Damascene, *De fide orth.* 4.27 (PG 94: 1224A–B; ed. Buytaert, p. 382, 82–86); see Alb., *De res.* tr. 1, q. 1 (ed. Colon. 26, p. 238, 14ff.).

67. Cf. Mt 27.51–52.

68. Greg., *Hom. in Ev.* 1 (PL 76: 1197C).

of resurrection." The act, however, of resurrection of the members, insofar as it is caused by Christ's resurrection, is proven by those who rose again when the graves opened at Christ's death, whose reason (*ratio*) [for rising then] was stated above.[69] On the other hand, the potential for Christ's resurrection is proven by the Transfiguration, whereas the act [of his resurrection is proven] by the appearances that follow after the resurrection. Moreover, the state of glory in both, namely in the head and in the members, is proven by Christ's Ascension and the ascension of those who ascended with Christ. For just as Amos says, Christ "ascended opening the way before them."[70]

2. To the query concerning other miracles, one must reply that they do not prove the resurrection. But the miracles that were performed before the Passion demonstrate that divinity was united with humanity, whereas the miracles at the Passion and death [of Christ] demonstrate that divinity was not separated from humanity by death.

3. To the last [objection] one must reply that human reason (*ratio*) is not the basis (*ratio*) of a miracle, and therefore faith can obtain some proof (*experimentum*) from a miracle. Or one can say that faith has no cause with respect to assent except the First Truth, but with respect to thought it can be assisted by some reason (*ratio*). And so rightly it [that is, thought] is helped by reason (*ratio*) to believe, but faith cannot [be so helped]. Indeed, Augustine says that "to believe is to think with assent."[71]

Art. 2. What transfiguration is[72]

To the second, one proceeds in this way:

Transfiguration denotes a change of shape (*figurae*). But bodies that rise again do not change shape, because shape is the delimitation of size,[73] and that remains the same. There-

69. Alb., *De res.* tr. 2, q. 4 (ed. Colon. 26, p. 262, 42ff.).

70. The reference is not to Amos, but rather to Mi 2.13. See Alb., *De res.* tr. 2, q. 9, art. 4 (ed. Colon. 26, p. 287, 50).

71. Aug., *De praedest.* 2.5 (PL 44: 963).

72. Alb., *Super Matth.* 17.2. On Albert's treatment of the Transfiguration in this text and his scriptural commentaries, see Aaron Canty, *Light and Glory: The Transfiguration of Christ in Early Franciscan and Dominican Theology* (Washington, DC: The Catholic University of America Press, 2011), 136–75.

73. Cf. Alb., *De praedic.* 5.8; *De anima* 2.4.6.

fore, it seems either that resurrection will not be proven by transfiguration, or that it should not be called transfiguration.

In addition, it was proven in the seventh book of the *Physics* that alteration does not occur with respect to form and shape.[74] Since, therefore, the Lord has revealed [his] resurrection by the alteration of his body, it seems that it is not properly called transfiguration.

Solution: One must reply that shape (*figura*) is understood in two ways, namely according to the substance of shape, and as it is perceptible to the common sense.[75] In the first way, shape is not changed, but in the second way it is. In fact, shape is the principle for recognizing this particular thing, insofar as it is this [particular thing], according as it is united to a specific sensible. And this is evident from the fact that to compare one sensible with another is an act of the common sense rather than of a specific sense, as the Philosopher says.[76] Since, therefore, a particular thing is discerned from [its] shape (*figuratio*) and specific sensible [properties]—and specific sensible [properties] like color can change while the discernment of the particular thing remains the same—it is clear that shape (*figuratio*) is the principle for recognizing a particular thing. An indication of this is that elderly people, once they are known, are immediately recognized even if they have been absent for a long time, whereas children are not. This is because in children shape is changed by the expansion and enlargement of [their] size, which does not happen in the elderly. We say, therefore, that shape, inasmuch as it is the principle of recognition, was altered, not to such a degree that he [that is, Christ] would not be recognized as the same [person] because of it, but so that, united to another quality, it would reveal another condition of the same [person].

And from this the solution to both of the objections is clear.

Art. 3. What the end-from-which (*terminus ex quo*) of the Transfiguration is

To the third, one proceeds in this way:

In Christ there was a heavenly power in the composition of

74. Ar., *Phys.* 7.3 (245b21–25).
75. Cf. Ar., *De anima* 3.1 (425a16–18).
76. Ar., *De anima* 3.2 (426b12–15).

his body, just as [there was] also in the bodies of others.[77] Likewise, there was a potential (*potentia*) for light there, stemming from the will's merit and similarly from the union [of his body] to divinity and to the rational soul. Since, therefore, the potential for light is an end in the change to light, it seems that such great [potencies] in Christ constituted the end from which (*terminus a quo*) the Transfiguration came.

To the contrary: That which is a potential for some act is a privation with respect to it. I say, however, that it is a potential, like that from which there is motion, as the Philosopher says in the *Physics*,[78] that white comes from non-white: and not from the non-white that is an end, but rather from black or a color in the middle that can become white. But these potencies also remained in the Transfiguration itself with the act in which they existed before the Transfiguration. Therefore, they were not the potencies and the end from which the Transfiguration came. But it is clear from the Gloss on Mt 17 that the middle [premise] is true: a mortal body is not disposed to immortality. And this is [a gloss] on the passage: "His face shone like the sun."[79]

Likewise, those powers that dispose [the body] to light dispose it to nothing but light, which is the reward and beatitude of the body. The light of the Transfiguration, however, was not this light, as the Gloss on the same passage says that the Lord did not reveal to them immortality, but a clarity similar to immortality. Therefore, the Transfiguration does not stem from those powers as if from an end.

Solution: Without offense one must reply that the Transfiguration's end-from-which was the outward appearance of his skin. For just as the objection stated, the condition of the body with regard to the nature of its mortality was not changed; and

77. Cf. Alb., *De homine* q. 78, sol. (ed. Colon. 27/2, pp. 571–72); *Quaest. super de animal.* 16, q. 8 (ed. Colon. 12, 63ff.; *QDA*, pp. 487–88); *De animal.* 20.1.7 (*SZ* 2: 1361); Alex. Hales, *Summa* III inq. un. tr. 6 q. 2 tit. 2 mem. 2 cap. 2 art. 1 ad 2 ("Aliter potest dici ... 2") (ed. Quarrachi, vol. IV, pp. 274–75).

78. Ar., *Phys.* 5.5 (229b14–20); cf. Alb., *Phys.* 5.3.5 and *De gen. et corr.* 1.1.30.

79. Mt 17.2. Not in the *Glossa ordinaria.* Cf. Alex. Hales, *Summa* III inq. un. tr. 6 q. 2 tit. 1 cap. 1 obj. 2 (ed. Quaracchi, vol. IV, p. 252: "Glossa Bedae").

since this power for light, which exists in us from the composition[80] of heavenly power or from the [body's] union with the soul, cannot exist in its own act, it is necessary for the elemental power to exist in active and passive qualities in act and for a heavenly power to exist as if in potency until the resurrection. And this is what the Gloss says, that there was [in the transfigured Christ] a clarity similar to the clarity of immortality, but not that clarity itself. For it was not produced throughout the entire nature of the body, as the clarity of the resurrection will be produced.

To the first objection, one must reply that those dispositions indicate only a potential for the light of the Resurrection and not [for the light] of the Transfiguration.

Art. 4. What the end-to-which (*terminus in quem*) of the Transfiguration is.

To the fourth, one proceeds in this way:

The interlinear gloss on Mt 17, "and he led them up onto a high mountain," says, "He was going to reveal [to them] the glory of [his] majesty."[81] Therefore, the Transfiguration was a change into the glory of majesty.

Likewise, in the same place [namely, the Gloss] on that text, "until they see the Son of Man coming in his kingdom,"[82] the interlinear gloss [says], "in that clarity in which he will exist after judgment has been completed." Therefore, he was changed into the clarity of the resurrection because he will exist in that [clarity] after judgment has been completed.

1. But to the contrary: The gloss in the same place [says]: He did not reveal [the clarity of] immortality, but a clarity similar to immortality.

Again, in the same place on that passage, "And responding, Peter said to Jesus, 'Lord, it is good for us to be here,'"[83] the interlinear gloss [says], "He had forgotten that the kingdom that was promised is not on earth but in heaven, and that those still enwrapped in mortal flesh cannot enter in." And from this, one

80. "Composition": perhaps "complexion."

81. *Glossa interl. super Matth.* 17.1.

82. Mt 16.28.

83. Mt 17.4.

understands that what appeared on the mountain in no way belonged to the kingdom of heaven, which will exist at the resurrection.

In addition, the power of the non-glorified eye is not proportionate to the sun's light on the disk [of the sun]; it is far less proportionate, then, to the light that shines forth from a glorified body, and especially to the light that exists in the glorious body of Christ. Therefore, if the light [of the transfigured Christ] were of this kind, the apostles would not have seen it. But they did see it; therefore, it was not of this kind.

2. Next, one asks whether at that time he assumed that dowry (*dos*) that is clarity, as some assert.[84] It seems so. It belongs to the highest wisdom to reveal something in the most fitting way in which it can be revealed. But the clarity of a glorious body cannot be revealed more fittingly than by assuming a clarity of the same nature (*ratio*). Therefore, it seems that he assumed that dowry. But then one asks whether that clarity existed in him or in the surrounding air. If it existed in him, then the same thing was at one and the same time subject both to mortality and immortality, which contradicts the Gloss noted above.[85] If, however, it existed in the surrounding air, then there will be deception in the highest truth, since he revealed in himself what he did not possess in himself.

Solution: As the Gloss says, he did not assume the dowry but a clarity similar to the dowry. This clarity that he assumed, however, can be considered according to intensity and according to the impression that it leaves in the subject, because, as a certain philosopher, Averroes, says,[86] every property leaves its own impressions in its subject. And with respect to these two considerations, it [that is, the clarity of the transfigured body] has no likeness [to the clarity of the resurrected body]; for the clarity of the resurrected body will be much greater. Likewise,

84. Cf. Alex. Hales, *Summa* III inq. un. tr. 6 q. 2 tit. 1 cap. 5 (ed. Quaracchi, vol. IV, pp. 257–58).

85. Not found in the Gloss, but see Alex. Hales, *Summa* III inq. un. tr. 6 q. 2 tit. 1 cap. 1 obj. 2 (ed. Quaracchi, vol. IV, p. 252: "Glossa Bedae"); Alb., *De res.* tr. 2, q. 7, art. 3 (ed. Colon. 26, p. 266, 43).

86. Averr., *In Porph.* 3 (ad sensum).

its impression in the subject will be immortality or the glory of the body, which is not the impression of what has illumined only the surface [of the body]. Moreover, [clarity] can be considered with regard to act, which is to illumine or to shine forth according to heavenly power, and in this way it possesses a certain likeness [to the clarity of the resurrected body].

1. One must solve the objection to the contrary in this way, that the reasons and authorities that prove that this clarity [of the Transfiguration] revealed the clarity of the immortality of resurrected bodies understand this clarity as a sign [of resurrected clarity] and not [this clarity] in itself absolutely. And it readily happens that the lesser is a sign of the greater through some likeness, as is evident among the signs of the sacraments.

2. To the last [objection], one must reply that he never assumed the dowry [of the clarity of the resurrected body] before the resurrection, and, moreover, that quality existed in his face and not in the surrounding air.[87]

Art. 5. Whether Christ alone was capable of transfiguration

To the fifth, one proceeds in this way:

1. Our resurrection has been revealed in certain others by the act of resurrection, and he who can do what is greater can do what is lesser, and what can receive the greater can receive the lesser. But we can receive the act of resurrection; therefore we can receive the act of transfiguration all the more. And so it follows that others were capable of transfiguration, just as Christ was.

2. In addition, this clearly seems to have occurred in Moses according to Exodus 34,[88] when Moses's face was made to shine so much "that the children of Israel were unable to look upon the clarity of his countenance."[89]

Solution: One must reply that God could transfigure anyone, but only Christ is transfigurable (*transfigurabilis*).[90]

1. To the objections, however, one must reply that transfigu-

87. "Face": cf. Mt 17.2.

88. Ex 34.30, 35.

89. 2 Cor 3.7.

90. Alb. seems to mean that although, hypothetically, any person *can* be transfigured, only in Christ is that potential realized.

ration indicates a light, which is a proof of the resurrection. But such a proof cannot exist in others apart from Christ because they are not the cause of salvation and of our resurrection.

2. To the objection concerning Moses, one must reply that the clarity of his countenance signified the clarity of the truth signified in the Law; the veil that he placed over his face, however, signified the shadow of the ceremonial laws and not the resurrection.

Art. 6. On the circumstances of the Transfiguration

To the sixth, one proceeds in this way:

1. One asks whether Moses rose again.[91] It seems so, because a certain gloss on Mt 17 says that the resurrection of the dead is signified by Moses, whereas the resurrection of those that will be found alive [at Christ's second coming] is signified by Elijah. And there is a long gloss of Rhabanus [Maurus] that begins in this way: "And behold, Moses and Elijah appeared to them. Luke indicates what things or what kind of things were said, etc."[92] Therefore, just as those who rise again while alive are signified by Elijah, who was alive, so too the dead who rise again are signified by Moses only if he himself rose again.

In addition, it is said in Lk 9[93] that "they appeared in majesty"; but majesty befits only those who have been resurrected.

2. Furthermore, one asks why these two [namely, Moses and Elijah], and not others, appeared [to them].

3. Additionally, [one asks about] the text (*lectio*) they read there.[94]

4. Besides, one asks about the white garments, since we will not have garments in glory.

5. Again, one asks about the cloud that cast a shadow on the

91. Cf. Alb., *Super Luc.* 9.30.

92. *Glossa ord. super Matth.* 17.3. See Lk 9.31.

93. Lk 9.31.

94. Although none of the synoptic accounts of the Transfiguration indicates explicitly that Moses and Elijah read any text on the mountain, all three make mention of their talking, discussing, or debating with the disciples and/or Jesus himself (see Mt 17.3; Mk 9.3; Lk 9.30). Furthermore, as Alb. indicates in his reply to 3 below, Lk 9.31 suggests (at least to Albert) that some scriptural text may have been the basis for their discussion: "They appeared in majesty, and they spoke of his death, which he would accomplish in Jerusalem."

mountain, since there will be nothing cloudy at the resurrection.[95]

6. Also, [one asks] about the voice of the Father, to what it was necessary to testify.

7. And one asks why the disciples fell down, since that light is not capable of damaging vision and the brain, but rather it is salubrious with respect to both.

Solution: One must reply that Moses did not rise again, but that his spirit was there [at the Transfiguration] in an assumed body, by means of which he formed sounds (*voces*) for the disciples to hear. If one asks, however, how he was able to do this, one must reply that there is a twofold power in the soul in relation to the body, namely the power capable of unifying or delimiting the body, as form unites and delimits matter, and the vivifying power and life in the body follow from this [power]. The soul has another [power in relation to the body, namely] the power capable of moving the body by progressive motion (*motu processivo*) throughout the whole body and by moving the organs to [their] organic acts, as it moves the tongue to produce meaningful speech and the hand to grasp objects.[96] And the soul possesses [both of] these conjoined powers in relation to a natural body, but it has only the latter [power] in relation to a body that has been assumed not naturally but [merely] for temporary use. And to learn what kind of body that is, see the discussion of the appearances of angels before the Incarnation.[97]

If one objects, however, that the Philosopher says that "to live" is said in many ways,[98] and one way is to be moved, one must reply that this is understood when the motive power is conjoined to preceding powers in relation to a natural body. Elijah, however, was able to be there [that is, at Christ's Transfiguration] in his own proper body.

1. To the objection to the contrary, one must say that the movement of all the saints toward the splendor of the clarity

95. Cf. Alb., *Super Matth.* 17.5.
96. This is the *vis motiva*, "the motive power."
97. Cf. Alb., *De IV coaequ.* Q. 61, a. 2.
98. Ar., *De anima* 2.2 (413a22–24).

of the risen Christ is signified by the movement [of Moses and Elijah] toward the light of the Transfiguration. And so it follows that they [namely, Moses and Elijah] signify the resurrection by [their natural bodily] movement [toward the light of the Transfiguration] and not by the fact that they themselves have been resurrected. If one objects, however, that "there is no redemption in hell,"[99] and that before [Christ's] descent into hell there was no fruition among the saints in hell (because fruition comes from the vision of glory) and so Moses could not come from hell and see the clarity [of the glorified Christ], one must reply that full redemption did not exist before Christ's Passion, nor does redemption come from leaving a [particular] place, but from participation in the blessed vision. Likewise, on the mountain Moses only saw glory in the image of that clarity which appeared there. Fruition, however, designates the vision of glory in splendor (*species*) and not in an image.

2. To the next [question regarding the circumstances of the Transfiguration], one must reply that Moses and Elijah, rather than others, appeared for three reasons. Two of these are touched on in the Gloss on Mt 17, which says this: Moses and Elijah "signify the oracles of the Law and the prophets, which were fulfilled in the Lord."[100] And the reason given in the Gloss is that Moses alone was the lawgiver who gave expression to the law of nature in the moral laws and prefigured the future truth in the ceremonial laws. Both of these will exist in the highest degree at the resurrection, because there nature will exist in the highest beauty of justice, and understanding will exist in perfect knowledge of the truth. Moreover, Elijah was the first and most distinguished of the prophets,[101] who received a sign of the future judgment at the resurrection in the descent of fire from heaven onto the two chief captains of fifty men, who signify the double multitude of those to be condemned.[102] Indeed, some [of the condemned], as Augustine says,[103] are con-

99. Resp. 7 in *Commemoratione omnium fidelium defunctorum*. See Alb., *De sacram.* tr. 6, pars 2, q. 3, art. 4, §1 (ed. Colon. 26, p. 125, 53).

100. *Glossa ord. super Matth.* 17.3.

101. Cf. ibid.

102. Cf. 2 Sm 1.14.

103. Ps. Aug., *Sermo* 77.4 (PL 39: 1896) (ad sensum).

demned and not judged, whereas others are both condemned and judged. Elijah also received the same sign of the ascension of the saints into glory with Christ by the fact that he was taken up into paradise by a fiery chariot.[104] I say "fiery," however, in terms of brightness and not in terms of heat. Moreover, Moses rendered a judgment by which the iniquitous will be judged, inasmuch as he established the Law, in which he introduced curses against transgressors.[105] And therefore it follows that each of them has a special significance for the condition of those to be condemned at the resurrection and of those to be glorified. Further down, the Gloss touches on the third reason, that the dead are signified by Moses, who is dead, whereas the living are signified by Elijah.[106] But this is an interpretation more than a reason.

3. To the next, one must reply that their text was about the end of redemption, that is, the Passion, and about the end of glory, that is, the glorious resurrection. And these two are understood by what Luke 9 says, that they spoke of his "death, which he would accomplish in Jerusalem."[107] In the long gloss noted above, Rhabanus [Maurus] explains that this passage is about death in the glory of the resurrection and about death in the redemption of the Passion.

4. To the next, one must reply that the radiance of the garment signifies the splendor proceeding from Christ into the saints. For just as brightness in the sun is light [itself] but on the surface [of something illuminated it is] a bright and clear radiance, so too in Christ glory exists in the manner of light [itself], but in the saints it exists in the manner of radiance—not absolutely, but in relation to him. For considered absolutely, all the saints "will shine forth as the sun in the kingdom of their Father."[108]

5. To the next, one must reply that the cloud signifies the un-

104. 2 Kgs 2.11.

105. See Dt 28.15–19.

106. That is, Moses signifies those who will have died before the day of resurrection, whereas Elijah signifies those who will still be alive on that day.

107. Lk 9.31; cf. *Glossa ord. super Matth.* 17.3.

108. Mt 13.43.

circumscribed and incomprehensible light that at that time descended on Mount Tabor, which means "mountain of light,"[109] that is, [that descended] on the radiant Church spiritually by the light of truth and corporeally by the clarity of physical beatitude. And it is called a cloud not because of [any] darkness that it possesses in itself, but on account of its incomprehensibility, for which reason it was necessary that it be clothed with definite arguments appropriate to the understanding of the blessed. And therefore it says in the text that there was "a bright cloud overshadowing them,"[110] so that the light refers to the object,[111] and the shadow to those looking upon it.

6. To the next, one must reply that the Father's voice gave testimony to Christ three times: first, at baptism with respect to the obedience of the sacraments;[112] second, on Mount Tabor with respect to the obedience of the precepts and the evangelical law, which were to be proclaimed by the disciples.[113] And on account of this, in both [of these manifestations] of his voice he said the same thing, adding "Listen to him." With his third testimony he confirmed the reward for those who were obedient before the Passion, when he said: "I have glorified it, and I will glorify it again,"[114] that is, I have glorified it in grace and I will glorify it again in glory.

7. To the last, one must reply that there is a certain light that, by the multiplication of [its] rays, disperses that on which it shines, and by dispersion it introduces heat, and such is the light of the sun on the eye. And because of this, when one looks [directly] at the disk of the sun, the crystalline moisture in the eye is dispersed, and vision is rendered disconnected[115] and confused, and the heat that has been stimulated consumes the [crystalline] moisture and even the brain's humor, which is, according to nature, cold and moist; and this is how the visible ob-

109. Cf. Aug., *Enarr. in Ps.* 83.13 (PL 37: 1127); Peter Lombard, *In Ps.* 88.13 (PL 191: 823A); Alb., *Super Matth.* 17.1 and *Super Luc.* 9.28.

110. Mt 17.5.

111. Namely, to the light itself that descended on Mt. Tabor, as interpreted above.

112. Mt 3.17.

113. Mt 17.5.

114. Jn 12.28.

115. Cf. Alb., *De anima* 2.3.13.

ject that exceeds [the capacity of the sense faculty] destroys the sense faculty, as the Philosopher says.[116] There is another light, shining forth brightly from a glorious body, which is not subject to the elemental qualities, and its light is not capable of moving the elements' qualities as is the light of the sun. But if it moves the sense faculty, it will move it in relation to reason, because reason, from having grasped the sensible object, is moved to wonder at the majesty shining forth in the sensible object or to consider the goodness shining in it, or to understand the truth signified by what is sensible. And so it was in the case of the Lord's clarity at the Transfiguration. The apostles fell down, therefore, not because of an opposition between the sensible and the sense faculty, but from the amazement of that wonder that was perceived (*intelligebatur*) through the sensible object. And this is what Gregory says in an interlinear gloss on Mt 17:[117] "And the disciples, hearing this, fell": "not only because of the majesty of the Father, but also because of the majesty of the Son." And Gregory [adds] in the *Moralia* [*on Job*][118] that we, who "cannot bear" that light "that we were created to behold," are in a wretched condition. It follows, then, that it is not a corporeal light for which we were created, but rather a spiritual light, which was understood through it [that is, corporeal light].

Art. 7. Concerning the proofs that were after death but before the Resurrection

Next one asks about those who were resurrected at the Passion, whether they were burned to ashes—that is, whether afterwards they died.[119] If so, then resurrection is not fittingly proven by them, just as it is not [proven] by Lazarus or by others who were resuscitated.

Furthermore, there is a distinction between resurrection and

116. Ar., *De anima* 3.2 (426a30–b3). Cf. Ar., *De gen. animal.* 5.1 (780a10ff.). Alb., *De animal.* 19.1.3.12 (*SZ* 2: 1338).

117. *Glossa interl. super Matth.* 17.6.

118. Rather, Greg., *Hom.* 8 *In Ezek.* 32 (PL 76: 869B).

119. See Alb., *De res.* tr. 1, q. 4 (ed. Colon. 26, p. 245, 60ff.). Alb. seems to be asking whether these people who were raised at Christ's Passion eventually died after this event: if so, they were not raised immortal (i.e., resurrected); if not, they experienced true resurrection.

resuscitation, and the Gospel says that they were resurrected.[120] Since, therefore, according to Damascene, "resurrection is the union with the soul of a body made incorruptible," it seems that afterwards they were not corrupted.[121]

In addition, Nicodemus says in his Gospel: "But listen to me now. All of us know the blessed Simeon, who received the infant Jesus in the Temple. And that Simeon had two sons, twin brothers, and we were all present at their dormition and burial. Take a walk, therefore, and see their graves; to be sure, they are open, because they rose again, and behold they are living together in the city of Arimathea."[122] And just below this he mentions their names, Carinus and Leucius, and describes how, coming to the priests, once the sign of the cross had been impressed on their tongues, they recounted the mystery of the Resurrection and the redemption of the Fathers from hell, and they concluded their report in this way: "The archangel Michael commanded us to walk across the Jordan into paradise (*in locum optimum*), where there were many who were resurrected with us as a testimony to the Lord Jesus Christ."[123]

We concede this, saying that afterwards they never died.

But the question that one could ask—where were they before the Ascension?—must be resolved by the authority mentioned, because they were beyond the Jordan in paradise, in the full enjoyment of Jesus's divinity. Therefore, it also describes there the joyful celebration that Elijah and Enoch had with them and with the thief.[124]

Question 8. Concerning the appearances of Jesus Christ after the Resurrection

Next one asks about the proofs, that is, the appearances, that were after the Resurrection. And first one asks why the appearances were multiplied; second, whether a glorious body is

120. Cf. Mt 27.52.

121. John Damascene, *De fide orth.* 4.27 (PG 94: 1224C; ed. Buytaert, p. 383, 96–97); Alb., *De res.* tr. 1, q. 2 (ed. Colon. 26, p. 242, 57ff.).

122. *Evang. Nicod.* pars 2.1(17).1 (ed. Tischendorff, p. 389).

123. *Evang. Nicod.* pars 2.11(27).1 (ed. Tischendorff, p. 407).

124. *Evang. Nicod.* pars 2.10 (26).1 (ed. Tischendorff, p. 405). For the thief, cf. Lk 23.42–43.

movable from place to place, and from its place; third, whether it is visible miraculously or without a miracle; fourth, whether it is palpable; fifth, concerning its food and consumption; sixth, concerning specific appearances.

Art. 1. Why the appearances were multiplied

To the first, one proceeds in this way:

1. With respect to faith, there is no intermediate between sight (*species*) and a mirror; therefore, with respect to the proofs of faith there will be no intermediate between a proof of faith in a mirror and its proof to sight.[125] But it [that is, faith] was proven in a mirror by the Incarnation; therefore, it ought to be proven to sight by the Resurrection. And so it follows that the appearances should not have happened, but rather [there should have been] the explicit revelation of glory.

2. Similarly, Augustine says: We love nothing in Christ except his flesh and his divinity.[126] Therefore, whereas Christ instructed his disciples to love his flesh through conversation and instruction before his Passion, after his Resurrection he was obliged immediately to send the Holy Spirit to instruct [them] to love [his] divinity.

3. Again, Augustine says on that text in Jn 17, "it is expedient for you that I go,"[127] that carnal love for the bodily presence of the Lord delayed the arrival of the Holy Spirit among the disciples.[128] Since, therefore, in his appearances after the Resurrection he revealed only a bodily presence, it seems instead that they [that is, the appearances] presented an obstacle to the perfection of faith and of love, which they [that is, the disciples] were going to receive through the [arrival of the] Holy Spirit, [perfection] which they [that is, the appearances] had confirmed. Therefore, it was fitting that the appearances should not have happened.

4. Next one asks why faith has proofs for the article on the Resurrection rather than for another [article].[129]

125. Cf. 2 Cor 5.7; 1 Cor 13.12.

126. Ps. Aug., *Sermo* 246.5 (PL 39: 2200).

127. Jn 16.7.

128. Aug., *In Joh.* 94.4 (PL 35: 1869).

129. "article": that is, the article in the creed professing faith in the Resurrection.

Solution: We say that from the necessity of the end—that is, of fittingness—it was necessary that the appearances happen, and for the reason that the power of the risen Lord had been entirely hidden under the weakness of the Passion. And so it would not have been easy to believe unless faith also had been led by the hand (*manuducta fuisset*) by means of the appearances.

1. To the first [objection], therefore, one must reply that regarding the object of faith, to which assent is given, there is no intermediary between truth in a mirror and truth according to sight. But because faith is united to us, one possesses thought about what is believed, and from that perspective one needs to be led by the hand by proofs, and especially concerning Christ's Resurrection, because through the weakness of the Passion a certain appearance was considered contrary to the Resurrection.

2. To the next [objection] one must reply: Just as Augustine says,[130] there is no transition from the carnal love of Christ to a purely spiritual love unless a person reasons concerning the spiritual things that have been revealed in the body of Christ. And that is called rational love by blessed Bernard,[131] and it is midway between carnal and spiritual love. And the disciples were instructed in that [love] by the appearances.

3. To the next [objection] one must reply that the argument does not hold up, unless he had revealed nothing but carnal things in the appearances.[132] But he revealed spiritual things by virtue of the fact that he entered through closed doors and the like. And on account of this, the appearances were not an obstacle to the arrival of the Holy Spirit, but rather they confirmed it.

4. To the last [objection] one must reply that our nature receives proofs against the Resurrection from the things that ap-

130. Aug., *In Joh.* 94.4 (PL 35: 1869–70) ad sensum.

131. Bern., *In Cant. serm.* 20.9 (PL 187: 871Df.).

132. Albert's Latin here reads: "… nisi in apparitionibus carnalia ostendisset." The editor indicates that, in keeping with the objection, one should read, "he had revealed nothing but (*nihil nisi*) carnal [things] in the appearances." See Alb., *De res.* tr. 2, q. 8, art. 2 (ed. Colon. 26, p. 271, n. 15).

pear to the eyes, which does not happen against other articles of faith. And therefore faith in this article [of faith] was especially in need of proofs.

Art. 2. Whether a glorious body is movable from place to place, and from its place[133]

To the second, one proceeds in this way:

1. If a glorious body is movable, it will be movable only by means of progressive motion, that is, motion that stems from an appetite of the will or of a desire for different regions of a place. But it is not movable by progressive motion, which I will prove. Therefore, it is altogether immobile. Proof: Everything movable by progressive motion has something outside itself that is desirable or is desired by it, and every such thing is incomplete with respect to what is desired, because it wants something that it does not have. But those who are glorified have everything that they want. Therefore, they do not desire anything more, and so it follows that they are not moved to acquire it.

2. Similarly, what does not exist from nature before the resurrection, according to the truth of [human] nature, likewise will not exist from nature after the resurrection. This is why we do not say that man will have wings for flight at that time. Since, therefore, before the resurrection man does not have the power to leave the place established for a mortal nature—for he cannot be raised up into the air or the fire [of heaven] whenever he wishes—so too neither after the resurrection will he have the power to leave the place that is established for glorified bodies, that is, the empyrean heaven. And so it [that is, the glorified body of Christ] will not be moved toward us by means of appearances.

If perhaps one should say that the fact that bodies cannot be moved beyond their place stems from weakness and not from the truth of nature, then to the contrary: If it stems from the truth of nature, then we have in the soul a certain power for that act, just as we have powers for speaking and walking and the like, as is evident among individual humans. But there is an

133. Cf. Alb., *De res.* tr. 4, q. 1, art. 16 (ed. Colon. 26, pp. 338–39); Alb., *IV Sent.* d. 44a a. 2, 3.

organ in the body that corresponds to every power when the power exists for the organ's act. Therefore, some organ would correspond to this power as well, which does not seem to be the case.

3. In addition, one asks whether its [that is, a glorious body's] motion exists in time or in an instant (*in nunc*). It seems that it is not in time because time is the measure of motion, where motion is the act or perfection of what is in potency insofar as it is in potency. But glorious bodies are not in potency to anything, and so it seems that their motion is not in time.[134]

If, however, its motion exists in an instant (*in nunc*), then it seems that they [namely, glorious bodies] will never be moved, because there are an infinite number of instants in any time [period] whatsoever. And so by their motion they cannot delimit a time [period], however brief.

4. Furthermore, one asks about a glorious body's place. To contain [is a property] of place. Since, therefore, there is no empty [place][135] in the order of the universe, what is placed (*locatum*) needs to be contained, and in this respect what is placed depends on a place (*locum*). But a glorious body depends on no other body. Therefore, it is not in a place.

5. Besides, for all places and things placed [in them], the place is nobler than what is placed. But a glorious body is nobler than every [other] body. Therefore, it does not exist in a place.

6. Similarly, of bodies in nature the noblest is the place for all [others], and it is not [itself] placed.[136] Therefore, analogously, the noblest bodies after the resurrection will be the place for all [others], and they will not be placed. And such will be glorious bodies. Therefore, etc.

7. In addition, one asks about its relationship to a place through which it is moved. For the Philosopher says at the end of the *Physics* that if the power of a mover were infinite, it would

134. Cf. Ar., *Phys.* 4.14 (233b15–16); cf. Alb., *Phys.* 4.3.17.

135. Cf. Ar., *De caelo et mundo* 1.4 (271a33); Alb., *De caelo et mundo* 1.1.10; *De res.* tr. 1, q. 1 (ed. Colon. 26, p. 239, 17–18).

136. Cf. Ar., *Phys.* 4.5 (212b17ff.); Alb., *Phys.* 4.1.13.

move the movable (*mobile*) in an instant (*in nunc*).[137] Since, therefore, the power of the mover in a glorious body surpasses without comparison every power of one that moves in nature, the measure of natural motion will be less than the measure of its motion without comparison. But this cannot be unless it were in an instant, because every time has a relationship to every [other] time. Therefore, its motion through a place will be in an instant.

To the contrary: every body, so far as it is contained under another body, is circumscribed by place. Proof: every body to which there is assigned a beginning, a middle, and an end in a place is circumscribed by place. But a glorious body is such as this, because a head or a foot is not just anywhere on it, but rather is here or there in a determined way. Every body, however, that is circumscribed by place, if it should be moved through a local space, exists—during its motion—partly at its end-from-which and partly at its end-to-which and does not exist <in>[138] indivisible [units] of space. Therefore, in this way a glorious body will be in a space. And every body of this kind is moved in time and not in an instant, because "before" and "after" in time are caused by the "from which" and "to which" with regard to place,[139] in which there is motion. Therefore, the motion of a glorious body with regard to place will be in time and not in an instant.

8. Next one asks whether two or more glorious bodies can exist in the same place.[140] It seems that they can, because the Lord entered through a closed door without breaking the door.[141] At some time, therefore, he existed in the same place as the door. If one should concede this, it will contradict the Philosopher, who proves that two bodies cannot exist in the same place.[142]

137. Ar., *Phys.* 8.10 (266a24–31); cf. Alb., *Phys.* 8.4.2.

138. Angle brackets indicate an addition by the editor of the Latin text.

139. Or: "by the place 'from which' and the place 'to which.'"

140. Cf. Alb., *IV Sent.* d. 44 a. 3.

141. Jn 20.26; cf. Alb., *Super Jn.* 20.19. The door through which Christ entered was not, of course, a glorious body. The question with which Albert is concerned here, then, is whether a glorious body can exist in the same place as any other body whatsoever.

142. Ar., *Phys.* 4.1 (209a6–7); cf. Alb., *Phys.* 4.1.3, 6–7.

9. Likewise, on account of what certain people say,[143] one asks whether a glorious body can exist in the smallest place whatsoever. It seems not, because Augustine says that they [that is, glorious bodies] retain the size of a thirty-year-old.[144] But a quantity so large could not exist—without its compression—in a place that is a palm's width. Much less, then, could it exist in the smallest place whatsoever.

Solution: One must say that a glorious body has the perfect power for progressive motion.

1. To the first [objection], one must reply that desire is moved by what is desirable outside itself, and, owing to its need, it moves by progressive motion, so as to be united to the desirable [object] that it does not have. And this kind of motion will not exist there, where there will be no need, but motion will exist as a demonstration of the motive power, according to which the power is directed by eternal wisdom to act. Indeed, in this way the basis (*ratio*) of glory exists in the motive power from God.

2. To the next [objection] one must reply: As Avicenna says,[145] weariness is induced in progressive motion from the opposition of the elemental nature, which has control over the body, to progressive motion. But at that time [that is, after the resurrection] that opposition will be removed, and there will be no basis (*ratio*) for the opposition that impedes the motion of every part.

To the objection that at that time that power [to move from place to place] ought to be made known to us by some organ, one must reply that the powers of a sensible soul are made known by organs, but not [the powers] of the rational soul, because that perfection does not belong to any part of the body in the way that the perfection that is, I say, tied to an organ belongs to that organ.[146] And therefore, since at that time pro-

143. See Alb., *IV Sent.* d. 44 a. 3; Thomas Aquinas, *IV Sent.* d. 44 q. 2 a. 2 qla. 5.

144. Peter Lombard, *In epist. Pauli* Eph 4.13 (PL 192: 201C); Aug., *De civ. Dei* 22.15 (PL 41: 777; CSEL 40/2: 623f.); Peter Lombard, *IV Sent.* d. 44 c. 1 (p. 1000); Alb., *De res.* tr. 2, q. 6 (ed. Colon. 26, p. 264, 6–7).

145. Avic., *Suff.* 1.5 (fol. 16vb in *Opera*).

146. Cf. Ar., *De anima* 1.5 (411b17–19); Alb., *De anima* 1.2.16; Alb., *De nat. et orig. animae* 1.6 (ed. Colon. 12, p. 14, 66–72).

gressive motion will come immediately from the rational soul's will, and the will exists with respect to all differences of place, the body's obedience will obtain in every different place. One ought not concede that at that time it [that is, the glorified body] will use feet as the organ for that motion, because, as was said, the power is not confined to a [particular] organ, but [rather] its power will exist in relation to the whole body. And so it does not follow, moreover, that we ought to have wings. For the power for flight is a power joined to a specific organ, and does not exist in relation to the whole body. Nonetheless we readily concede that at that time bodies will not be moved except perhaps on account of our need, just as the body of the Lord was moved in order to prove the resurrection to the disciples.

To the objection that nothing can be moved beyond its natural place, one must reply that this is true for bodies that, owing to their imperfection, depend on [their] place. Even though, however, a glorious body will be in a place, nevertheless it does not depend on it, as will become evident in the following.[147]

3. To the next [objection] one must reply that because, according to Augustine,[148] a glorious body retains the size of a thirty-year-old, it is impossible for its motion to be in an instant.

To the objection that it [that is, the glorious body] seems to exist in potency, one must reply that there is a certain potency that is not opposed to a body's perfection, as is the potency to a [particular] position (*ad situm*) in local motion. This is evident in the most perfect body, which exists in potency to different positions and nonetheless is the most perfect [body] in nature, like heaven.[149]

If one objects, however, that it is said of the impious, "and their time will be forever,"[150] yet it is said of the saints that their

147. Alb., *De res.* tr. 2, q. 8, art. 2 (ed. Colon. 26, p. 273, 24ff.).

148. See Peter Lombard, *In epist. Pauli* Eph 4.13 (PL 192: 201C); Aug., *De civ. Dei* 22.15 (PL 41: 777; CSEL 40/2: 623f.); Peter Lombard, *IV Sent.* d. 44 c. 1 (p. 1000); Alb., *De res.* tr. 2, q. 6; tr. 2, q. 8, art. 2 (ed. Colon. 26, p. 264, 6–7 and p. 272, 32).

149. Cf. Ar., *De caelo et mundo* 2.2 (285a27ff.); Alb., *De caelo et mundo* 2.1.5.

150. Ps 80.16.

bodies will be everlasting and immutable,[151] one must reply that time is the measure of motion changing something in an instant (*in subito*), as alteration in the soul happens through changes in the emotions, and in the body through changes in punishments.[152] And one understands what is said—"and their time will be forever" —to concern this time. And there is time that is related to motion that changes nothing in an instant (*in subito*), that is, [related to] a change of place, and in this respect time can exist in the motion of a non-temporal object, that is, an object that does not exist in time according to its nature. This is clear by way of an analogy: although heaven is necessary with respect to [its] nature, nonetheless its motion exists in time and is measured by time. But there is a difference in this respect: that heaven produces something in another, although not in itself, by means of [its] motion; that is, it produces generation and corruption in lower [bodies]. But a glorious body does not produce anything in itself through motion, because its potency is perfected in itself before it is demonstrated by an act. And so it is also clear that it does not follow that if it is moved in time, then it exists in time.

4. To the question concerning place, one must reply that glorious bodies exist in a place and are circumscribed in it.[153]

To the objection to the contrary, one must reply that place is investigated in many ways. To the extent that place can be ordered among the categories,[154] it is investigated by logic. To the extent that it is a type (*species*) of continuous immobile quantity, it is part of the subject matter of geometry; and in this respect the Philosopher says in the fourth book of the *Physics* that mathematicians also investigate place.[155] To the extent that place is one of the principles of motion, it is investigated by the natural philosopher. From this it is clear that place is not always understood from the point of view of that container that is the

151. Cf. Wis 5.16; Sir 44.14.

152. Cf. Ar., *Cat.* 8 (8b35–36; 9a28–29); Boethius, transl. ant. PL 64: 214A, 245D; Alb., *De praedic.* 5.2.6.

153. Cf. Alb., *De praedic.* 3.10.

154. That is, as one of Aristotle's ten categories.

155. Ar., *Phys.* 4.1 (208b22–23; 208a26ff.); Alb., *Phys.* 4.1.1.

act of form with respect to [what is] imperfect; for it is understood in this way only in nature, where place is reduced to a formal principle. To the extent, however, that the act of place is to measure [something] by an external boundary, place belongs to mathematical objects; and in this way it is appointed for a glorious body.

5. From this a solution to the second [objection concerning the place of a glorious body] is evident, because the noblest body does not exist in a place in such a way that it is contained by place; but it can have a boundary, and this will not be contrary to its nobility. For just as it is not contrary to a noble nature to be measured by [its] intrinsic quantity—namely, by length, width, and depth—so too neither [is it contrary to a noble nature to be measured] by [its] permanent extrinsic quantity, which is place.

6. To the next [objection] one must reply that a place exists for the noblest body not insofar as it is of such a kind [namely, the noblest body as placed], but rather insofar as it is the noblest and the last [body], within which all things exist. And from this it is clear that that objection does not make progress.

7. To the question that is raised about its motion through a place, one must reply that it has been proven that "before" and "after" in time are caused by the "before" and "after" in motion and in space, and no body that is divisible in quantity can be moved through indivisible [units] of space because it would not pass through.[156] And on account of this, it is necessary for the medium through which it is moved always to have the aspect (*ratio*) of the end-from-which and the end-to-which, from which the "before" and "after" is caused in the measure of motion, which is time.

To the Philosopher's objection, however, one must reply that he understands this of a power that exists in a movable body [and] that is divisible according to its quantity, just as "force of weight" (*virtus gravis*) exists for motion. For it does follow correctly that, if the [arithmetic] proportion of one "weight" (*gravitas*) is determined to be ten and it moves something movable through a certain space in four hours, another "force of weight" determined to be twenty will move the same movable

156. See Alb., *De res.* tr. 2, q. 8, art. 2 (ed. Colon. 26, p. 272, 13ff.).

through the same space in two hours. And [it also follows that], if there is another [power] that is determined to be infinite, it will move [the movable] to infinity in a measure [of time] less than four hours, that is, in an instant (*in nunc*). But if the power is not divisible with respect to the quantity of the subject, as the Philosopher himself says of the power of the Prime Mover—that it is neither finite nor infinite with respect to the quantity of any body, but it is indivisible and incommunicable, not having magnitude at all[157]—it will move [the movable] with respect to time, even if it is not proportionate to it, as is the case with the power of the rational soul, which will move glorious bodies by progressive motion. For just as the power of the Prime Mover does not have the same basis (*ratio*) as any power that moves bodies, and therefore has neither a finite nor an infinite relation to it, so too the power of the rational soul, since it does not have the same basis (*ratio*) as heaviness (*gravitas*) and lightness, has no relation to them. And yet it will not move [the movable] in an instant (*in nunc*), but in time.

Therefore, one must assert that the motion of a glorious body occurs in an imperceptible time [period], and it occurs suddenly and without regard to the size of the space. Hence we readily concede that the motion occurs more quickly toward the middle of the space than toward the outer boundary,[158] but nonetheless in a manner imperceptible to us. And Augustine provides as an analogy the ray that moves out from the eye to a visible object, no matter how distant. To be sure, the ray exists first in the space nearer to the eye rather than in one more remote, but nonetheless in a manner imperceptible to us.[159]

8. To the question whether two bodies can exist in the same place, one must reply that there are two [things to consider] in something that is placed (*in locato*), namely the extension of the substance through an intrinsic quantity, and [its] repletion from gross matter. In glorious bodies, however, whatever pertains to inferiority, that is, repletion from gross matter, is removed, and

157. Ar., *Phys.* 8.10 (267b25–26).

158. Because of the attractive power of the center.

159. Aug., *Sermo* 277.11 (PL 38: 1263). Cf. *Epist.* 102.5 (PL 33: 372; CSEL 34: 548f.).

whatever belongs to the truth of human nature remains. And according to this, a glorious body can exist in the same place with another [body]. And an analogy can be established according to the opinion of certain people who say that heaven,[160] through a certain spiritual nature of its own, which is said to be diaphanous or clear, exists in the same place with air and water; how much more, then, will a spiritual body, which is more subtle than heaven, [exist in the same place with another body]. Nor does this contradict the Philosopher, because he is speaking of bodies in which the repletive power of matter exists.

9. To the last question, we concede that a glorious body can only exist in a place equal to it with respect to the extent of [its] quantity. Nonetheless, there are those who say that this is true after the resurrection, when the elements will be glorified, but that before the resurrection it [that is, a glorified body] can exist in a [place] smaller than it with respect to quantity, which exists in potency in that place.[161] For just as from one handful of water there arise ten [handfuls] of air,[162] so it follows, they say, that from a place having a small size there will come a large size through glorification of the elements. But this opinion is false for two reasons. One is that the glorification of the world will not come about through the rarefaction and extension of the elements, as will be proved below.[163] The other is that the glorious body of Christ and of the others who rose with him existed, after the resurrection, in a place in act and not only in potency. Therefore, its [that is, the glorious body's] place existed in act and not only in potency.

But whatever objection could be raised concerning the body of Christ on the altar has been fully discussed and resolved in the treatise *On the Eucharist*.[164]

Art. 3. Whether a glorious body is visible miraculously or without a miracle[165]

160. "Certain people": Cf. Ps. Odo Rigaldi (fol. 24rb); Alb., *De IV coaequ.* q. 12 a. 1 sol.; *De caelo et mundo* 2.1.2; *De anima* 2.3.8.

161. Cf. Alb., *De sacram.* 5.1, q. 4 a.1.2; *IV Sent.* d. 44 a.2.

162. Ar., *De gen. et corr.* 2.6 (333a21–22).

163. See Alb., *De res.* tr. 2, q. 10, art. 3 (ed. Colon. 26, p. 292, 63ff.).

164. Alb., *De sacram.* 5.1, q. 4 a. 4 (ed. Colon. 26, p. 64, 4ff.).

165. Cf. Alb., *Super Jn.* 20.27.

To the third, one proceeds in this way:

1. Gregory says, [commenting] on the end of Luke, that every visible object is corruptible.[166] Therefore, if a glorious body is visible, it will be corruptible. But it is not corruptible; therefore, etc.

2. Likewise, the Philosopher says that all sensible bodies are subject to generation and corruption.[167] But every visible object is sensible. Therefore, every visible object is subject to generation and corruption. If, therefore, a glorious body is visible, it is corruptible, which is false.

3. Additionally, Boethius says that the power of an agent is considered not only according to the power of the agent, but also according to the power of the patient.[168] For example, the sun is not said to have the power to illuminate mud, because mud does not have the power to be illuminated, although the sun has the power to illuminate. Therefore, if a glorious body is visible, it is necessary that the eye be capable of receiving its light. But this is not true.

4. Proof: A power that cannot [act] on the lesser cannot [act] on the greater, as the Philosopher says in the second book of *On Heaven and Earth,* when explaining the proposition: "Strength is the limit of a thing's power."[169] But our eye cannot [act] on the lesser, unless perhaps with its own destruction, as is [the case when it looks directly at] the light of the sun. Therefore, it cannot [act] on the light of a glorious body.

5. Again, Alpetragius[170] says in his *Astrology*[171] that the light of the ninth orb, that is, of the heaven that exists beyond the sphere of fixed stars—which, at the end of the second book of

166. Greg., *Hom.* 26 *In Ev.* 1 (PL 76: 1198A).

167. Ar., *De gen. et corr.* 2.1 (328b32–33).

168. *secundum potestatem patientis:* i.e., according to the power or potential of the one that suffers, undergoes, or passively experiences the change effected by the agent. Boethius, *De cons. phil.* 5, pros. 4 (PL 63: 848Cf.; CSEL 67, p. 117, 12–14). Cf. Alb., *Super Dion. Epist.* 5, q. 1; *De sacram.* 3, q. 1 a. 5 sol. (ed. Colon. 26, p. 32, 62).

169. Ar., *De caelo et mundo* 1 (not 2).11 (281a11–17).

170. I.e., Al-Bitruji (d. 1204), an Islamic astronomer from Al-Andalus known in the West as Alpetragius.

171. Alpetragius, *De mot. cael.* 7.14 (ed. F. J. Carmody, p. 90); Cf. Alb., *De caelo et mundo* 2.3.1.

On Heaven and Earth, the Philosopher calls the hidden heaven[172]—is so subtle and simple that its light is not accessible to sight, even though it is luminous throughout. Since, therefore, a glorious body, and most especially the body of Christ, exists incomparably in a simpler light, it will not be visible.

6. To the contrary: Gregory says [in his comments on] the end of Luke that the Lord presented to the disciples a visible body to be touched. Also, the Lord himself said to the disciples, "Touch [me] and see, for a ghost does not have flesh and bones, as you see that I have."[173] Therefore, it was visible.

7. Next one asks about what some say,[174] that it is within its power—that is, [the power] of a glorious body—to be seen and to be hidden when it wishes. It seems that this is not true. Indeed, a body's qualities have extension according to its position, and these [qualities] are not subject to the will. It seems, therefore, that if that [body] is visible or invisible by its own light, neither of these is subject to its will.

8. After this, one asks again about the affirmation of the ancients[175] who say that the Lord was seen by the disciples not in his own appearance but in an assumed appearance, namely one that has color (*colorati*).[176]

Opposed to this is the fact that then deception would fall within the First Truth.

Additionally, since his appearance is a proof of the resurrection—as it is said at the beginning of Acts that he appeared to them "by many proofs"[177]—the proof will be apparent and non-existent.

9. On account of this, some say[178] that the form and the appearance (*species*) differ. For form is said in relation to that of

172. Ar., *De caelo et mundo* 1 (not 2).9 (279a29); cf. Alb., *De caelo et mundo* 1.3.10.

173. Lk 24.39.

174. Cf. Alex. Hales, *Summa* III inq. un. tr. 6 q. 2 tit. 2 mem. 2 cap. 1 (ed. Quarrachi, vol. IV, pp. 268–71).

175. Cf. Wm. of Auxerre, *Summa aurea* IV tr. 18 cap. 2 q. 3 sol. (ed. Ribaillier, vol. 4, pp. 488–89).

176. Cf. Alb., *IV Sent.* d. 44 a. 27 arg. 2.

177. Acts 1.3.

178. Cf. Wm. of Auxerre, *Summa aurea* IV tr. 18 cap. 2 q. 3 sol. (ed. Ribaillier, vol. 4, pp. 488–89).

which it is the form—that is, in relation to a subject—whereas the appearance [is said] in relation to the knower. And they say that the Lord appeared in his own, namely luminous, form; but this form was assumed from the form of a colored body for the sake of the appearance.[179]

Opposed to this is the fact that the nature (*ratio*) of knowledge is taken from the nature of the knowable. Since, therefore, there was no basis (*ratio*) for color in the knowable, there will be no perception of color in knowledge.

10. For this reason, others say that the form of the colored did not exist in him, but [rather] in the eyes of those looking at him.[180]

Opposed to this is the fact that the sensible form, which exists in sense, is generated by an object altering sense. Therefore, it is necessary either for the one generating and the one generated to have different natures, which is unfitting, or for a form not to be perceived by sight other than the one that exists in the object.

Furthermore, we see from this that a luminous [object] does not imprint color, but rather light, on our eye.

In addition, others say[181] that it [that is, the glorified body of Christ] altered the eye according to light, but on account of a defect in the non-glorified eye it was perceived as colored. And they propose that it is analogous to having a weak eye by reason of a humor flowing down into the pupil. For it does not see a luminous [object] according to the act of a luminous [object], but under redness. There is also an analogy among the colors that appear in the sky, like [the colors] of a rainbow,[182] which are caused because the sun's rays are reflected over an aqueous cloud more or less profusely. If there is only a little of the cloud's moisture among the rays, a bright red is generated; and if there is more [moisture], it begins to tend toward a blood-red

179. Alb. seems to mean that some believe that the Lord's body had to have color in order to be visible to sense.

180. Cf. Wm. of Auxerre, *Summa aurea* IV tr. 18 cap. 2 q. 3 sol. (ed. Ribaillier, vol. 4, pp. 488–89).

181. Cf. Alex. Hales, *Summa* III inq. un. tr. 6 q. 2 tit. 2 mem. 2 cap. 1 sol. (ed. Quarrachi, vol. IV, p. 270); Alb., *IV Sent.* d. 13 a. 3 ad 3.

182. Cf. Alb., *Meteora* 3.4.2.

color; and over another part [of the cloud], where the moisture is [even] more dense, green is generated; and in the middle a dark blue [is generated]. And if the cloud is not aqueous but has a subtle vapor, and if there is a lot of vapor, a golden color tending toward red is generated, as happens at daybreak and evening. And other colors too, like the color of fleece[183] or of blackness, are produced according to differences of this sort in an aqueous or earthy cloud.

11. Opposed to this seems to be the fact that one Lord was seen at the Transfiguration before the Resurrection and another in the appearances after the Resurrection. Therefore, it seems that this [change] does not occur on the part of the eye, but from the nature of the one who changes.

12. Also, when no weakness exists in the eye, a luminous [object] is not drawn elsewhere (*ad aliud*) but is perceived in the light, especially since the light of a glorious body does not corrupt vision, as was maintained above in the question on the Transfiguration.[184]

13. After this, one asks about an assertion of certain people:[185] Supposing that everything that is seen is seen under [the form of] a triangle, whose base is as large as the size of the object seen, and [supposing that] there is an acute angle formed in the eye by the lines resting on the base, and [supposing that] the glorious body is seen by the glorious eye and by the non-glorious eye, one may ask whether the base of the angle that is in the non-glorious eye is the same size as the base of the angle that is in the glorious eye. It seems not, for we see Christ's body in the sacrament, whose size does not extend beyond the visible species and more than a small distance. But the glorious eye sees him according to the size of a thirty-year-old.

14. Some people concede this and say that it is the same for other glorious bodies according to the statement of the Apostle, who says that "he will reform the body of our lowliness, conformed to the body of his clarity."[186]

183. Cf. Alb., *Meteora* 1.4.10.
184. Alb., *De res.* tr. 2, q. 7, art. 2ff. (ed. Colon. 26, pp. 265, 83ff.).
185. Cf. Alb., *Quaestio de sens. corp. glor.* art. 2 §1 (ed. Colon. 25/2, pp. 115–18).
186. Phil 3.21.

But opposed to this is the fact that according to this view a glorious body will be seen not only according to a different quality but also according to a different quantity. This is false, since quantity belongs to the truth of human nature, which remains the same both here and there, as Augustine[187] and Anselm say.[188]

Solution: We say that a glorious body is not visible to a non-glorious [eye] without a miracle, but that it is visible to a glorious [eye] without a miracle. A distinction must be drawn, however, between the power to effect change and the power to undergo change. Now, the power to effect change in a non-glorious eye does not exist in a glorious body without a miracle, but once [this] change has happened by means of a miracle, the reception of the form of the one that effects change can occur without a miracle according to the power of a non-glorious eye. And so the appearance (*visio*) of a bounded elemental body, that is, of one like glass that transmits something seen, does not occur except under the form of color. If, however, once [this] change has happened by a miracle, reception [of the form] should again occur through an amplified visual power, then a glorious body will be seen under [the form of] light, and then there will be a double miracle: one on the part of the one that effects change, and the other on the part of the one that undergoes [change] or sees [the glorious body].

1–5. From these [words], a solution appears to the first five arguments. For we concede that anything that is seen according to the power of a non-glorious eye as an object of sight, and not as an act of sight and of the visible [reality] and of the medium—this entire [object] is corruptible. I call, however, the act of the visible [reality] and of sight and of the medium that which is luminous of its own nature, like the sun. For this can be non-corruptible, if it exists apart from [its] active and passive elemental qualities, as does the light of heaven.

6. From this a solution to the objection to the contrary is

187. Aug., *Enchir.* 88 (PL 40: 273).

188. Anselm, *Cur deus homo* 2.11 (PL 158: 410CD; ed. Schmitt, 2: 109, 13–15); cf. Alb., *De res.* tr. 1, q. 6, art. 4 (ed. Colon. 26, p. 251, 15–16); Alb., *De incarn.* 5, q. 2 a. 3 (ed. Colon. 26, p. 215, 60).

also clear, because such a change was produced by a miracle on the part of the one effecting change, although not on the part of the one undergoing [the change]. But why this was so will be articulated below in the sixth article.[189]

7. To what was asked next, we concede that it is not in the power of a glorious body to be seen and not to be seen when it wishes. But the fact that sometimes it is seen, and sometimes not, stems from the power of divine wisdom, which moves inferior objects not only by nature, but also—for the benefit of the faithful—by a miracle.

8. To the question about the ancients' opinion that he [that is, Christ] appeared under an alien form, we say that it is not true.

9. To the question about species and form, similarly we say that it is not true, unless it is understood such that species designates the nature (*ratio*) of the form according to what has been received, and not according to what is effecting change.

10. To the following opinion we say that it is true, but imperfectly explained. For in a porous,[190] vaporous, or moist body, the dispersed rays that are emitted by a luminous body or by the eye cause various colors, as was said. But if light shall be perceived in a bounded body without any medium interposed between the one seeing and the visible [object], then it will be seen under a color. This is clear from the statement of the Philosopher in *On Sense and the Sensed*, who says that "color is the extremity of the transparent" or of the clear "in a bounded body."[191] And Alfarabi, in his commentary on this passage, says that color is nothing but the mixture of light with the nature of a bounded body's surface.[192] Since, therefore, a glorious body is not subject to rarefaction, but is bounded by the very same parts of matter that it has now, although not under the same qualities, it is clear that its light will be bounded light. But bounded light is perceived as color and not as light, not from

189. Cf. Alb., *De res.* tr. 2, q. 8, art. 6 (ed. Colon. 26, p. 278, 58ff).

190. "Porous" [*rarus*], or thin, or subtle.

191. Ar., *De sensu et sens.* 3 (439b11–12).

192. Alfarabi: rather, Averr., *Compend. libri Arist. De sensu et sensato* (CCAA 7: 15, 37–38, 16, 54); *De anima* 2, text comm. 67 (CCAA 6/1: p. 231, 25–27).

an expanded visual power [but] from a defect in the one seeing and from the nature (*ratio*) of the bounded [body].

11, 12. From this a solution to the objections against that opinion is clear. For that perception is caused by two things: namely, by a defect in the power of a non-glorious eye, and by the delimitation of the body that is seen. Its delimitation is in the combination and mingling of elements with respect to substance, although active and passive qualities are not in it in act. To be sure, the first objection proceeds from accidental weakness, whereas the second proceeds from a luminous non-elemental bounded [body].

13. To the question concerning the base of the angle of sight, we say that the size of the base of the one is the same as that of the other.

To the objection concerning the Lord's body in the sacrament, we say that Christ's body does not exist in the sacrament as in a place, but as in a sign containing within itself the truth and essence of the thing signified. And Christ's body possesses this [that is, the truth and essence of Christ] insofar as it is divine, not insofar as it is glorious, as is said in the question on the Eucharist.[193] And for this reason, this is no objection.

14. To the objection concerning the Apostle, one must reply that that conformation is understood of the likeness of participation in the dowries (*dotibus*) alone and not in other things that are found in the body of Christ, such as that it is united to divinity and that it is spiritual food in the sacrament.

Art. 4. Whether a glorious body is palpable

To the fourth, one proceeds in this way:

1. Every tangible object is distinguished by tactile qualities. A glorious body is tangible. Therefore, it is distinguished by tactile qualities. Proof of the minor [premise]: Gregory says: "He presented his body to the disciples as tangible or palpable."[194] But everything distinguished by tactile qualities is hot,

193. Cf. Alb., *De sacram.* 5.1, q. 4 a.1.2 (ed. Colon. 26, p. 63, 50ff.). Cf. Alb., *Super Jn.* 20.20.

194. *Glossa ord. super Luc.* 24.39 (under Gregory's name); Alb., *De res.* tr. 2, q. 8, art. 3 (ed. Colon. 26, p. 275, 17).

cold, dry, and moist,[195] which is not suitable for a glorious body.

2. Furthermore, one asks whether, if it is touched, it yields to or resists touch. If it yields [to touch], then it is soft, because the Philosopher says in book two of *On Generation and Corruption* that the soft is what yields to touch.[196] If it does not yield [to touch], however, then it is hard, because he says in the same place that the hard is what does not yield to touch.[197]

Solution:

1. One must reply that in a glorious body none of the elemental qualities exists in act, but only in root. On the other hand, the properties of a celestial body, such as brightness, subtlety, and the like, do exist in it in act. And one must distinguish the tangible just as the visible [has been distinguished]. To be sure, a glorious body is not tangible to a non-glorious [body] except by means of a miracle. And if a change in the sense of touch should occur miraculously, it [that is, a glorious body] will be touched only in accordance with the power of a non-glorious body, as was said above concerning a visible object, because at bottom these questions are the same.[198]

2. To the objection, however, concerning the hard and the soft, some solve this [by saying] that not yielding to touch arises from two causes, one of which is the firmness of the earthy parts, in which dryness prevails;[199] and the Philosopher defined the hard in this way. Another is the impossibility of being affected (*patiendi*) by something external. And in accordance with this, heaven does not yield to touch or to external pressure, and nevertheless it is neither hard nor soft.

It could even be said that the sense of touch is oriented toward two [classes of tangibles], namely toward those things that are sensibles contrary to its touch *per se,* such as the hot, cold, moist, dry, hard, and soft, and others of this sort; and with respect to these qualities touch only exists through a medium

195. "hot, cold, dry, and moist": i.e., the four humoral qualities of the body.

196. Ar., *De gen. et corr.* 2.2 (330a8–9). Cf. Alb., *De gen. et corr.* 2.1.7; *Meteora* 4.2.3.

197. Ar., *De gen. et corr.* 2.2 (330a11–12).

198. Alb., *De res.* tr. 2, q. 8, art. 3 (ed. Colon. 26, p. 276, 46–48).

199. Cf. Alex. Hales, *Summa* III inq. un. tr. 6 q. 2 tit. 2 mem. 2 cap. 2 art. 1 ad 1 ("Aliter potest dici 1") (ed. Quarrachi, vol. IV, p. 274).

and an organ distinct in act from these qualities. The sense of touch is also oriented toward what exists prior to these qualities according to nature, namely for the perception of an indivisible continuous [body] or a divided non-continuous [body]. And it touches these tangibles, according to which it is joined to the common sense, to which it pertains to perceive magnitude in an object.[200] Therefore, one can say that a glorious body effects change in the sense of touch by means of this second class [of tangibles], and not through the first. And it does not follow from this that it is corruptible or hot or cold, etc., because these [qualities] have one nature (*ratio*) in a corruptible body and [another] in an incorruptible body, and one [nature] in an elemental body and [another] in a non-elemental body.

Art. 5. Concerning its food and consumption[201]

To the fifth, one proceeds in this way:

1. Everyone who really eats transforms food's nourishment into himself by means of the nutritive power. But the Lord really ate after the Resurrection, because there was no deception in him. Therefore, he transformed food into himself.

To the contrary: Some loss of the body's substance occurs in everyone who really eats. Therefore, in someone in whom there can be no loss of the body's substance, there is no real eating. But no loss of the body can occur in a glorious body. Therefore, etc.

2. Next, one asks what happened to the food. And Augustine solves this in book twenty-one of the *City of God,* [saying] that the heat of the sun absorbs water in one way and the thirsty ground does so in another way, intending thereby to distinguish among bodies that take in food.[202] For some transfer the food into themselves, and these are similar to the earth that thirsts for and drinks up water into itself. Others, like glorious bodies, do not transfer the food into themselves, and these are similar to the rays of the sun that consume water.

3. But then one asks whether another glorious body has the same power with respect to food that Christ's body has.

200. Cf. Alb., *De homine,* q. 35 a.4 sol. (ed. Colon., 27/2, p. 276).

201. Cf. Alb., *Super Luc.* 24.30; *Super Jn.* 21.13.

202. Aug., *Epist.* 102, q. 1, 6 (PL 33: 372; CSEL 34/2: 549, 18–19), and not *De civ. dei.*

Solution:

1. One must reply with Augustine in the Gloss on the end of Luke[203] that there are two modes of consumption, namely one that indicates power and one that stems from need.[204] The consumption that indicates power is the one that, through the external act of eating, indicates that there is such power in the person eating and, through this power, [indicates] the truth of human nature of the person who eats. And the Lord ate in this way after the Resurrection. The consumption of need occurs when there is a very intense need for food for the sake of restoring what has been lost. This need does not belong to the truth of human nature, but only the power [to eat] does. From this a solution to the first [objection] is apparent.

2. To the question concerning what happens to the food, one can say with Augustine that just as those things that were created for the sake of man are subject to man's use,[205] such as food for refreshment and the like, so too they are subject to a glorious body as a demonstration of power; and therefore they are converted into a subtle, airy matter [in a glorious body], just as now they are converted into nutriment.

3. To the last question, one must reply that the same reason for the truth of the power of eating exists in all glorious bodies. But there is not the same reason of fittingness for why it is demonstrated in all. To be sure, the demonstration of the power is a proof of the resurrection. Proofs of the resurrection, however, are only introduced for the Resurrection of the head, and the resurrection of others is deduced from the Resurrection of the head, as is clear from the progress of the Apostle's discourse in 1 Cor 15. For there he proves the Resurrection of Christ first from [his] appearances, saying that "he was seen by Cephas, and after that," etc.[206] Then, having proved the resurrection of Christ, he arrives at a conclusion concerning the resurrection of others.

203. *Glossa ord. super Luc.* 24.41.

204. Albert's Latin is *comestio potestativa* and *comestio indigentiae.*

205. Aug., *De civ. dei* 13.22 (PL 41: 395; CSEL 40/1: 647, 13–14).

206. 1 Cor 15.5–8.

Art. 6. Concerning specific appearances

Concerning the sixth, ten things are asked corresponding to the ten appearances that are recounted at the end of the Gospels. And an eleventh question is raised, concerning what principally distinguishes the appearances, and why other appearances that are reported by the Apostle are not numbered among them.

§1. On the appearance in which he appeared to Mary Magdalene

First, one asks about the appearance in which he appeared to Mary Magdalene, in Jn 20.[207]

1. And first one asks why it was necessary for the first messengers of the Resurrection to be angels.

2. Second, [John] Chrysostom asks[208] why the woman speaking with the angels turned around.[209]

3. Third, since it is clear from what was said earlier that Christ did not appear in any form in which he did not exist,[210] why then was he perceived by Mary Magdalene in the form (*forma*) of a gardener?[211]

Solution:

1. Chrysostom replies to the first that the arrangement of the linen cloths[212] was a proof by which the woman would believe the Resurrection, but feebly, saying in *Homily* 86 on John, "An attitude full of much ardor and grace: Now because the woman's mind was not lifted up [to spiritual realities], something more occurred so that she might accept the resurrection based on [the evidence of] the cloths (*sudariis*):[213] she saw an-

207. Jn 20.11–14.

208. John Chrysos., *Hom.* 86 *in Joh.* 1 (PG 59: 467–68).

209. Jn 20.14.

210. Alb., *De res.* tr. 2, q. 8, art. 3 (ed. Colon. 26, p. 276, 83–85).

211. Jn 20.15.

212. Cf. Jn 20.5–7.

213. Jn 20.7 refers to the singular *sudarium,* or sweat cloth, which by the Middle Ages had popularly become associated with the veil of Veronica: "que sudarium siue Veronica uulgariter appellatur." William Durand, *Ratione divinorum officiorum* 6.19.6, ed. A. Davril and T. M. Thibodeau, CCCM 140A (Turnhout: Brepols, 1998); see also Ewa Kuryluk, *Veronica and Her Cloth: History, Symbolism, and Structure of a 'True' Image* (Oxford: Blackwell, 1991).

gels sitting with a joyful attitude, so that meanwhile she herself might be raised up from suffering and be soothed."

Another reason can be given, because two things belong to faith, namely assent and thought. And although assent arises immediately from the First Truth and in the First Truth, nevertheless the thought associated with faith and the determination of the time of an event in the dispensation belongs to the angels. And for this reason, they announced the time of the Incarnation at the nativity and the [time of the] nativity [itself] to [his] mother and to the shepherds. In fact, the revelations that come from the first [one] are perceived by angels by means of a first report, and are perceived by men through the angels from a second report.[214]

2. To the second, one must reply as does Chrysostom[215] on the passage, "She turned around,"[216] saying: "And what follows from the fact that, speaking to them and not yet hearing [from them], she turned around to what was behind her? It seems to me that while she was speaking, the fact that Christ appeared silently behind her stupefied the angels, and they, contemplating their Ruler, showed immediately in [their] posture and manner of looking and movement that they saw the Lord. And this caused the woman to turn around to [see] what was behind her."

3. To the last, one must reply that there are two reasons why he was seen in the appearance (*specie*) of a gardener, although he was in his own appearance (*specie propria*): namely, reason's doubt concerning the Resurrection, and the outward circumstances of the place presented to sense perception. Indeed, reason's doubt supposed that the one whom she was seeking was not alive, as Gregory says in a homily.[217] The circumstances of the place presented to sense also led [her] to believe that it was the gardener. For although he was in his own form (*figura propria*), which he had before the Passion, nevertheless for these

214. Cf. Alfred of Sareshel, *De motu cordis* prol. 1 (ed. Cl. Baeumker, Beiträge 23,1–2: 2, 8–9). Alb., *De incarn.* q. 1, art. 2 (ed. Colon. 26, p. 173, 62). Dion., *De eccle. hier.* 5, §4 (PG 3: 504ff.; Dionysiaca 2: 1330ff.). Alb., *Super Is.* 63.1 (ed. Colon. 19, p. 591, 16–18).

215. John Chrysos., *Hom.* 86 *in Joh.* 1 (PG 59: 468). Cf. Alb., *Super Jn.* 20.14.

216. Jn 20.14.

217. Greg., *Hom.* 25 *In Ev.* 4 (PL 76: 1192B).

two reasons she did not recognize him, but instead thought that he was someone else. In the same way it often happens among those who are suffering from fevers that, from the internal movement of the imagination, a slight juxtaposition of lines presented to sense perception appears externally to be the frightful form of an animal;[218] and the slight sound of the wind or of something else externally presented to sensation, when joined to what is in the imagination, appears to be the uprising of an army. This is why, moreover, it does not say that he *was* the gardener, but rather that she *thought* that he was the gardener.

§2. On the appearance in which he appeared to the women

Second, one asks about the appearance in which he appeared to the women, at the end of Matthew.[219]

1. First, one asks why the angel appeared to the guards with a frightful appearance but to the women with a joyful appearance.

2. Second, [one asks] why the stone was rolled back, since a glorious body has the property of exiting and entering through closed doors.

3. Third, why the women, and not the apostles, were the first to announce the Resurrection.

4. Fourth, why he came to meet the women before he came to the apostles.

5. Fifth, why he allowed the women to touch his feet, since, at his first appearance, he prohibited Mary Magdalene [from touching him].[220]

6. Sixth, why he sent the disciples to the brothers in Galilee, since, before they arrived, he appeared to them very often in Jerusalem.

1. To the first, one must reply, in agreement with Gregory in a homily,[221] that by means of that [frightful] appearance (*habitus*) the angels revealed the great fear of the risen Judge among the reprobate, whereas [they revealed] to the women

218. Cf. Ar., *De insomniis* 2 (460b11–13; ed. Droissart Lulofs, p. 18, 1–3); Alb., *De somno et vig.* 2.1.7.

219. Mt 28.1–10.

220. See Jn 20.17.

221. Greg., *Hom.* 21 *in Ev.* 3 (PL 76: 1171B).

the Judge's grace toward [his] friends. Therefore, on the text, "Do not fear,"[222] Gregory [says]: "What do you fear, you who have seen your fellow citizens? Let those who do not belong to their company fear."[223]

2. To the next, one must reply that the stone was rolled back to provide a proof to sense perception, not to reason. And this is shown by the statement of the angels, when they say: "Come, and see the place."[224]

3. To the third, one must reply, in agreement with the saints, that although the Passion was the cause of salvation, nevertheless the Resurrection was the first entrance into [eternal] life. And that [entry into eternal life] had to correspond to what happened at the entry into death, just as the entry into grace corresponds to the same [entry into death]: for death began with a woman, grace began with Mary, and the joy of the Resurrection began with the women. And this is Gregory's explanation in a homily.[225]

Elsewhere, in *On Job,* Gregory says the same thing on that text,[226] "The flesh being consumed, my bone cleaved to my skin":[227] [he says] that the skin signifies the women, among whom a greater faith remained after the Passion than among the apostles, and the flesh signifies the apostles, who were consumed by so much doubt that even the chief among them denied him. And this is what the Lord says in the Gospel of John 16: "Do you now believe? The hour is coming when you will be scattered and will leave me alone."[228] Indeed, everyone but his mother doubted, but the women less than the apostles. And for this reason they deserved to be the messengers of the Resurrection first.

4. To the next, one must reply that he appeared to them on the way as a greater proof of the Resurrection, so that they would announce it to the disciples with more certainty.

222. Mt 28.5.
223. Greg., *Glossa ord. super Matth.* 28.5.
224. Mt 28.6.
225. Greg., *Hom.* 25 *in Ev.* 6 (PL 76: 1194A).
226. Greg., *Moral.* 14.49.57 (PL 75: 1068B–C). Cf. *Glossa ord. super Job* 19.20.
227. Jb 19.20.
228. Jn 16.31–32.

5. To the next, one must reply, in agreement with Augustine,[229] that the first appearance did not completely confirm in Mary Magdalene faith in the Resurrection. And for this reason she was not fit to touch him, but a second appearance provided proof for her. Hence on that [passage], "For I have not yet ascended to my Father,"[230] Augustine says: "Not that he did not want to be touched until he had ascended, since we read that both the women and others on earth touched him and not while he was sitting in heaven. He wants, therefore, to be touched spiritually, that is, such that he is believed to be equal to the Father. And because she was still believing in him, whom she wept over as just a man, in a carnal way, she heard: 'Do not touch me, for I have not yet ascended to my Father';[231] that is, in your heart you do not yet believe that I am equal to the Father. You will touch me in the future, when you believe that we are not unequal."

6. To the last, one must reply that he immediately mentioned Galilee in order to recall to their memory a proof that had preceded the Resurrection, namely the Transfiguration on Mount Tabor, which is located in Galilee. Indeed, it was there that he had shown the power of rising again, which was revealed in every act of the appearances.

§3. On the appearance in which he appeared to Simon

Third, one asks about the appearance in which he appeared to Simon [Peter] before the other apostles, at the end of Luke where it is said: "The Lord has risen indeed, and has appeared to Simon."[232] Here the Gloss says, "He appeared to Peter first among all men. Even though the evangelist does not say when or where this happened, nevertheless he does not remain silent about the fact that it did happen."[233] One asks, therefore, why he appeared to Peter first among men.

To this, one must reply that there are two reasons why he appeared to Peter first: One, so that Peter would not fall into

229. Aug., *In Joh.* 121.3 (PL 35: 1957).
230. Jn 20.17.
231. Ibid.
232. Lk 24.34.
233. *Glossa interl.*

despair for having denied him. Therefore, the angel also said to the women, "Tell Peter and his disciples,"[234] specifically naming Peter. Another reason is one that the Lord himself had mentioned before the Passion, that Satan had fallen upon the apostles at that time in order to sift them through the sieve of doubt.[235] And Peter, who, as Dionysius says,[236] was the head of the apostles, "once he had turned back again" after [his] denial by means of the Lord's appearance, was responsible for strengthening his brothers.

§4. On the appearance in which he appeared to the two disciples going to Emmaus[237]

Fourth, one asks about the appearance in which he appeared to two disciples going to Emmaus, namely Cleopas and Luke, at the end of [the Gospel of] Luke.[238]

1. First, one asks about the form (*forma*) of the stranger.[239]

2. Second, [one asks] about the discussion concerning the Scriptures, and why he did not reveal himself immediately.

3. Third, why he pretended that he was going to go farther, considering that there should be no deceit in him.[240]

4. Fourth, why they recognized him in the breaking of the bread rather than in another sign.

5. Fifth, why he vanished from their sight.[241]

6. Sixth, about the burning in the apostles' heart.

1. To the first, one must reply, as was said earlier about the appearance (*species*) of the gardener, that although he revealed himself to them in his own proper form (*propria figura*), nevertheless they were not led by this form to the recognition of Christ because reason, constrained by doubt, did not refer this form to [its proper] subject, but to another [subject]. Moreover, given the circumstances of place, because he came on a festival day, he took on the form of a stranger.

234. Mk 16.7.
235. Lk 22.31–32.
236. Dion., *De div. nom.* 3, §2 (PG 3: 681D; Dionysiaca 1: 136).
237. Cf. Alb., *IV Sent.* d. 13 a. 3.
238. Lk 24.13–53; cf. Alb., *Super Luc.* 24.13.
239. Lk 24.18.
240. Lk 24.28.
241. Lk 24.31.

2. To the next, one must reply that faith in the Resurrection is more certain when reason coincides with sense perception. Indeed, he could have revealed immediately that he was alive, but the circumstances surrounding the time of the Resurrection are not proved from sense perception, but from Scripture, namely that it was fitting for him first to suffer and afterwards to rise again and in this way to enter into his glory.

3. To the next, one must reply that deceit can be attributed to an act or to an end. If it is attributed to the act, then there was no deceit in Christ, but rather in the disciples' assessment [of the act]. If, however, it is attributed to the end, then there was no deceit [in him] but a real sign of truth and the cause of the disciples' merit. For, according to Augustine,[242] by pretending that he was going to go farther, he intended to show that the disciples, in whose minds he was a stranger, were not fit to remain with him. And according to this, it was a sign of truth. According to Bede,[243] however, he intended to show that "strangers should not only be invited to, but also taken to a lodging." And this is similar to Gn 19, where the angels who were invited by Lot replied, "Certainly not; we will remain in the street,"[244] although they decided to remain with him nonetheless.

4. To the next, one must reply that there was a particular mode (*specialis modus*) of the Lord's breaking of the bread with a particular blessing,[245] which they had been accustomed to seeing in his presence.

5. To the next, one must reply that he disappeared in order to distinguish between faith in resuscitation and faith in the resurrection. For it does not belong to those who have been resuscitated to be made invisible, but it does belong to those who rise again.

6. To the last, one must reply that the heart's burning was

242. Not Aug. but Greg., *Hom.* 23 *In Ev.* 1 (PL 76: 1182B–C). Cf. Aug., *Quaest. Ev.* 2.51 (PL 35: 1362).

243. Bede, *In Luc.* 19.28 (PL 92: 627B). Cf. Greg., *Hom.* 23 *In Ev.* 1 (PL 76: 1182D).

244. Gn 19.2.

245. Cf. Lk 24.30.

caused by two things, which properly converged (*conveniebant*) in Christ: namely, his own form (*figura propria*), and the fact that when he was interpreting the Scriptures he spoke "as one having power."[246] This is why they also said that "he was a prophet, mighty in deed and word."[247]

Furthermore, it can be said that the soul is led by a certain extension into the presence of something that it seeks, even before it knows it. And there are two reasons why this happens: one is that the discovery of signs is better expressed in one thing than in another, and this cause exists on the part of sense perception that is oriented toward reason. Another is from the light of the agent intellect, by whose power, as Alfarabi says,[248] there arise certain revelations—although confused and indistinct—as happens in the phantasms of dreams. The special power of his divinity, which moved their minds, could be assigned as yet another reason.

§5. On the appearance in which he appeared to the disciples through closed doors

Fifth, one asks about the appearance in which he appeared to the disciples through closed doors, when Thomas was not with them, in Jn 20.[249]

1. First one asks why he entered through closed doors.

2. Then, since peace is the effect of the Passion, [one asks] why he greeted them by offering peace, and especially why he repeated the [offer of] peace.

3. Third, why he showed [them his] hands and side, considering that scars seem to indicate a deformity in a glorious body.

4. Fourth, why he sent them into the world, considering that in another appearance that is [recounted] at the end of Luke he tells them that they should wait until they are clothed with power from on high by the coming of the Holy Spirit at Pentecost.[250]

246. Mt 7.29.

247. Lk 24.19.

248. Al-Farabi: rather, Averr., *Compend. libri Arist. De somno et vig.* (CCCA 7: 100–103). Cf. Alb., *De homine* q. 45 a.1 (ed. Colon. 27/2, pp. 362–63).

249. Jn 20.19–24.

250. Cf. Lk 24.49.

5. Fifth, why he breathed on them and said, "Receive the Holy Spirit."[251] For this breathing on them does not seem to have had an effect prior to the coming of the Holy Spirit at Pentecost.

6. Sixth, one asks why he repeated his appearances so many times on the first day, because there were five appearances on the first day.

1. To the first, one must reply that several things are to be observed in the Resurrection, two of which are revealed principally in this appearance and are caused by Christ in the members. A third is also revealed [in this appearance] and is fitting for Christ alone. The first is the glory of the dowries, and this is revealed by the spiritual state of a body entering through closed doors. The second is the identity of nature in the one dying and the one rising again, and that is revealed by the display of his side and hands.

3. To the objection concerning deformity, however, one must reply that a wound causes deformity in the sense that it is destructive of the appropriate disposition in the body's form, but this is not the case in a glorious body. But insofar as it [that is, a wound] attests to a strength that does not concede defeat to the most terrible sufferings, in this way it bears witness to the glory of the martyr, and so it remains as a sign of a particular act of one who is going to be glorified.

2. To the next, one must reply that peace consists in the removal of evil, and this is caused by the Passion. And there is peace in advancing toward the God who glorifies, and this is caused by the Resurrection. The repetition of the peace, moreover, signifies the peace of the apostles and of those who believe through the apostles, for the apostles possessed peace and caused peace in the world. And for this reason, after he said, "Peace be with you" a second time, he followed immediately with "As the Father sent me," etc.[252]

4. To the next, one must reply that two things are required for a sending forth (*missionem*), namely a gathering of power and its release in act. And as far as the first [is concerned], they

251. Jn 20.22.
252. Jn 20.21.

are sent here; as far as the second [is concerned], [they are sent] on the day of Pentecost.

5. To the next, one must reply similarly that the Holy Spirit is conferred for two reasons: namely, for the power to administer the sacraments, and in this way the Holy Spirit is conferred here; and for the sanctity and strengthening of ministers, and in this way it is conferred on the day of Pentecost. And for this reason, there follows here a statement concerning the use of the keys: "Whose sins you forgive," etc.[253] And these last three things—namely peace, the sending forth (*missio*), and the conferral of the Holy Spirit—demonstrate what specifically befits the risen Christ, insofar as he was head of the Church. And for this reason he also said at the end of Matthew, "All power has been given to me," etc.[254]

6. To the last, one must reply that it was fitting for the proofs to be multiplied on the first day, because that day was determined by him for the Resurrection and for the consolation of the grieving apostles, as Chrysostom says.[255]

§6. On the appearance in which he appeared to the disciples when Thomas was present

Sixth, one asks about the appearance in which he appeared to the disciples after eight days, when Thomas was present, in Jn 20.[256]

1. And one asks first how Thomas was able to insert his finger and hands into the places of the nails and the lance.

2. Second, how this appearance differs from the preceding one.

1. To the first, one must reply that Thomas's touch was directed only to an awareness (*cognitionem*) of the wounds, and therefore it was not necessary for the wounds on the body to be open.[257] And his touch [here] is understood in this way, as was discussed above concerning the touch of a glorious body.[258]

253. Jn 20.23.
254. Mt 28.18.
255. John Chrysos., *Hom.* 86 *in Joh.* 3 (PG 59: 470f.).
256. Jn 20.26–29.
257. Cf. Alb., *Super Jn.* 20.27.
258. Cf. Alb., *Super Jn.* 20.29.

2. To the next, one must reply that this appearance principally shows that the truth of nature is the same in the resurrected body and the crucified body. And therefore it also shows the nature of a continuous body by means of the sense perception that is especially able to verify it. But the preceding [appearance] principally showed the glory and power of the risen Christ, and the one that followed it [showed] the identity of the risen and the crucified [body].

§7. On the appearance in which he appeared to the disciples at the sea of Tiberias

Seventh, one asks about the appearance in which he appeared to the disciples at the Sea of Tiberias, when Peter and Thomas and Nathaniel and the sons of Zebedee, namely John the Evangelist and James the elder, and two other disciples who are not named were at a place for fishing.[259]

1. And first one asks why they caught nothing, after spending the entire night working.[260]

2. Second, why Jesus stood on the shore, whereas before the Passion he walked on the sea.

3. Third, why Peter came through [the water of] the sea while the other disciples came by boat.[261]

4. Fourth, what the hot coals signify, and the fish placed upon them and the bread.

5. Fifth, why it was necessary to bring the fish they had caught, in order to eat with him whom they found by the coals.

6. Sixth, why it is fitting that he committed the care of the flock to Peter at that time, after asking about [his] love three times.

7. Seventh, what the reason of the distinction in the manner in which the disciples follow [Jesus] is, namely that Peter follows through the Passion, whereas John does not. For in the same passage [Jesus] said to Peter: "When you were younger, you girded yourself," etc.[262] And when Peter asked about John,

259. Jn 21.1–23.
260. Jn 21.3.
261. Cf. Jn 21.7.
262. Jn 21.18.

"What will this man do?"[263] he [Jesus] replied to him, "I want him to remain in this way," etc.[264]

1. To the first, one must reply that the night's work was providential, that is, they labored all night without result by the Lord's dispensation. This signified, as the Gloss states, that while laboring at the tasks of this world and drawing away from the vivid representation (*ab illustratione*) of the Lord's Resurrection, they are consumed by empty labor.[265] And for this reason, moreover, he appeared in the morning, that is, at dawn of the day of the Resurrection, and not at night.

2. To the next, one must reply that before the Passion the Lord had a corruptible nature which, nonetheless, by the power of divinity, trod upon every temporal reality of this world. And this was signified by the fact that before the Passion he walked on the sea; in fact, the waves of the passions of this corruptible life, in which Christ existed, are the sea, but he trod upon it by overcoming them. But after the Resurrection he stood on the firm ground of eternity, as Gregory says in the *Homilies*.[266]

3. To the third, one must reply that Peter's primacy over the universal Church, which exists among the waves of the passions, was signified by the fact that he came through [the water of] the sea. The fact that the other apostles came by boat signified the local churches (*determinatae ecclesiae*) over which they ruled.[267]

4. To the next, one must reply that "the broiled fish [signifies that] Christ suffered," as Augustine says,[268] whereas the bread signifies the strength of his divinity, [and] the coals the power of the Passion. And these signify the refreshment we will have in Christ according to [his] divine and [his] human nature when we arrive on the shore of eternity.

5. To the fifth, one must reply that the fish signify those who

263. Jn 21.21.

264. Jn 21.22.

265. Not found in the Gloss. Cf. Greg., *Hom.* 24 *in Ev.* 2 (PL 76: 1184Df.).

266. Greg., *Hom.* 24 *in Ev.* 2 (PL 76: 1184Df.).

267. Cf. Jn 21.7–8. Local churches are those that are determined or delimited by place, of course.

268. Aug., *In Joh.* 123.2 (PL 35: 1966). Cf. *Glossa ord. super Jn.* 21.12.

were converted by the apostles, as Damascene says,[269] namely those whom they drew out of the deep of faithlessness by a net of miracles and of preaching. And the refreshment of those fish signifies the refreshment that we will have from God among his saints.

6. To the sixth, one must reply that in that appearance the sign of Peter's sovereignty appeared, as has been said,[270] and similarly a special sign of the Lord's love in the fact that according to Mt 14 he had strengthened him, lest he be fearful among the waves, saying: "O you of little faith, why did you doubt?"[271] And therefore, as the reality (*veritas*) following the sign, the care of the flock is entrusted to Peter after Jesus asks him three times about [his] love.

7. To the last, one must reply that in the distinction of the disciples is signified the twofold condition of glorifying God by following, namely by the confession of penance and by the confession of martyrdom. Actually a sign of these two had gone before, one at Mt 14[272] and another in the appearance at Mk 6.[273] To be sure, the strong wind signifies the flood of persecution against the martyrs, and the labor of the oarsmen signifies acts of penance.

§8. On the appearance in which he appeared on Mount Tabor in Galilee

Eighth, one asks about the appearance in which he appeared on Mount Tabor in Galilee, at the end of [the Gospel of] Matthew.[274]

1. And first, one asks why he appeared in Galilee and on a mountain.

2. Second, how some doubted it.

3. Third, for whom, principally, that appearance was revelatory.

269. John Damascene, *De fide orth.* 1.3 (PG 94: 793C; ed. Buytaert, p. 16, 13–15). Cf. *Glossa inter super Jn.* 21.5.

270. Alb., *De res.* tr. 2, q. 8, art. 6, §7 (ed. Colon. 26, p. 282, 80f.).

271. Mt 14.31.

272. Mt 14.30.

273. Mk 6.48.

274. Mt 28.16.

4. Fourth, [one asks] about what he says to the disciples: "Go, therefore, teach all nations," etc.,[275] and just below that, "Behold, I am with you always, even to the end of the age."[276]

1. To the first, one must reply, as above,[277] that he had been transfigured on the same mountain in Galilee. Therefore, where the power to rise again had been demonstrated, so also the act was demonstrated there.

Gregory has another reason, that "Galilee" means "a wheel,"[278] and signifies the endlessness of eternity.[279] Therefore, he appeared there so that from the very circumstances of the place he could make manifest the eternity of a risen body. Likewise, he appeared on Mount Tabor, which means "mountain of light," so that from that place he might reveal the conspicuous clarity of risen bodies.[280]

2. To the second, one must reply, as the Gloss says, that "the disciples' doubt increases our faith,"[281] so that more abundant proofs of the Resurrection are provided.

3. To the next one, one must reply that, as Bede's gloss says, that appearance was revelatory of the power of a nature, which, before the Resurrection, owing to its passibility, was made "a little lower than the angels," and after the Resurrection was crowned "with glory and honor" and placed above all things.[282] And this is why he says: "All power has been given to me," etc.[283]

4. To the last, one must reply that a certain eminence of the one that is risen exists in the fact that, for believers, Christ was the cause of salvation in obedience to the precepts and in the

275. Mt 28.19.

276. Mt 28.20.

277. Cf. Alb., *De res.* tr. 2, q. 6, art. 6; tr. 2, q. 8, art. 6, §2 (ed. Colon. 26, p. 269, 31–32; p. 280, 31ff.).

278. "Wheel": or, perhaps, "circuit."

279. Greg., *Hom.* 21 *in Ev.* 5 (PL 76: 1172A). Cf. Bonaventure, *Coll.in Ioannem*, cap. 2, coll. 8, *Opera* 6: 545b.

280. Cf. Aug., *Enarr. in Ps.* 83.13 (PL 37: 1127); Peter Lombard, *In Ps.* 88.13 (PL 191: 823A); Alb., *Super Matth.* 17.1 and *Super Luc.* 9.28; Alb., *De res.* tr. 2, q. 6, art. 6 (ed. Colon. 26, p. 269, 31).

281. *Glossa interl. super Matth.* 28.17. Cf. Bede's gloss, *In Matth.* 28.18 (PL 92: 130C).

282. Cf. Ps 8.6 and Heb 2.7.

283. Mt 28.18.

reception of the sacraments. And for this reason, after mentioning his power, he said that they were to teach all peoples, baptizing them, that is, administering the sacraments, and teaching them to observe the commandments, and that he himself would be with them in the future in these two [acts], working salvation for believers "until the end of the age."[284]

§9. On the appearance that was in Jerusalem, when he ate with the disciples

Ninth, one asks about the appearance that was in Jerusalem, when he ate with the disciples, as is recounted at the end of Luke,[285] and, as is said at the end of Mark, he "upbraided their incredulity."[286]

1. And first one asks what, principally, that appearance reveals.

2. Second, what the honeycomb eaten with fish signifies.[287]

1. To the first, one must reply that this appearance is revelatory of the very same power in a mortal body and in a glorious body, such as is the comestive power (*potestas comestiva*).[288]

2. To the next, one must reply, as the Gloss says on the same passage,[289] that the honeycomb signifies the internal sweetness of divinity, in which we will perceive the refreshment of Christ in the glory of those who are risen. And for that reason, after

284. Cf. ibid.

285. Lk 24.36–51.

286. Mk 16.14.

287. Cf. Lk 24.42.

288. "Comestive power" (*potestas comestiva*): To our knowledge, Alb. uses this expression in only two other texts, viz., *Summa theologiae (sive de mirabili scientia Dei)* I, tr. 18, q. 75, m. 4 (ed. Borgnet 31, p. 790a), and *De IV coaequ.* tr. 4, q. 30, art.1 (ed. Borgnet 34, p. 499a). In the latter text Alb. argues, as in *De res.*, that after his resurrection the Lord's "comestive power" allowed him to eat with his disciples in order to offer them proof of life, even though in himself he had no need of food or nourishment. In the former, Alb. insists that an angel's assumed body has a "comestive power," i.e., a power to consume food or nourishment, not because an angel has any need of food or nourishment but only in order to demonstrate the presence of a higher or "noble power." This "comestive power" does not lead to the complete digestion of the nourishment consumed, however, for neither angels' bodies nor the glorified body of the Lord fully digests and evacuates what has been consumed. Cf. *supra*, n. 204.

289. *Glossa ord. super Luc.* 24.42.

these two testimonies, namely, proof that there is the very same power for eating and proof of glory in the kind of food eaten, lest one believe that this was done by magical arts, as the Gloss says,[290] he opened their senses for them, so that they would understand the Scriptures. And this was to upbraid them for their incredulity.

§10. On the appearance when he led them out from Jerusalem to Bethany

Tenth, one asks about the appearance when he led them out from Jerusalem to Bethany onto the Mount of Olives, as is said at the end of Luke[291] and at the beginning of Acts.[292] This appearance was on the Day of the Ascension.[293]

1. And first one asks what the circumstance of place signifies.

2. Second, what the blessing with which he blessed them with raised hands was.

3. Third, what this appearance reveals.

1. To the first, one must reply, as the Gloss says,[294] that Bethany means "house of obedience," and it signifies that we, when we are obedient, perfect the ascent that we prepare in our hearts by ascending "from virtue to virtue."[295] Moreover, the Mount of Olives signifies the mercy of God that draws one along, as is said in Song of Songs 1:[296] "Draw me; we will run after you to the fragrance of your ointments." Ointments signify the same thing as oil.

2. To the next, one must reply that the blessing was nothing other than a confirmation of the faith among the apostles that was built up by the many proofs for the Resurrection, "appearing to them over forty days," etc.[297]

3. To the last, one must reply that this final appearance reveals the transition of the blessed to the one who beatifies through an ascent to a place of eternal contemplation.

290. *Glossa ord. super Luc.* 24.43.
291. Lk 24.50. Cf. Alb., *Super Luc.* 24.49.
292. Acts 1.12.
293. The Ascension occurred 40 days after the Resurrection.
294. *Glossa ord. super Luc.* 24.50.
295. Ps 83.8.
296. Song 1.3.
297. Acts 1.3.

§11. For what purpose (*penes quid*) the appearances are multiplied[298]

1–2. Eleventh, one asks for what purpose the appearances are multiplied, and why the other appearances are not numbered among those that, nonetheless, are read to have occurred.

1. To the first, one must reply that the appearances are multiplied along with those that provide proof for resurrection (*in resurgente*) and among the very people for whom the appearances were produced. The first [appearance], therefore, which was produced for Mary Magdalene, absolutely provides proof of life. The second, which was produced for the women when they held his feet, provides proof of life with the reality (*veritas*) of a tangible body. The third provides proof of a property of Christ that he does not share in common with the members [of his body, the Church], that is, the remission of sin [that comes] from the mercy of the Passion, which preceded the resurrection. And that [appearance] was produced for Peter, who had denied him. The fourth, which was produced for the disciples going to Emmaus, provides an argument (*ratio*) for the entry into the glory of the Resurrection through the Passion and death. By the entrance through closed doors, the fifth provides proof of the spiritual state of the glorious body, and in the passage that follows, God is revealed as risen from the fact that he grants the Holy Spirit.[299] By means of the wounds that Thomas touched, the sixth [appearance] provides proof of the numerical identity of the one who arose and the one who died. The seventh provides proof of the immobility of the immutable body of eternity and of the immutability of Christ himself, who directs the Church, which still stands fixed under the changeableness of this age. It does so first from the fact that he stands on the shore, [and] second from the fact that, removed from every danger of the sea, he directed the disciples on the sea. The eighth provides proof of the crown of glory and honor, by which Christ's nature was elevated above every crea-

298. The locution *penes quid* is odd here, but a manuscript variant is *quare*. See Alb., *De res.* tr. 2, q. 8, art. 6, §11 (ed. Colon. 26, p. 284, n. 41).

299. Jn 20.22.

ture through the Resurrection. This occurred in Galilee on Mount Tabor, when he received power in heaven and on earth. The ninth provides proof of the truth [of his nature] from the identity of the natural power according to the comestive power (*vim comestivam*). This occurred in Jerusalem when he ate with the disciples. The tenth provides proof of the transition of the blessed who rise to the one who beatifies, because, as a certain philosopher says,[300] union with the Prime Mover—that is, with God—is the goal of well-being.

2. To the next, one must reply that the other appearances, of which the Apostle spoke in 1 Cor 15,[301] are not numbered along with these because they did not add anything decisive concerning a risen body, but rather they offered consolation or correction to specific persons. Now, it is said in the *Elucidarium* that first he appeared to Joseph [of Arimathea],[302] and second to his own mother. But because this book contains many heresies, one does not believe it. It is also declared, as is said in the first letter to the Corinthians 15, that he appeared to James and "to five hundred brothers at the same time."[303] Now James had vowed, as is said, that he would never eat [again] until he saw him.[304] Ambrose says in his book *On Virginity:* "The Blessed Virgin saw him first and believed, but the Magdalene first saw him afterward and did not believe."[305] Therefore, he appeared first to his mother, but among the non-believers he appeared first to Mary Magdalene.

Question 9. On the Ascension[306]

Next one asks about the Ascension. And first, one asks about the Ascension in itself; second, about the Ascension in relation to the Assumption and in relation to being lifted up (*evolationem*).

300. Cf. *Summa Alexandrinorum,* ed. Marchesi, p. lxxxiv, 19–20.

301. 1 Cor 15.5–8.

302. Honor. August., *Elucid.* 1.23 (PL 172: 1127B); cf. *L'Elucidarium et les Lucidaires,* 1.170, ed. Yves Lefèvre (Paris: E. De Boccard, 1954), p. 391.

303. 1 Cor 15.6.

304. Honor. August., *Elucid.* 1.23 (PL 172: 1127B); cf. *L'Elucidarium et les Lucidaires,* 1.170.

305. Ambrose, *De virginit.* 3.14 (PL 16: 283C).

306. Cf. Alb., *De IV coaequ.* q. 10 a. 3. ad q. 1.

On the Ascension in Itself

Concerning the first, one asks three questions: first, whether the Ascension pertains to the human or the divine nature; second, whether it is to a place, or to a rank, or to both; third, to what place or to what rank.

Art. 1. Whether the Ascension pertains to the human or the divine nature[307]

To the first, one proceeds in the following way:

1. It is said in Jn 3[308] that "no one has ascended into heaven, except him who descended from heaven," etc. But no one has descended except the Son of God according to the divine nature. Therefore, no one ascended [to heaven] except the Son of God according to the divine nature.

2. Again, in the same passage it is said that "no one has ascended into heaven except the Son of man, who is in heaven."[309] If we speak in relation to the time when this statement was made, it follows that the Son of man was not then in heaven according to [his] human nature.

3. Again, on Isaiah 63[310]—"Who is this that comes from Edom"—Jerome says that the angels were amazed by one ascending by his own power.[311] But nothing ascends by its own power except the divine nature. This is proved in the Song [of Songs], where it is said of the holy soul ascending [from the desert] that it "ascended leaning upon [its] beloved."[312] Therefore, ascension pertained to the divine nature.

4. Opposed to this is what Damascene says, that it pertains to bodies to ascend and descend.[313]

In addition, there seems to be a disagreement between Augustine and Damascene, because Damascene says that both,

307. Cf. Alb., *III Sent.* d. 22 a. 7; *Super Jn.* 3.13.

308. Jn 3.13.

309. Ibid.

310. Is 63.1.

311. Jerome, *In Is.* 63.1 (PL 24: 634A). Cf. Alb., *Super Is.* 63.1 (ed. Colon. 19, p. 590, 32ff.).

312. Song 8.5.

313. John Damascene, *De fide orth.* 4.1 (PG 94: 1104B; ed. Buytaert, p. 278, 18–19).

namely both ascent and descent, pertain to bodies, whereas Augustine says that he [that is, Christ] descended insofar as he is God and ascended insofar as he is man.[314]

5. In addition, Augustine seems to say something false, because for one whose being exists everywhere there is no movement to any particular place. But the divine nature's being (*esse*) exists everywhere. Therefore, descent does not pertain to it.

Solution: One must say that he ascended insofar as he is man, and he descended insofar as he is God, as Augustine says.

1–2. To the first two arguments one must reply that there is a misleading figure of speech there, because "he who" or "who" is implied, which indicates a person, [and] "according to what," which indicates a condition of nature.

3. To the next, one must reply that "one's own power" (*propria virtus*) is referred to a person; that is, he did not ascend by another person's power. Now, every created person only ascends by another person's power, namely by the power of the divine person. I say, however, "another person's" in the sense that "another" indicates an essential distinction between a person and a person, because Christ ascended by his own power, which is the same power that belongs to the Father and to the Holy Spirit. But he did not ascend by the power of another person who is essentially distinct from him.

4. One must reply to the opinion of Damascene that he spoke of ascent and descent according to the proper definition (*ratio*) of each, and he was not referring to the ascent and descent of Christ. And so there is no disagreement between him and Augustine.

5. To the last, one must reply that, properly speaking, God did not descend nor did he move, but, as Augustine says,[315] his descent means nothing other than that he became visible in the flesh he assumed.

Art. 2. Whether ascension is to a place, or to a rank, or to both[316]

To the second, one proceeds in this way:

314. Aug., *Enarr. in Ps.* 122.1 (PL 37: 1630).
315. Ps. Aug., *De fide contra Manich.* 26 (PL 42: 1147).
316. Cf. Alb., *III Sent.* d. 22 a. 8.

On the passage in Col 3, "Therefore, if you are risen with Christ, seek the things that are above,"[317] the Gloss says, above in rank (*dignitas*), not in place.[318] Therefore, when they ask about those things that are "where Christ is sitting," Christ is sitting above in rank, not in place.

Opposed to this is another gloss on Eph 4, on the passage, "But that he ascended, what is it except that he [also] descended?"[319] The gloss indicates that he ascended to a place and to a rank: in regard to "ascending," the gloss says, "in place and rank."[320]

Solution: We concede that he ascended to a place and to a rank.

To the first gloss, therefore, one must reply that something is considered to be above insofar as it produces merit, and, insofar as it is of this sort, it is not above in place, but in rank. And this is clear from what follows in the Gloss, because it says that the virtues are above.[321]

Art. 3. To what place or to what rank he ascended[322]

To the third, one proceeds in this way:

1. The Apostle says, "he ascended above all the heavens."[323] But there is no place that is beyond all the heavens, unless heaven is called the place of the Trinity through metalepsis, because the Trinity is not enclosed in any created or corporeal place, and for that reason the heaven of the Trinity will be neither created nor corporeal, but will be the Trinity itself.[324] Insofar as it is said that God exists in himself, the "in" denotes the container (*continentiam*) of the Trinity's heaven. Therefore, in accord with this it appears that Christ ascended into the Trinity's heaven.

2. Again, on Isaiah 14, "I will ascend into heaven," etc.,[325] the

317. Col 3.1.

318. Peter Lombard, *In epist. Pauli* Col 3.1 (PL 192: 279C).

319. Eph 4.9.

320. *Glossa interl. super Eph.* 4.8.

321. Cf. Alb., *De bono* 3 q.1 a. 1 (ed. Colon. 28, p. 121, 38); *III Sent.* d. 22 a. 8 sed contra 1.

322. Cf. Alb., *III Sent.* d. 22 a. 8.

323. Eph 4.10.

324. Cf. Alb., *II Sent.* d. 2 a. 8; *De IV coaequ.* q. 10 a. 1.2.

325. Is 14.13.

Gloss[326] says that this is the statement of Lucifer, who was in the empyrean heaven and willed to ascend higher to be equal to God in the Trinity's heaven. And because of this he said, "I will be like the Most High."[327] And blessed Bernard provides the explanation (*ratio*) that he [Lucifer] foresaw that in the future a creature ought to ascend there, and since at that time he was the highest among creatures, he saw and he became envious that anyone would ascend above him, and he willed to ascend there himself.[328] And therefore, since he foresaw that a creature was going to ascend there, and that it was none other than Christ, Christ ascended there.

3. In addition, one asks what the right hand of the Father, at which Christ sits, is. For the right is said relative to the left, and these are said of a nature in which power is [sometimes] absent and [sometimes] abounds, which is not fitting for God, where power exists in the highest according to equality.

4. In addition, it is said that to be at the right hand of the Father is to be "among the superior goods."[329] Therefore, one asks what it means to be "among the superior goods."

5. Besides, Christ seems to possess nothing special from the fact that he sits at the right hand of the Father, since he will cause all the saints to stand on the right, but the wicked will be on the left. And it is said in the Song of Songs that "his right hand will embrace me."[330]

Solution:

1. One must reply that Christ, insofar as he is human, never ascended to equality with God nor into the Trinity's heaven, which is the same thing. And when the Apostle says that "he ascended above all the heavens," one has to make a distinction with respect to the noun "heaven," because heaven is equivocal in meaning, referring both to the container (*ad continens*) and to the mode of life that exists in heaven. Therefore, the

326. *Glossa ord. super Is.* 14.13. Cf. Alb., *Super Is.* 14.13 (ed. Colon. 19, pp. 206ff.).

327. Is 14.14.

328. Bernard, *In Cant. serm.* 17.5 (PL 183: 857B–C). Cf. Alb., *Super Is.* 14.14 (ed. Colon. 19, p. 207, 64).

329. Cf. Peter Lombard, *In epist. Pauli* Rom 8.34 (PL 191: 1452C).

330. Song 2.6; 8.3.

angels' modes of contemplation are called in that passage "all the heavens," which [phrase] means the whole of heaven, as the blessed Dionysius maintains,[331] because the motion of an intelligence that contemplates blissfully is circular, that is, [going] from the same [thing] to the same [thing]. To be sure, contemplation among the blessed begins with God and roams through everything whatsoever, whether through themselves (*per se*) or through other creatures, and then returns to him again through praise and the act of giving thanks.

2. To the objection concerning Isaiah, it can be said that that interpretation was offered as an opinion, because Anselm, in his book *On the Fall of the Devil* (*De casu daemonis*), clearly proves that the devil never desired anything but what he would have attained had he stood firm.[332] If, however, someone wishes to save both interpretations, he ought to distinguish between what he desired and the mode of desiring. With respect to what he desired, he never willed to be God or to be like God. With respect to the mode of desiring, however—namely, that he willed to have complete power by his own power (*propria virtute*) without divine aid—he willed to be just like God, because this belongs to God alone. And Christ ascended in this way, because he ascended by his own power, so it follows that one's own power (*propria virtus*) refers to a person. If, however, it is said that he said, "I will ascend to heaven," when he was in the empyrean, one must reply that heaven connotes a higher mode of having complete power, as was said. If it is said that he [Lucifer] foresaw that a creature would sit there, it should be understood that he saw only in part and not completely, because that creature is not a creature in the simple sense, nor did he have to sit there insofar as he is a creature, but insofar as he is God.

3. To the next [objection], one must reply that God's right hand and left hand do not refer to power in itself, but to the manifestation of power in God's works. And because the eter-

331. Dion., *De div.nom.* 4 §8 (PG 3: 704D; Dionysiaca 1: 189). Cf. Alb., *Super Dion. De div. nom.* 4, 98 (ed. Colon. 37/1, pp. 199–200).

332. Anselm, *De casu diab.* 4.6 (PL 158: 332Aff. and 334Df.; ed. Schmitt 1: 240, 15ff. and 244, 1–2). Cf. Alb., *Super Is.* 14.13 (ed. Colon. 19, p. 206, 96). Bonaventure, *II Sent.* d. 5 a. 1 q. 1, *Opera* 2: 148.

nal goods of the blessed manifest that power better than do fallen and infernal things, for this reason those who are blessed are said to be on the right, and those who exist in damnation or among temporal goods are said to be on the left, although differently—the damned, because liberating grace (*gratia liberans*) is not manifested in them; and those who still abide in temporal things, however, because the highest power (*virtus*) of freedom from sin and punishment does not appear in them.

4. To the next [objection], one must reply that the highest mode of possessing beatitude is said to be the superior goods, according to which Isidore says that the Trinity is known to itself alone and to the human assumed [in the Incarnation].[333]

5. To the last [objection], one must reply that it is said antonomastically of the human Christ that he is at the right hand of the Father. Of others, however, it is said in an ordinary manner.

One must understand, nonetheless, that all these things are said of the human Christ. To be sure, insofar as he is the Son of God, he never departed from equality with the Father.

On the Ascension in Comparison to the Assumption and to being Lifted Up (*evolationem*)

With regard to the second, two questions are raised. First, one asks about the difference between the Ascension and the Assumption and being lifted up [to heaven].[334]

Second, one asks about the difference of place to which there is lifting up and ascension and assumption.

Art. 4. On Ascension's difference relative to the Assumption and to being lifted up

To the first, one proceeds in this way:

It is said in the prophecy of Micah 2, "He will ascend, opening the way before them,"[335] and again in the Gospel of John, "I go to prepare a place for you."[336] And so it seems that [his] as-

333. Isid., *Sent.* 1.3.1 (PL 83: 543A). Cf. Bonaventure, *III Sent.* d. 14 a. 1 q. 2, *Opera* 3: 299.

334. Cf. Lk 24.51, where Jesus is "carried up into heaven" [*ferebatur in caelum*].

335. Mi 2.13.

336. Jn 14.2.

cension is the causal basis for being lifted up (*evolationem*) and for the assumption, and so these differ in the same way that the cause does from the caused.

Moreover, it is said in the Gospel of Luke: "And it happened that the beggar died and was carried by the angels," etc.[337] Therefore, by analogy others too are carried by the angels into heaven. And so there seems to be this difference between them, that the ascension occurs by the proper power (*propria virtute*) of the one ascending, whereas being lifted up occurs by the ministry of the angels.[338]

Again, assumption indicates a violent motion, which is attraction, and so it seems that that motion is by the power of the one attracting or assuming. And so the difference among these three seems to be that ascension occurs by the proper power of the one ascending, whereas assumption occurs by the power of Christ who assumes, not by the [power of the] one assumed, and being lifted up occurs by the ministry of angels.

1. In opposition to this, one objects that the soul experiences enjoyment immediately when it departs from the body, unless sin presents an obstacle. And so it seems that being lifted does not pertain to a distance to a place.

2. In addition, if we follow the metaphor (*metaphora*), then one that struggles upward by the power of wings is said to be lifted up. The 'wings' of the soul, however, are intellect and affection (*affectus*), whereas [its] plumes are the intellectual and

337. Lk 16.22.

338. The distinction here between Ascension, Assumption, and being lifted up is affirmed more clearly by a text that was sometimes attributed to Albert or to his Franciscan contemporary, St. Bonaventure, but now is recognized as more likely by the Dominican Hugh Ripelin of Strassburg (d. c. 1270), and which remarks that the term "ascension" refers to Christ, the term "assumption" to Mary, and the term *evolatio* to the other saints. In each case, the causal modality differs. Christ ascends by virtue of his own power; Mary is assumed by the power of Christ, who assumes; and the saints are lifted up by the power of ministering angels. "Differentia est inter ascensionem et assumptionem, et evolationem: quoniam ascensio pertinet ad Christum; assumptio, ad beatam Virginem; evolatio autem, ad alios sanctos. Et ratio hujus est, quoniam ascensio fit propria virtute ascendentis; assumptio autem, virtute Christi assumentis, quia filius specialiter obsequitur matri; evolatio vero fit ministerio angelorum" (*Compend. theol. veritatis* 4.24, ed. Borgnet 34, p. 149).

affective powers. And so it seems that those who are lifted up are not raised up by the ministry of angels.

Solution: We concede that the principal differences have been demonstrated.

1. To the objection to the contrary, however, one must reply that being lifted up, ascension and assumption, insofar as they indicate local motion, indicate motion only according to the place that is suitable for the condition of the blessed, which place is the empyrean heaven. And for this reason, although they experience enjoyment immediately, movement is still required according to the suitability of place, as has been said.

2. To the next, one must reply that what the objection proves is true. But nonetheless the ministry of angels also exists there, not in such a way that angels properly carry souls, but because angels were a certain cause of the merit and blessedness of souls by the effect of their protection, for which reason they are said to carry them on their shoulders. And the works of protection are called "shoulders." If, however, one asks whether angels accompany souls, one can concede that they do accompany them, but they carry them only in the sense that souls refer the effect of their being lifted up to the angels' service.

Concerning the Assumption, however, we concede that in this, Christ properly serves [his] mother, drawing to himself, as it were, her whose part he united (*univerat*) to himself, as is described more fully above in the question on the Annunciation.[339]

Art. 5. On the difference of place to which there is lifting up and ascension and assumption

To the second, one proceeds in this way:

Blessed Jerome says in a sermon on the Assumption of the Blessed Virgin that all the souls of the saints are assumed next to the choirs of angels, with the exception of the Blessed Virgin, who was assumed above all the choirs of angels.[340] Therefore, it seems that the place of those lifted up is distinct from the place

339. Alb., *De incarn.* 2, q. 3 (ed. Colon. 26, p. 188, 66ff.), where Alb. discusses whether Jesus was conceived from Mary's flesh or from her blood.

340. Ps. Jerome, *Epist.* 9 (*ad Paul. et Eust.*) *De assumptione b. M. v.* 7 (PL 30: 132D). Cf. Alb., *Summa* I, tr. 19, q. 77 m. 3 a. 3 q. 3 (ed. Borgnet 31, p. 821b).

of the choirs [of angels], whereas the place of the Blessed Virgin is beyond the choirs, and the place of Christ ascending is beyond the place of the Blessed Virgin, who has been assumed.

Moreover, differences of rank correspond to differences of place. But a threefold gradation (*gradus*) is found in the rank of a nature that is ascending, one that is assumed, and one that is lifted up. Therefore, a threefold difference of place will correspond to it.

1. To the contrary: Hierarchies are distinguished according to gradations of blessedness. If, therefore, there is a twofold gradation above the hierarchies of angels, it seems as if that twofold gradation establishes two hierarchies.

If perhaps one should say that hierarchy is a name appropriate [only] for the angels, it is clear that this is manifestly false, because a supercelestial hierarchy exists in God the Trinity.[341]

Moreover, the definition (*ratio*) of the term indicates nothing more than a sacred supremacy (*sacrum principatum*), and that is very fitting for both Christ and the Blessed Virgin.

2. Moreover, every nature, whether it is lifted up or assumed or ascending, exists in the empyrean heaven, because nothing exists beyond the last heaven, as the Philosopher says.[342] Therefore, it seems that there is no difference with respect to place.

Solution: We concede the principal differences.

1. To the objection concerning hierarchies, however, one must reply that hierarchies are distinguished by the means whereby a lower nature is led back (*reductio*) to God. And in accord with this, the lowest hierarchy is said to be in heaven, the hierarchy that leads humans back [to God]. The middle hierarchy is said to be the one that leads the lower angels according to the ministering power back [to God]. The superior hierarchy is said to be the one that leads the middle angels back according to the sitting power,[343] as is evident from the names of the choirs [of angels], which are among the hierarchies of Seraphim, Cherubim, [and] Thrones, whose names reveal only

341. Cf. Alb., *II Sent.* d. 9 a. 1; *Super Dion. De cael. hier.* 3 §1 dub. ad 5. Cf. *De IV coaequ.* q. 36 a. 1; *Summa* II q. 38 m. 1.

342. Ar., *De caelo et mundo* 1.9 (279a16–18). Cf. Alb., *De caelo et mundo* 1.3.9, 10.

343. "Sitting power": *vim assistricem.* Cf. Wis 9.4, which identifies wisdom as sitting by the throne of God (*assistricem sapientiam*).

what pertains to the sitting power. Also in the middle hierarchy there are dominions, virtues, [and] powers, whose names, again, reveal only what pertains to the ministering power. In the last hierarchy [are] the principalities, archangels, [and] angels, whose names, again, reveal only what pertains to the management and governance of men. Therefore one must reply that according to the hierarchic act,[344] which is to lead lower [natures] back to God either in this way or that, Christ is in the third hierarchy together with [his] mother. According to the mode of participating in blessedness, however, and according to place, they are beyond all the angels. Nor does it follow from this that they comprise some special hierarchy,[345] because two hierarchies are not distinguished in this way. Otherwise, there will be many hierarchies even in one choir.

2. To the next, one must reply that the empyrean heaven is the place shared by all the blessed. But specific places in the empyrean heaven are distinguished according to the specific ranks of the blessed.

Question 10. On the return for judgment

Next, one asks about the return of the Judge for judgment, and how he will deliver the kingdom to God and to the Father. And three questions are raised: first, concerning the fire that will precede the appearance of the Judge; second, on the order of judgment; and third, how it will deliver the kingdom to God and to the Father.

On the Fire that will go Before the Appearance of the Judge[346]

Concerning the first [inquiry], eight questions are raised. First, one asks whether that fire will be corporeal and in the same species with fire, the element; second, whether it is in the same species with the fire of hell and of purgatory; third, what

344. "hierarchic act": cf. Dion., *De cael. hier.* 3 §1 (PG 3: 164D; Dionysiaca 2: 785f.). Alb., *Super Dion. De cael. hier.* 3 §1 dub., sol. (ed Colon. 36/1, pp. 44–46).

345. Cf. Alb., *II Sent.* d. 9 a. 8 ad 6.

346. See, e.g., 2 Pt 3.7–12.

its effect on the world will be; fourth, what its effect will be on humans who will be found alive at that time; fifth, according to what nature that fire and the other fires—namely, the fires of hell and of purgatory—will act upon souls and bodies; sixth, whether it precedes or follows judgment; seventh, where it will remain after judgment; eighth, what its matter, in which it will be perpetuated, is and what will perpetuate it.

Art. 1. Whether that fire will be corporeal and in the same species with fire, the element[347]

To the first, one proceeds in this way:

1. The power of an element is more abundant in comparison to other elements only when in its proper place. Therefore, if fire has to be more abundant than other elements, it will be in its proper place. Therefore, by means of a locus from opposites (*per locum ab oppositis*),[348] in a contrary place its power will be defective, and elements that exist naturally in their own place will prevail over it. But the place contrary to fire is down below. Therefore, it will not prevail there, but will be prevailed over. But the fire that goes before the appearance of the Judge will prevail over the inferior elements, as the saints say.[349] Therefore, it will not have the same nature (*ratio*) as fire, the element.

We see proof of the first proposition with our eyes. To be sure, the part of fire in the lower [regions] is converted by smoke and flame into air, and the earthy parts cool by themselves into coals; similarly, air close to water becomes humid. And if, conversely, inferior [elements] have to be changed into superior ones and overcome by them, it is necessary for them to be raised up as vapor (*vaporaliter*) to superior places where the action of the superior ones is strong. And this occurs on account of two propositions, one of which the Philosopher states in *On Generation and Corruption*,[350] namely that if one has to act and the other to be acted upon, it is necessary for the

347. Cf. Alb., *IV Sent.* d. 47 a. 6.

348. That is, a logical argument that proceeds through negation, as when one argues that Socrates is not black; therefore, Socrates is white. Cf. Alb., *Anal. Prior.* 2.7.7 (ed. Borgnet 1, p. 801b).

349. Cf. Aug., *De civ. dei* 20.16 (PL 41: 682; CSEL 40/2: 465, 14–15).

350. Ar., *De gen. et corr.* 1.7 (324b7–9).

one acting to be near the one being acted upon, and conversely. The other proposition is that, if a change has to occur, it is necessary for the one acting to prevail over the one being acted upon.

2. Again, nothing in an element's nature acts beyond its own species. But fire will burn the surface of the entire world, as the saints say.[351] Therefore, it will burn itself, and in this way it will act beyond its own species because it will change its own matter into another [matter] outside its own species. Therefore, that fire will not have the same nature (*ratio*) as fire, the element.

3. Besides, an elemental action according to nature exists only in that which has a matter univocal to it with a contrary form. But the act of this fire will exist in that which has matter that is both univocal and equivocal. Therefore, it will not have the same nature (*ratio*) as fire, the element. The proof of the first is taken from the Philosopher,[352] [and] the proof of the second [is taken] from Peter in the second canonical [epistle], the last chapter, who says that the heavens that exist now will be destroyed by fire.[353] But that heaven and the elements have equivocal matter is maintained at *Metaphysics* 8,[354] where the Philosopher says that heaven's matter is in potency only with respect to place, but an element's matter [is in potency] with respect to every change.

4. Again, according to nature fire does not act upon something stronger than it is. But that fire will act upon something stronger than it, because [it will act] upon heaven. Therefore, it will not be an element.

To the contrary: Of those things for which there is one operation according to nature, there is one species.[355] But to burn is fire's operation according to nature. Therefore, anything that will have the same operation will be fire. But that fire will have the same operation. Therefore, it will have the same nature and species.

351. Cf. Aug., *De civ. dei* 20.16 (PL 41: 682; CSEL 40/2: 465, 14–15).

352. Ar., *De gen. et corr.* 1.7 (323b31–33). Cf. Alb., *De gen. et corr.* 1.5.4.

353. 2 Pt 3.10.

354. Ar., *Metaph.* 8.4 (1044b7–8).

355. John Damascene, *De fide orth.* 2.23 (PG 94: 949A; ed. Buytaert, p. 142, 7–8); 3.15 (PG 94: 1052B, p. 232, 2–3). Alb., *IV Sent.* d. 47 a. 6 sed contra.

Moreover, all the saints call it fire, and do not distinguish among different uses of the word.

Solution: We concede that that fire will be fire, the element. But one must draw a distinction between a fire that is one thing in its proper sphere and something else in the lower [regions]. For in its own sphere it exists in matter that has no privation and no contrary to its species. In the lower [region], however, it exists in matter that is still under contrary dispositions, and on account of this in inferior [regions] it exists only according to the nature (*ratio*) of a flame or a coal. We say, then, that that fire will be generated in the lower part of air in matter belonging to air and to water according to the nature (*ratio*) of a flame or of burned [water] vapor, [and] in parts of the earth according to the nature (*ratio*) of [burned] coal.[356]

If one asks, however, what will generate that [fire], I say that it is brought forth (*educitur*) from the matter of the lower elements, in which it exists in potency. What brings it forth (*educens*), however, will be the power of justice (*potentia iustitiae*), which has authority to judge the world and in relation to which every creature has been commanded to act to serve justice. I do not concede what some say,[357] that that fire will be brought forth from the reflections of rays upon the lower, solid bodies—those flat and concave and convex—because such an eduction of fire does not occur in all places in equal measure, but rather it abounds over radiant bodies, and over other bodies it only brings forth heat, and sometimes a weak heat.

1. Therefore, we say to the first that that fire has power in the lower regions in a qualified way (*secundum quid*) but not absolutely (*simpliciter*), namely only so far as something combustible is present (*extenditur*); and when that does not exist, it will

356. In other words, in the sub-lunar realm, fire, one of the four primary elements (fire, water, earth, and air) does not appear by itself, but only in conjunction with the other elements and their properties. For a more detailed discussion of fire and its relationship to the other elements, as well as its appearance both in its own matter and in foreign matter, see especially Albert the Great's *On the Causes of the Properties of the Elements* (*Liber de causis proprietatum elementorum*), 1.1.1; 1.2.12 (trans. Resnick, pp. 21ff.; 80–83).

357. Cf. Alb., *IV Sent.* d. 47 a. 6 ad 2. Bonaventure, *IV Sent.* d. 47 a. 2 q. 1, *Opera* 4: 976a.

not exist further in that place. And on account of this, it will not prevail over the inferior elements completely, but only insofar as they are combustible, that is, insofar as they are infected by the exercise of sin, as the saints say.[358]

2. To the next, one must reply that that fire does not act beyond its own species, but rather it will be bounded within it, and it does not burn itself. If one objects, however, that fire also existed for the use of sinners and so it ought to be burned and purged just like the other elements, one must say that all the fire that is in use among humans is changed into inferior elements, and it is purged in them, and not in any other way.

3. To the next, one must reply that no heaven will be burned up except the airy heaven. And this is the heaven mentioned by Peter and the saints.

4. And from this a solution to the last [objection] is clear.

Art. 2. Whether it is in the same species with the fire of hell and of purgatory

To the second, one proceeds in this way:

1. Damascene says of the fire of hell and of purgatory that that fire is not corporeal, but "God certainly knows what kind [it is]."[359] But that fire that precedes the appearance of the Judge will be corporeal, as has been said. Therefore, it will not belong to the same species with that.

2. Besides, "it is impossible for a non-body to be moved by a body," as is said in *On Six Principles.*[360] But souls are a non body. Therefore, they are not moved by a body. And so it seems that the fire of hell and of purgatory will not be corporeal, since it acts upon souls.

3. Again, among those things that do not share matter in common, there is no action and passion with respect to one another.[361] There is not one [shared] matter for the soul and for corporeal fire. Therefore, etc.

4. Moreover, the corporeal [cause] is less powerful than the

358. Cf. *Glossa interl. super* 2 Petr. 3.7. Alb., *IV Sent.* d. 47 a. 7 ad 5.

359. John Damascene, *De fide orth.* 4.27 (PG 94: 1228A; ed. Buytaert, p. 385, 144–46).

360. Gilb. Porr., *De sex princ.* 2.6 (PL 188: 1260D; ed. Heysse 12, 20–21).

361. Ar., *De gen. et corr.* 1.3 (319a29ff.).

incorporeal, and if one has to move the other, the incorporeal will be the one moving, and the corporeal the one moved. This is clear among the movers of the planets and among souls, for which there is something that moves [them] with respect to their body. Therefore, if there are action and passion between them, the corporeal will be the one acted upon and the incorporeal will be the one acting (*agens*), and so the soul will act on fire rather than the other way around.

To the contrary: Basil, Augustine, and Gregory say that the fire that exists in hell and purgatory is corporeal.[362] Therefore, it will have the same nature (*ratio*) as the fire that precedes the appearance of the Judge.

1. We concede this, replying to the first [objection] that Damascene's statement is understood with respect to the immediate torment of souls. And this is the impression (*intentio*) that is received of something harmful, which is not corporeal but spiritual, but nonetheless has been abstracted from a body, as will be clear later.[363]

2. To the next, one must reply that it is true according to local motion if the proposition is understood *per se*. To be sure, a non-body that exists in a moved body is moved by it locally in an accidental fashion (*per accidens*). Likewise, the proposition is true concerning alteration, if one accepts that alteration occurs according to the active and passive qualities of a body through the being (*per esse*) that they have in a body. If motion is understood, however, by means of an impression (*intentio*) abstracted from a contrary body, as the soul abstracts an impression, according to which sadness and joy exist, then it is clear that it is not true, because we see joy and sadness in the soul continuously according to abstracted impressions.

3. And from this a solution to the next one is apparent. To be sure, that proposition is understood concerning those that act physically—that is, of an action that exists according to qualities, with respect to which they have being (*esse*) in matter.

362. Basil, *In Hexaem. hom.* 6.3 (PG 29: 121D); cf. Bonaventure, *IV Sent.* d. 44 a. 2 q. 1, *Opera* 4: 925. Aug., *De civ. dei* 21.10.1 (PL 41: 724f.; CSEL 40/2: 537, 24ff.). Greg., *Dial.* 4.29 (PL 77: 368C).

363. Cf. Alb., *IV Sent.* d. 20 a. 5.

4. To the last, one must reply that according to the nature of the corporeal and the incorporeal, the incorporeal exists above the corporeal; but on account of some defect in goodness of a nature, [a defect] that is introduced to the incorporeal, nothing prevents the incorporeal from being ordered beneath the corporeal. And sin is such a defect, because it is a corruption of the goodness of a nature in a spiritual creature, as Augustine says.[364] Indeed, the soul submits itself to fault by the freedom of the will, [and] once it has submitted to it, it is subject to punishment by the necessity of justice, because otherwise evil would remain disordered, which would be unfitting.[365]

Art. 3. What its effect on the world will be[366]

To the third, one proceeds in this way:

1. The glorification of the elements will be the world's renewal, as is said [in the Gloss] on the Apostle[367] in Rom 8: "creation itself will be delivered from the servitude of corruption."[368] And it is said in Isaiah that "the light of the moon will be like the light of the sun, and the light of the sun will be sevenfold, as the light of seven days."[369]

Likewise, Isidore says that the earth will glitter like glass,[370] and Bede [says that] the air will be strengthened with light.[371] And such an effect does not seem to be a power of fire, since it is not in accord with fire's species and nothing acts otherwise than according to its own species.

2. Next after this, one asks why such a renewal is necessary. If it is said that the elements have provided a service and ought to be rewarded, then to the contrary: The elements' action does not exist with the intention of meriting, but rather from an im-

364. Not explicitly found in Augustine, but cf. Peter Lombard, *II Sent.* d. 35 c. 5 (p. 497f.).

365. Cf. Anselm, *Cur deus homo* 1.12 (PL 158: 377B; ed. Schmitt 2: 69, 12–13).

366. Cf. Alb., *IV Sent.* d. 47 a. 7 sol.; *Super Marc.* 9.31.

367. *Glossa ord. super Rom.* 8.22.

368. Rom 8.21.

369. Is 30.26.

370. The source in Isidore of Seville has not been located. Cf. Alb., *IV Sent.* d. 47 a. 7 sol.; *Super Marc* 9.31.

371. Bede, *In Epist. 2 Petr.* 3.10 (PL 93: 82C). Cf. *Glossa ord. super Petr.* 3.10.

pulse of nature, and reward corresponds only to the intention of meriting. Therefore, they ought not to be rewarded.

3. Besides, the Gloss on Rom 8[372] says that every creature now discharges its functions with labor, but renewal will free it from the servitude of labor. Therefore, one asks what this labor is. Indeed, what exists entirely according to nature is not laborious, but is fitting and pleasant. The functions of creatures exist according to their natures, and for that reason heaven is not wearied by its revolutions, nor is fire wearied by burning, and so too for the others. Therefore, there is no labor for them in these functions, because Avicenna says that only what exists in some way contrary to nature is laborious.[373]

4. Next, one asks again to what extent that fire will consume the world. And Bede says on the last [chapter] in the second canonical [epistle] of Peter that that last fire will entirely consume two elements,[374] whereas it will transform two [others] into a better species, because it is said in the penultimate [chapter of] Isaiah, "Behold, I create a new heaven and a new earth,"[375] and in the Apocalypse, "I saw a new heaven and a new earth."[376] And so the air, which is called heaven, and the earth will be renewed. But concerning water, one reads in the Apocalypse that "the sea is now no more."[377] And concerning fire also, one does not read that it will remain. And so fire and water will be consumed in their entirety, whereas the air and earth will be transformed into a better form.

But the opposite of this was maintained above, namely that fire does not destroy itself.[378]

Besides, it seems that there is another gloss that contradicts Bede's on the same passage,[379] which says that that fire will not rise higher than the water did during the flood. But the flood

372. Rom 8.22.
373. Avic., *De caelo* 5 (fol. 38va in *Opera*). Cf. Alb., *Super Matth.* 11.28.
374. Bede, *In Epist. 2 Petr.* 3.10 (PL 93: 82C). Cf. *Glossa ord. super Petr.* 3.10.
375. Is 65.17.
376. Rv 21.1.
377. Ibid.
378. Cf. Alb., *De res.* tr. 2, q. 10, art. 2 (ed. Colon. 26, p. 290, 23ff.).
379. *Glossa ord. super Petr.* 3.10. Cf. Peter Lombard, *IV Sent.* d. 47 c. 4 (p. 1021).

did not rise as far as fire. Therefore, neither will fire rise as far as fire, and so it will not consume fire.

5. In addition, a gloss on the same passage says that it will rise only as far as the elements that have been infected from association with sin.[380] But this is only as far as the place of generation and corruption on earth. And so it seems that it will not burn the elements entirely.

6. Furthermore, since sin occurred in heaven and in paradise, it seems that both of them ought to be burned by fire.

7. Next, one asks again why it is fitting for that purgation to be accomplished by fire rather than by some other element.

Solution:

1. One must reply to the first that there is a twofold end (*terminus*) for the renewal of the world, namely an end-from-which (*terminus a quo*) and an end-to-which (*terminus ad quem*). The end-from-which is movement away from a disposition preventing glorification or renewal. The end-to-which, however, is that very form according to which renewal occurs. We say, therefore, that fire's action aims at the movement away from the contrary disposition, and not at the bestowal of the form of renewal; indeed, only divine action aims at the latter. If, however, one asks what the contrary form is, one must reply that [it is] only that infection that exists in the elements on account of the fact that the exercise of sin was in them, and it is not a natural form *per se*. And so in this way a solution to the first is evident, that that fire will not act beyond its own species.

2. To the next, one must reply that desire is twofold, namely that belonging to matter and that belonging to what is animated. With respect to matter's desire, the Philosopher says that matter desires form and it desires a better form to a greater extent;[381] this is the desire for a glorious form. That desire, however, that belongs to what is animated does not exist in irrational creatures. And they will also receive recompense according to the mode whereby they possess desire, and this is a reward only in a qualified sense (*secundum quid*). To be sure, [the reward] is nothing other than the transformation of matter toward an

380. See *Glossa ord. super 2 Petr.* 3.7.

381. Ar., *Phys.* 1.9 (192a22–23).

act that is better according to the same species but according to different qualities. Recompense, however, properly exists in one who acts according to the intention of reason and recognizes the recompense that has been received.

3. To the question concerning labor, one must reply that power is twofold in a creature, namely in relation to the Prime Mover and in relation to the qualities according to which action and passion exist in nature. The Prime Mover moves, however, by intending the end.[382] Man is, however, the end of all things, because all things were made on account of man. And for this reason, when man descended by means of sin, all things flowed down to a worse condition. In fact, it is necessary that whatever exists for an end be proportioned to the end. Since, then, the nature of the end has been rendered ignoble on account of sin, and since the things of this world are oriented to it in a material way, it is necessary that they have been made ignoble too. And from that ignobility they contract a certain disobedience toward the Mover, such that they do not easily produce those things for whose sake they were created, as they would do if there were no sin. And this is said to be the labor of creatures, to which the reward of glorification corresponds. In themselves and in their qualities, however, they do not have labor.

4. To the question concerning how much of the world will be consumed, one must reply that according to substance and species, nothing will be consumed in the world's agent principles or material [principles]. But among those that originated from elemental matter, nothing but man will remain; so it follows that the beginnings (*principia*) and the end of the world will remain but the middle things (*media*) will be consumed. Similarly, one must distinguish among the principles, for just as man will exist [then] with other qualities according to the same species, so too the world [will exist] according to its own principles (*principia*), which are the five bodies,[383] four active and passive [qualities] and only one that is a motive [principle]. Man, how-

382. Ar., *Phys.* 2.2 (194a35). Alb., *Phys.* 2.1.11.

383. The five bodies refer, presumably, to the five planets—Saturn, Jupiter, Mars, Mercury, and Venus. The sun and the moon are often added to these five, to produce seven celestial bodies.

ever, will have double qualities, namely those that are congruent with the justice that imposes punishment on the damned, who will be considered later,[384] and those that are congruent with the blessedness found among the glorified. And for this reason the world will be divided into two. To be sure, what is noble among the five bodies will tend upward to the place of the blessed, whereas what is ignoble—like burning heat, icy cold, coarse earth, and opaque blackness—will tend downward to the place of the damned. Therefore, glorification occurs through the separation of the noble from the ignoble and not by means of rarefaction, as some have said.[385] For otherwise it would be necessary to concede that heaven will be stretched to a greater capacity, since everything that is rarefied demands more space than what is non-rarefied. But that this is true, [namely] that the glorification of man will not be through rarefaction, is clear, since Augustine says that nothing of the truth of our body will be lost, not even a hair. And for this reason, properly speaking such bodies are not called "rare," but rather subtle spiritual [bodies]. And from this, a solution to [the question of] how the elements will remain and how they will not is clear.

To the authority of Bede, we say that there are two elements in which active qualities exist, namely fire and water. One of these is defined by heat and the other by cold, as the Philosopher says in *On Generation and Corruption*.[386] At that time the Lord will divide them, as Basil says on that [passage], "The voice of the Lord who divides the flame of fire,"[387] such that the burning heat and the icy cold will tend downward, and the transparent clarity in water and the light of fire will remain up above in their places. Therefore, because these elements are defined now by qualities that at that time will be stripped from them, for that reason the saints say that two elements will cross over.[388] Regarding the other two elements, however, there is no definition by

384. See Alb., *De res.* tr. 3, q. 2 (ed. Colon. 26, p. 306, 34ff.).

385. Cf. Ps. Guerricus (fol. 174ra).

386. Ar., *De gen. et corr.* 2.3 (330b3–5); cf. ibid., 330b11–13. Alb., *De gen. et corr.* 2.1.5.

387. Ps 28.7.

388. Cf. Bede, *In Epist. 2 Petr.* 3.10 (PL 93: 82C). Cf. *Glossa ord. super Petr.* 3.10.

means of active qualities that are capable of inflicting punishment, and therefore one does not say of them that they will be changed entirely through that division.

If one should object, however, that those qualities are the substantial forms of the elements, one must reply that that is not true. Actually, although the Philosopher distinguishes the elements in precisely these respects (*penes ipsas*) in the second book of *On Generation and Corruption*,[389] nevertheless it does not follow from this that they are substantial [forms]. For he does not make a determination there concerning the principles of the elements according to substance, but he speaks of them inasmuch as they are a cause of continuous transformation through the active and passive qualities that exist in them. Therefore, although they will lose these qualities altogether (*in toto*), they can still retain [their] species under properties that are striving for a nobler form.

Nonetheless, if someone wishes to maintain that they are substantial forms, it is necessary that double qualities be distinguished, namely the specific (*specificae*), which are simple, and the accidental. And according to this [distinction], those that are simple do not have a contrary, for substantial forms do not have a contrary. Similarly, in a change (*transmutatio*), the change will be simple, not in time, but suddenly. But change in the others will occur in time and through a medium. And in this sense it can be conceded that those specific qualities will remain, but the active and the passive [qualities] will be divided.

Moreover, there are some who say that the active and passive elemental qualities will remain neither in act nor in potency, but [only] in their roots, in which it is impossible for them to be restored to act.[390] And the act of light descending from heaven will prevail at that time in all things, but in different ways. Indeed, the two superior elements—namely fire and air—will resemble heaven, because both of them will be luminous without darkness. But the two inferior elements[391] will be brilliantly clear, but not to the point of being subtle.

If, however, one should ask, since division also occurs in the

389. Ar., *De gen. et corr.* 2.3 (330a30ff.).
390. Cf. Ps. Odo Rigaldi (fol. 250rb).
391. That is, water and earth.

two other elements—namely, in air and earth—why they are not said to cross over whole in themselves just like the other two,[392] one must reply that the stripping away [of qualities] does not occur in them in the same way as in the others, because they are not defined by active qualities that are capable of inflicting punishment, but rather earth is defined by the dry and air is defined by the moist.[393] The dry, however, is that which is bounded by its own boundary,[394] and according to this act it does not express contrariety to the form of renewal, in which all things will be bounded by their own boundaries. The moist, however, exists in two acts. There is one [act in which the moist] is poorly bounded by its own boundary,[395] according to which act it will not remain there. There is another, however, according to which it is said that the moist is capable of connecting (*continuativum*) parts, according to which it causes one part to flow into [another] part and thus there exists continuity among the parts.[396] And according to this act, again, it expresses no contrariety to the form of glory. It is clear, therefore, that the moist will not be stripped away with regard to every act. And so it follows that since there are four qualities, two active and two passive, in respect of which (*penes quas*) the elements are defined, the active [qualities] will be stripped away with regard to all acts, but the passive [qualities] will not be [stripped away] with regard to all. And therefore the two elements that are defined with respect to the active [qualities] are said to be consumed altogether (*in toto*), whereas the other two, with respect to the passive [qualities], are not consumed altogether.

5. To the next one, a solution is clear from what has already been said, because fire will not rise up higher than the infection [from sin], nor is glorification an act of fire except through the removal of that infection from sin, as has been said.[397]

392. I.e., like fire and water.

393. Elsewhere Alb. identifies earth as the heaviest of the four elements, because it is both dry and cold in complexion. Next heaviest is water, which is moist and cold. Next is air, which is moist and hot, whereas fire, which is hot and dry, is not heavy at all. Cf. *On the Causes of the Properties of the Elements* 1.1.1, p. 21.

394. Cf. Ar., *De gen. et corr.* 2.2 (329b31–32).

395. E.g., water is not bounded by itself, but only by a container that holds it.

396. Cf. Ar., *De gen. et corr.* 2.2 (329b30–31). Alb., *De gen. et corr.* 2.1.5.

397. Alb., *De res.* tr. 2, q. 10, art. 3 (ed. Colon. 26, p. 292, 3ff.).

6. To the objection concerning heaven and paradise, one must say without offense that fire will not exist there. Although sin occurred in these places, nevertheless sinners were expelled because of [their] opposition (*contrarietatem*) to the delightfulness in these places, and so purgation followed immediately after the sin was perpetrated. Nevertheless, these places will be glorified just like the rest, but not through fire.

7. To the last one, one must reply that there are two active qualities: the hot and the cold—one that exists in an absolute way (*simpliciter*), and the other in a qualified way (*secundum quid*). Since, then, there are two judgments of the world, one in a qualified way (*secundum quid*) when some were punished, it was fitting for this to be accomplished by water, which is defined by the cold. The other [judgment], however, is absolute (*simpliciter*), and it is fitting that it be accomplished by fire, which is active in an absolute way. Besides, this occurs according to what is appropriate for sin. For at the time of the Flood the sin of carnal concupiscence, whose tinder (*fomes*) exists in the fire of lust, was at its highest. And for this reason it was fitting that judgment be rendered by means of a contrary, by means of a cold element. At the end, however, "the charity of many will grow cold"[398] as is said in the Gospel, and this from the icy frost of avarice. And for this reason that judgment will be rendered by means of a contrary: by means of the heat that exists in fire.

Art. 4. What its effect will be on humans who will be found alive at that time[399]

To the fourth, one proceeds in this way:

1. On the Day of Judgment, different kinds of people will be found, namely the very bad and the very good, the moderately bad and the moderately good.[400] Since, therefore, that fire attacks the infection of sin, it seems that it will be necessary for the fire to be diversified according to those who have sinned.

2. Besides, since purgatory is not going to exist after Judg-

398. Mt 24.12.

399. Cf. Alb., *IV Sent.* d. 47 a. 8.

400. See Alb., *De res.* tr. 2, q. 10, art. 11, §2 (ed. Colon. 26, p. 300, 24f.).

ment [Day], one asks how that fire purges in a moment (*in momento*)[401] those who are in need of greater or lesser purgation.

3. In addition, since there are some, like the innocents, who have not sinned at all, it seems that that fire will have no power over them. And so it follows that some will exist in the fire who will not be burned [to ashes by it].

Solution: We say with Haimo that all those who will be found alive will be burned to ashes in that fire,[402] because, as was shown above, the general resurrection is from ashes.

1. To the first, therefore, one must reply that among the good, voluntarily suffering fire makes the fire a kind of martyrdom for them, so that whatever impurity existed in them will be cut away by the scythe of that martyrdom. And blessed Jerome says something similar about the thief who voluntarily suffers [on Calvary] and about the Sodomites—if any of them did penance, however, among the flames (*inter ignes*)—and about those who perished in the waters of the Flood.[403] And so it is necessary for the fire to be diversified only with respect to good and bad [people].

2. In this way, a solution to the second is also apparent, because the voluntary devotion to suffering supplies what is lacking in time.

There are some, however, who say, just as the objection proceeds, that the fire is diversified in severity according to the variety of sins, but not in terms of time.[404]

3. To the third, one must reply that the infection of the tinder (*fomes*) will exist in all people, for which reason death was introduced to nature, and as a result that fire will have power over all as far as introducing death to nature and burning the body to ashes, because it was shown above that the reduction to ashes corresponds to the tinder of concupiscence.[405]

401. Cf. 1 Cor 15.52: *in momento, in ictu oculi:* "in a moment, in the twinkling of an eye ..."

402. Cf. Haimo of Auxerre, *In Rom.* 5.10 (PL 117: 405C).

403. Jerome, *Epist.* 58.1 (PL 22: 580; CSEL 54: 528, 15–16).

404. "In terms of time": that is, in duration. Cf. Thomas Aquinas, *IV Sent.* d. 47 q. 2 a. 3 qla. 2 ad 5.

405. Cf. Alb., *De res.* tr. 1, q. 4 (ed. Colon. 26, p. 246, 26ff.).

Art. 5. According to what nature that fire and the other fires —namely that of hell and of purgatory—will act upon souls and bodies[406]

To the fifth, one proceeds in this way:

Blessed Gregory says in the *Dialogue* that what it means for spirits to burn in fire is that they see fire.[407] One asks, therefore, what [kind of] vision is intended [here]. For he does not mean external vision, which is a sense, because the demons do not have sensation. He means, then, the vision of the intellect. Therefore, to understand fire will be what it means to see fire. But we learn from experience that punishment does not stem from this, because we also understand fire but nevertheless we do not suffer on account of it.

In addition, fire only acts on matter, in which it exists according to being (*esse*). It does not exist in the intellect, however, according to being (*esse*), but according to the impression of a universal on the intellect (*secundum intentionem universali intellecti*). Therefore, it does not act on the intellect. And thus to see fire will not be the same as to burn in fire.

Besides, understanding (*intellectus*) occurs only by means of the assimilation of the intellective power to the intelligible. Therefore, in understanding fire, fire has been assimilated to the nature of the intellective power according to simplicity (*secundum simplicitatem*). Between like things, however, there is no suffering, but rather pleasure. And so it follows that there will be no suffering in that vision of fire.

Owing to this, others say that spirits exist in a material fire and are burned by that very fire.[408] And they have a reason for their statement, namely that if to burn in fire were only to see fire by means of the understanding (*intellectus*), then those who are in the fire and those who are outside the fire would suffer equally, because the understanding (*intellectus*) apprehends apart from the presence of matter.

If, however, one asks of them according to what nature fire

406. Cf. Alb., *IV Sent.* d. 44 a. 40.
407. Greg., *Dial.* 4.29 (PL 77: 368A).
408. Cf. Greg., *Dial.* 4.29 (PL 77: 368A).

will act upon them, they say that it acts virtually (*virtualiter*).[409] And they distinguish between "to act virtually" and "to act according to the nature of its own species." To be sure, although it cannot act upon souls according to the nature of its own species, nevertheless it can act according to power (*secundum virtutem*). But this statement is said to be confused, because whatever acts acts according to power.

In addition, one asks whether the fire would act according to the same power upon good souls, if they were in it.[410] If so, then good souls would be capable of suffering (*passibiles*), which would be contrary to nature and to their [state of] grace. If not, since that power does not exist according to the species of fire, as they say, it is necessary that it exist, insofar as it acts, by the divine power. And in this way the debate with them ceases.

Solution: One must say with blessed Gregory that spirits are united to fires, not in the sense that they will endow the fires with life, as blessed Gregory says, but because they derive punishment from the fires.[411] And to derive punishment from the fires is what it means to see fire. And one must concede that he understands this to concern vision by means of the intellect (*per intellectum*).[412] But the intellect is twofold, namely the speculative intellect, which apprehends the object (*res*) only insofar as it is the source of knowledge, and this [speculative intellect] does not lead to punishment. There is also the practical intellect, which apprehends the object in terms of what is suitable and harmful, and this, if it should apprehend the harmful as imminent, can lead to punishment.

Similarly, one must draw a distinction between the fire that is apprehended as fire according to nature and species, and in this way it has no contrariety (*contrarietatem*) to spirits, and [the fire] that is apprehended as an instrument of retributive justice (*iustitia vindicantis*), and in this way it can have contrariety.

409. "Virtually," *virtualiter:* i.e., by its power [*virtus*]. Cf. Thomas Aquinas, *IV Sent.* d. 44 q. 3 a. 3 qla. 3 sol.

410. Cf. Alb., *IV Sent.* d. 47 a. 10.

411. Not Greg., but Aug., *De civ. dei* 21.10 (PL 41: 725; CSEL 40/2: 538, 1–7).

412. Cf. Alb., *De homine* q. 63 a. 4 (ed. Colon. 27/2, pp. 484–85).

Similarly, one must draw a distinction with regard to spirit. There is spirit that is spirit according its own nature, and in this way is not inferior to any corporeal power. There is also spirit that exists under the defect of sin, to which it submitted itself voluntarily, and in this way it can have contrariety to the power of fire insofar as it is an instrument of retributive justice.

Likewise, one must draw a distinction between understanding in an absolute sense (*simpliciter*) and understanding in the mode of vision. Indeed, understanding in an absolute sense (*simpliciter*) has to do with an object that is not present, but understanding in the mode of vision has to do only with a present object, as Basil says in the beginning of *On the Beginning of Proverbs*.[413]

Likewise, one must draw a distinction concerning the assimilation of the intelligible to the intellect. Indeed, there is one assimilation of the abstracted species considered absolutely (*simpliciter*), that is, when it has the same simplicity as the intellect—that is, when it does not have material being (*esse*)—and then it can be the form of the intellect. And according to this mode there is always assimilation and there is never any contrariety between the intellective power and the intellective species. And neither what is harmful nor what is suitable is said to be apprehended according to this mode, because every such apprehension is assimilated, and indeed according to this mode it does not move one to a feeling of good or evil or sadness or joy. According to another mode, however, the species is considered as it is capable of leading to the object of which it is the species. And in this way the suitable or the harmful is distinguished, so long as it is properly (*debite*) oriented to the object, as is clear from the preceding distinctions. Indeed, the species of fire has to exist, not only insofar as it is fire, but insofar as it is the instrument of retributive justice; and in this way nothing will prevent it from having contrariety to a soul that is subject to fault.

And from these distinctions a solution to the entire [question] is clear.

413. Basil, *Hom.* 5 *In Princ. Prov.* 13 (Rufinus's trans.; PG 31: 1776A).

Art. 6. Whether [that fire] precedes or follows judgment[414]

To the sixth, one proceeds in this way:

It seems that it precedes judgment, because the Gloss on Romans[415] says, "we read that there will be two fires," one of which will precede the appearance of the Judge, just as the Psalm says, "A fire will go before him."[416] But what precedes the Judge precedes judgment. Therefore, that fire will come before judgment.

To the contrary: The execution of a sentence should not occur before judgment. But that that fire will envelop the wicked is the execution of the sentence. Therefore, this will come after judgment.

But further along, the Gloss says that that fire will purge the elect and envelop the reprobate. Therefore, it will come before judgment.[417]

To this we say that that fire will precede judgment. To be sure, judgment leads to a new condition for the elect and the reprobate, and on account of this [new condition] it [that is, judgment] will occur once the elements in the world have been renewed.

To the objection to the contrary, one should reply that that enveloping fire is understood with respect to [fire's] division. Indeed, once the division has been accomplished, the heat in fire will remain in hell with the damned, not before judgment but after.

Art. 7. Where [that fire] will remain after judgment[418]

To the seventh, one proceeds in this way:

1. Nothing exists in nature in vain. But what does not exist for some end exists in vain.[419] But once the renewal of the world has been accomplished, that fire seems to exist for no purpose. Therefore, it follows that if it endures, it will endure in vain.

414. Cf. Alb., *IV Sent.* d. 47 a. 11.

415. Rather, Peter Lombard, *In epist. Pauli* 1 Cor 3.13 (PL 191: 1558A–B).

416. Ps 96.3.

417. Peter Lombard, *In epist. Pauli* 1 Cor 3.13 (PL 191: 1558A–B). Cf. *Glossa ord. super Is.*, 66.15.

418. Cf. Alb., *IV Sent.* d. 47 a. 9.

419. Ar., *De caelo et mundo* 1.4 (271a33).

2. In addition, since there are two natures in fire, namely lightness (*leve*) and heat, why is it said to remain below because of the nature of heat rather than to remain up above because of the nature of lightness?

3. Also, since Basil says that the Lord will divide the flame of fire[420] and that the luminous will remain above and the heat will descend below to the lowest part, one also asks where the dryness that is in the fire will remain.

Solution:

1. We say that the nature of that fire will remain in hell, and therefore it does not exist in vain, because it will burn up the damned.

2. To the next one, we say that lightness (*levitas*) is a quality of the matter [of fire], but heat and dryness are elemental qualities that determine the nature of fire more than lightness does. And for this reason that fire is said to remain in hell because of these,[421] rather than [to remain] above because of lightness.

3. To the last one, one must reply that fire's dryness will remain in hell, but the saints do not mention it because it is not an active, but rather a passive, quality [of the fire].

Art. 8. What its [that is, that fire's] matter, in which it will be perpetuated, is, and what will perpetuate it

To the last one, one proceeds in this way:

Sin is a defect. A defect does not prevail for perpetuity, however. Therefore, it does not seem that that fire is perpetuated by sin.

In reply to this, some say, in accord with Gregory,[422] that because man sinned in his eternity, it is just for him to be punished in God's eternity. But it does not seem that someone should be punished for eternity for a momentary sin.

Blessed Bernard replies to this in [his] fifth [letter] to [Pope]

420. Cf. Alb., *De res.* tr. 2, q. 5 (ed. Colon. 26, p. 263, 25). Basil, *Super Ps.* 28.7.6 (PG 29: 297A–C); *In hexaem. hom.* 6.3 (PG 29: 121C–D; transl. Eustathii Afri., PG 30: 925B). Cf. Bonaventure, *I Sent.* d. 42 a. 1 q. 3, *Opera* 1: 750; *IV Sent.* d. 43 dub. 3, *Opera* 4: 903b.

421. I.e., the elemental qualities of heat and dryness.

422. "Some": cf. Ps. Guerricus (fol. 175vb). Greg., *Dial.* 4.3 (PL 77: 321B). Cf. Bonaventure, *IV Sent.* d. 44 a. 1 q. 1, *Opera* 4: 922a.

Eugenius, saying: "Although the deed was done in time, the fact that it was done remains forever (*sempiternum*). What transcends time does not pass away with time. Therefore, it is necessary for it to cause torment for eternity, so that you might remember for eternity the wrong that you did."[423]

But it seems that this is nonsense, because according to this even a venial [sin] would be punished for eternity, since this too would persist in memory, and one's having done it would not pass away, although the doing of the deed would pass away.

For this reason, others say[424] that the will to sin is perpetual. Indeed, because man is "a spirit that goes forth and does not return,"[425] one who consents to sin consents, as a result, to be subject to perpetual sin.

But this does not seem to be true because, although willing is an act of the soul, it can attend well to one thing separately and not [to] that to which it is inseparably united, as [when one says,] "I want (*volo*) to be an abbot and not a monk."[426] And for this reason the will is not to remain in perpetual sin.

And this is why others say that the will to sin is perpetual.[427] To be sure, the will desires to enjoy the sweetness of sin without end, and for this reason it is just that it be punished without end.

But one objects to this that it is known to be impossible to enjoy the sweetness of sin without end, and for this reason it does not seem to move the appetite or will.

But they easily respond to this by saying with Aristotle in the *Ethics* that [there is] "a will for impossible [things]."[428]

After this, one asks how punishment for venial sin is perpetuated in one who departs life in [a state of] mortal and venial [sin]. In fact, if he is punished in eternity, then it seems that God is unjust.[429]

The question is the same for a mortal sin that has become

423. Bern., *De consid.* 5.12.29 (PL 182: 803C).

424. Cf. Richard Fishacre (fol. 352rb).

425. Ps 77.39.

426. Cf. Alb., *De bono* 5 q 2 a.1 (ed. Colon. 28, p. 282, 53ff.).

427. Cf. Ps. Guerricus (fol. 175vb).

428. Ar., *Eth. Nic.* 3.4 (1111b22). Cf. Ar., *Top.* 3.1 (116b23ff.); Boethius, trans. ant. PL 64: 935C. Alb., *Top.* 3.1.3.

429. Cf. Alb., *IV Sent.* d. 21 a. 8.

venial through contrition and later is joined again to a mortal [sin], and someone departs life in this way.

We respond to this with Chrysostom on [the Gospel of] John,[430] that the fire's severity corresponds to the sin. But the fact that it is perpetual occurs *per accidens,* namely because the sinner departed life without grace. But no sin, whether mortal or venial, is forgiven without grace, and one cannot obtain grace after death. Therefore, it follows that he will remain under sin forever (*in perpetuum*). Since, then, that fire attacks sin, it happens that that fire is perpetuated both against venial and against mortal [sin], but with a severity that is not the same.

To the first, one must reply that although sin is in itself a defect, nevertheless it acquires the quality of lasting forever (*perpetuitatem*) by reason of an incorruptible subject, especially since the will, which is the cause of sin, remains depraved forever.

One must reply to all the others that there are certain accommodations and arrangements that consider the appropriateness of the punishment based on the disposition of the fault.

On the Order of Judgment

Next one asks about the order of judgment, in three ways: namely, first about judgment on the part of the Judge; second, on the part of the [judicial] sentence; third, on the part of those who are to be judged.

Art. 9. Concerning judgment on the part of the Judge[431]

With respect to the first, one asks who will judge.

1. Now it seems that [it is] the Son, who says in the Gospel of John: "The Father does not judge any man, but has given all judgment to the Son."[432]

And then one asks whether he [that is, the Son] will judge in the form of God or in the form of a servant. It seems that it will be in the form of a servant, because Augustine says:[433] "Surely

430. John Chrysos., *Hom.* 38 *In Joh.* 1 (PG 59: 211); cf. ibid. *Hom.* 10.2 (PG 59: 73) and *Hom.* 28.1 (PG 59: 161).

431. Cf. Alb., *IV Sent.* d. 48 a.1.

432. Jn 5.22.

433. According to Peter Lombard, *IV Sent.* d. 48 c. 1 (p. 1022); according to Aug., *In Joh.* 21.13 (PL 35: 1571). Cf. Alb., *IV Sent.* d. 48 a. 1 sol.

he will judge in the form of a servant, which [form] will appear to all at judgment, so that the wicked might see [judgment] in the one whom they pierced."[434]

One sees the same thing in the Gospel, where it is said: "And he has given him power to execute judgment, because he is the Son of Man."[435]

In Daniel it appears contrariwise that the Father will judge, where it says, "The Ancient of Days sat," and, "and the books were opened."[436] The Ancient of Days signifies the Father. And so it seems that the Father will judge.

2. Likewise, it seems that the saints will judge, because Christ says to the Apostles: "You who have left all things and followed me, you will sit on the seats judging the twelve tribes of Israel."[437] Similarly, Wisdom [says]: "The saints will judge the nations and rule over the peoples."[438]

3. Likewise, it seems that the whole world will judge, for we read in Wisdom 5: "And his zeal will take armor, and he will arm the creature for the revenge of [his] enemies. He will put on justice as a breastplate, and will take true judgment as a helmet. He will take equity for an invincible shield. And he will sharpen his stern wrath into a spear, and the whole world will fight together with him against the foolish."[439]

4. After this, one asks, if Christ will judge in the form of a servant, whether he will appear in a glorious or non-glorious form.[440] It seems that [he will appear] in a glorious form, because he exists in a glorious [form] and it does not belong to truth to pretend or to fashion phantasms.

But Isaiah says to the contrary, "Let the impious man be taken away, lest he see the glory of the Lord."[441]

434. Cf. Rv 1.7.
435. Jn 5.27.
436. Dn 7.9 and 10.
437. Mt 19.27 and 28.
438. Wis 3.8.
439. Wis 5.18–21.
440. Cf. Alb., *IV Sent.* d. 48 a. 3.
441. Cf. Is 26.10. See Peter Lombard, *IV Sent.* d. 48 c. 2 (p. 1023); but cf. Alb., *Super Is.* 26.10 (ed. Colon. 19, p. 293, 88–91) and *Super Is.* 35.2 (p. 372, 89–91).

In addition, a non-glorious eye cannot see a glorious body. But the damned will not have glorious eyes. Therefore, etc.[442]

1. To this, one must reply, as Augustine says, that the Son will judge in the form of a servant although with the power of divinity, and just as there is one divine nature (*divinitas*) of the Father and of the Son and of the Holy Spirit, in the same way there is one judgment. And those authorities who say that the Father or the Son or the Holy Spirit will judge are to be understood in this way.

If one should ask, however, why the Son will judge as a human being (*in persona hominis*), we say in accord with Augustine that this is for three reasons.[443] One is that as a human being he gave the Law, according to which there has to be a judgment, and it belongs to the legislator to pass judgment according to the Law. Second is that redemption was accomplished within the human race (*in humanitate*) through the Son. Therefore, since he himself was established as the Redeemer, it is appropriate that he also should be the Judge of those who are contemptuous of redemption. Third is that in the form of a servant he was judged by men, and on account of this he merited [to possess] judiciary power.

4. To the question whether he will judge in a glorious or non-glorious form, we say that it will be in a glorious [form]. But the damned will not see him in a glorious form, but rather in the form in which "they pierced him"[444]—and nevertheless there is no illusion (*phantasia*) there. What kind [of form] it may be was indicated in the question concerning the proofs for the glorious Resurrection.[445] Nonetheless, the good will see him in a glorious form, and this will be everlasting joy for them, just as Augustine says.[446]

2. To the question concerning the saints, one must reply that it is different for the saints who have performed privileged

442. See Alb., *De res.* tr. 2, q. 5, art. 3 (ed. Colon. 26, p. 274, 49ff.).

443. Alb. takes the reference to three causes in Aug. from Peter Lombard, *IV Sent.* d. 48 c. 2 (p. 1023). Cf. Aug., *De trin.* 1.13.28f. (PL 42: 840f.).

444. Rv 1.7.

445. Alb., *De res.* tr. 2, q. 5, art. 3 (ed. Colon. 26, p. 274, 49ff.).

446. Cf. Aug., *De trin.* 1.13.28 (PL 42: 841). Cf. Alb., *IV Sent.* d. 48 a. 2.

works, such as abandoning all things and following Christ, and teaching the faith, and laying down one's body for the faith, and others of this sort. Indeed, it is said of these [saints] that they will sit "on the twelve seats judging the twelve tribes of Israel."[447] And the masters[448] say that they [that is, the saints] will judge with a judgment of comparison or confirmation, because by comparison with them others will be judged and they will also confirm the sentence of the Judge. But this is insufficient, because according to this [text] all the saints sit on seats. In fact, judiciary power is indicated by the seats, [and] the collective body (*universitas*)[449] through the twelve. And for this reason we say, just as John and Daniel and Gregory and Richard of St. Victor do,[450] that the books of conscience will be opened then,[451] which [books] have been written in a twofold way with respect to the saints. To be sure, in some [books] the deeds are written, and in others the divine judgments [are written] with the deeds. The conscience of every individual will lie open to each book at that time. And for the damned, this will be the sentence of condemnation or judgment received from apostolic men, namely to read the decrees of divine truth in their consciences. And all of this is understood from the words of Richard in the book *On the Sentence of the Judge,* which speaks thus:[452] "What are the consciences of those who are going to be judged except certain actions of Scripture, so to speak, and what indeed are the hearts of those being judged, [hearts] that have been divinely instructed in every truth, if not certain decrees of the canons, as it were? From this double Scripture, therefore, every sentence is drawn, whence every one who is going to be judged is damned or absolved. Therefore, that those to be judged open the books (*codices*) of their own actions before the judges means nothing other than that they are unable to hide their consciences from the judges. But for the judges to read in

447. Mt 19.27 and 28.

448. Cf. Ps. Odo Rigaldi (fol. 248va).

449. *Universitas:* cf. Aug., *Enarr. in Ps.* 86.4 (PL 37: 1104).

450. Greg., *Dial.* 24.8.16 (PL 76: 295B–C); Richard of St. Victor, *De judiciaria potestate* (PL 196: 1182A–C).

451. Cf. Rv 20.12; Dn 7.10.

452. Richard of St. Victor, *De judiciaria potestate* (PL 196: 1182A–C).

books of this sort is nothing other than to penetrate the hidden places of their consciences with clear vision and to know beyond all doubt on that basis who will be rewarded and who will be soiled. For the judges to open the books of their decrees before those being judged, however, is to permit all inferiors to see the inspection of hearts and to reveal their own thoughts about those things that pertain to the basis (*ratio*) of judgment. To be sure, those being judged, when they read among the canonical decrees of this sort, they find the sentence of retribution that each one deserves and the basis of the sentence. Therefore, to read a text of this sort will be to have received the sentence of judgment on them; on the other hand, for the apostolic men to judge any of those being judged will be to present to their eyes the basis for the sentence being given."

Therefore, we say, in accord with the preceding words, that the perfect (*perfecti*) and the contemplatives (*contemplativi*) in this life are fashioned, by continuously gazing at the divine truth that they contemplate, into a [wax] seal, as it were, of divine judgment. Thereby they will reveal to the good and the wicked who are going to be judged the basis of and understanding for their judgments on the Day of Judgment, and this is what it means for them to judge. Other saints who are active and not perfect (*sancti activi non-perfecti*), however, inscribe upon themselves now only good deeds, according to which judgment is determined.[453] And for this reason these [saints] will judge only by a judgment of comparison and confirmation, and this confirmation is described as "two-edged swords in their hands."[454]

3. To the question concerning all creatures, one must reply that creatures will punish but they will not judge. And this means nothing other than, at the time of the world's renewal, to move quickly whatever is ignoble in the world to the place of punishments and to increase the horror of the prison in that place. And this is what is said in Wisdom 5: "Hailstones full of

453. Alb.'s distinction here is that of saints engaged in either of the two basic modes of religious life, namely those who live an active mode of life in the world, on the one hand, and those who lead a contemplative life that sets them apart from the world, on the other.

454. Ps 149.6.

wrath will be hurled from a rocky place, and the water of the sea will rage against them, and the rivers will run together relentlessly."[455]

From this a solution to the whole is apparent.

Art. 10. Concerning judgment on the part of the [judicial] sentence[456]

To the second, one proceeds in this way:

It has been maintained that Christ will judge in the form of man.[457] But man's judgment occurs by means of the vocal expression of man's sentence. Therefore, the sentence will be vocalized.

Furthermore, the Gospel seems to say this explicitly, where it says that the king "will say to those who are on the left, 'Go, you cursed,'"[458] and, "to those who are on the right, 'Come, you blessed, I was hungry,'" etc.[459]

But to the contrary, a very great multitude will be in that place. Therefore, if he has to be heard, it is necessary that the sentence be [proclaimed] with a loud cry. If perhaps it is said that it will happen miraculously and by the power of God that each one can hear that voice, by the same reasoning it will be assumed [to be] a miracle that that voice will be heard by the heart and not [come] from the mouth.

In addition, from the statement in the Gospel, "He will say to those," etc.,[460] it is not proved that the voice must be corporeal, because it is also said in the Gospel that "the hour will come when all who are in their tombs will hear the voice of the Son of God."[461] Nevertheless, Augustine says that "voice" is understood there to mean the power that the Son of God has to raise the bodies of the dead.[462]

455. Wis 5.23.
456. Cf. Alb., *IV Sent.* d. 47 a. 2–4.
457. Alb., *De res.* tr. 2, q. 10, art. 9 (ed. Colon. 26, p. 297, 56ff.).
458. Mt 25.41.
459. Mt 25.34–35.
460. Mt 25.41.
461. Cf. Jn 5.25.
462. Aug., *Epist.* 140, 34.78 (PL 33: 573; CSEL 44: 226ff.). Cf. Alb., *De res.* tr. 1, q. 5 (ed. Colon. 26, p. 247, 31). Peter Lombard, *IV Sent.* d. 43 c. 2 (p. 996).

Furthermore, the Apostle speaks of the voice of the archangel and the trumpet of God,[463] though neither of these will be corporeal, as was maintained above in the question on the resurrection of Christ.[464]

Moreover, it is said that during that judgment an accusing conscience will stand.[465] Therefore, the voice of witnesses will not be corporeal. Therefore, by analogy, neither will the Judge's examination occur by means of a corporeal voice.

Also, it is said that judgment will be "in a moment and in the twinkling of an eye."[466] This could not happen if such a long examination as is mentioned in the Gospel had to take place with words.[467]

In the *Sentences* the Master responds to this [by saying] that "it is not clear how to explain this" because "Scripture does not determine clearly" whether it will happen by means of a corporeal voice or whether the efficient power of the Judge is signified by speech.[468] Without offense, then, we say, with blessed Bernard[469] and with Richard of St. Victor,[470] that the sentence will not be vocalized but, as we said above,[471] that to permit those being judged to see the basis for their sentence in the conscience of Christ means for them to have received the sentence of judgment with their consciences presenting testimony.[472] And we say that the truth shining in the book of the canon of judgment is called the light by which the Lord "will illuminate the hidden things of darkness and will reveal the hearts' counsels."[473] And just as corporeal light, owing to its

463. 1 Thes 4.16 (Vulg.).

464. Alb., *De res.* tr. 2, q. 2; tr. 1, q. 5 (ed. Colon. 26, p. 260, 20–21; p. 247, 61ff.).

465. Cf. Aug., *De civ. dei* 20.14 (PL 41: 680; CSEL 40/2: 462, 4–8). Cf. Peter Lombard, *IV Sent.* d. 43 c. 4 (p. 997); d. 47, a. 1 (p. 1018).

466. 1 Cor 15.52.

467. Mt 25.31–46.

468. Peter Lombard, *IV Sent.* d. 47 c. 1 (p. 1018).

469. Ps. Bern., *Medit. piissimae de cognitione humanae condicionis* 2.4 (PL 184: 488A).

470. Richard of St. Victor, *De judiciaria potestate* (PL 196: 1179C, 1183A).

471. Alb., *De res.* tr. 2, q. 10, art. 9 (ed. Colon. 26, p. 298, 34ff.).

472. Cf. Rom 2.15.

473. 1 Cor 4.5.

spirituality and subtlety, instantly changes the entire fabric of the sensible world, in such a way the eternal truth shining forth in the heart of Christ and of apostolic men will illuminate all things much more through revelation, and by that light all the unjust ones are accused and all the righteous ones are praised. And this is understood through judgment's examination: "For I was hungry," etc.[474]

To that first objection, therefore, we say that when an ordinary human (*purus homo*)[475] judges, he only judges the things that are according to appearance (*secundum faciem*), and for this reason he needs the expression of the voice.[476] But when the Man-God judges, and in accord with divine judgments, then he judges the things that belong to the heart and according to the testimony of the heart, and therefore he does not need the expression of the corporeal voice.

Art. 11. Concerning the order of judgment on the part of those being judged

Two [questions] are raised concerning the third [investigation], namely about the order of those being judged in a place and about the order of those being judged among themselves.

§1. On the order of those being judged in a place[477]

One asks about the place where those being judged will stand.

1. If it is said that [they will stand] in the valley of Jehosaphat, then one asks about the capacity of that place, [and] how they all can be contained there.

In addition, one asks about the elect, who will be taken up "in the clouds to meet Christ, into the air, and so always will be with the Lord."[478] Therefore, not all will be in the valley of Jeho-

474. Cf. Mt 25.35.

475. By *purus homo,* Alb. means a simple or ordinary human being, in contrast to Christ, the Son of God, an eternal, divine Person who assumed a human nature in time in order to accomplish human salvation.

476. Cf. Mk 12.14.

477. Cf. Alb., *IV Sent.* d. 48 a. 6; *Super Luc.* 17.21.

478. 1 Thes 4.16 (Vulg.). This "rapture" was discussed in medieval texts. See Dyan Elliott, "The Physiology of Rapture and Female Spirituality," in *Medieval Theology and the Natural Body,* ed. Peter Biller and A. J. Minnis (Woodbridge, Suffolk: York Medieval Press, 1997), 141–73.

saphat, because some of the elect will act as judges, as is clear in the Gospel.[479]

2. Next one asks about the right and the left [hand] of the Judge, where the sheep and the goats are said to be placed.[480] In fact, it seems that this will not be true, but rather [they will be placed] below and above, because, as Augustine says,[481] the impious will remain on the earth, which they have loved, whereas the just will be taken up above into the air. And so they will be above and below rather than to the right and to the left.

Solution:

1. We say that the valley of Jehosaphat is meant according to the meaning [of the name] and not literally, for Jehosaphat means "the judgment of the Lord."[482] Therefore, the valley of Jehosaphat is nothing other than the valley of the Lord's judgment, and that will be this [whole] world. Nevertheless, some say[483] that they will be gathered together facing the valley of Jehosaphat and not in it.

2. To the objection concerning the right and the left [hand], we say that according to the philosophers[484] right and left are understood in two ways, namely according to power and according to [external] form (*figura*). According to power, the right is where the principle of motion and the abundance of power exist, whereas the left is where there is a slowing or reversal of motion owing to a lessening of motive power.[485] According to [external] form, however, right and left exist in animals and in likenesses.[486]

One must reply, therefore, that the abundance of power for the purpose of glorifying and beatifying is called the right

479. Mt 19.28.

480. Cf. Mt 25.33.

481. Aug., *Enarr. in Ps.* 71.5.9 (PL 37: 1626); cf. *Glossa ord. super Joel* 3.2. Peter Lombard, *IV Sent.* d. 48 c. 4 (p. 1025).

482. Cf. Jerome, *Epist.* 18.3 (PL 22: 362; CSEL 54: 77, 13–14). Alb., *Super Joel* 3.2 (ed. Borgnet 19, p. 169).

483. Cf. Peter Lombard, *IV Sent.* d. 48 c. 4 (p. 1025). *Glossa ord. super Joel* 3.2.

484. Cf. Ar., *De caelo et mundo* 2.2 (285b1–4). Cf. Alb., *De caelo et mundo* 2.1.5.

485. For Ar., the principle of motion is on the right side of the body. See *De incessu animalium* (705b35f). Cf. Alb., *Quaest. super de animal.* 1, q. 40, resp. (ed. Colon. 12, pp. 102–3; *QDA*, p. 65).

486. E.g., in paintings and statues.

[hand] of Christ, whereas his left is the lessening of the same [power]—not that a defect is posited in Christ, but rather in the damned, who have not merited to receive beatitude. From this a solution is clear, because "below" and "above" are understood with respect to place, whereas "right" and "left" [are understood] with respect to the power of beatifying.

§2. On the order of those being judged among themselves[487]

Second, one asks about the order of those being judged among themselves. And Gregory says that there will be four orders in judgment.[488] For some will be judged and saved, some will be judged and condemned, some will be saved and not judged, and some will be condemned and not judged.

What is said in Acts, where it is said that "Christ was appointed as the Judge of the living and the dead," seems to contradict this.[489] Therefore, all will be judged.

In addition, the Apostle says of himself and of others: "It is necessary for us all to appear before the judgment seat of Christ."[490] But only those who must be judged appear before the judgment seat. Therefore, all will be judged, both the apostles and others.

Furthermore, Master Richard of St. Victor says, "It seems that all either will judge or will be judged, and indeed some of those to be judged will be saved and others will be damned."[491] Therefore, there seem to be only three orders in that future judgment.

Additionally, it seems that there are five [orders]. For some are among those for whom salvation is certain and nevertheless will not judge, such as infants who have died after baptism; and others are among those for whom salvation is certain, and they will rise in the place of those [saints] who judge. Similarly, some are among those for whom damnation is certain, and others are among those for whom damnation is uncertain

487. Cf. Alb., *IV Sent.* d. 47 a.5.

488. Greg., *Moral.* 26.27.50 (PL 76: 378C). Cf. Ps. Aug., *Sermo* 77.4 (PL 39: 1896); *Glossa ord. super Ps.* 1.5. Peter Lombard, *In Ps.* 1.5 (PL 191: 65A).

489. Acts 10.42.

490. 2 Cor 5.10.

491. Richard of St. Victor, *De iudiciaria potestate* (PL 196: 1179B).

but who will be damned, and still others are among those for whom salvation is uncertain but who will be saved. And Master Richard actually posits these five orders.[492]

Solution: We say that God's judgment is threefold, namely, uniform, multiform, and omniform. Uniform judgment is the judgment of the present Church, and this is called uniform because he [that is, God] renders judgment only concerning the quality alone of compensatory acts and only in a general way (*in genere*)—namely, that good things will be repaid for good deeds and evil things for evil deeds, but he [that is, the person in this present life] does not know the number and extent of the compensatory acts. And this judgment takes place only in [his] thinking about the sentence of judgment. Another judgment is multiform, and this is the judgment that someone experiences at death, when receiving a sentence according to all the good or evil deeds that he performed. But he does not receive all the good or evil things immediately, because he receives [the sentence] only in the soul, and for this reason it is called multiform. Omniform [judgment], however, is the Last Judgment, when he receives recompense in the body and the soul for good or evil [deeds] according to their quality and number and extent. And these two last judgments[493] consist in experiencing the sentence, not only in thinking [about it]. And this is the distinction of Master Richard.[494]

Concerning the Last Judgment, we say that it can be considered in two ways, namely in relation to the cause of the sentence or in relation to the effect. If [it is considered] in relation to the effect, then there are only two orders, because there is only a double effect—namely, the possession of life and the possession of death. And so there will be two orders: those judged and saved, and those judged and condemned. And in this way one understands what the Apostle says, "It is necessary for us all to appear [before the judgment seat of Christ],"[495] and the

492. Richard of St. Victor, *De iudiciaria potestate* (PL 196: 1177C–D).

493. That is, the judgment is double because it is experienced in both the soul and the body.

494. Richard of St. Victor, *De iudiciaria potestate* (PL 196: 1181A–C).

495. 2 Cor 5.10.

article of the creed, that "he will come to judge the living and the dead, at whose coming all men have to rise again," etc.[496]

If judgment is understood in relation to the cause, however, then it is understood according to a consideration of the cause either as now or as then. If considered as now, then there are five orders, for the cause of judgment is merit, and this is certain in some and doubtful in others. Doubtful merit produces two orders: those being judged and saved, and those being judged and condemned. Certain merit is either good or evil. If evil, it produces one order, namely those being damned while not being judged, because they have already been judged. Certain good [merit] produces two orders, namely those being saved while not being judged or judging, and those being saved while not being judged but judging. And if one objects that there ought to be a sixth order consisting only of infants who died in [a state of] Original [Sin] (*in originali*), one must reply that this is not so, because the Apostle says that they appear before the seat of judgment in order to receive "the proper things of the body" (*propria corporis*),[497] but infants will only have another's (*alienum*).[498] Moreover, judgment is either to fire or to eternal life, but infants receive a judgment leading to neither.

But if merit, which is the cause of the sentence, is understood as then, there will be four orders, as Gregory says: for that merit is very evil, or very good, or moderately evil, or moderately good. If very evil, they will be condemned [but] not judged, because their sins have been clearly revealed for judgment. If very good, they will be saved [but] not judged, because their virtue will be clearly revealed for salvation. If moderately good, they will be judged and saved, because their virtue is clearly revealed as the reason for the sentence, when it is said:

496. Athanasian Creed; see Heinrich Denzinger, *The Sources of Catholic Dogma*, trans. Roy J. Deferrari (Fitzwilliam, NH: Loreto Publications, 2002), sections 39–40.

497. 2 Cor 5.10; "the proper things of the body": namely, reward or punishment for the deeds performed while in the body.

498. *Alienum:* Infants who die prior to baptism, that is, in a state of Original Sin, receive a judgment based not on their own personal sins, but rather on the sin they inherit from another, namely from Adam.

"For I was hungry, and you gave me something to eat," etc.[499] If moderately evil, they will be judged and damned, because their sins are clearly revealed as the reason for the sentence, when it is said: "For I was hungry, and you did not give me something to eat," etc.[500]

Also, note that the Lord intimated only two groups, namely the sheep and the goats. And this division is understood according to the general differences of merit, namely good and evil.

Likewise, there is another division with regard to the nature of those being judged, and in this way there are humans and angels. And this is how one understands what is said in the Gospel, "Have you come to destroy us before the time?"[501] because he will destroy them in judgment, and [how one understands] the authority of Peter, that God delivered into hell those demons that were drawn down, keeping them there for the Day of Judgment.[502]

Similarly, another division could be made with regard to the division of lots in the place of judgment, and in this way there are two orders,[503] because the good will share the air with the Lord, and the impious will share the earth, which they have loved.

Again, a division could be made with regard to what is received through the sentence, and then there are three orders, as Master Richard says in that authoritative opinion noted above.[504] For death is received through the sentence, and in this way they are judged and condemned; or life alone is received, and in this way they are judged and saved; or life is received with judicial power and in this way they are saved and judging.

499. Mt 25.35.
500. Mt 25.42.
501. Mk 1.24.
502. Cf. 2 Pt 2.4 and 9.
503. See Alb., *De res.* tr. 2, q. 10, art. 11, §1 (ed. Colon. 26, p. 299, 60–65).
504. Mt 25.35, 42.

What it Means to Deliver the Kingdom to God and to the Father

Next one asks what it means to deliver the kingdom to God and to the Father.[505] And two questions are raised: first one asks what "the kingdom" there means; second, how it will be delivered to the Father.

Art. 12. What "the kingdom" there means

To the first [question], one proceeds in this way:

Dionysius says in the book *On the Divine Names,* chapter 12: "The kingdom is the distribution of every end (*finis*) and of splendor (*ornatus*) and of law and of order."[506] But such distribution is not delivered to the Father by the Son. Therefore, it seems that the kingdom is not delivered to the Father by the Son. Now the end is established there for the sake of the good, because the highest good is the end, whereas splendor is for the sake of the beautiful according to reason, law is for the sake of a rule governing behavior (*in moribus*), whereas order is for the sake of virtue, because, as Augustine says, "Virtue is the order of love."[507] The Son, however, delivers none of these to the Father.

If perhaps one should say that the kingdom there is not understood in this way, but according to what Basil says at the beginning of *On the Beginning of Proverbs,* that "the kingdom is a certain legitimate care and establishment that looks after all in common, and is not based on a consideration of what is useful for the individual. Indeed, a king differs from a tyrant in that the latter attends to what is useful for himself, whereas the former attends to [what is useful] for all."[508] According to this, again it does not seem that the Son will deliver the kingdom to God the Father. For the establishment of what pertains to the common use of all by providence, which here is called care, is common to the three persons [of the Trinity]. And therefore it will not be delivered to the Father by the Son.

505. Cf. 1 Cor 15.24.

506. Dion., *De div. nom.* 12, §2 (PG 3: 969B; Dionysiaca 1: 529). Cf. Alb., *Super Dion. De div. nom.* 12, 1–9 (ed. Colon. 37/1, pp. 427–31).

507. Aug., *De civ. dei* 15.22 (PL 41: 467; CSEL 40/2: 109, 5–6).

508. Basil, *Hom.* 5 *In princ. Prov.* 2 (Rufinus's trans.; PG 31: 1763A).

If, again, one should say that the faithful there, in whom Christ reigns, are called the kingdom, again it seems to be false. For Christ himself says in John 10 that the Father gave the sheep to him, and that no one will snatch them from his hand because he and the Father are one.[509]

Furthermore, it seems that the Son receives the kingdom from the Father, because in the first chapter of 2 Peter it says: "For he received honor and glory from the Father."[510] And Hilary says that the king begot a king.[511]

To this, one must reply that "the kingdom" is understood there in an occasional sense to refer to those in whom Christ reigns through instructions from the care of providence according to counsels and precepts, and through the distribution of what is good and fitting or beautiful and of law and order.

To the objection that the Son received these from the Father, one must reply that that kingdom can be considered in two ways, namely according to the going forth (*exitum*) into a being (*esse*) of nature and of grace from the First Principle, which is God, and in this way the kingdom is delivered to the Son from the Father, because these are from the Father through the Son. It can also be considered according to the return (*in reditu*) to God as to the ultimate end, and in this way it is delivered from the Son to the Father, because the Son is the form through which they are led back to the Father. And these two considerations are understood at the end of the Apocalypse, where it is said: "I am the Alpha and the Omega, the beginning and the end."[512] Therefore, in the ninth book of *On the Councils* Hilary [says]: "We refer all things through the Son to one Originator (*initiabilem*), the beginning of all things."[513]

But then it appears that by the same argument the kingdom should be delivered to God and to the Father by the Holy Spirit, especially since in the book *On the Spirit and the Soul* Augustine

509. Jn 10.28–30.

510. 2 Pt 1.17.

511. Hil., *De synod.* 33 (PL 10: 505B).

512. Rv 22.13.

513. Hil., *De synod.* 59.26 (PL 10: 521A). Cf. Alb., *I Sent.* d. 31 a. 14 qla. 2; *Summa* I q. 41 m. 2 a. 2.

says that the Holy Spirit is the person nearest to us, because those who are led back to God are led back to God by the gifts of the Holy Spirit and by the Holy Spirit.[514]

To that we say that it is not similar concerning the Son and the Holy Spirit, because the Holy Spirit proceeds by way of the good and of love, and owing to this is analogous to the dispositions that incline us to return. But the Son possesses an analogy, moreover, to nature and proceeds from the Father in the manner of a likeness according to form and definition (*ratio*), because generation is the flow of one from another according to the likeness of nature and of species or form.[515] And owing to this it is fitting for the Son to return the kingdom. But the dispositions, according to which there is a return, befit the Holy Spirit.

Art. 13. How the kingdom will be delivered to God and to the Father

Concerning the second, one asks how the kingdom will be delivered to God and to the Father.

1. And the Gloss says that to deliver the kingdom is "to show that the Father reigns, which is believed now, whereas then [in the future] it will become clear by sight (*per speciem*) and manifestation."[516]

2. But it seems that it is the opposite. So it is said in Phil 2: "He gave to him a name that is above every name."[517] And the Gloss says that "after the Resurrection he gave to him the name that God is called, because it was set forth as evident at that time so that demons and men might know it. And an event is said to occur at the time when it becomes known."[518] And one understands from this that the Son is called God and King, to whom "every knee should bow, of those who are in heaven, on earth, and under the earth."[519] He receives [these names] from

514. Ps. Aug., *De spir. et anima* 6 (PL 40: 783).

515. Cf. John Damascene, *De fide orth.* 1.8 (PG 94: 812C; ed. Buytaert, p. 31, 68–69). Alb., *I Sent.* d. 4 a. 2 sol.; *Summa* I q. 30 m. 2 ad 2.

516. Peter Lombard, *In epist. Pauli* 1 Cor 15.24 (PL 191: 1679B).

517. Phil 2.9.

518. Peter Lombard, *In epist. Pauli* Phil 2.9 (PL 192: 236C).

519. Phil 2.10.

God the Father, and so it seems that he does not deliver [the kingdom] to him.

3. In addition, one asks about the meaning of what the Apostle says in 1 Cor 15: "When he will have destroyed every principality, and power, and virtue."[520] The Gloss there says: "While the world endures, angels preside over angels, demons preside over demons, and men preside over men to benefit or deceive the living. But when all have been gathered together, every prelacy will cease, because it will not be necessary."[521] According to this, then, it seems that the choirs of angels will not exist after the Day of Judgment. Similarly, it seems that the ranks among the demons will cease to exist, according to which one is said to belong to the powers, another to the virtues, another to the principalities, and so on for the others.

But this does not seem to be so. For in the kingdom of heaven an angel will still be higher than another angel. And since it belongs to the superior to lead the inferior back to divine glory (*illuminationes*), as Dionysius says in *On the Celestial Hierarchy*,[522] so it seems that principalities and powers will still remain, as will the others also.

4. After this, one asks again about the meaning of what the Apostle says in the same place: "When all things have been made subject to the Father, then the Son himself also will be subject to the one who subjected all things to himself, so that God may be all in all."[523] For this does not seem to be fitting (*convenire*) for the Son according to divinity, because according to divinity he is not subject to the Father. Therefore, this text seems to imply that he will deliver the kingdom to the Father in such a way that he will not retain [possession of] it, and this is false.

5. In addition, it does not seem that at that time [in the future] God will be "all in all" because there will still exist the

520. 1 Cor 15.24.

521. Peter Lombard, *In epist. Pauli* 1 Cor 15.24 (PL 191: 1679C). Cf. Peter Lombard, *II Sent.* d. 6 c. 4 (p. 331).

522. Dion., *De cael. hier.* 7 §3 (PG 3: 209A; Dionysiaca 2: 853). Cf. Alb., *Super Dion. De cael. hier.* 7 (ed. Colon. 36/1, pp. 110–11).

523. 1 Cor 15.28.

distinct essences of the heavens, the elements, men, and angels, which are not God.

If, however, one wishes to say, in accord with the Gloss,[524] that God will be "all in all" in the sense that in all things there will be nothing contrary to his will, as is the case now, then to the contrary: At that time hell will not be outside his kingdom, and nevertheless an evil will, which is opposed to the will of God, will exist in hell.

6. If it is said that God will be "all in all" in the sense that his will will be fulfilled throughout the whole creation, or that his will will be done concerning it, as Augustine says,[525] to the contrary: This is the case even now, because everything that exists does the will of God, as the good do, or the will of God is done concerning them, as is the case with the wicked.

Solution:

1. We say with the Gloss[526] that to deliver the kingdom to God and to the Father is to show to the Father the elect, in whom he manifestly rules, and the impious, who have been trampled under his feet, in whom he rules by justice.

2. To the next [objection] we say that nothing prevents the Son from receiving the kingdom from the Father and, conversely, from delivering it in different ways, as was said above.[527] For insofar as the Father is the principle of glory for the elect, in this way the kingdom is from the Father through the Son. Insofar as the Father is the end to which there is a return, however, in this way the kingdom is returned to the Father through the Son, as was said above in the authoritative opinion of Hilary.

3. To what is asked after this—how every principality and power will be destroyed—one must reply that the angelic orders possess two things: one is that which indicates a rank of dignity based on the excellence of a gratuitous gift and of nature, and this will never be destroyed. The other is that which considers the [angelic] office, and this is twofold. For the office

524. Peter Lombard, *In epist. Pauli* 1 Cor 15.28 (PL 191: 1682B–C).

525. Aug., *In epist. Pauli* Gal 3.2 (PL 35: 2128).

526. See Alb., *De res.* tr. 2, q. 10, art. 13 (ed. Colon. 26, p. 302, 54). Cf. Haimo of Auxerre, *In epist. Pauli* 1 Cor 15.24 (PL 117: 596D).

527. Cf. Alb., *De res.* tr. 2, q. 10, art. 12 (ed. Colon. 26, p. 302, 31).

possesses the act of ruling according to the governance of the world and of the elect with regard to merit along the road to the [heavenly] homeland, and in this respect angelic prelacies (*praelationes angelici*) over men and angels will cease. The office possesses another act according to which superiors have to lead inferiors back to theophanies of glory, and in this respect the office of prelacy will not cease, but instead superiors will lead inferiors back forever.

In the same way we speak of demons, though contrariwise, because in demons there is malice that corresponds to a gratuitous gift and to nature—and that rank will never be destroyed. And there is an office that has a double act.[528] One [act] is to tempt those who are on the journey [in this present life], and so far as this one is concerned, it will be destroyed. The other [act] is to revile and to irritate, according to which one provokes another with regard to malice, and this is not destroyed, because "the pride of those who hate you always ascends."[529] And in this way one understands what is said in Isaiah 14: "Hell below was in an uproar to meet you at your coming."[530] Indeed, the uproar of hell is nothing but the reviling of those that are in hell.

Concerning the prelacies of men, however, there is no doubt that they will cease, because the prelacies of men are deans,[531] centurions, chiliarchs,[532] and others of this sort.

Concerning the prelacy of creatures, in truth one must say that it will also cease insofar as the office is concerned, because at that time [in the future] superiors will not move inferiors.

4. To what is asked after this—how the Son will be subject to the Father—one must reply that this is understood according to the human nature in the Son, as Augustine's gloss on the same text states.[533] For according to that [nature], he himself is part of the body that is subject to God, namely [the

528. Cf. Alb., *II Sent.* d. 6 a. 4.

529. Ps 73.23.

530. Is 14.9. Cf. Alb., *Super Is.* 14.9 (ed. Colon. 19, p. 204, 87–89).

531. That is, a chief or commander over ten men (a *decanus*).

532. In ancient Greece (and later) chiliarchs were military commanders over 1,000 men. Cf. Mk 6.21; Acts 25.23.

533. Peter Lombard, *In epist. Pauli* 1 Cor 15.28 (PL 191: 1681A). Cf. Aug., *Contra serm. Arian.* 87 (PL 42: 708).

body] of the Church, because he is the head of the Church.

To the objection that he seems not to retain [possession of] the kingdom, one must reply that this is not true, especially since the Apostle says that he must reign "until he has put [all] his enemies under his feet."[534] In fact, although he was made subject [to the Father] in his human nature, nevertheless he himself, existing also in the divine nature, is king together with the Father. But if he existed only in a human nature, then the objection would follow.

If, however, one asks what the "until" signifies when it is said, "until he has put [all] his enemies [under his feet]," one must reply that it denotes the continuity of the Son's kingdom without the delivery [of it] that he will make to the Father. To be sure, that delivery, as the Gloss says,[535] is the manifestation that the Father rules over the elect, which now one believes but which then will be seen by means of clear vision. Therefore, even now, without this delivery, the Son reigns, because his and the Father's kingdom is now hidden. And this is what the Gloss says: "He must reign—add, in a hidden way—until he has put [all] his enemies," etc. "And then he will reign openly." Therefore, the "until" signifies the finitude of the hidden kingdom but not the finitude of the kingdom.

5. To what is asked next, one must reply in accord with the Gloss that God will be all in all because his will will be fulfilled concerning all things or throughout all things.

6. To the objection that in this respect even now he is all in all, one must reply that this is hidden now but then it will be revealed, "and an event is said to occur at the time when it becomes known." And this is Augustine's solution.[536]

It could also be said that now he is not all in all, because iniquitous wills are not now ordered to punishment, as they will be then, although they are ordered toward something else, namely toward proving the virtue of the elect.

534. 1 Cor 15.25. Cf. Ps 109.1.

535. Peter Lombard, *In epist. Pauli* 1 Cor 15.25 (PL 191: 1680A). Cf. Alb., *De res.* tr. 2, q. 10, art. 13 (ed. Colon. 26, p. 302, 59).

536. Aug., *De div. quaest.*, q. 69.4 (PL 40: 75). Albert seems to have taken this from Peter Lombard, *In epist. Pauli* Phil 2.9 (PL 192: 236C); cf. Alb., *De res.* tr. 2, q. 10, art. 13 (ed. Colon. 26, p. 302, 59–62).

TRACTATE THREE

ON RESURRECTION ON THE PART OF THE WICKED ALONE

NEXT, ONE ASKS about the Resurrection on the part of the wicked alone. And one asks first about the [bodily] members of the wicked; second, about the punishments of the wicked in the body; third, about their punishments in the soul; fourth, about their punishments so far as they [that is, body and soul] are conjoined; fifth, about the places of punishment, in which they suffer affliction.

Question 1. On the [bodily] members of the wicked[1]

Concerning the first [question], one asks whether the wicked who are hump-backed here will rise again hump-backed, and whether those who are leprous here [will rise again] leprous.

1. It seems so, because Augustine says in the book *On the City of God* that the wicked will rise again with their deformities.[2] But to be hump-backed or leprous are deformities. Therefore, they will rise again with these.

2. Again, at the resurrection only justice imparts beauty (*decor*), and the impious do not have justice. Therefore, they will not have the beauty of justice.

3. Again, the Apostle says in 1 Cor 15, "We will all rise again, but we will not all be changed."[3] But it is necessary for one

1. Cf. Alb., *IV Sent.* d. 43 a. 24, d. 44 a. 33.

2. Aug., *De civ. dei* 22.20.3 (PL 41: 783; CSEL 40/2: 633, 25–26). Cf. Alb., *De res.* tr. 1, q. 6, art. 7 (ed. Colon. 26, p. 252, 66). Peter Lombard, *IV Sent.* d. 43 c. 7 (p. 999), d. 44 c. 4 (p. 1002).

3. 1 Cor 15.51.

who is hump-backed to be changed if he has to be made non-hump-backed. And so it follows that he will not be changed.

4. After this, one also asks about those who are born without certain members, such as without a hand or a foot or without eyes, whether they ought to rise again in this condition.

It seems so, because if they should rise again with those members, an injustice will be done them because they will be afflicted in those [members] but they did not sin in them.

Solution: We say that the general resurrection will correct two things in nature, namely error and defect—error in the deformity of members (*in monstruositate membrorum*), defect in a body's diminished stature. And for that reason the damned will rise again in the fullness of [the body's] members and the fullness of stature that they had or would have had at thirty years of age if nature had not erred.

1. Therefore, we say to the first that the defects of which Augustine speaks are the body's coarseness and weight and animal nature (*animalitas*) and things of this sort, and not that it is hump-backed and lame.

2. To the next we say that iniquity deserves the actual punishment of fire. But nature exists prior to iniquity. Therefore, iniquity does not impede the correction of nature by means of the resurrection.

3. To the next we say that "to be changed" indicates the reception of a glorious form, and the damned are not changed in this respect. But nothing prevents them from being changed in some respect.

4. To the next we say that although some of the damned may not have had the [bodily] instruments for sinning while they were living, nonetheless they had a will and the powers of the soul, which are the movers of those instruments, and they sinned in these. And for the sake of these powers the members ought to be restored to them, so that they might suffer affliction in them.

Question 2. On the punishments of the wicked in the body[4]

Second, one asks which punishments they will have to endure in the body, whether they will have fevers and blisters and the like.

1. It seems so, because just as the sum total of all joys will exist among the elect, so it seems that the sum total of all punishments ought to exist among the damned, and so it follows that they will have fever.

If perhaps one should say that the elemental qualities in their bodies will not be active and passive (*agentes et patientes*), but that a balanced proportion will exist there that impedes imbalance (*distemperantiam*), it seems that this is false, because a place and what is placed in it have the same nature.[5] But the fire in hell will have an active quality, by means of which it will afflict the reprobate. So it seems to follow as well that the reprobate themselves [will have active and passive elemental qualities].[6]

2. In addition, the division of an element only occurs when it is glorified in a part, as is clear in fire. For the luminous [part] is glorified, and the heat will descend. But an element in the body of the damned is not glorified in any part. Therefore, it seems that the qualities will remain active in the elemental parts of the bodies of the damned.[7]

To the contrary: Everything that is composed from active and passive contraries is subject to dissolution.[8] None of the bodies of the damned is subject to dissolution. Therefore, none of the bodies of the damned is composed from active and passive contraries.

We concede this, asserting that the bodies of the damned are indissoluble from the fact that the contraries in them have

4. Cf. Alb., *IV Sent.* d. 43 a. 25. Alb. refers to this question at *De IV coaequ.* q. 67 a. 5. Cf. Alb., *De res.* tr. 3, q. 3 (ed. Colon. 26, p. 307, 65).

5. Cf. Ar., *De caelo et mundo* 4.3 (310b7ff.). Alb., *De caelo et mundo* 4.2.1; *De nat. loc.* 1.3; *II Sent.* d. 2 a. 3 sed contra 3; *Summa* II q. 12 m. 1.

6. Cf. Alb., *De res.* tr. 2, q. 8, art. 4 (ed. Colon. 26, p. 277, 56ff.).

7. Cf. Alb., *De res.* tr. 2, q. 6; tr. 2, q. 10, art. 3 (ed. Colon. 26, p. 263, 25ff.; p. 292, 81–84).

8. Cf. Ar., *De caelo et mundo* 1.12 (283b20–21). Alb., *De caelo et mundo* 1,4,10.

been restored to an indissoluble balance. And God's justice produces this restoration among the punishments, so that their body can be an everlasting subject of punishments.[9] Therefore, we concede that they will not have fevers and blisters and the like, because these are caused by an imbalance of contraries.

1. To the first, therefore, one must reply that damnation does not take into consideration nature as cause, but [only] merit. And owing to this, it is not necessary that they have those punishments that arise from a defect of the body's nature.

2. To the next, we say that the fire that exists in hell will have an active quality in one sense, and in another sense not. It will not have [an active quality] for generation and corruption, but it will have a burning [quality] that does not consume, only for the purpose of afflicting [bodies]. Likewise, in the bodies of the damned there will exist an elemental quality that does not lead to corruption or consumption, but preserves the passible subject in being (*in esse*) in the midst of punishments.

If anyone wishes, therefore, to summarize the punishments of the bodies of the damned, he will distinguish [among them] in this way: that the punishment of the body is either punishment of the damned or punishment of the sense [faculty]. If it is punishment of the damned, then there is an absence of the four dowries (*dotes*) of the [glorified] body. For they [that is, damned bodies] are passible in contradistinction to an impassible [body], and animal or coarse in contradistinction to spiritual, and dark in contradistinction to luminous, and heavy in contradistinction to agile. The punishment of the sense [faculty], however, is understood in two ways, namely as the cause and as the effect of punishment. As cause, there are two active qualities—cold and heat. In fact, they [that is, those being punished according to sense faculty] will "pass over from the snow waters [to excessive heat]," etc.[10] If [understood] as effect, then there will be weeping and gnashing of teeth:[11] weeping because of the fire, and gnashing of teeth because of the cold.

But then one asks whether cold tempers the heat, and again,

9. Cf. Alb., *De res.* tr. 1, q. 6, art. 7 (ed. Colon. 26, p. 253, 19ff.).
10. Jb 24.19.
11. Cf. Mt 8.12. Alb., *Super Matth.* 8.12.

whether cold exists there in any subject, as heat exists in fire, and again, why the moist and dry, which are also elemental qualities, do not exist there.

To this [question] we say that the one does not temper the other, because one does not act on the other, nor does one suffer from the other. Every increase (*intensio*) and abatement occurs, however, according to the action and passion (*actionem et passionem*) of contraries.[12] Since that act, however, is directed to generation and corruption, the contraries will not have it there, but the action of cold and heat will exist there at the same time, such that neither impedes the other. And it is similar in someone who suffers a tertian fever,[13] for whom cold does not cause the heat to abate, nor does heat cause the cold to abate.

To the next, one must reply that of all the elements, the ignoble will descend to hell, as was said above,[14] and cold will exist in parts of the elements, and heat will exist in other parts, as in a subject.

To the next, one must reply that the moist and the dry are not vigorously active qualities, and for this reason the damned are not said to be afflicted by them vigorously.

Additionally, from what has been said, a solution to a certain [question] that could be asked is clear, namely, whether weeping [there] will produce tears. Since tears are certain discharges of the body, and those bodies will not be subject to discharges, it is necessary that weeping not produce tears. But because weeping is the ultimate sign of grief, their ultimate grief is shown by weeping.

Question 3. On their punishments in the soul

1. Third, one asks about the punishments that they will endure in the soul, concerning which Bernard says in the fifth [book] to [Pope] Eugenius, "Woe to those opposed wills, which actually bring the sole punishment of their aversion upon

12. Cf. Ar., *De caelo et mundo* 2.6 (288b12ff.). Alb., *De caelo et mundo* 2.2.5.

13. Tertian fever: one that recurs periodically, every third day.

14. Cf. Alb., *De res.* tr. 2, q. 5; tr. 2, q. 10, art. 3; tr. 2, q. 10, art. 6 (ed. Colon. 26, p. 263, 25ff.; p. 292, 75ff.; p. 295, 76ff.).

themselves."[15] And from this, one understands that aversion is the sole punishment with respect to the will.

But opposed to this is what the very same Bernard says elsewhere, that the iniquitous will burn in hell.[16]

2. In addition, in the same place Bernard speaks of the will and enumerates other punishments, saying: "What punishment is as great as always to will what never will be? What is so damned as a will that is enslaved to the necessity of willing and nilling so that, whichever way it is moved, it is moved only perversely and only wretchedly? It will not obtain in eternity what it wills, and it will endure in eternity what it does not will."[17]

3. He says the same thing concerning the worm of conscience:[18] "The worm that does not die is the memory of things past. Once introduced, or rather born within through sin, it adheres firmly and can never be plucked out thereafter. Nor does it cease to gnaw on the conscience, and, fed on food that cannot be consumed, it perpetuates [its] life." And according to this, it seems that the punishment of the soul will be twofold, namely the strengthening of the will in wickedness and the strengthening of the worm of conscience.

4. Again, Dionysius says in the fourth chapter of *On the Divine Names,* that a demon's evil is threefold, namely "irrational anger, demented concupiscence, and violent illusion."[19] Since, therefore, the intellectual soul and a demon will be damned in the same ways, it seems then that the soul's punishment also will be threefold.

5. Similarly, one raises a question about what Ezekiel 32 says, that those who fell asleep, having been killed by the sword, were buried in hell with their weapons, and their swords [were laid] under their heads, and their "iniquities were in their bones."[20] Namely, one asks what are called "weapons" there, and what [are called] "swords," and what [are called] "iniquities."

15. Bern., *De consid.* 5.12.25 (PL 182: 802C).

16. Bern., *De gratia et lib. arb.* 9.31 (PL 182: 1018A).

17. Bern., *De consid.* 5.12.25–D (PL 182: 802C).

18. Bern., *De consid.* 5.12.25 (PL 182: 803B). See also Is 66.24 and Mk 9.43, 45, 47.

19. Dion., *De div. nom.* 4 §23 (PG 3: 725B; Dionysiaca 1: 280). Cf. Alb., *Super Dion. De div. nom.* 4, 191–92 (ed. Colon. 37/1, pp. 274–75).

20. Ezek 32.26–27.

6. Again, concerning what is said in the Gospel, that "the rich man died and was buried in hell,"[21] one asks what it means to be buried in hell, and what the tongue and the flame and the cooling drop that he [the rich man] requested[22] are, and what Lazarus's finger is.

7. Next, one asks again about Gregory's statement on that passage in Job,[23] "Whether his children come to honor or dishonor," the impious man (supply, after death) "will not understand,"[24] where Gregory says that the damned will be unaware of the things that are done here concerning their loved ones.[25] But this seems false, because the rich man spoke of his brothers.[26]

8. Similarly, next one asks whether the impious in hell will see the elect.[27] It seems so, because the rich man saw Lazarus.[28]

But this is contrary to what is said in the *Sentences,* namely that the elect will see the damned, but not the reverse.[29]

9. In addition, one asks why what has been fixed between the elect and the damned is called chaos.[30]

10. Besides, one asks about what the Lord says in the Gospel,[31] "Cast him into the outer darkness,"[32] where Augustine says that there is a certain inner darkness.[33] And one asks what these are.

Solution:

1. We say to the first that the aversion of the will is said to be the sole punishment by way of cause, since it is the sole cause of punishment, as blessed Bernard says elsewhere in *On the Song of*

21. Lk 16.22. Cf. Alb., *IV Sent.* d. 50 a. 9.
22. Lk 16.24.
23. Cf. Alb., *IV Sent.* d. 50 a. 7.
24. Jb 14.21.
25. Greg., *Moral.* 12.21.26 (PL 75: 999B). Cf. *Glossa ord. super Job* 14.21.
26. Lk 16.27–28.
27. Cf. Alb., *IV Sent.* d. 50 a. 10.
28. Lk 16.23.
29. Peter Lombard, *IV Sent.* d. 50 c. 5 (p. 1096).
30. Lk 16.26. Cf. Alb., *IV Sent.* d. 50 a. 10.
31. Cf. Alb., *IV Sent.* d. 50 a. 10.
32. Mt 22.13.
33. Aug., *Glossa interl. super Matth.* 22.13. Cf. Greg., *Hom.* 38 *In Ev.* 13 (PL 76: 1290A). Peter Lombard, *IV Sent.* d. 18 c. 8 (p. 865).

Songs: "Remove your own will, and at once hell does not exist."[34]

2. To the next, one must reply that the punishment that blessed Bernard touches on there belongs to the will, insofar as it is the universal mover turning itself to whatever is willed and to the other powers of the soul, because in this way it is immediately strengthened in opposition to justice, so that it never wills what is fitting (neither in itself nor in the other powers), and nonetheless it never arrives at what is pleasing.[35]

3. To the next we say, as he himself[36] says, that the worm of conscience is the worm that never dies.[37] And it exists for the sake of three things: namely, for the evil that has been committed; and for the good that has been omitted; and for the scandal that was caused to little ones by a bad example, because to be scandalized pertains to little ones. And note that sometimes there are said to be many worms, as it is affirmed in Isaiah 14: "The moth will be stretched out under you, and worms will be your covering."[38] And he calls hidden sins emerging from the interior corruption of the tinder (*fomes*) "the moth." And for this reason they are spoken of as "under" and "the moth"—"under" because they are hidden, and "the moth" because they emerge from the interior. He calls public and manifest sins "worms." And they are said to be a "covering" for this reason: a "covering" because they are public, and "worms" because they are born from the putrid matter drawn to the outside, that is, from concupiscence made manifest in deed.

4. They say that those three [demonic evils] that blessed Dionysius enumerates[39] are, in fact, the perverse evil of the soul's two parts in opposition to the triple object of blessedness. For truth, which satisfies the intellect, is the first object of blessedness; the second is the good that is pleasurable,[40] satisfying the

34. Bern., *Sermo 3 temp. resurr.* 3 (PL 183: 290A).

35. Bern., *De consid.* 5.12.25 (PL182: 802D); cf. Alb., *De res.* tr. 3 , q. 3 (ed. Colon. 26, p. 308, 19ff.).

36. That is, Bernard.

37. Cf. Alb., *De sacram.* tr. 6 pars 2 q. 3 a. 4 §2 (ed. Colon. 26, p. 126, 48ff.); *IV Sent.* d. 45 a. 3 sol.

38. Is 14.11. Cf. Alb., *Super Is* 14.11 (ed. Colon. 19, p. 206, 2ff.).

39. See n. 19 above.

40. The *bonum delectabile,* or a good that is pleasant, evokes Aristotle's assertion

will (*affectum*) as far as one part of it [is concerned], namely the concupiscible; the third is what is on high, which is unfailing and powerful, satisfying the will as far as another of its parts is concerned, namely the irascible. And the damned perversely position themselves in opposition to these three [objects]. Contentious illusion (*proterva phantasia*) exists in opposition to truth; to be sure, contentiousness (*protervitas*) is resistance to the truth stemming from a perverse will.[41] And the understanding of one who is damned, and [the understanding] of a demon, is called an illusion on account of the fact that it has been hidden from the first light. How this is so has to be investigated in the "Disputations on Demons."[42] Perversity is a demented concupiscence in opposition to the good that is pleasurable, which satisfies the concupiscible. It is said to be demented because it is not ruled by the mind, and it is called concupiscence because it desires (*concupiscit*) what is illicit because, as blessed Bernard says, it never desires what is appropriate.[43] To be sure, the madness (*furor*) that satisfies the irascible [part] is an irrational perversity that is powerful and unfailing in its opposition to what is lofty. And it is called madness because it rages indignantly against the good, and it is called irrational because it is not ruled by reason. And note that through [the terms] "demented" and "irrational" a privation of reason is posited for the irascible and the concupiscible, because these two powers have to be ordered by reason.[44] Similarly, contentiousness is posited for the rational [power], which indicates the will's lack of order (*inordinationem*) toward reason when moving, with the result that in this way a double corruption is observed in each of these powers: one with respect to the object, which is signified by the name of a corrupt act. For illusion (*phantasia*) is a corrupt act in relation to the truth. Similarly, concupiscence

---

that the will's choice is determined by three things: the good, the useful, and the pleasurable. Cf. *Eth. Nic.* 1103b30ff. Note that Thomas Aquinas also identifies the *bonum delectabile* as the object of the concupiscible part. See *ST* IaIIae q. 30 a. 2 co.

41. Cf. Alb., *De IV coaequ.* q. 67 a. 5.

42. Cf. Alb., *De IV coaequ.* q. 67 a. 5; *II Sent.* d. 7 a. 4.

43. Bern., *De consid.* 5.12.25 (PL 182: 802D).

44. Cf. Alb., *De bono* tr. 1 q. 6 a. 1 (ed. Colon. 28, p. 80, 21ff.).

is a corrupt act in relation to the good that is pleasurable. In the same way, a powerful madness is a corrupt act in relation to what is on high. But the perfect acts in relation to these three [objects of blessedness] are to understand by means of sight (*per speciem*), to love fervently, and to comprehend fully (*feliciter*). But the perversity that exists in these powers, so far as one is related to the other, is known through additions (*per adjectiva*) to these three. For reason is ordered to the will just as one that rules it, yet [it is] moved by itself to act because it deliberates freely apart from the will. But it ought to rule the will in the sense that it [that is, the will] ought to acquiesce to a known truth. And Dionysius indicates the corruption of this order by what he calls "contentiousness," because it struggles against a known truth from the perversity of the will. Similarly, the irascible and concupiscible ought to be ruled by reason, and he designates the corruption of this order as the "demented" and the "irrational."

5. To the question concerning Ezekiel, one must reply that the "weapons," by which justice is impugned, are the wicked struggles that will endure among the damned forever.[45] The "swords," moreover, are nothing but the sinners' acts, with which they slay each other by a bad example, which will abide in its effect, namely in the punishment that corresponds to sin. The "iniquities in the bones," however, are the blemishes of sin in the worst habits that exist in the soul's powers; for the soul's "bones" are the powers of the soul, as Augustine says.[46]

6. To the question concerning the Gospel, one must reply that a sepulcher is a house of death, as is said in the Psalm: "Their sepulchers will be their houses forever."[47] And this sepulcher is nothing but a certain lot or portion of the infernal place, as it were, and of infernal punishments according to the degree (*quantitas*) of [one's] impiety. Augustine calls this a mansion,[48] but according to the Gospel and the Psalm it is

45. Cf. Alb., *II Sent.* d. 5 a. 6 sol.

46. Aug., *Enarr. in Ps.* 6.4 (PL 36: 92).

47. Ps 48.12.

48. Rather, Peter Lombard, *IV Sent.* d. 49 c. 1 (p. 1027); cf. Aug., *Enchir.* 111 (PL 40: 284).

properly called a sepulcher, because a sepulcher is a house for death, and a mansion is a house for life, as will be discussed below in the question on the mansions.[49] To be sure, the tongue of the rich man is nothing other than the power of taste and of speech (*vis gustativa et interpretativa*), each of which was in the tongue, because the tongue's function "consists in two acts," as the Philosopher says.[50] This power was severely tormented, because concerning that rich man one reads more about sins of the tongue, such as ravenousness, and, as Gregory says,[51] loquacity customarily abounds in the midst of ravenousness. The flame is actually the fire's burning heat. Lazarus's finger, however, signifies a very slight support, because the act of indicating (*ostensio*) occurs by means of the finger and assistance [occurs] by means of the hand. In this way it [that is, the finger] signifies the act of indicating assistance, as it is said in Exodus, "This is the finger of God,"[52] that is, an act of indicating divine power. Water, however, signifies the cool refreshment of indulgence that is provided by the saints, and a drop of that water signifies a very little bit of cool refreshment, so that although the punishment associated with sin is not removed, nonetheless it will be mitigated to some degree.[53]

7. To the objection of blessed Gregory on Job, that they [the damned] will have no knowledge of what occurs here, one must reply that what occurs here occurs in two ways: namely, [in one way] there are things that are subject to free will, and, just like the demons, they [that is, the damned] will have no knowledge of those things, because these are known only by means of revelation in the Word, which Word the damned do not contemplate. Things that proceed from the course of nature, however, both the demons and these [that is, the damned] know, because their damnation is not greater than that of the demons. The mode of knowing that will exist in them will be made clear

49. Although Albert makes reference to this question at *De res.* tr. 3, q. 9; tr. 4, q. 1 (ed. Colon. 26, p. 321, 25; 322, 5), it is not found.

50. Ar., *De anima* 2.8 (420b17–18); cf. Alb., *De anima* 2.3.22.

51. Greg., *Hom.* 40 *in Ev.* 5 (PL 76: 1307A).

52. Ex 8.19.

53. Cf. Alb., *De sacram.* tr. 6 pars 2 q. 3 a. 4 §1 (ed. Colon. 26, p. 125, 45).

in what follows, when we will discuss the mode of knowing that will exist after death.[54]

8. To the question whether the wicked will see the elect, one must reply that they will not see their glory, just as Gregory says,[55] because they could see their glory only in the Word shining either in itself or in those having been glorified, which the damned are unable to see.

To the objection that the rich man saw Lazarus and Abraham, one must reply that this was in limbo, before they crossed over to the enjoyment of God.

9. To the question that was raised concerning chaos, one must reply that chaos is said there metaphorically. Indeed, chaos is an impassable abyss and symbolizes the unchangeable nature of the judgment that confirms the just in beatitude and the damned in punishments.[56] The desire among the elect, however, to cross over to the damned is the natural inclination of compassion to provide assistance, if only the unchangeable nature of judgment were not preventing it. The desire among the damned, however, to cross over is a desire to escape punishment simply (*absolute*) considered.

10. To the question concerning the inner darkness, one must reply that the inner darkness is the absence of the light that exists in the vision of God.

Consider, therefore, the punishments of the soul in this way: The soul's punishment is either a punishment of condemnation or of disorder [in the soul] or of sense perception (*sensus*), such that [the punishment] of sense perception may be called the experience of pain. If [the punishment] of condemnation, then it is the inner darkness. If of disorder, either it is a disorder of a power in relation to a power, or of a power in relation to an object, or of a power in relation to an act. Dionysius enumerated the first two modes sufficiently, as was shown above.[57] In the third there are two modes, for the reason that there are two things that cause the disorder (*deordinantia*) of a power in

54. *De res.* tr. 3, q. 4 (ed. Colon. 26, p. 311, 74ff.).
55. Greg., *Hom.* 40 *in Ev.* 2 (PL 76: 1303C).
56. Cf. Greg., *Hom.* 40 *in Ev.* 6 (PL 76: 1308A–B).
57. See *De res.* tr. 3, q. 3 (ed. Colon. 26, p. 307, 17ff.).

relation to an act, namely the tinder (*fomes*) of Original [Sin] and the habit (*habitus*) that remains because of actual [sin]. According to the first mode, the moth and the worm and the like are underneath, as was maintained above.[58] According to the second mode, iniquities are sealed in the bones and the like, which are reduced to this. If, however, it [that is, punishment] is by the experience of pain, then it exists either from an internal or an external agent. If from an internal [agent], then this is the bite of the worm according to its variation established above.[59] If from an external [agent], then this is the experience of heat or cold having been sensed.

Question 4. On the punishments on the part of the conjoined [body and soul]

Fourth, one asks about the punishments on the part of the conjoined [body and soul].

1. And one asks first whether the struggle of the flesh against the spirit will remain in them.

And it seems not, because that [struggle] exists in relation to a future sin. At that time, however, there will be no future sin, because then they will sin no more. Therefore, that struggle should not remain.

To the contrary: that struggle is removed only by grace or by glory, neither of which the damned will possess.

In addition, Augustine says in the book *On the Good of Marriage*[60] that it is the daughter of sin. But the generation of sin is not removed from them, because the generation of sin is only removed by grace.

2. Furthermore, since the acts of the conjoined [body and soul] are also acts of the individual parts, one asks about the acts of the damned not only on the part of the body but also on the part of the soul.[61] On the part of the body, one asks wheth-

58. See *De res.* tr. 3, q. 3 (ed. Colon. 26, p. 307, 69ff.).

59. See *De res.* tr. 3, q. 3 (ed. Colon. 26, p. 307, 65ff.).

60. Rather, Aug., *De nupt. et conc.* 1.24.27 (PL 44: 429; CSEL 42: 240, 4–5). Cf. Aug., *De bono conjugali* 2.2 (PL 40: 374; CSEL 41: 189, 9). Alb., *II Sent.* d. 30 a. 1 sol.

61. Cf. Alb., *De bono* tr. 1 q. 3 a. 1 ad 4,5 (ed. Colon. 28, p. 38, 57–58).

er they [that is, the bodies of the damned] will be moved into different regions of hell from punishment to punishment. To be sure, this passage seems to imply this: "They will pass over from the snow waters," etc.[62]

But the contrary seems to be the case, because they are distinguished in place and in degree of punishments (*quantitate poenarum*) according to [their] merits. Therefore, just as merit is unchangeable (*immobile*), in the same way they seem to be immovable (*immobiles*) according to place.

Moreover, the Lord says in the Gospel that they are cast into the outer darkness, bound by the hands and feet.[63]

If perhaps one should say that they are dragged around by demons, just as the saints say[64] that tormentors hold in [their] punishments those whom instigators hold in [their] faults, this does not seem to be true, because, as was determined above,[65] fire exists equally everywhere in hell, and sin is the reason why they suffer more or less, and this exists equally everywhere. And so it does not seem that there is a reason why they would be moved or dragged here and there.

3. On this basis, one asks what are the chains on the hands and feet of which Bernard speaks in *Sermon 14 on the Song of Songs*:[66] "'Who will give water to my head, and a fountain of tears to my eyes,'[67] so that with tears of weeping I may forestall the gnashing of teeth, and the harsh chains on the hands and feet, and the heavy bonds that oppress, that strangle, that burn and never consume?"

4. Again, one asks about speech, whether they [that is, the damned] will speak to one another. For this seems to be the case according to Isaiah 14: "All who have seen you will turn toward you and behold you,[68] saying, 'You too have been wounded just as we have, and you have become like us.'"[69]

62. Jb 24.19. Cf. Alb., *Super Is* 50.11 (ed. Colon. 19, 502, 24–25; 541, 12–13).

63. Mt 22.13.

64. Cf. Peter Lombard, *IV Sent.* d. 47 c. 5 (p. 1022); Jerome, *In Is* 14.9 (PL 24: 225D).

65. *De sacram.* tr. 6 pars 2 q. 3 a. 4 §1 (ed. Colon. 26, p. 125, 31ff.).

66. Bern., *In Cant. serm.* 16.7 (PL 183: 852B).

67. Jer 9.1.

68. Is 14.16.

69. Is 14.10.

But, on the other hand, it seems that they will not speak, because, as Basil says, "The God who created us granted to us the use of speech for this purpose, so that we might reveal the secrets of the heart to one another through the ministry of the word, and so that from a common inclination of nature in one another each one of us might divulge secret counsels to his neighbor as if from certain private dwelling places."[70] But there no one wills to reveal a secret to another. Therefore, it seems that speech will not exist there.

Moreover, demons have no speech, and [there] humans abide among demons and vice versa.

5. Next one raises a question about their senses, whether at that time they will perceive by receiving [something] within.[71] And if, by chance, not, then an objection arises concerning sight, because they exist in outer darkness. Nonetheless, Isaiah says: "All who have seen you will turn toward you and behold you."[72]

In addition, some sensations (*sensus*) occur through an external medium, others through an internal medium, and those that occur through an external medium have air or water as a medium.[73] At that time, however, the air will be glorified, and a glorified body does not undergo change. From there, one proceeds in this way: Every sensation (*sensus*) that occurs through an external medium occurs by means of a change in the medium. No medium that can be changed will exist at that time. Therefore, there will be no sensation through an external medium.

In addition, sound occurs from air striking against a solid surface, and this seems consistent only with air that is subject to alteration (*passibili*) and change.[74]

Likewise, odor arises only from a mediating evaporative dry-

70. Basil, *Hom. In Dt* 15.9.1; Rufinus's transl. (PG 31: 1733D–1734A).

71. Sight or vision provides the best known case, and often debated was the question "utrum visus fiat intus suscipiendo?"—whether vision occurs because something is received into the eye. Cf. Roger Marston, in *Quodlibeta quatuor: Ad fidem codicum nunc primum edita,* quod. 1, q. 19, ed. Gerard I. Etzkorn and Ignatius C. Brady (Grottaferrata: Collegio S. Bonaventura, 1994), p. 56. Albert considers sight and hearing under this same rubric. See *Top.* 1.4.2 (ed. Borgnet 2, p. 278a).

72. Is 14.16.

73. Cf. Alb., *De homine* q. 34 a. 4 (ed. Colon. 27/2, p. 265).

74. Cf. Ar., *De anima* 2.8 (416b9ff.). Alb., *De anima* 2.3.17.

ness. Every such evaporation, however, occurs with some disintegration of bodies, but at that time no body will be subject to disintegration.[75] Therefore, there will be no odor, and so it follows that there will not be the sense of smell.

What the saints say seems to run contrary to this,[76] namely that the foul odor of dead bodies rises up to their noses, as it is said in Isaiah 14: "But you, as if a useless branch, have been cast out of your grave, just like one polluted and covered with bloody pus."[77]

Similarly, there is an objection concerning the two senses (*sensus*) that arise through an internal medium. And the first concerns taste, which is a "sort of touch" as the Philosopher says,[78] and whether it will exist there.

It seems so. For blessed Bernard says in the place mentioned previously: "My mother, woe to me that you have given birth to me, a man of sorrows, a child of eternal bitterness."[79] But bitterness is perceived by taste.

To the contrary: taste serves the nutritive [power]. And nourishment will not exist there. Therefore, neither will taste exist there in act.

One asks about touch in a similar way, whether it will occur [at that time] by receiving [something] within, as some assert.[80]

It seems not. For when a surpassing sensible is received into [sense], a change (*passio*) [to the sense faculty] occurs to a greater extent,[81] and every such [change] detracts from [its] substance, as is said in the sixth book of the *Topics*.[82] Therefore, there would be a destruction of substance, which is false, because in this way the corruption and disintegration of bodies would occur.[83]

In addition, the measure (*modus*) of the punishments will be

75. Cf. Ar., *De sensu et sens.* 5 (442b27ff.). Alb., *De sensu et sens.* 1.2.9–10 (ed. Colon. 7/2, pp. 80–83).

76. Cf. *Glossa ord. super Is.* 30.33; *Glossa ord. super Rv* 14.10.

77. Is 14.19. But cf. Alb., *Super Is.* 14.19 (ed. Colon. 19, p. 209, 28–29).

78. Ar., *De anima* 3.12 (434b18); 2.10 (422a8); Alb., *De animal.* 1.2.10.235, 249 (*SZ* 1: 134, 139). But cf. *De animal.* 1.3.1.516 (*SZ* 1: 243).

79. Bern., *In Cant. serm.* 16.7 (PL 183: 852B).

80. "Some": see Alb., *De anima* 2.3.31; Ar., *De anima* 2.11 (422b22–23).

81. Alb., *De anima* 2.4.9, p. 161, 38ff.

82. See *De sacram.* tr. 6, pars 2, q. 3, art. 1, §5, 1 (ed. Colon. 26, p. 113, 48).

83. Cf. Alb., *De animal.* 20.1.5.23 (SZ 2: 1370).

in accordance with the proportion of the sin. But sin either does not exist in the body, or it exists in the body through the soul, such that the body is an instrument, as it were. Therefore, by the same reasoning, infernal punishment, which is punishment for sin, will exist in the body from the soul. Hence, one proceeds in this way: Every change (*passio*) caused by the senses receiving [something] within is a change that occurs in the soul from the body. No infernal punishment is a change that occurs in the soul from the body. Therefore, no infernal punishment occurs from a sense [faculty] receiving [something] within.

Furthermore, a sense [faculty] that receives [something] within is worn out by sensing, and so it requires rest through sleep. Proof of this is taken from the eleventh book of the *Metaphysics*,[84] where it is said of the First Intellect: "And first, if it does not understand, but is a potency, it is necessary that the pursuit of understanding cause weariness in it." On account of this, it is maintained that every passive potency—being at first in potency, later in act—is exhausted by the pursuit of act and requires rest. And so it seems that those who are in hell do not perceive by receiving [something] within either according to touch or according to another sense.

6. One asks further concerning imagination (*phantasia*) whether it will exist in act. For if imagination is "a change (*motus*) produced by sense according to act," as the Philosopher says in the second book of *On the Soul*,[85] and [in hell] there will be no reception [of anything] into sense according to act, it seems that no change in imagination will occur.

7. Additionally, one asks concerning the intellect whether it will exist then by abstracting from a phantasm, just as it does now. If so, then it will be necessary to posit powers that perform abstraction, receiving something internally just like sense and other [powers], which was disproved above.[86]

Moreover, the souls of the damned know in the same way that demons do, and demons do not know by abstraction. Therefore, neither do the souls of the damned.

84. Ar., *Metaph.* 12.9 (1074b28–29).
85. Ar., *De anima* 3.3 (429a1–2); cf. Alb., *De anima* 3.1.9.
86. See *De res.* tr. 3, q. 4 (ed. Colon. 26, p. 310, 30ff.).

8. In addition, one asks about inhalation and exhalation. Indeed, it seems that these should not occur in the future, because they occur now in order to mitigate the heat in the chest,[87] lest an animal suffocate, which will not be necessary at that time because the animal[88] cannot be suffocated [then].

Solution:

1. To the foregoing objections one must reply, without offense (*sine praeiudicio*),[89] that the struggle of the flesh against the spirit will remain in the damned, such that by "the flesh" one may understand, according to Augustine's exposition,[90] the inferior part of the soul inordinately desiring (*concupiscens*) in the flesh, and it drags down the mind, which is united to an innate moral consciousness (*synderesis*). And this is understood from Bernard's statement noted above, in the fifth [book] to [Pope] Eugenius, that "it will not obtain in eternity what it wills, and it will endure in eternity what it does not will."[91] But it [that is, the struggle] will not remain for the purpose of sinning, but in order that the struggle's opposition might cause a multiplication of punishments, with respect to which Job says: "O keeper of men, why have you set me in opposition to yourself, and I have become a burden to myself?"[92]

2. Concerning the question about local motion, I say without offense that those who exist in hell will be immovable; that is, they will not be moved according to place, as was proved. But they will be moved locally into hell from the place of judgment.

And concerning the objection based on the words of Job,[93] I say that that passing over is understood according to the vicissitudes of punishments.

And concerning the objection regarding demons, that they

87. Cf. Ar., *De anima* 2.8 (420b22ff.); Alb., *De anima* 2.3.22; *Quaest. super de animal.* 1, q. 4 (ed. Colon. 12, p. 81f.; *QDA*, pp. 21–22).

88. Namely, the damned human.

89. *Sine praeiudicio:* "without offense"; perhaps Albert intends this as shorthand for the not uncommon expression *sine praeiudicio melioris sententie,* "while remaining open to a better opinion."

90. Aug., *Enarr. in Ps.* 145, 5 (PL 37: 1887).

91. See *De res.* tr. 3, q. 3 (ed. Colon. 26, p. 307, 7–8).

92. Jb 7.20.

93. Namely, Jb 24.19, quoted in objection 2 above.

are tormentors, I say that this is understood as pertaining to [their] reviling [those who are damned].

3. To the question about the bonds, one must reply that the indissoluble fetter of punishment for fault is understood from the weight of the chains, drawing power from divine assistance. Moreover, from the fact that they are said to be bound by [their] hands and feet, one understands the lack of power to flee by means of the feet and the lack of power to defend [themselves] by means of the hands.

4. To the objection concerning speech, there is a twofold response. For it can be said that speech will exist there, not in order to disclose the hidden counsels of the heart, but insofar as one reviles another and laments over himself. In another way it could be said that vocalized speech will not exist there, because that cannot occur without drawing in and exhaling air, but a spiritual speech will exist there, insofar as angels and demons and souls that have departed the body speak to themselves. How that occurs has to be determined in the question on the speech of spirits and angels.[94]

5. To the question concerning the senses, we say that if some kind of sight will exist there, I concede that it will not perceive by receiving [something] within, on account of the arguments presented.

Concerning the sense of smell and taste, however, I say that there is no doubt that they will not exist there according to act.

But if one should ask me how sense perceptions will exist there, I respond that there is one path for receiving knowledge (*cognitio*) before death, and another after. Before death, knowledge is received from sense and ascends through the imagination (*per phantasiam*) to the intellect, whereas after death it will be the reverse, and sensible knowledge will descend from the intelligible. And according to this mode, all the senses of the wicked will perceive the appearance (*species*) of a contrary that is afflicting it. And in this sense the objection is true, that just as sin exists in the body from the soul, so too does punishment. How that happens will be made clear below where

94. Cf. Alb., *De IV coaequ.* q. 60.

the knowledge (*cognitio*) belonging to the elect is discussed.[95] And I say that sensations (*sensus*) exist in these acts, [but] not according to any things received from outside. And according to this mode [of sensation], there will exist [there] taste in the presence of bitterness, and the sense of smell in the presence of what is foul, and sight in the presence of horrible ugliness, and hearing in the presence of doleful sound, and touch in the presence of the cold and the hot.

If someone should say, however, that it would be unfitting for a knowable type (*species cognoscibilis*) of something harmful to descend from higher into lower powers, one must reply that this is not unfitting according to the philosophers,[96] because a superior power (*potentia*) readily moves an inferior one, as is clear in the phantasms of dreams, which move the bodily instruments to terrors and pleasures according to different types of dreams.

From this a solution to all the objections concerning the senses is clear.

If perhaps one objects that, according to this view, infernal punishments will be dream-like visions and not real punishments—for in a dream, someone is affected by an image (*idolum*) just as [he would be] by the reality (*res*),[97] and therefore movement follows in the body, yet it is deceiving because the reality is not there—one must reply that if there is only a fictive image in sensible knowledge and imagination, then the objection will be valid, because this is how it is in a dream. But we say that the true reality (*veritas rei*) exists there. But nonetheless the image is not confined within the bounds of that true reality that stands outside in front of sense perception (*ante sensum*), as happens here [and] now when we are awake, but it is confined within the bounds of the true reality that exists in the intellect. Indeed, the intellect receives the true realities. And this is what

95. See *De res.* tr. 4, q. 2, art. 4 (ed. Colon. 26, pp. 342–44).

96. Ar., *De insomniis* 2 (460b11–13), ed. Drosssart Lulofs p. 18, 1–3; Alb., *De somno et vig.* 2.1.7; cf. Alb., *De incarn.* 4, q. 2 a.3 (ed. Colon. 26, p. 209, 27); *De res.* tr. 2, q. 8, art. 6, §1 (ed. Colon. 26, p. 279, 33ff.).

97. Cf. Ar., *De somno et vig.* 2.3 (462a29–31), ed. Drosssart Lulofs p. 30, 4–6, and 3.2 (464b8–9), p. 46, 4–5; Alb., *De somno et vig.* 2.2.4, 3.2.9; *De homine* q. 46 (ed. Colon. 27/2, p. 371).

Gregory said above,[98] that what it means for them to burn in fire is that they see fire.

6. To the objection concerning imagination, that is, mental images, a solution is already apparent, because mental images will exist there, but not insofar as there is movement produced from sense perception, but insofar as there is movement downward from the intellect.

7. To the question concerning the intellect, one must reply that they will not have an intellect, as they do now, that receives [an impression] from a phantasm, but they will have an intellect filled with ideal forms created for it at the same time. Through these forms they understand whatever they understand. And this question will be determined more fully below.[99]

8. To the last question concerning respiration, it can be resolved in two ways. In fact, respiration exists for two reasons: one is for the mitigation of heat in the chest, and it will not exist for this purpose, as the objection proves. Another is so that the source for the sound of the voice (*materia vocis*) will exist in the vocal instruments. And if we posit vocalized sound there, it is necessary to posit there the source of sound in respiration. If, however, one should say that there will be no vocalized sound there, then it is not necessary to posit respiration; rather, by means of natural spirits the soul will vivify the body conjoined to it, and it will not need inhalation and respiration.

On the Places of Punishment, where Souls are Afflicted

Fifth, one asks about the places of punishment where souls are afflicted. And first, one asks about hell; second, about purgatory; and third, about the limbo of infants; fourth, about the limbo of the fathers; fifth, about all of these [places] generally.

Question 5. On hell

To the first, one proceeds by dividing it in this way, so that first one asks whether hell is a physical place; second, where it is; third, about the punishments that exist in it; [and] fourth, whether those punishments exist in time or in eternity.

98. *De res.* tr. 2, q. 10, art. 5 (ed. Colon. 26, p. 294, 46).
99. *De res.* tr. 4, q. 2, art. 4, §2 (ed. Colon. 26, p. 344, 46).

Art. 1. Whether hell is a physical place (*locus corporeus*)[100]

To the first, one proceeds in this way:

1. A place for a body is a physical place. Souls and demons, however, are not bodies. Therefore, they are not contained in physical places. Therefore, etc.

2. Also, the fire that is in hell is not physical (*corporeus*), as Damascene says, "but God certainly knows what kind it is."[101] If, therefore, what is put [in hell] is not corporeal, the place will also be incorporeal.

3. In addition, demons are always in hell and in the midst of infernal punishments, as 2 Peter chapter 2 says: "[God] delivered them, drawn down by infernal ropes to the lower hell, into torments to be reserved for the Day of Judgment."[102] And yet demons are here with us [now]. Since, therefore, our place here is not hell, and there is not another physical place here, it is necessarily the case that their hell is not a physical place.

To the contrary, Augustine says: "If anyone thinks that souls separated from bodies are contained in physical places, even though they have no body, there will be no shortage of people who agree [with this view]."[103]

Also, Gregory asserts this explicitly in the *Dialogue*.[104]

We concede what they affirm, that hell is a physical place.

1. To the first [objection], which is opposed to this, we say that something is contained in a place in two ways, namely circumscriptively (*circumscriptive*), which is to assign a beginning and a middle and an end [to the thing] in a place according to [different] parts of the place, and in this way only a body exists in a place.[105] In another way, something is contained in a place demonstratively (*definitive*), namely, when something exists where its acting or being acted upon (*operatio eius vel passio*)—

100. Cf, Alb., *IV Sent.* d. 44 a. 38.

101. John Damascene, *De fide ortho.* 4.27 (PG 94: 1228A; ed. Buytaert, p. 385, 145–46); cf. *De res.* tr. 2, q. 10, art. 2 (ed. Colon. 26, p. 290, 37).

102. 2 Pt 2.4 and 9.

103. Aug., *De gen. ad litt.* 8.5.9 (PL 34: 376; CSEL 28/1, p. 237, 8–11). Cf. Peter Lombard, *IV Sent.* d. 50 c. 4 (p. 1036).

104. Greg., *Dial.* 4.28ff. (PL 27: 365ff.).

105. Cf. *De res.* tr. 4, q. 1 (ed. Colon. 26, p. 328, 75); Alb., *Phys.* 4.1.1; John Damascene, *De fide ortho.* 1.13 (PG 94: 852ff.; ed. Buytaert, p. 56ff.).

which is restricted to a body—exists, and in this way a spiritual substance exists in a place where it acts upon a body or is acted upon by a body. And in this way souls and demons are in hell.

2. To the next, one must reply that the fire that afflicts souls and demons, to the extent that it is unmediated, is incorporeal. What kind [of fire] it is was determined above in the question on the renewal of the world.[106]

3. To the third, one must reply that there is a twofold hell: interior and exterior. The interior one is nothing other than the punishment that holds the damned [in bondage], wherever they may be. And demons are in this hell when they are here with us. The exterior one, however, is a physical place, in which they do not exist when they are here with us, but they will be there after Judgment Day. And those [demons] delivered to the interior hell are reserved for torment until the Day of Judgment.[107]

Art. 2. Where hell is

To the second [article], one proceeds in this way:

Isaiah 14 says, "Hell below was in an uproar."[108] The Gloss there [says]: "the place for punishments." Therefore, hell is under the earth.

Similarly, Isidore [says] in the book *On Creatures:* "After Judgment [Day] the sun will receive the reward for its labor. Therefore, the prophet [says], 'It will shine sevenfold,'[109] and neither the sun nor the moon will come to set, but rather they will stay in the order in which they were created, lest the impious placed under the earth in torments enjoy their light."[110] Therefore, hell is under the earth.

Likewise, Job 17 [says]: "All that I have will go down into the deepest hell."[111] Gregory's gloss[112] on that passage [says] that

106. Cf. Alb., *De IV coaequ.* q. 67 a. 6 sol.

107. Cf. Alb., *IV Sent.* d. 44 a. 38, d. 48 a. 11–12.

108. Is 14.9.

109. Cf. Is 30.26.

110. See Peter Lombard, *IV Sent.* d. 48 c. 5 (p. 1026). Cf. Isid., *De ord. creat.* c. 5, 6.7 (PL 83: 924Cf.). Alb., *IV Sent.* d. 44 a. 38.

111. Jb 17.16.

112. Cf. Greg., *Moral.* 13.48.53 (PL 75: 1040BC); *Dial.* 4.42 (PL 77: 400CD).

the upper air is hell, and our [earthly] dwelling place is the deeper hell, and purgatory or limbo is the deepest. Since, then, limbo is under the earth, much more so will hell be under the earth.

1. To the contrary: The Lord's judgment exists for the purpose of ordering whatever is disordered. Therefore, how much more will he perfect that order in which he created creatures. But he created fire so that it would rise up. Therefore, at that time he will not make it descend down below. But hell is where there is corporeal fire. Therefore, hell will not be down below.

2. Similarly, the beauty of justice is such that the punishment for iniquity appears where the iniquity has been perpetrated, just as Elijah said to Ahab that where he slew Naboth, an Israelite citizen, dogs would lick his blood in that same place.[113] And it is also apparent in cities[114] that crimes are punished in the same place where they were committed. Therefore, it seems that the hell of the damned ought to be on earth, where they committed [their] sin.

Solution: We say that hell is in the heart of the earth, just as the holy fathers say.[115]

1. To the objection to the contrary, we say that fire exists for a twofold purpose, namely for generation and corruption, and in this way it exists up above. But it is also an instrument of retributive justice (*iustitiae vindicantis*), as was said above,[116] and in this way it will descend to the place of wickedness, where retribution is administered. For just as at creation God separated by the greatest distance what is most ignoble as regards the generation of bodies from what is noble by setting the earth in the deepest place and heaven in the highest place, so too at the Last Judgment he will separate by the greatest distance what is most ignoble as regards the rational creature from what is most noble; that is, [he will separate] the damned from the saved. Since, therefore, the saved will be in heaven, it is necessary that the damned be in the deepest place of the earth.

113. Cf. 1 Kgs 21.18–19.
114. In contrast to the countryside in which the vineyard of Naboth stood.
115. Cf. Greg., *Dial.* 4.42 (PL 77: 401A). *Glossa interl.* On Jon 2.4.
116. *De res.* tr. 2, q. 10, art. 5 (ed. Colon. 26, p. 295, 22–32).

2. To the next, we say that the judgment of a city sequesters the condemned in an unclean place, which nevertheless is within that city's jurisdiction and is visible to all passersby, so that justice will be praised when their punishment is seen. Likewise, at the Last Judgment the Lord will separate evildoers in the unclean place of hell, where their punishment will be apparent to all of the elect, so that they might glory in the justice of God. And this is what is said at the end of Isaiah, "And they will go out,"[117] namely the elect will go out by steps of contemplation, "and see the carcasses of the men who have transgressed against me. Their worm will not die, and their fire will not be extinguished, and they will be a loathsome sight to all flesh," that is, to the elect, who, the Gloss says, are called there "all flesh."[118]

Art. 3. On the punishments that exist in hell[119]

To the third [article], one proceeds in this way:

The Lord commands that the damned be cast out into outer darkness.[120] And one asks the reason why there is an outer darkness in hell.

Likewise, [one asks] whether it is called this from a privation of spiritual and corporeal light, or whether there is another reason altogether. Actually, it seems that there will be corporeal light there, since it is said in Isaiah[121] that the damned saw Nebuchadnezzar in hell,[122] and corporeal sight occurs with light as a medium.

Similarly, one asks about what the Lord says, that the adversary will deliver the damned into prison, and prison is the name of a horrible place.[123]

To these [queries] and others like them we respond that in the place called hell there is a threefold punishment beyond

117. Is 66.24.

118. Cf. Alb., *Super Is.* 66.24 (ed. Colon. 19, p. 632, 84–85).

119. Cf. Alb., *IV Sent.* d. 50 a. 4.

120. Cf. Mt 22.13; 25.30.

121. Cf. Is 14.9.

122. Cf. Alb., *Super Is.* 14.9 (ed. Colon. 19, p. 205, 40ff.); Jerome, *In Is.* 14.9 (PL 24: 225Cff.).

123. Cf. Lk 12.58.

those [punishments] enumerated above;[124] and [we respond] that, apart from the interior hell, the exterior hell has these three punishments, namely [1] a darkness that is the absence of both [spiritual and corporeal] light, and [2] an abhorrence for the place because that place is an abyss into which the excrement of all creatures descends at the renewal of the world, and [3] the stench of the [evil] community.

And to the objection to the contrary, one must reply that that sight [in the outer darkness of hell] will have a different basis from this one [that is, sight in this present life]. For it will descend from the intellect, as was said above.[125] And for this reason it will not need external corporeal light.

Art. 4. Whether infernal punishments exist in time or in eternity[126]

Finally, one asks whether infernal punishments exist in time or in eternity.

1. It seems that they do not exist in time, because Augustine says that what [once] existed in time is not [now], and what will exist is not yet.[127] But among the damned nothing crosses over into the past because nothing is cast off, and nothing is awaited in the future because punishments always exist in the same way, and none of such as these exists in time. Therefore, these punishments are not in time.

2. Moreover, what will have no end is perpetual, and these punishments will have no end. Therefore, they will not exist in time but rather in perpetuity, because time is the measure of things that have an end and a beginning.

3. In addition, Dionysius says in a chapter on the everlasting (*de aevo*) and on time that time is what is measured by generation and corruption.[128] But there will be no generation and corruption there. Therefore, the measure of time will not exist there.

124. *De res.* tr. 3, q. 2; tr. 3, q. 3; tr. 3, q. 4 (ed. Colon. 26, p. 306, 38ff., p. 309, 33ff., p. 311, 27ff.).

125. *De res.* tr. 3, q. 4 (ed. Colon. 26, p. 311, 78ff.).

126. Cf. Alb., *IV Sent.* d. 46 a. 7.

127. Aug., *Conf.* 11.15.18 (PL 32: 816; CSEL 32, p. 292, 27f.).

128. Dion., *De div. nom.* c. 10 §3 (PG 3: 937CD; *Dionysiaca* I, 490–91), transl. Sarr. Cf. Alb., *Super Dion. De div. nom.* 10, 16–17 (ed. Colon. 37/1, pp. 407–9).

But to the contrary, it is said in the Psalm, "their time will be forever."[129]

4. Besides, Boethius says, "eternity is the possession of unending life all at once."[130] Therefore, if they existed in eternity, they would have the possession of life, which is false. In fact, they have the possession of death.

Solution: We say that these punishments will be temporal.

1. To the first, which contradicts this, we say that there is nothing past and nothing future with regard to the substance of the damned. But their pain does not exist all at once according to duration, although it will exist all at once with respect to intensity. To be sure, a part of the duration [in time] passes by, and a part exists in the future. And according to this argument, it encompasses both past and future.

2. To the next we say that the time that has an end refers to the time that is the measure of the motion of the First Movable (*primi mobilis*),[131] and not to the time that is the measure of the punishments of hell.

3. To the next we say that generation and corruption are understood there in a broad sense to refer to unqualified generation and qualified generation, and likewise for corruption. And thus it includes every change that changes something in a subject, and so it also includes the change that exists in the vicissitude of hell's punishments.

But it still seems that they exist in eternity, because it is said in the Psalm that "their sepulchers will be their houses forever."[132] And blessed Bernard says [of the damned person] that "he will not obtain in eternity what he wills, and he will endure in eternity what he does not will."[133]

Likewise, it is the common way of speaking to say that their damnation is eternal.

To this we say that the punishments are temporal so far as

129. Ps 80.16.

130. Boethius, *De cons. phil.* 5, prose 6 (PL 63: 858A; CSEL 67, p. 122, 12–13).

131. The First Movable is the most distant heavenly body or sphere through which all local movement begins.

132. Ps 48.12.

133. Bern., *De consid.* 5.12.25 (PL 182: 802CD); cf. *De res.* tr. 3, q. 3 (ed. Colon. 26, p. 307, 7–8).

concerns the measure [of time], but they are perpetual so far as concerns duration relative to an end.

4. To the objection that "eternity is the possession of unending life," etc., one must reply that this definition was given for eternity insofar as it exists in an eternal subject. And with regard to this definition, the punishments of the damned are not eternal; but they are in this regard: that they share with eternity the fact that they have no end.

Question 6. On purgatory

Next, one asks about purgatory. And two questions are asked: namely, where it is and what its punishments are.[134]

Art. 1. Where Purgatory is

To the first [article], one proceeds in this way:

It was maintained above that the souls' abodes are physical places.[135] But in the *Dialogue,* Gregory speaks of some that are purged here.[136] According to this it seems that purgatory is here.

Again, it is written in the *Life of Blessed Patrick* that he obtained for his own [people] that they might enter a certain place at the borders of Ireland in order to be purged there.[137]

Next, one again asks whether purgatory is a perpetual place or one that is temporary.[138]

Solution: We say that purgatory is a place next to hell and is the upper part of hell. And concerning the objections based on Gregory and Patrick, [we say that] this[139] was done by [special] dispensation for the sake of their correction.

To the question whether it is perpetual or not, we say that it is not. In fact, no purgation is perpetual, but rather it will last until the Day of Judgment.

134. Cf. Alb., *IV Sent.* d. 20 a. 6.

135. *De res.* tr. 3, q. 5 , art. 1 (ed. Colon. 26, p. 312, 81ff.).

136. Greg., *Dial.* 4.40 (PL 77: 397AB).

137. See *Acta Sanct. Mart.* (vol. 2, p. 587ff., Mart. 17). Bonaventure, *IV Sent.* d. 20 a. 1 q. 6, *Opera* 4: 526b.

138. Cf. Alb., *IV Sent.* d. 20 a. 7.

139. Namely, that certain people are purged here on earth, whether at the borders of Ireland or elsewhere.

Art. 2. On its punishments

Concerning the second [article] three questions are raised: First, one asks what the matter (*materia*) for the punishments of purgatory is. Second, [one asks] about the punishments. Third, [one asks] about the intensity of the punishments.

§1. What the matter for the punishments of purgatory is

To the first, one proceeds in this way:[140]

1. Master Hugh of St. Victor says, "The dross of sins is consumed by the fire (*incendium*) of purgatory."[141] It seems, then, that sin is the matter of purgatory. Therefore, one asks which sin, whether any sin whatsoever or some particular sin. But not any sin whatsoever, because mortal sin is consumed in Gehenna. Therefore, some particular sin [is the matter of purgatory].

2. And the Apostle appears to say in 1 Cor 3 that wood, hay, and stubble burn in purgatory.[142] But then one asks what should be called wood, hay, and stubble. If it is any venial [sin] whatsoever, this is false, because this [category of sin] has a greater diversity (*est maioris distinctionis*) than three categories.[143]

In addition, one asks what it means to build upon wood, hay, and stubble.[144] Venial sin, in fact, is customarily called wood, hay, and stubble. And Augustine says he builds upon such things "who reflects on the things of the world and how he might please the world, who is bound by a certain carnal affection to his wealth and nevertheless gives many alms from it and does not undertake any fraud or theft for its sake."[145] And on this basis there seems to be only one distinguishing feature (*differentia*) of [venial] sin, namely cupidity. And so he [that is, the Apostle Paul] should not have said "wood, hay, and stubble."

140. Cf. Alb., *IV Sent.* d. 21 a. 1–3.

141. Rather, Richard of St. Victor, *De potest. lig. et solv.* c. 25 (PL 196: 1177A). Cf. Bonaventure, *IV Sent.* d. 21 a. 2 q. 1, *Opera* 4: 552, where this is attributed to Hugh of St. Victor.

142. 1 Cor 3.12.

143. *trimembris:* three categories; a reference, presumably, to the wood, hay, and stubble mentioned in 1 Cor 3.12.

144. 1 Cor 3.12.

145. Aug., *De fide et operibus* 16.27 (PL 40: 215). Alb. seems to have taken this passage from Peter Lombard, *IV Sent.* d. 21 c. 5 (p. 882).

Moreover, it is customary to draw a threefold distinction concerning venial sin,[146] namely with respect to genus, to cause, and to a specific case (*casus*): with respect to genus, such as idleness, because all idleness is a venial sin; with respect to cause, such as a sin of ignorance or weakness or piety, which has a cause for forgiveness attached to it, such as the midwife's sin which resulted from piety;[147] [and] from a specific case, such as when a mortal sin becomes venial[148] through penance. Therefore, one asks whether these three may be signified by the three things the Apostle mentions. And it seems not, because on the basis of the cause a venial [sin] often is mortal, and so will be consumed in hell, not in purgatory. Likewise, Augustine says of the venial in general that "there is no [sin] so venial that it cannot become mortal when it pleases." And when it becomes mortal, it will burn in hell.

3. After this, one asks to whom it pertains to build [with wood, hay, and stubble]. Actually, Augustine says that the perfect do not build with wood, hay, or stubble, but with gold, silver, and precious stones, and he calls the perfect "contemplatives." Therefore, contemplatives will not enter purgatory.

Moreover, if the desires for earthly things are called wood, hay, and stubble, as Augustine says, it seems that those who are poor in spirit, since they have left all [earthly] things behind, will not be punished in purgatory.

4. If perhaps this is conceded, the opposite seems to be the case, because it is possible that ones like this will depart [from the world] with a venial [sin] such as idleness or some carnal pleasure. And no one enters the kingdom unless he has been purged. Therefore, it is necessary for them to be purged after death.

5. In addition, since there is the sin of fornication and of pride and of envy, etc., why does Augustine make a distinction regarding the cupidity of avarice rather than regarding the cupidity of other sins?

146. Cf. Alb., *II Sent.* d. 22 a. 4 ad 2; *IV Sent.* d. 17 a. 55 sol.; *Summa* II q. 114 m. 4 a. 2 sol.

147. See Ex 1.15–19.

148. *veniale:* subject to forgiveness.

6. Again, one asks about the solution of certain people who say that wood, hay, and stubble denote a lesser, a greater, and a moderate attachment (*adhaerentia*);[149] for it seems that there are many desires (*cupiditates*) between the moderate and the smallest, and likewise between the moderate and the greatest.

7. In addition, virtue exists in the middle, whereas sin exists in excesses, and so it seems that no distinction exists between the moderate and the excesses of cupidity.

8. Again, to desire what should not be desired is an act of excess, and every sin of cupidity, no matter how small, possesses that [act]. Therefore, every sin of cupidity exists in excess, and none exists in its opposite (*in minimo*).

Solution:

1. We say that Master Hugh speaks the truth, that venial sin, with respect to genus or to a specific case (*casu*), is consumed in purgatory.

2. To the authority of the Apostle we say, with Augustine, that desires (*cupiditates*) for earthly things are called wood, hay, and stubble. And the basis for this statement is the greater or lesser resistance of venial sin itself to fire. For wood is more resistant to fire than hay, and hay is more resistant than stubble. Again, a greater desire is more resistant to fire and is not purged as quickly as a moderate or lesser one.

6. And to the objection that more than one [desire] exists between the extremes, we say, as is said in the *Ethics*,[150] that what is thought to be very close to the moderate [desire] is in the middle; likewise, what is thought to be very close to excess is in excess.[151]

7. To the objection that virtue exists in the middle, etc., we say that this distinction among the excesses and the moderate and a lack does not apply as it does for virtue or for sin, but this distinction applies to the manner of desiring that which has to be desired on account of the necessity of this [present] life.

8. And from this, the following [objection] is solved, because,

149. "Certain people": cf. Peter Lombard, *In epist. Pauli* 1 Cor 3.12 (PL 191: 1557C).

150. Ar., *Eth. Nic.* 2.9 (1109b18–19). Cf. Alb., *De bono* tr. 1, q. 5 a. 1 (ed. Colon. 28, p. 75, 34–36).

151. The numbering here reflects the numbering in the printed edition.

although to desire what should not be desired will always exist in [an act of] excess, nonetheless to desire what is permitted can have three degrees with respect to the manner of desiring.

5. To the question why it [that is, cupidity] is distinguished with respect to avarice rather than with respect to another [sin], we say that it can be distinguished with respect to any [sin] but to a greater extent with respect to this one, since it clings [to it] more according to the necessity of this [present] age.

3. To what is asked concerning to whom it pertains to build this, one must distinguish between the state [of life] and the person. For if the state is considered, because those who are active [in the world] have to think about the things that are of the world (owing to the many cares that the world imposes), they build with wood, hay, and stubble. But those who are contemplative, because they only have to think about what pertains to God, build with gold, silver, and precious stones—with gold while contemplating, with silver while meditating, and with precious stones while praying; or, with gold in purity of heart, with silver in usefulness of speech, and with precious stones in integrity of action. Or, according to Augustine, contemplation of God is understood by gold, love of neighbor by silver, and good works by precious stones. If only persons are considered, however, then some active [persons] build with gold, silver, etc., and some contemplatives with wood, hay, and stubble.

4. To the objection that some contemplative may depart [from the world] in venial [sin] we say that this is the least [sin] and has no notable resistance to fire, and on account of this it cannot be called wood, hay, or stubble. Know, too, that these are built on a foundation, and the foundation is formed faith. Gold, silver, precious stones, and others are built up directly, however, and just as things immovable are. But wood, hay, and stubble [are built up] indirectly, namely just like those things that are rendered subject to destruction by virtue of their foundation, apart from which they would be indestructible. Actually, venial sin that is united to mortal sin is not destroyed for eternity in hell.

Nevertheless, some say[152] that when the Apostle says, "If any-

152. "Some": see Alex. Hales, *Glossa* 4 d.21.6 (ed. Quar. p. 369, 14–15). Alb., *IV Sent.* d. 21 a. 3.

one has built upon this foundation ... wood, hay, stubble,"[153] he substitutes "upon" (*super*) for "close by" (*iuxta*), just as in the passage: "Upon (*super*) the rivers of Babylon,"[154] that is, close by the rivers.[155]

§2. What the punishments of purgatory are

Second, one asks what the punishments of purgatory are. Gregory says that fire is one of the punishments.[156] And similarly the Apostle says, "He himself will be saved, yet in such a way as by fire."[157]

1. But one asks whether they experience the worm of conscience. It seems so, because the worm of conscience stems from sin. And they themselves are consumed by fire on account of sin. Therefore, etc.

2. In addition, one asks whether souls experience demons as tormentors, or whether souls punish themselves.[158] It seems not, because souls are holy, and so they ought rather to be corrected by a good angel or by the Lord himself.

3. Again, one asks whether they experience inner darkness. It seems not, because inner darkness, which evildoers suffer even now, is the privation of the light of formed faith, and souls that are in purgatory are not deprived of such light.

But to the contrary: They do not possess the vision of God, and this is a certain inner darkness. Therefore, etc.

4. Again one asks whether they suffer an outer darkness. It seems so, because if hell is under the earth, the light of this world cannot exist there.

5. Again one asks whether they suffer an icy cold.[159] It seems so, because there are two active qualities,[160] and they suffer from the one, and therefore from the other also.

Solution: We say that to pass judgment on questions of this

153. 1 Cor 3.12.

154. Ps 136.1.

155. Cf. Alb., *IV Sent.* d. 21 a. 5.

156. Greg., *Dial.* 4.39 (PL 77: 396A).

157. 1 Cor 3.15.

158. Cf. Alb., *IV Sent.* d. 21 a. 9.

159. Cf. Alb., *IV Sent.* d. 21 a. 5 sol.

160. The active qualities are heat and cold. Cf. Alb., *De gen. et corr.* 2.4 (ed. Colon. 5/2, p.138).

sort is very complex. Speaking without offense, however, we say that the only punishment they suffer is the punishment of fire.

1. To the objection concerning the worm, we say that the worm does not exist for a sin amended through penance, because otherwise the saints would suffer the worm of conscience in the kingdom (*in patria*).

3. To the next, we say that they do not suffer inner darkness, since the light of formed faith and the light of grace shine forth in them.[161] Nor is it true that the absence of the vision of God by means of sight (*per speciem*) is called inner darkness. Nonetheless, they do not lack the vision of God absolutely, but it is postponed for them for a time.

2. To the question concerning demons, whether they are their tormentors, one must say that they are not in any way other than by leading them to punishments.[162]

5. To the question concerning icy cold, we say that they do not suffer an icy cold. In fact, this is a quality (*passio*) of those whose love has cooled, but this does not occur in souls being purged.

§3. On the intensity of purgatory's punishments[163]

Third, one asks about the intensity of purgatory's punishments.

1. Augustine says that this punishment ought to be greatly feared, for it is greater than all the punishment of this world.[164] But this appears to be false, because God is not unjust, such that he would punish more than a human deserves; rather, he punishes less [than one deserves] on account of [his] mercy; and a human being does not deserve the maximum punishment of this world for the smallest venial sin, even according to human judgment.

2. Again, one asks whether what certain people say is true,[165]

161. N.B. the numbering in the text.

162. Cf. Alb., *De sacrif. missae* tr. 3 c. 16, 1.

163. Cf. Alb., *IV Sent.* d. 20 a. 8.

164. Aug., *Enarr. in Ps.* 36.3 (PL 37: 397). Cf. Ps. Aug., *De vera et falsa paenit.* 18.34 (PL 40: 1128). Peter Lombard, *IV Sent.* d. 20 c. 1 (p. 874).

165. "Certain people": cf. Wm. of Auxerre, *Summa aurea* IV tr. 18 cap. 4 q. 1 a. 2 (ed. Ribaillier, vol. 4, pp. 540–42).

that the punishment of purgatory is related to Gehenna in the same way that a fire in a painting is related to a real fire, and as a point is related to a line.

Solution:

1. We say to the first that the authoritative statement of Augustine is understood to concern those building upon wood, hay, and stubble, and not to concern the smallest venial sin whatsoever. And besides, it is understood to concern those who build such things in some sense (*quoad quid*). Actually, a saintly soul who has departed from the body desires to be united to God more than to its own body or to anything it loves in this world. And for that reason, separating it from union with God will be a greater burden than to remove or separate it from its own body or from anything it loved in this world. And Augustine's statement is understood in this respect and not with respect to the severity of the punishment of the fire. Indeed, its severity is determined only by the magnitude of sin, and the magnitude of a venial sin is rather small.

2. To the next we say that, according to the Philosopher,[166] every finite exists in relation to any finite whatsoever. And on account of this, since the severity of the fire of hell is finite and so too is the severity of the fire of purgatory, they have a relation according to this [finite] mode, and in this way the statement above is false. If they are compared, however, according to duration, then it is true.

Question 7. On the limbo of infants[167]

Next, one asks about the limbo of infants. And first one asks about the infants who are in limbo; second, about the place itself that is called limbo; [and] third, about the punishments of those [who are there].

166. Ar., *Phys.* 3.6 (206b11–12); cf. Alb., *Phys.* 5.2.11 (ed. Colon. 4/1, p. 190).

167. Cf. Alb., *IV Sent.* d. 45 a. 6. For Albert's contribution to scholastic debates on limbo, see Donald Mowbray, "A Community of Sufferers and the Authority of Masters: The Development of the Idea of Limbo by Masters of Theology at the University of Paris (c. 1230–c. 1300)," in *Authority and Community in the Middle Ages,* ed. Donald Mowbray et al. (Stroud: Sutton, 1999), 43–68.

Art. 1. Why infants descend to limbo

1. Concerning the first [article], one asks why infants descend to limbo. If it is said to be because of Original Sin, then to the contrary: their Original Sin is without guilt (*sine culpa*). Therefore, it seems to be associated with them unjustly if they are punished for this.

2. Again, one asks at what age they will rise again and in what condition (*dispositio*) their body will remain, for they will not have the endowments (*dotes*) of the [resurrected] body, because they will not be blessed. Similarly, they will not have the ignoble qualities of the wicked, because they will not be damned.

1. To this one, we say that children descend to limbo deservedly (*merito*) for Original Sin. And this is just, for the reason that the whole nature was vitiated in Adam; had he remained steadfast, it would have also been confirmed in [its] powers by him. Therefore, because it would have reaped the benefit from him, it was just that it reap the damage. And this is the sin of the nature specifically, not [the sin] of the person.

2. To the next, we say that they will rise again with a stature that coincides with thirty years of age, and they will have the same kind of bodily condition that Adam had, that is, an animal body, but with the sole exception that they will not need food or sleep.

If one asks, however, whether the defect of the tinder (*fomes*) remains in them, one must reply that it does not remain according to concupiscence, but it does remain insofar as it impedes the glorification of the body.

Art. 2. Where the limbo of infants is

Second, one asks where the limbo of infants is.

1. On the basis of the name, it seems that it is the outer boundary (*extremitas*) of hell; for a *limbus* is a border and a part of a garment. Therefore, similarly, the *limbus* of hell will be a border and a part of hell.

2. But to the contrary: the heat of the fire exists throughout the whole of hell. But the heat of the fire does not exist in limbo. Therefore, limbo is not a part of hell.

3. Next one asks again whether the limbo of infants is closer

to Gehenna, or whether purgatory is. It seems that purgatory is closer, because it accords with it [that is, Gehenna] in several ways: for the punishment of fire exists there [that is, in purgatory], whereas here [in limbo] it does not.

The opposite seems to be the case, however, from the fact that the limbo of infants is perpetual, just like hell, whereas purgatory is not, because it lasts only until [the Last] Judgment.

Solution:

1. We say that the limbo of infants is close to Gehenna, just as the first objection demonstrates.

2. To the objection to the contrary, one must reply that limbo is nevertheless different from Gehenna, although it is close by it. And therefore fire can be in Gehenna but not in limbo.

3. To the question whether limbo or purgatory is closer [to Gehenna], one must reply that limbo is, because infants in limbo are more distant from God than the holy souls that are in purgatory, although the latter experience fire.

Art. 3. On the punishments of limbo

Third, one asks about the punishments of limbo.

1. And one asks whether they experience the worm of conscience. It seems so, because the worm results from an unpardonable sin, and their sin is unpardonable.

2. Moreover, Augustine says,[168] and it is established in the fourth book of the *Sentences* in the treatise *On Penance,* that children experience damnation and torment, but they do not experience the torment of fire. Therefore, they experience the torment of the worm, since there is no torment except from fire or from the worm.

If perhaps one should say that the torment [there] is the absence of the vision of God, this is plainly false, because torment indicates a punishment perceptible to sense, whereas the absence of the vision of God is a punishment for the damned according to the privation of some good.

3. In addition, one asks whether they suffer inner darkness. It seems so, because it was maintained above[169] based on the

168. Aug.: Fulg., *De fide ad Petrum* 27 (PL 40: 774). Peter Lombard, *IV Sent.* d. 4 (in the treatise on baptism) c.4 (p. 769).

169. *De res.* tr. 3, q. 3 (ed. Colon. 26, p. 307, 51 and 309, 30–32).

words of Augustine that inner darkness is the absence of the light of faith and the absence of the vision of God by means of sight (*per speciem*), and the infants [in limbo] experience the absence of both of these. Therefore, they suffer inner darkness.

4. Similarly, one asks about outer darkness, namely whether they are in it. It seems to be so, because they are under the earth. But it seems not to be so, because they have not deserved to lose the corporeal light. Therefore, they are treated unjustly if they are deprived of the light of this world.

Solution:

1. We say that infants do not suffer the worm, because the worm results from an unpardonable sin that was committed voluntarily by one's own fault (*culpa*). But infants have only another's guilt (*culpa*).[170]

2. To the objection from Augustine, we say without a doubt that it is proposed improperly as torment and proposed improperly as the absence of the vision of God, which is a punishment for the damned and not a punishment of the sensible part of the soul (*poena sensus*).

3. To the next we say that it is one thing to suffer inner darkness, and it is another to exist in it. Indeed, they for whom conscience dictates that they exist in it suffer it from their own fault, because they are tormented by the worm from the loss of light. But there are those who exist in it and do not suffer it, who indeed do not possess inner light, but this stems from another's fault and not from their own. They possess, nevertheless, a natural knowledge of God and of all creatures, not by grace nor from that [knowledge] that is in the Word, because no one is deprived of natural knowledge after death—not the damned, nor even the devil—just as Dionysius says in *On Divine Names,* chapter four: "We say that 'natural gifts,' namely being, life, and understanding, 'were granted to them,' namely to demons, [and] 'that they are never changed, but remain whole and most splendid.'"[171]

170. Children in limbo have only the guilt or blame that accompanies Original Sin. Therefore, the guilt is not properly theirs, but Adam's, and they suffer for the sin of nature rather than for personal sin.

171. Dion., *De div. nom.* c. 4 §23 (PG 3: 725C; Dionysiaca I, 281–82) transl. Sarr. Alb., *De IV coaequ.* q. 67 a. 2 sol.; *De homine* q. 75 art. un. (ed. Colon. 27/2,

4. To the question concerning outer darkness, one must reply that that place is dark, but this does not harm the infants, because after the resurrection vision and the acts of the bodily senses will not be informed from the outside, but from the inside, as will become apparent later and as was partly explained above.[172]

Question 8. On the limbo of the holy fathers[173]

Next, one asks about the limbo of the holy fathers who died before the advent of Christ. And one asks first how, according to justice, the fathers descended to limbo. Second, [one asks] where [that] limbo is, and whether it is temporary or eternal. Third, [one asks] which punishments are in limbo, if there are any.

Art. 1. How, according to justice, the fathers descended to limbo[174]

To the first, one proceeds in this way:

Gregory says that Original Sin was remitted by the faith of the parents and by both sacrifice and circumcision, whereas actual sin was forgiven by penance.[175] Now the holy fathers performed each of these.[176] Therefore, they had neither Original nor actual sin. It seems, therefore, that they descended to limbo without regard for justice.

If perhaps one should say that it was because the door to paradise was not open, it seems that this is not [why they descended]. Actually, the closed door only required that they remained outside of heaven, and not that they descended to hell. In fact, what descends descends because of some weight that is in it.

---

p. 558); *II Sent.* d. 9 a. 7 qla. 1, d. 23 a. 6 sol.; *Super Dion. De div. nom.* 4, 23 (ed. Colon. 37/1, pp. 189–90, 193); *Summa* I q. 71 sol. ad. 3; II q. 25 m. 1 a. 2 sol. Cf. Alb., *De IV coaequ.* q. 67 a. 3.

172. *De res.* tr. 4, art. 4, q. 4 (ed. Colon. 26, pp. 342–44); *De res.* tr. 3, q. 4 (ed. Colon. 26, p. 311, 74ff.).

173. Cf. Alb., *IV Sent.* d. 1 a. 20.

174. Cf. Alb., *IV Sent.* d. 45 a. 5.

175. Greg., *Dial.* 4.3 (PL 75: 635B).

176. Namely, sacrifice and circumcision, on the one hand, and penance, on the other.

To this we say that two things are required for the satisfaction of Original Sin: one is personal [satisfaction], which someone makes on his own behalf, and the fathers had this; the other is universal, which only Christ could make. What this is, moreover, was determined above in the "Question on the Necessity of the Incarnation."[177] Therefore, on account of that portion [of satisfaction], before the advent of Christ, Original Sin remained unextinguished and dragged the fathers down to hell by its weight.

Art. 2. Where the limbo of the fathers is

Second, one asks where the limbo of the fathers is and whether it still exists.

1. It seems that it is not close to hell. For the abodes of souls are differentiated according to merit. But the merit of the fathers was far removed from the merits of those who are in hell. Therefore, the place was far removed as well.

It appears likewise from what is said in the Gospel: "When the rich man was in torment, raising his eyes he saw Abraham," etc.[178] But Abraham and Lazarus were in limbo, because the bosom of Abraham was limbo, as Jerome says.[179]

To the contrary: Christ descended to hell, as both the Apostle's Creed and the Athanasian Creed say, and it follows that he did not descend only to limbo for, as the Damascene says, "the deified soul descended to hell."[180]

2. After this, one asks whether that limbo still exists. It seems so, for it does not seem to be the case that a place is removed because what is placed [in it] has been removed.

Solution:

1. We say that the limbo of the fathers is close to hell, just as the Creed says, and it is the border of hell joined to the limbo of infants. The distance of which the Gospel speaks, however, is understood with respect to the distance of merit and of conso-

177. Alb., *De incarn.* tr. 1 (ed. Colon. 26, p. 171).

178. Lk 16.23.

179. Jerome, *In Is.* 65.7 (PL 24: 659D).

180. John Damascene, *De fide orth.* 3.29 (PG: 1101A); transl. Burg. (ed. Buytaert, p. 276, 3). Cf. Alb., *De incarn.* tr. 6, q. 4 (ed. Colon. 26, p. 234, 37; 235, 27–29).

lation, and also the place is higher than hell with respect to the place of the damned.

2. To the question whether it still endures, we say that only the limbo of infants exists now. Therefore, it has endured with respect to substance, but not with respect to purpose such that it could be called the limbo of the fathers.

Art. 3. Whether there were any punishments there

Third, one asks whether there were any punishments there. And it follows from what was said above that neither the worm [of conscience] nor fire existed there.[181]

But one asks about outer darkness. For Zachariah, the father of John, says: "To enlighten those who sit in darkness and in the shadow of death."[182] Therefore, outer darkness was there, because inner darkness is not the shadow of death.

Similarly, one asks whether outer darkness existed there as a punishment. It seems not, because a soul that has departed from the body is related equally to corporeal light and darkness.

Solution: We say that the fathers in limbo experienced no punishment perceptible to sense, nor did they experience inner darkness, but rather they possessed the light of faith. But the postponement of the vision [of God] by sight (*per speciem*) because of the impediment of Original Sin is called "the shadow of death."

To the question concerning outer darkness, we say that punishments do not exist for a soul that has departed from the body except with respect to the indignity of the place in which the soul is forced to exist.

Question 9. On the places of punishment [treated] all together[183]

Next, one asks about all of these together, and how the number and distinction of the aforementioned places should be understood.

181. See *De res.* tr. 3, q. 7, art. 3 (ed. Colon. 26, p. 319, 3ff.).
182. Lk 1.79.
183. Cf. Alb., *IV Sent.* d. 44 a. 45 sol.

To this we say that the abode of the soul is either the end of the journey or it is on the journey. If the end, then [it is] either with joy or with punishment. If with joy, then it is the kingdom of heaven. If with punishment, then either it is the punishment of damnation only, or with the punishment of the senses and damnation, because there cannot exist any place with the punishment of the senses only, because the punishment of the senses implies the punishment of damnation. If [there is punishment] in the first way, then it is the limbo of infants; if in the second way, then it is Gehenna. If it is on the journey to the end, however, then again it is either with the punishment of damnation only, which is only the postponement of the vision [of God] and is not a lack [of vision] absolutely, or it is with the punishment of the senses and of damnation. If [there is punishment] in the first way, it is the limbo of the fathers; if in the second way, it is purgatory.

Again, they are differentiated in this way according to the cause of merit. Merit is either good, or it is bad, or it is good joined to bad. If good only, then the kingdom of heaven will accord with it. If bad only, then either from one's own fault (*culpa*) or from someone else's. If from one's own, then Gehenna will accord with it; if from someone else's, then the limbo of infants. If it is good joined to bad, however, this bad cannot be a mortal [sin], because the good of grace is not joined to that. Therefore, it will be a venial [sin]. Therefore, either it is joined to a venial sin (*malo veniali*) that stems from one's own fault or from someone else's fault. If in the first way, purgatory will accord with this; if in the second way, the limbo of the fathers.

Again, these are differentiated according to what exists in these places. These are four [in number]: affliction, darkness, bright light, and joy. If joy and bright light, this will be the kingdom of heaven, in which the contraries, namely affliction and darkness, cannot exist. If affliction and darkness, however, then it will be Gehenna. To be sure, if [there is] unqualified affliction but a qualified darkness, namely so far as concerns the postponement of the vision [of God], this will be purgatory. But if there is absolute darkness and no affliction, this will be the limbo of infants. If [there is] a qualified darkness and no affliction, however, this will be the limbo of the fathers.

If someone objects to this division, however, that there ought to be a place that should have only bright light, just as there is one that has only darkness, and that there should be one that has bright light in a qualified way, just as there is one that has [qualified] darkness, and that there should be one that has only affliction, and one that has only joy, and one that has qualified affliction, and one that has qualified joy, and one that has neither affliction nor joy nor darkness nor bright light, because only then would there be a complete division: we say that those divisions (*membra*) cannot exist because bright light is the cause of joy. Therefore, every luminous place is joyful. Likewise, affliction implies darkness, and therefore every place of affliction is a place of darkness as well. Similarly, affliction only exists as a result of fire, and therefore every affliction is absolute affliction. But darkness exists from a double cause: namely, from the absence of the light of formed faith, and from the absence of the vision of God by means of sight (*per speciem*). And therefore something that lacks light in both ways can be absolute darkness, and something that has only one or the other light can be darkness in a qualified way. Similarly, there cannot be qualified bright light, because bright light only exists from the vision of God by sight (*per speciem*), and this always presupposes that light that follows faith in the soul. And from this it is also clear that there cannot be qualified joy, because absolute bright light implies absolute joy.

But if someone objects, according to a middle division, that there are many distinctions of merit among those to be saved, those to be damned, and those to be purged because some have merited more than others and some have sinned more than others, and according to this there ought to be more than five abodes [for souls]: one must reply that the abodes are understood on the basis of general divisions of merit. In fact, the mansions are distinguished among the abodes according to specific [merits], as will be argued below.

TRACTATE FOUR

ON THE RESURRECTION ON THE PART OF THE GOOD ALONE

NEXT, ONE ASKS about the resurrection on the part of the good alone. And one asks first about the dowries (*de dotibus*);[1] second, about eternal life; third, about eternal beatitude; fourth, about the eternal crowns; fifth, about the dwelling of God and the mansions [of heaven].

Question 1. On dowries

The questions concerning dowries are divided into two, namely [those] concerning dowries in general and [those] concerning dowries in particular.

On Dowries in General

First, concerning dowries in general, one asks whether there is a dowry; second, what a dowry is; third, for what reason a

1. Medieval scholastic theologians described and understood the divine gifts conferred on the blessed, both soul and body, in the next life as "dowries" (*dotes*), on the analogy of the betrothal gifts given by a bride and/or her family to the groom. Albert teaches here (aa. 9–17 below) that there are three dowries of the blessed soul—namely, the vision of God by sight, love, and comprehension—and four dowries of the resurrected body—luminosity, impassibility, subtlety, and agility. For more on the dowries in scholastic theology generally, see, e.g., Nikolaus Wicki, *Die Lehre von der himmlischen Seligkeit in der mittelalterlichen Scholastik von Petrus Lombardi bis Thomas Aquin* (Freiburg: Universitätsverlag, 1954); Joseph Goering, "The *De Dotibus* of Robert Grosseteste," *Mediaeval Studies* 44 (1982): 83–109; Carlo Leget, "Eschatology," in *The Theology of Thomas Aquinas*, ed. Rik van Nieuwenhove and Joseph Wawrykow (Notre Dame, IN: University of Notre Dame Press, 2005), 365–85, esp. 377 and 380; and Aaron Canty, *Light & Glory, passim*, esp. 17, 37–38, and 197.

dowry is owed to the human; fourth, whether a dowry is owed to the human alone or to the angels as well; fifth, whether a dowry is owed to one who is merely human (*puro homini*) or to Christ also; sixth, whether it is owed to one who is merely human only on the journey [of this life] (*in via*), or while in the kingdom [of heaven] (*in patria*) and on the journey [of life]; seventh, one asks whether a dowry is principally owed to the human equally according to the body and according to the soul, or, first and foremost, according to the soul; eighth, one asks from whom, as from the one giving it, the dowry comes.

Art. 1. Whether there is a dowry

One proceeds in this way concerning the first [question]:

1. The reason for a dowry is that it is given on account of the burdens of marriage. But there will be no burdens in the future. Therefore, there will be no dowry in the future.[2]

2. In addition, a dowry is given owing to the bridegroom's lack of goods, or to his poverty in relation to supporting a wife and children. But the eternal spouse suffers no lack of goods. Therefore, there will be no dowry for marriage in the future.

3. Similarly, a dowry consists of external goods. This is clear because if the bride (*sponsa*) is beautiful or virtuous, this is not calculated in the price of the dowry. But whatever [gifts] will be given in the future, they will be inner goods. Therefore, they cannot be called dowries.

Solution: We say that there will be a dowry in the future when the Church is united to Christ, its bridegroom. Indeed, Christ's marriage is not more deficient than human marriage. Therefore, since there is a dowry in human marriage, so too there will be a dowry in Christ's marriage.

1. To the first, therefore, we say that although in the future there will be no burdens, nevertheless a dowry will be given. In fact, a dowry is given to remove the burdens that would exist in the future, were there no dowry. And it will be the same in the future [marriage], because on account of the defects of the soul and the body there would not be a free union of man to God unless man were enriched with dowries.

2. Cf. *De res.* tr. 4, q. 1, art. 2 (ed. Colon. 26, p. 323, 1–3).

2. To the next we say that there is no analogy here, namely as far as the bridegroom's lack of goods is concerned, but on account of other analogies the name "dowry" is transferred to an eternal dowry. Or, better yet, one could say that a dowry is given to a bridegroom for two reasons: namely, owing to a lack of goods and owing to the bride's affection offered to the bridegroom, because she does not want to be burdensome to him, since he is self-sufficient with his own goods. And in this respect there exists a certain analogy to man's eternal dowry, which is given to the bride by the father of the bride and of the bridegroom, owing to the bridegroom's affection.

3. To the next we say that among human beings a dowry consists of external goods for the reason that internal ones are not fully sufficient when weighed against the burdens of marriage. But if internal goods were fully sufficient, it would not be necessary for the dowry to consist of external goods. Therefore, it happens that it consists of external goods. In the future, however, when there will be a complete abundance of internal goods, it will not be necessary to introduce external goods.

Art. 2. What a dowry is[3]

Second, one asks what a dowry is. And the definition should be taken from those who have to inquire into the dowry and the law of the dowry, that is from those skilled in law, who say that "a dowry is a gift (*donatio*) made to the man on behalf of the woman on account of the burdens of marriage."[4]

1. And, first, it seems that according to this definition, the term "dowry" should not be transferred to those things that will be given in the future marriage, because the bride will give nothing to the bridegroom but rather will receive [something] from him. And so it seems that what will be given in the future marriage should be called "a gift (*donatio*) on account of wedding nuptials" rather than a dowry (*dos*).

3. Cf. Alb., *Quaestio de dotibus sanctorum in patria,* art. 1: *Quid sit dos* (ed. Colon. 25/2, pp. 102–4).

4. "Skilled in law": Cf. Justinian, *Dig.* 23, t. 3 lex 56 §1. Bernardus Papiensis, *Summa decretalium* 4 tit. 21 §1 (ed. E. A. Th. Laspeyres, Regensburg, 1860, p. 190). Cf. Raymund de Pennafort, *Summa* 4 tit. 25 §1. Tancredus, *Summa de matrimonio* tit. 39 (ed. A. Wunderlich, Gottingen, 1841, p. 108).

2. Likewise, after the husband's death, the dowry is restored to the woman for the sake of a second marriage. And it is clear from this that it was not given by the husband to the woman, as some say,[5] but rather it was given by the woman. And again it is clear from this that the fictitious account (*fictio*) provided by certain people—that according to the canons the dowry is given by the husband to the wife—is false,[6] and according to the laws it is the other way around, especially since those who know the canons do not make this distinction.

3. In addition, if there will be a dowry in the future marriage, one asks whether there will also be a gift on account of wedding nuptials[7] and *parapherna*,[8] so that what the bridegroom gives to the bride for the sake of the wedding nuptials may be called a gift (*donatio*), and what the bride possesses alongside the dowry may be called the *parapherna*.

Solution:

1. We say that there will be a dowry in the future, given by the father of the bride to the bridegroom on account of the bridegroom's affection. But the difference is that among human beings the dowry is given to the bridegroom for his use, and it is given to the bride as her possession, whereas among the divine [persons] God the Father gives a dowry indeed to the bride as a possession, but he gives it to the bridegroom for his glory and honor rather than for his use, because he has no need of our goods.[9] And from this a solution to the first [objection] is apparent.

2. To the next, we say that among human beings there is consideration for second wedding nuptials [that take place] because of the defect of death, which can break the bond of marriage. But in the future, when there will be no defect, this consideration is not necessary.

5. Cf. Greg. IX, *Decretal.* 4 t. 20 c. 6 (Innoc. III: Potthast, Reg. pont. Rom. 1193). Cf. Justinian, *Cod.* 5 t. 3 lex 20.

6. "Certain people": Cf. Hugh of St. Cher (fol. 303ra).

7. Cf. Justinian, *Inst.* 2 t. 7 §3, and *Cod.* 5 t. 3. Bernardus Papiensis, *Summa decretalium* 1 c. §3 (ibid., p. 191). Tancredus, 1. C. (ibid., p. 109).

8. *Parapherna* is the property of a woman that was not part of her dowry and thus remained her own after her marriage. Cf. Justinian, *Cod.* 5 t. 14. Bernardus Papiensis, *Summa decretalium* 1 c. §3 (ibid.). Tancredus 1. C. (ibid.).

9. Cf. Ps 15.2.

3. To the last, we say that the *parapherna* will exist in the future among the joys that are not dowries, and especially in the joy that will be possessed from the company of the blessed.[10] The gift (*donatio*) on account of wedding nuptials, however, is the joy that we will have in the vision of Christ the man, for we will see him as God and man, but the angels will not see him as an angel.

Art. 3. For what reason a dowry is owed to the human

Third, one asks for what reason a dowry that exists in marriage is owed to the human.

1. Since there exists a double union in marriage, namely a union of hearts and a union of natures in carnal intercourse, correspondingly there will be a double union in spiritual marriage, namely a union in love according to which the soul is made one spirit with God,[11] and a union of natures in the one person of Christ. One asks, then, by reason of which union is a dowry owed to the human.

It seems that it is by reason of the first union, which is in one spirit, because a dowry is not owed to unbelievers and to evildoers, and nevertheless they have an analogue to the union of natures in the one person of Christ, because they have one and the same nature with Christ in species (*in specie*) at least. Therefore, since the just, to whom the dowry is owed, have only the union in one spirit beyond this union [in species], a dowry is owed to them for that reason.

2. Likewise, let us suppose that Christ had not been united to flesh. There still would have been another mode of liberation that was possible, according to Augustine, and the dowries would be given.[12] Therefore, the dowries do not essentially pertain to the union of natures in Christ. But, supposing that a union in one spirit does not exist, the dowries will not be given. Therefore, the giving of the dowry pertains essentially to that union, because once that [union] is posited, the giving of the dowry is implied, and once that [union] is destroyed, it [the giving of the dowry] is destroyed.

10. Cf. Alb., *De mul. forti* c. 20 §3 (ed. Borgnet 18).

11. Cf. 1 Cor 6.17.

12. Aug., *De trin.* 13.10.13 (PL 42: 1024); cf. *De res.* tr. 2, q. 1 (ed. Colon. 26, p. 258, 61).

3. Likewise, some of the dowries denote the perfection of the union in one spirit, such as love (*dilectio*). None, however, denotes the perfection of the union in nature. Therefore, it pertains essentially to the first union and not the second.

4. But to the contrary: The future dowry will be everlasting. Therefore, by reason of what is everlasting in a spiritual marriage it will be given to those joined by marriage. But the union of love (*caritatis*) in one spirit is not everlasting, because we see constantly that various [people] have fallen out of love. The union of natures in Christ, however, is everlasting. Therefore, the giving of the dowry will be by reason of that [union].

5. Similarly, at the husband's death the dowry is placed under the bride's control so far as use and possession are concerned. But Christ, who according to the divine nature is joined to us in one spirit, does not die according to the divine [nature]. Therefore, although the dowry is given to the bride for her use and possession in the future, it is not given by reason of this union, but by reason of that union of nature in which he was able to die and was dead.

6. Also, angels are well united in one spirit, and nevertheless they do not have a dowry properly. Therefore, the dowry does not pertain to that union, as it seems.

Solution: One must distinguish between the promise to give the dowry and the collection of the dowry itself. The promise of the dowry exists in the contract of marriage, but the collection consists in the delivery of the bride. There is an analogy here in spiritual marriage: for marriage is contracted in the present by means of the bond of love, but <the bride> is delivered to the house of the bridegroom and to the marriage bed in the passage to the kingdom after death. And so we say that both unions produce something for the collection of the dowry: one according to potency, and the other according to act. For the conformity of nature to the bridegroom makes it possible for a human being (*homo*) to be a bride, but the conformity of love makes the human being a bride in act.

(4–6) And from this a solution to the last three arguments is clear. For the fact that angels do not have dowries stems from a lack of the potential to be brides, because they do not possess a conformity of nature with God, of the kind that ought to exist between a bridegroom and a bride.

1. To the first, however, we say that sinners have the potential for dowries and for a spiritual marriage with God, but they do not have the act of union in one spirit, and because of this they will not have dowries.

2. To the next we say that it is based on an error, because if God had not become human, we would not have enjoyed the conformity of nature with him, and thus there would have been no real basis for marriage between him and us. Therefore, although another mode of liberation would have been possible, as Augustine says, nevertheless there was no other mode of betrothal, if one attends to the proper definition (*ratio*) of marriage.

3. To the third we say that the dowry pertains more closely to a union according to act than according to potency, and there it is designated rather by the former.

Art. 4. Whether a dowry is owed to the human alone or also to the angel[13]

Fourth, one asks whether a dowry is owed to the human alone or also to the angel.

1. It seems that [it is owed] to the angel. For the angel was first united to God by grace and afterwards through glory and confirmation. Therefore, it seems that marriage was contracted there and also the induction of the bride.[14] But a dowry is owed for marriage. Therefore, also to the angels.

2. Likewise, there is one head of the Church, as was said above in the "Question on the Head and the Members."[15] Since, then, angels share one head with us, it seems also that they have one bridegroom with us, and so [they are owed] dowries just as we are.

3. Also, in the Song of Songs: "One is my dove, the beauti-

13. Cf. Alb., *Quaestio de dotibus sanctorum in patria,* art. 3: *Cui debeatur dos* (ed. Colon. 25/2, pp. 105–6).

14. "Induction of the bride": *traductio sponsae,* i.e., her introduction to the home of the bridegroom.

15. Cf. Alb., *De incarn.* tr. 5, q. 2, art. 5 (ed. Colon. 25, p. 216, 54ff.).

ful one, the delight of [her] mother."[16] And the Gloss on that passage says the Church, which is the bride of Christ, is one for both human beings and angels.[17] Therefore, by the same reasoning, they share with us the reception of dowries.

4. Similarly, on that passage in Luke, "You are like humans who wait for their Lord when he returns," etc.,[18] Gregory says[19] that God contracted marriage with the angels in heaven. And thus, as earlier, a dowry is owed them because of the wedding nuptials.

5. Likewise, angels possess love, knowledge, and understanding, just as we do, and these are said to be dowries. Therefore, etc.

Solution: We say that angels do not have dowries according to the proper and complete definition (*ratio*) of a dowry, but according to a partial [definition], namely according to the union in one spirit only.

1–4. To the first, and to the others except the last one, we say that there is a union in one spirit in which the angels are like us, and according to this they are said to be one bride with us, and this is in a qualified way (*secundum quid*). But beyond this, the human has the union of the conformity of nature, which the angel does not have, and so far as this is concerned [the human] has a special basis (*ratio*) for betrothal. And for that reason, he has a special basis for the dowries, according to which basis the angel cannot have dowries.

5. To the last we say that angels possess what is called a dowry, but not under the definition (*ratio*) of a dowry. And for this reason, the last argument errs with respect to something accidental.

Art. 5. Whether Christ possesses dowries

Fifth, one asks whether Christ possesses dowries.[20]

16. Cf. Song 6.8 and 2.10.

17. Not found in the Gloss on this passage. But cf. *Glossa ord. super Is.* 65.18; Wm. of Auxerre, *Summa aurea* IV tr. 16 cap. 3 obj. 2 (ed. Ribaillier, vol. 4, p. 375); Thomas Aquinas, *IV Sent.* d. 49 q. 4 a. 4.

18. Lk 12.36.

19. Greg., *Hom. 13 in Ev.* 2 (PL 76: 1124B).

20. Cf. Alb., *Quaestio De dotibus sanctorum in patria*, art. 4: *Utrum Christo debeantur dotes* (ed. Colon. 25/2, pp. 106–8).

1. It seems so, because the Apostle says in Philippians, "He will reform the body of our lowliness, conformed to the body of his glory."[21] If, therefore, we will possess dowries of the body analogous to the dowries of Christ's body, it seems that we will also possess the dowries of the soul analogous to the dowries of Christ's soul.

2. Moreover, "He is the firstborn among many brothers,"[22] as the Apostle says, and he participated in body and blood, and "it behooved him to be made like his brothers in all things," as he says in Hebrews 2.[23] Therefore, it behooved him to be made like his brothers in this as well.

Solution: We say that Christ does not possess dowries according to the definition (*ratio*) of dowries, for three reasons: The first and most important reason is that he himself is the bridegroom, and a dowry is in the possession of the bride, as was said above.[24] Another reason is that a dowry is given to the one who is brought into the home of the bridegroom, and Christ was always in the home, because he was the possessor (*comprehensor*) [of the home] from the moment of conception. But a [mere] human, who is a wayfarer and not a *comprehensor,* is brought in when he is made a *comprehensor.*[25] The third reason is that, upon the death of the bridegroom, a dowry is executed for the use and possession of the bride. But this was not the case in Christ, because before his death he who is the bridegroom had the use and possession of the dowries of the soul. And three arguments in opposition can be formed from these three [reasons].

21. Phil 3.21.

22. Rom 8.29.

23. Heb 2.17.

24. *De res.* tr. 4, q. 1, art. 2 (ed. Colon. 26, p. 323, 23ff.).

25. A *comprehensor* is a human who enjoys the beatific vision of God, that is, who sees or comprehends God as he is. Among mere or ordinary humans, this comprehensive vision of God is possessed only in the life of the world to come and only by the elect. Christ, by contrast, as understood by Alb. and other scholastic theologians, most notably Aquinas, was a *comprehensor* who enjoyed the beatific vision of God the Father from the first moment of his conception as a human. For an excellent study of Aquinas's teaching on Christ's beatific vision, see Simon Francis Gaine, *Did the Saviour See the Father? Christ, Salvation and the Vision of God* (London: Bloomsbury T&T Clark, 2015).

1. To the first, however, we say that the argument contains the accident fallacy,[26] namely that if he possesses those things that are dowries in the body, on that account he possesses them under the definition of a dowry.

2. To the next we say that he [that is, Christ] is like his brethren in nature, and the Apostle's statement is understood in this way.

Art. 6. Whether a dowry is owed to the human only in the kingdom [of heaven], or both in the kingdom and on the journey [of this life]

Sixth, one asks whether a dowry is owed to the human only in the kingdom or both in the kingdom and on the journey.

It seems that [it is owed] in the kingdom and on the journey, because each of the unions of marriage, namely [the union] in one spirit and in the conformity of nature, exists on the journey; therefore, the dowry will exist on the journey as well.

To the contrary: A dowry is given at induction (*traductio*), and one will only be inducted after death. Therefore, the dowry will only be given in the kingdom after death.

Also, a dowry has a certain basis in reward, and there is no reward on the journey, but rather [only] in the kingdom. Therefore, etc.

We concede this, saying to the first that the union of the conformity of nature creates the possibility of [receiving] the dowry, whereas the union in one spirit creates the obligation [to receive it]; but induction causes the presentation [of the dowry].

Art. 7. Whether a dowry is principally owed to the human equally according to the body and the soul, or, first and foremost, according to the soul[27]

Seventh, one asks whether a dowry is principally owed to the human equally according to the body and the soul, or, first and foremost, according to the soul.

26. Cf. Alb., *De Soph. el.* 1, tr. 3 c. 3–4 (ed. Borgnet 2, pp. 560–64).The accident fallacy occurs when an attempt is made to apply a general rule to all cases even though there are clear exceptions to the rule.

27. Cf. Alb., *Quaestio De dotibus sanctorum in patria,* art. 3: *Cui debeatur dos* (ed. Colon. 25/2, pp. 105–6).

1. It seems principally according to both equally, because divinity was united in an unmediated way to flesh and to the soul. Since, therefore, a dowry is owed for the union, the dowry will be [due] principally to both equally. If one objects that Augustine says that it [that is, the divinity] is united to the intellect and to the soul through the intellect, and to the body through the soul,[28] this was resolved above in the "Question on the Union."[29]

2. Moreover, if superiority (*vis*) results from the number of dowries, the body benefits from many more dowries than does the soul, and in this way it [the body] seems to partake of dowries more principally than or equally with the soul.

But to the contrary: a dowry is owed for the union. But the soul is united with the bridegroom according to nature and will, whereas the body [is united] according to nature alone. Therefore, the dowry is owed more principally to the soul than to the body.

Similarly, a dowry is a part of a reward. Therefore, it takes merit into account. But merit exists principally in the soul, and it exists in the body only through the soul. Therefore, the reward too will exist principally in the soul, and it will exist in the body by its disposition toward it.[30]

1. This we concede, saying to the first that the conformity of nature creates only the potential for receiving a dowry, as has been said. Conformity of the will, however, creates the obligation. Hence, the conformity of nature cannot bring about the excellence of reception. But why the divinity was united in an unmediated way to the body as well as to the soul has to be investigated among the things said above.[31]

2. To the next we say that the number of dowries does not produce greater excellence, but rather the nobility and the mode of the dowry do. The soul's dowries, however, are nobler than the body's. Likewise, the mode of the soul's dowry, since it bespeaks an unmediated union with God, is nobler than the

28. Aug., *De agone Christ.* c. 18, 20 (PL 40: 300; CSEL 41, p. 121, 1–2).

29. *De incarn.* tr. 3, q. 2, art. 3 (ed. Colon. 26, p. 197, 66ff.).

30. "It": *ad illud,* i.e., the reward or merit.

31. *De res.* tr. 4, q. 1, art. 6 (ed. Colon. 26, p. 325, 59–61).

mode of the body's dowry, since the body's dowry is nothing but the perfected disposition of the body to the glorified soul.

Art. 8. From whom, as from the one giving it, the dowry comes[32]

Eighth, one asks from whom, as from the one giving it, the dowry comes, whether from the Father or from the Son or from the Holy Spirit or from the whole Trinity.

It seems that it comes from the whole Trinity, because grace, which merits the dowry, comes from the whole Trinity.

Likewise, a dowry is what is given by the woman's father, as those skilled in the law say.[33] But the father of the woman, that is, [the father] of the human, is the Trinity. Indeed, we say to the whole Trinity: "Our Father, who art [in heaven]," etc.[34] Therefore, the eternal dowry will be from the whole Trinity.

To the contrary: It does not pertain to the bridegroom to give the dowry, according to its proper definition, as the laws say.[35] Therefore, it does not pertain to the Son to give the dowry, because the Son is the bridegroom.

Likewise, those who come from the [family of the] bridegroom do not properly give the dowry, but if they do give something, it will be a present (*donatio*) for the wedding nuptials. Since, therefore, the Holy Spirit comes from the Son, the Holy Spirit will not give the dowry under the definition of the dowry. It remains, then, that it pertains to the Father to give the dowry.

But opposed to this is the fact that the Father is naturally the father of the bridegroom, and by a conformity of image and of grace he is the father of the bride. And so he is more principally the father of the bridegroom than of the bride. But what is given by the bridegroom's father is not called a dowry. Therefore, the eternal dowry will not be given by the Father, so it seems.

Solution: Without offense to those who say otherwise,[36] we

32. Cf. Alb., *Quaestio De dotibus sanctorum in patria,* art. 5: *Cuius sit dare dotes* (ed. Colon. 25/2, pp. 108–9).

33. Cf. Alb., *De res.* tr. 4, q. 1, art. 2 (ed. Colon. 26, p. 323, 1).

34. Mt 6.9. Cf. Alb., *Super Matth.* 6.9.

35. Cf. *De res.* tr. 4, q. 1, art. 2 (ed. Colon. 26, p. 323, 1).

36. Cf. Hugh of St. Cher, *Quaestio de dotibus* (fol. 304va).

say that the dowry is from the whole Trinity, just as the first arguments prove, but nonetheless the presentation (*donatio*) of the dowry is attributed especially to the Father, as the two penultimate arguments demonstrate.

To the last argument, however, we say that when the bridegroom and the bride do not have the same father, then what is given by the bridegroom's father is not called a dowry, but rather a present on account of the wedding nuptials. But when they have the same father, then nothing prevents what is given by the bridegroom's father from being called a dowry, just as if Adam had given one to his children who were joined in marriage.

And note that in all questions of this sort, some reply differently, and this is because they make two false assumptions,[37] namely that the dowry is something that is given to the woman on behalf of the husband, and that the dowry is an honor (*ornatus*), although the dowry is not an honor, but rather the dowry is a relief for the burden of marriage.

On Individual Dowries considered Separately

Next, one asks about individual dowries separately, and first about the vision [of God] by sight (*per speciem*).

And there are three questions: namely, whether the vision [of God] is a dowry; second, what it means to see [God] face-to-face or by sight; third, on the difference between that vision and other visions of God.

Art. 9. On the vision [of God] by sight

§1. Whether the vision [of God] is a dowry[38]

One proceeds in this way concerning the first:

1. It is said in the Gospel of John [chapter] 1: "No one has ever seen God."[39] But some humans have possessed the dowries of the soul. Therefore, the vision of God is not a dowry.

37. Greg. IX, *Decretal.* 4.20.6 (Innoc. III; Potthast, Reg. Pont. Rom. N. 1193); cf. Justinian, *Cod.* 5.3.20; cf. Alb., *De res.* tr. 4, q. 1, art. 2 (ed. Colon. 26, p. 323, 12, 13–14); Hugh of St. Cher, *Quaestio de dotibus* (fol. 303ra).

38. Cf. Alb., *De IV coaequ.* q. 32 a. 1 ad q. 1.

39. Jn 1.18.

If perhaps one should say that the Gospel is speaking about the vision on the journey and not the vision of the kingdom [of heaven], opposed to this is the authority of Chrysostom on the same passage in John in the original [language, that is, Greek], which says that not even the celestial essences themselves, by which I mean the Cherubim and Seraphim, have ever been able to see God as he is.[40] And in that same place he proposes two arguments for this. One argument is: How will the created see the uncreated? And he seems to suppose that the created could not be in the uncreated. The second argument is that the divine nature is simple. If, therefore, they have seen it, they all equally have seen it, and they have seen nothing in it but the One. But this is false, because one [celestial essence] praises it [that is, the divine nature] as glory, and another praises it as majesty, and another praises it as holiness, and another as wisdom, etc. Therefore, they have not seen it, but instead something under it.

2. Similarly, Dionysius [says] in the first Letter to the monk Gaius: "If anyone seeing God understood what he saw, he did not see him, but rather something of those things that are his, which exist and are known."[41]

3. Again, in the same place: "According to a better [interpretation], perfect ignorance is the knowledge of him who is beyond all things that are known."[42]

4. Again, in *On the Celestial Hierarchy,* chap. 1: "As a matter of fact, it is not possible for the divine ray to illumine us in any way other than by a variety of sacred veils surrounding him anagogically, prepared by paternal providence connaturally and properly from those that exist with respect to us (*secundum nos*)."[43] One understands from this that God is not seen in his proper substance, but rather something that exists from him is seen, and God is known in that. And Dionysius seems to say

40. John Chrysos., *Hom.* 15(14) in Joh. 1 (PG 59: 98). Cf. Alb., *I Sent.* d. 1 a. 15: "Quaestio de visione"; *Super Dion. De div. nom.* c. 1, 19 (ed. Colon. 37/1, pp. 9–10). Cf. Thomas Aquinas, *IV Sent.* d. 49 q. 2 a. 1.

41. Dion., *Epist.* 1 (PG 3: 1065A); Dionysiaca I, 606–7); transl. Sarr.

42. Dion., ibid., 1066A; 607, transl. Sarr.

43. Dion., *De cael. hier.* c. 1 §2 (PG 3: 121BC; Dionysiaca II, 733); transl. Sarr. Cf. Alb., *Super Dion. De cael. hier.* 1 (ed. Colon. 36/1, pp. 12–14).

further along in *On the Celestial Hierarchy* that he is known only in theophanies.[44]

5. The same thing is apparent from an argument. For in every potency, if it has to be completed by act, it is necessary to assume a proportion and capacity of the potency to that act. But there is no proportion or capacity between the finite and the infinite. Therefore, a finite potency never has to be completed by an infinite act.[45] But every created intellect is finite. Therefore, it does not have to be completed by an infinite intelligible. But God is an infinite intelligible. Therefore, it does not understand God. And to see, as is assumed here, means to understand. Therefore, there will be no vision of God in his proper substance.

6. Similarly, if vision has to be according to the intellect, it is necessary for the intellect to be assimilated to the thing understood. Indeed, every intellect exists through assimilation. Therefore, either the intellect will be assimilated to God according to substance or according to a condition (*habitus*) or some formal species. It follows that it is not in the first way, because the intellect will not be God. If in the second way, however, it follows that vision exists only in theophanies. For the form or light received by the intellect is not God, but it is something in which and through which God is known.[46]

7. Likewise, understanding of what is distinct from the intellect according to substance and form does not come from the intellect, except through abstraction or through an ideal form that has been concreated for the intellect.[47] For example, our intellect's understanding of a rock exists only through the abstraction of the species of rock from a [particular] rock, but the understanding of a rock by an angel's intellect is through an ideal form concreated for the angel, because it is necessary for

44. Dion., *De cael. hier.* c. 4 §3 (PG 3: 180C; Dionysiaca II, 810). Cf. Alb., *Super Dion. De cael. hier.* 4 (ed. Colon. 36/1, pp. 68–71).

45. Ar., *De caelo et mundo* 1.6 (274a7–8). Cf. Alb., *De caelo et mundo* 1.2.3.

46. Cf. Alb., *Super Dion. De cael. hier.* c. 4 §6.

47. "Concreated": i.e., created together or at the same time. At *Summa de creaturis* 2, q. 56, art. 5, sol. (ed. Borgnet 35, p. 486), Albert remarks that ideal forms are concreated with the rational soul. For discussion, see Markus Führer, "Albert the Great and Mystical Epistemology," in *A Companion to Albert the Great. Theology, Philosophy, and the Sciences,* ed. Irven M. Resnick (Leiden: Brill, 2013), 137–61 (esp. 147–50).

the intelligible to be united to the intellect in some way. Since, therefore, God is distinct from the intellect of a glorified soul, it will understand him either in the one way or in the other. If it understands by abstraction, since every abstraction arises from a particular—and that which is abstracted is the universal—it is necessary that both the universal and the particular exist in God, and thus that he be composite, which is false. Moreover, it would be necessary for powers (*virtutes*) to exist there by whose mediation abstraction would occur, such as sensation (*sensus*) and imagination, because the intellect is found to be moved only by a phantasm.

If, however, it [understanding] exists through an ideal form that has been united to it, once again it follows that we will not see [God] without a medium. But vision without a medium is proposed as the dowry. Therefore, that dowry will not exist. In addition, an ideal form is posited with respect to creatures, not with respect to God, because only creatures are represented by ideas (*ideatae sunt*). And so it seems that we will not see God as he is.

To the contrary: John in the first canonical [epistle says]: "When he has appeared, we will be like him, and we will see him as he is."[48]

Likewise, Augustine says that we will see [him] in the kingdom face-to-face without a medium. To be sure, he says that the [divine] dispensation of signs (*dispensatio similitudinum*) is useful for us so long as we are on the journey.[49]

Also, John, a certain expositor, [says]: "The Lord says: 'These things I have spoken in proverbs, but the hour is coming when I will no longer speak to you in proverbs.'[50] Understand proverbs to mean the symbols and figures by which God is seen. Therefore, he will speak openly, not in proverbs, when, after the darkness has been dispersed from our mind, he makes himself known by a clear vision and reveals himself through the visible appearance (*species*) of his majesty."[51]

48. 1 Jn 3.2.
49. Aug., *De trin.* 1.8.16 (PL 42: 831).
50. Jn 16.25.
51. Joh. Sarr., *Comm. super Dion. De cael. hier.* c. 1 §2 (PG 3: 122B).

Similarly, Master Hugh of St. Victor [says]: "What does it mean that God can be seen only in theophanies, and cannot be seen outside of them, except that he is never truly seen and that the truth is never seen? Indeed, if it is always the image alone that is seen, the truth is never seen, since the image is not the truth, even when it is from the truth. Let them remove their phantasms, with which they strive to overshadow the light of our minds, and let them not separate our God from us with our estimative likenesses, for just as nothing but God can satisfy us, so too nothing can lead us all the way to him."[52]

Besides, the same Hugh [says]: "We do not interpose anything between our God and us, but we make the journey immediately both from us to him and from him to us, so that we may be in him and he may be in us, so that there is nothing outside of him in which we are beatified, just as there could be none other than he by whom we were created."[53]

Gregory says the same thing in the Gloss on that passage in Exodus 33, "No man will see me and live."[54]

The same thing is demonstrated by reason in this way: Every agent establishes an end for its action by means of [its] purpose. The intellect is capable of understanding (*intelligens*) by means of purpose. Therefore, it establishes an end only in order to be united to the truth, and especially to the First Truth. And in the same way, the purpose of every intelligence will be useless if it cannot be united to the First Truth *per se*.[55]

In addition, the Philosopher says in the first book of the *Metaphysics* that divine science is the goddess of sciences (*dea scientiarum*).[56] And on [book] 11, the Commentator says that the investigation regarding the intellect and the knowledge of God *per se* "is desired by all."[57]

Also, if something exists in the intellect essentially (*per*

52. Hugh of St. Victor, *Comm. in hier. cael.* 2 (PL 175: 955A), commenting on Dion., *De cael. hier.* c. 1 §3 (PG 3: 124A).

53. Hugh of St. Victor, ibid., PL 175: 955BC.

54. Ex 33.20; *Glossa ord. super Ex* 33.20. Cf. Greg., *Moral.* 18.54 (PL 76: 92–93).

55. Cf. Ar., *Phys.* 2.3 (194b29ff.). Alb., *Phys.* 2.2.4.

56. Ar., *Metaph.* 1.2 (983a6–7); *Metaph. vetus,* ed. Steele, p. 259, 23–24.

57. Averr., *Metaph.* 11 text comm. 51.

seipsum), the only thing necessary for it to be seen or understood is to remove whatever prevents its view or understanding. But God is in the intellect essentially (*per seipsum*), that is, substantially, because he is in every essence whatsoever. Therefore, in order to be seen as he is, it is necessary only to remove an impediment. There are two impediments, however: namely, the imperfection of wretchedness, and turning away to something else. Since, therefore, both of these are removed by beatitude, in beatitude we will see him as he is.

This we concede, saying that we will see God in the kingdom as he is. In fact, just as God sees himself without a medium, so too he will offer himself to us without any medium. And this vision will be a dowry of the soul. But nevertheless a distinction must be made, because it is one thing to see *that* God is, and it is something else to see *what* God is, just as it is one thing to see that something is, and something else to see what something is. Indeed, to see *that* something is is to see the thing's being or the essence of the thing (*esse rei sive essentia rei*). To see *what* something is, however, is to see its proper definition including all the thing's attributes (*terminos*). And these two are different, according as the questions concerning them are different. For when seeking after what is simple and incomposite, first we ask whether the thing exists, and that question is answered since we know that the thing is and has being (*esse*) that has been caused by the First Cause. In fact, the First Cause only establishes being (*esse*), and it adds no distinction beyond that. With this in mind, therefore, we inquire into *what* a thing is, wishing to know the complete definition of the thing by means of the attributes (*terminos*) that comprehend the thing's entire being in such a way that there is nothing of its being [that remains] outside those attributes. And for an understanding of the first question, it is only necessary to reach the thing according to the intellect. For an understanding of the second question, however, it is necessary to comprehend the thing truly, insofar as comprehension is the intellect's encounter with the thing's attributes. Thus, concerning God we say that we reach his being (*esse ipsius*) by means of the intellect without a medium, but we never comprehend it. And this is what Augustine says, that we can see God with the mind, but in truth we can hardly comprehend him at all,[58] and Damascene [says] in book 1, chap. 17: "Indeed, something is circumscribable that is comprehended in terms of place or time or understanding, whereas the uncircumscribable is contained by none of these. Therefore, God alone is uncircumscribable, a being (*ens*) without beginning and without end, both containing all things and contained by no understanding (*comprehensione*). He alone is incomprehensible and without end, known by no one; truly he alone is the contemplator of himself."[59]

1. And based on these [arguments], a solution to Chrysostom's first authority is evident. Moreover, to his arguments we say that Chrysostom understands that the finite cannot [see] into the infinite insofar as it is infinite, but insofar as it is finite it can [see] into it in some manner.[60] Indeed, it remains to consider God's substance in two ways, namely according to "what he is" (*quid est*) and according to being (*esse*), as it is said. According to "what he is," he is not bounded by our intellect; but according to being, he is reached by means of any attribute whatsoever that belongs to the essence of God.

And from this a solution appears to the argument that follows, because although any attribute whatsoever may belong to the divine essence according to what is in God, nevertheless, according to what is perceived by the intellect, the attributes are distinguished by what they signify (*connotata*). And for this reason one [celestial essence] praises [it] as glory, another as wisdom, and another as majesty.

2. To the objection from Dionysius, one must reply that what he means by [the phrase] "not to see him" is "not to see what he is," and what he means by "to see something of [those things that are] his" is "to see him according to a particular attribute."

3. To the next authority from Dionysius, one must reply that

58. Aug., *Sermo* 117, 3.5 (PL 38: 663); cf. *Epist.* 147, 9.21 (PL 33: 606; CSEL 44, p. 295).

59. John Damascene, *De fide orth.* 1.13, and not chap. 17, as in text (PG 94: 853B); transl. Burg. (ed. Buytaert, p. 59, 48–54).

60. Cf. Alb., *De res.* tr. 4, q. 1, art. 9, §1 (ed. Colon. 26, p. 328, 50ff.).

"perfect ignorance" is said to be ignorance of the one who is perfect, that is, ignorance of him with respect to "what he is." Indeed, the most perfect knowledge of God is the vision of his very own being (*esse*), with a recognition of [our] powerlessness to reach "what he is." For in this way he is known to be beyond all knowledge and beyond every mind. And this is what Job says, that all who see him perceive from a distance.[61]

4. To the objection from *On the Celestial Hierarchy,* one must reply that it does not refer to the [divine] ray of truth in the kingdom, but to the ray of truth on the journey, and that [ray] is covered by a variety of mystical and symbolic veils.

5. From the aforementioned, a solution to all the arguments introduced is apparent.[62] In fact, it has been shown that once the imperfection of wretchedness, which stems from the flesh and from sin, has been removed from the intellect by blessedness, and once the turning away to another has been removed through attention to God, in some sense the intellect is rendered capable [of knowing] God in himself. And in this way the first argument is solved.

6. Similarly, it was maintained that God is in the intellect essentially and he is intimate to it and contains it.[63] And in this way, just as the intellect turns to what is above itself without a medium, so too it turns to God without a medium.[64] And Master Hugh of St. Victor shows how this happens by an analogy, saying: "Just as these are two things—light and the body that receives light—and these two produce one [reality] that is luminous, and the one luminous [reality] is in a certain way an image and a likeness of the light insofar as it shines just as the light itself does, so too our God is light and is true light, and rational souls that are clean and pure receive that light itself, and from it they are made luminous; and these are not themselves

61. Cf. Jb 36.25.

62. *De res.* tr. 4, q. 1, art. 9, §1 (ed. Colon. 26, p. 328, 43–46).

63. *De res.* tr. 4, q. 1, art. 9, §1 (ed. Colon. 26, p. 328, 40–41).

64. Cf. William J. Hoye, "Heil und Auferstehung nach Albert dem Grossen," in *Albert der Grosse: Seine Zeit, sein Werk, seine Wirkung. Papers from the 22nd Kölner Mediävistentagung held at the Thomas-Institut, University of Cologne, 3–6 September 1980,* ed. Albert Zimmermann and Gudrun Vuillemin-Diem, Miscellanea Mediaevalia 14 (Berlin: Walter de Gruyter, 1981), 61–77, here 69–70.

an image of the light insofar as they exist, but insofar as they shine because of the light, just as the light itself shines."[65]

7. To the last objection also a solution is clear, because, as was maintained,[66] that which is essentially remote from the intellect is seen through form. But God exists essentially in the intellect. Therefore, it is only necessary that he be seen through his own essence immediately.

§2. What vision is a dowry

Second, one asks what vision is a dowry.

1. If it is said that it is to see [God] face-to-face, then one asks what that means. In fact, a simple substance does not have a face. If it is said that it [the vision] is knowledge of his substance, then again it seems that we will see [him] face-to-face, because we will have some knowledge of his substance as well, especially since it is said in Genesis, "I have seen the Lord face-to-face," etc.[67]

2. In addition, one asks whether this is the same thing as to see in the Word. And it seems that it is, because they will see the Word and they will see in the Word, just as Gregory says.[68]

Moreover, Augustine says in *The Literal Interpretation of Genesis* that the morning vision of the angels, which is a vision of light and a beatifying vision, is in the Word.[69] Therefore, in like manner, the vision that beatifies souls will be in the Word. And this goes back to this question [under consideration]: what is the vision with respect to which there is a dowry?

Solution: We say that the vision-dowry is the vision of what is beloved and possessed without a medium for the sake of glorification. And insofar as it is without a medium, it is said to be face-to-face. Insofar as it is without a sign (*symbolo*) and without obscurity, it is said to be a vision by means of sight (*per speciem*).

65. Hugh of St. Victor, *Comm. In hier. cael.* 2 (PL 175: 955AB), who explicates Dion., *De cael. hier.* c. 1 §3 (PG 3: 124A). Cf. Alb., *De IV coaequ.* q. 32 a. 2 sol.

66. *De res.* tr. 4, q. 1, art. 9, §1 (ed. Colon. 26, p. 327, 51ff.).

67. Gn 32.30.

68. Greg., *Dial.* 4.33 (PL 77: 367B). Cf. *Moral.* 2.3.3 (PL 75: 556f.). Peter Lombard, *II Sent.* d. 11 c. 2 (p. 357).

69. Aug., *De gen. ad litt.* 4.23–24.40f. (PL 34: 312ff.; CSEL 28.1, p. 122, 26ff.). Cf. Alb., *De IV coaequ.* q. 24 a. 3 part. 1; *Summa* II q. 14 a. 2 part. 2.

For here the proper nature of God is called "sight," according to which it is the principle for knowing his substance according to "what he is" (*quid est*). And this is derived from the authority of Maximus [the Confessor], who says: "'The death of his saints is precious in the sight of the Lord';[70] it is the precious transition of completely purified souls into intimate contemplation of the truth, which is indeed true beatitude and eternity. And this is the death by which those who live religiously, seeking their God piously and chastely,[71] are dying already (while still fixed in this mortal life), seeing what they seek in a mirror and dimly. In the future, however, they will return to the pristine dignity of the divine image according to which they were created, and they will see God himself face-to-face, as far as is possible for a creature [capable of knowing what is] comprehensible and intelligible, and when exalted above all things they will see the incomprehensible and unintelligible cause of everything face-to-face. As the Apostle says, 'We see now in a mirror and dimly, but then face-to-face,'[72] calling the appearance of divine truth, which cannot be perceived by any creature through itself, that is comprehensible to the human intellect, the 'face.'"[73]

1. To the objection, therefore, that even here it is [possible] to see [God] face-to-face, we say that this occurs suddenly and in rapture. And for this reason it is not a dowry, because the dowry is a quiet, everlasting possession.

2. To the question concerning vision in the Word, one must reply that vision in the Word differs from this [vision] according to definition (*rationem*). For vision in the Word denotes an illumination apprehended from the Word with respect to something knowable, whether pertaining to glory or pertaining to the governance of the world. With respect to this, Augustine says that the angels saw creation going to be created in the

70. Ps 115.15.

71. Cf. Ti 2.12.

72. 1 Cor 13.12.

73. *Glossae super Dion.* (*De eccl. hier.* c. 3 §9; PG 3: 437C), attributed to Maximus, Cod. Paris, B. N. 15630, fols. 22va–b. Cf. Alb., *Super Is.* 14.19 (ed. Colon. 19, p. 209, 50). John Scotus Eriugena, *De divisione naturae* 5.27 (PL 122: 922BC). H.-F. Dondaine, *Le corpus Dionysien*, p. 13.

Word and that the prophets also read in the Word.[74] But the vision by sight (*per speciem*) is a vision of the divine nature that is beloved and embraced for the glorification of the one seeing him.

From these [remarks], a solution is apparent to something that could be asked, namely whether the truth that is seen is only an intellectual truth (*veritas intellectiva*), according to which the Philosopher says that "truth is the goal of speculative intelligence,"[75] or whether it is an affective truth (*veritas affectiva*) known along with the intellect, that is, affecting [one] through the intellect: [the solution is] that it is certain that it exists in the last way. Indeed, otherwise it would not be the bride's dowry, for the bride attends to love and affection.

§3. How this vision differs from other visions

Third, one asks how this vision differs from other visions, and especially from the vision that follows upon faith, and from the one that comes after the gifts (*dona*) of prudence and knowledge and counsel and understanding and wisdom.[76]

And it seems that it does not differ at all, because the saints[77] say that the vision by sight (*per speciem*) follows upon faith, and this vision is the dowry discussed above.

Similarly, if anything comes after wisdom and understanding, it seems that it is nothing but knowledge of the divine substance, because, as Augustine says, wisdom is the knowledge of things divine.[78]

To this we say, without offense (*sine praeiudicio*), that these visions differ in two ways from each other, namely on the part of the one who sees and on the part of what is seen. And for this to be understood appropriately, one must propose an analogy

74. Aug., *De gen. ad litt.* 4.23–24.40f. (PL 34: 312ff.; CSEL 28.1, p. 123, 23ff.). Cf. Wm. of Auxerre, *Summa aurea* II tr. 6 cap. 1 (ed. Ribaillier, vol. 2/1, pp. 124–30).

75. Ar., *Metaph.* 2.1 (993b20–21); *Metaph. vetus,* ed. Steele 282, 45; cf. Alb., *De res.* tr. l, q. 6, art.1 (ed. Colon. 26, p. 248, 60).

76. Here we have some of the traditionally seven gifts of the Holy Spirit.

77. Cf. Peter Lombard, *In epist. Pauli* Phil 3.15 (PL 192: 249B); *In epist. Pauli* 1 Cor 13.10 (PL 191: 1662B). Aug., *De doc. Christ.* 1.38.42 (PL 34: 35).

78. Aug., *De trin.* 14.1.3 (PL 42: 1037). Cf. Peter Lombard, *III Sent.* d. 35 c. 1 (p. 707f.).

to the visual power that exists in the eye of an animal. For there is a certain visual power that exists in the eye that is strengthened by the compressed (*calcatum*)[79] and dense and unified light that is in that eye, as is the visual power in the eye of a lynx.[80] There is also a certain visual power that does not have sufficient light in the eye, but that requires external light, with respect to which Chalcidius [commenting] on Plato says that our vision is perfected when a ray is emitted by an internal light that exists in the eye, which ray is joined to a ray of external light, so that in this way by the assistance of the two lights the visual power may be perfected for seeing.[81] And the combination and condensing of that light exists in various animals to a greater or lesser degree. It exists a great deal in the eagle, as the Philosopher says, and for this reason it beholds the sun in the orb.[82] But it does not exist in the same way in a human, and for this reason he cannot behold the sun in this way, but sees in the sun's light that is diffused in the air. In some eyes it [the light] is not dense, but nonetheless it is unified, such as in the eye of the screech owl (*noctua*), and for this reason the screech owl is repelled by a great deal of light, but sees correctly in light mixed with shade, such as the light at dusk and the light at night. And there is another visual power in an eye with a weak and non-unified (*non-adunatum*) light, and this [eye] requires the cover of darkness so that it will not be repelled, just like the visual power in the eye of the mole, which has eyes under the skin, as the Philosopher says,[83] and this is because its habitation is, for the most part, underground.

Likewise, one must note that the sensible form received

79. On *calcatus*, cf. Alb., *De IV coaequ.* q. 15 a. 2; *De caelo et mundo* 2.3.6; *Summa* II q. 57 m. 2 sol.

80. Alb. often remarks that the lynx's acute eyesight surpasses that of humans, and may in one sense be said to be superior to ours. Cf. *De animal.* 21.1.4 (*SZ* 2: 1411); *Quaest. super de animal.* 2, q. 29 ad 2 (ed. Colon. 12, pp. 120–21; *QDA*, p. 106).

81. Chalc., *Comm. in Tim.* C. 244 (ed. Wrobel, p. 278, 10ff.).

82. Ar., *De hist. animal.* 9.34 (620a1–2). Cf. Alb., *De animal.* 8.2.6.106 (*SZ* 1: 714), and 23.7(1) (*SZ* 2: 1547).

83. Ar., *De hist. animal.* 1.9 (491b28). Cf. Alb., *De animal.* 1.2.3.141 (*SZ* 1: 98–99).

by sense exists in two modes. For there is one [sensible form] through which an object is seen, but it [the form] is not seen in it. And of this [form] the Philosopher says that "sense is capable of receiving the sensible species without matter" when the object is present.[84] Indeed, there is an image (*idolum*) in the eye through which we see, but not in which we see, the object. But the image that exists in a mirror is that in which we see the object.

Having treated these things, let us proceed to a distinction. I say, therefore, that the vision of faith on the journey [of this life] is just like vision united to light that is non-unified and condensed, perceiving the visible object as in a mirror. For just as light exists in the eye, so too the habit of faith exists in the intellect; and just as the visual power [is] in the eye, so too the intellective power [is] in the intellect; and just as an image [is] in a mirror in which we see an object, to which the image leads, so too [there is] a symbolic or mystical mirror of creation in which is seen the First Truth, which is God, because it leads to that [Truth]. What follows upon faith, however, is like a light that is condensed and unified on the part of the one who sees, and just like the object itself on the part of the object seen. The vision of wisdom, on the other hand, is like experiential knowledge from those [properties] that a man possesses in himself here from divine gifts through grace, [but which he will possess] in the future through glory. But the intellectual vision of the gift is like a light generated from illuminations received through doctrine or revelation. Therefore, Gregory says that it confers understanding when it illumines the mind concerning things that have been heard.[85] But the light that follows upon counsel is just like a light united to the basis (*ratio*) of the counsels. In fact, the basis of all counsels is illumination by way of grace or glory for those works [of human action] that exist beyond a [moral] precept. And this light, elevating the intellect, will exist in the kingdom [of heaven] so that one may see the divine basis itself of counsels and may glory in it. What follows upon the gift of knowledge is a light perfected for the knowl-

84. Ar., *De anima* 2.12 (424a17–19). Cf. Alb., *De anima* 2.4.1.

85. Greg., *Moral.* 1.32.44 (PL 75: 547A). Cf. *Glosssa ord. super Iob* 1.4.

edge of God, insofar as he himself is the source of those works (*operabilium*)[86] that regulate the interaction of humans with one another. Similarly, the light that follows upon prudence is a perfected light uniting the intellect with God, insofar as in him there shines forth the basis (*ratio*) of all choices directed toward works of virtue.

And note that the eternal vision and vision in the journey [of this life] are not the same. Indeed, on the journey [of life], over and above the light that strengthens the visual power, it is necessary for us to have a likeness through which we may see an object. But in the kingdom [of heaven] we will see the object immediately and without a likeness under a light that replaces the graces defined above. The light of the vision of the dowry, however, differs from all these in that it is a light given from above to the bride, not replacing any power that it had on the journey [of this life], and it is given to her in order to complete the most noble union of lover and beloved.

If, however, one should object that the vision of God is in all of these and thus one object (*res*) seems to exist in them all, one must reply that an act is drawn into the appearance by reason of the object of the act and by reason of the one by whom it is an act. Therefore, although one object is seen, namely God, nevertheless it is not [seen] in the same way (*sub eadem ratione*), as is clear from what has been said. Similarly, it is not seen from the same light, and for that reason the vision will not be one vision but multiform.

Art. 10. On the second dowry, which is love (*dilectio*)

Next, one asks about the second dowry, which is love. And first, one asks whether love is [a dowry]; second, what it is, insofar as it is a dowry; third, [one asks] about the difference between it and charity (*caritas*), which is a virtue.[87]

86. On the *operabilia* among scholastic authors, cf. Jeremiah Hackett, "Epilogue: Roger Bacon's Moral Science," in *Roger Bacon and the Sciences: Commemorative Essays* (Leiden: Brill, 1996), 406–7.

87. On the three forms of love (*amor*)—*caritas, dilectio, and amicitia*—in the work of Thomas Aquinas, cf. Mark-Robin Hoogland, *God, Passion and Power: Thomas Aquinas on Christ Crucified and the Almightiness of God* (Leuven: Peeters, 2003), 92–93.

§1. Whether love (*dilectio*) is a dowry

To the first question, one proceeds in this way:

1. A dowry is what is given to a bride when she is inducted to the marriage bed and to the home of the bridegroom. But she possesses love before induction. Therefore, love does not seem to be a dowry.

2. Also, it is commonly said that the dowry is an everlasting adornment, or an everlasting gift (*donum*).[88] Charity (*caritas*), however, insofar as it is [something] of this sort, is not an everlasting gift, because if it were an everlasting gift then necessarily one would never lose it after possessing it. Therefore, love (*dilectio*) does not seem to be a dowry.

3. Also, every dowry is part of the glory of the blessed. But charity (*caritas*) is part of merit rather than of glory. Therefore, it is not a dowry.

4. Also, all the other dowries of body and soul will be possessed only in the kingdom and not while on the journey. Charity (*caritas*), however, will be possessed here on the journey. Therefore, it does not seem to be a dowry.

To the contrary: Love (*dilectio*) is a genuine affection for the bride. Therefore, she ought to be especially endowed with this in her union to the bridegroom.

Also, a dowry is given to the bride so that, once onerous impediments to the joy of the union have been removed, she will be better able to be joined to the bridegroom. But nothing is better able to effect the marital union than love (*amor*), because Augustine says that love is the band that binds the lover tightly to the beloved.[89] Therefore, this [love] especially ought to be the dowry.

1. This we concede, saying to the first that there is a love (*dilectio*) that desires and a love (*dilectio*) that binds. The love that desires belongs to the journey; the love that binds, however, belongs to the kingdom, and the latter is a dowry.

88. See Alb., *De res.* tr. 4, q. 1, art. 8 (ed. Colon. 26, p. 326, 61–62).

89. "the beloved": here, *amato*, masculine; i.e., the bridegroom. Aug., *De trin.* 8.10.14 (PL 42: 960). Cf. Alb., *Super Dion. De div. nom.* c. 4, 135 (ed. Colon. 37/1, pp. 224–25); *Eth. Quaest.* 1.78; *infra*, p. 347, 4; *III Sent.* d. 27 a. 4. Bonaventure, *III Sent.* d. 27 dub. 1, *Opera* 3: 615a. Alex. Hales, *Glossa* 3 d. 27, 22 (p. 330, 29–31).

2. To the next we say that love (*dilectio*) is related to the lover in two ways: it is related to him as directing the affection of the lover, which affection is nonetheless disposed to the contrary because of the tinder of sin (*fomes*). And in this way charity (*caritas*) is not an everlasting gift (*donum*), but one that can be lost. It is related to the lover in another way, namely as obtaining the affection removed from every disposition to the contrary and confirmed with respect to one [person]. And in this way it is a dowry, because in this way it is everlasting.

3. To the next, one must say that there is a love (*dilectio*) moving free will flexibly into each part, and there is a love uniting the will with the ultimate object of the will. And the first produces merit, and the second is a part of glory.

4. To the last, one must say that the most perfect of the virtues is love (*dilectio*). And for this reason, in one respect it can exist on the journey and in another respect in the kingdom. And this is because it perfects the will, which, when wholly free, exists purely among the powers of the soul, because it is not dependent in act on the flesh, unlike the intellect, which, so long as it is united to the phantasm, cannot see clearly but rather sees in a mirror. And for this reason faith, which perfects the intellect, cannot exist both on the journey and in the kingdom in the same way as love, which perfects the affection.

§2. How love (*dilectio*) is a dowry

Second, one asks how love is a dowry.

1. If one says that this is because love is a virtue, this does not seem to be so, because a dowry and blessedness are different parts of the reward, and the virtue charity (*caritas*) is part of blessedness. Therefore, it seems that love (*dilectio*) the virtue is not the same as love (*dilectio*) the dowry.

2. Moreover, since there are many virtues, like justice, temperance, etc., there is no reason why one of these should be a dowry more than another. Therefore, all will be dowries (*dotes*) or none.

3. Moreover, since a gift (*donum*) and a fruit and blessedness are habits (*habitus*) more noble than a virtue, there is more reason for a dowry (*dos*) (which is the noblest gift [*donum*]), to be a gift (*donum*) or a fruit, but it is not. Therefore, neither is it a virtue.

Solution:

1. One must say that nothing prevents one and the same thing from being, under different definitions (*rationes*), a dowry and a virtue or something following a virtue, just as is the case for vision and understanding, one of which follows faith and the other follows hope, although under these definitions they are not said to be dowries. We speak similarly concerning love (*dilectio*), for insofar as the first goodness is understood to be its end and object, it is a virtue and part of blessedness. In fact, love (*dilectio*) as a virtue loves the highest Good because it is the highest Good. It is a dowry, however, to the extent that it unites into one spirit, and such a union is the reason for loving. In this way a solution is apparent to the first.

2. To the next we say that there are certain virtues of which God is the end and the object, so far as he is the source of beatitude, to wit, insofar as he is the highest Truth and the highest Goodness and the unfailing source of power, just as faith, hope, and charity (*caritas*), and the acts of the dowries are assumed to accord with those that follow from them. There are others, however, that do not have God as their proper object but as an end, like the four cardinal [virtues],[90] and it is not necessary to assume that the acts of the dowries accord with them.

3. To the last one, one must say that although a gift (*donum*) and a fruit are habits (*habitus*) nobler than a virtue, nonetheless there is no habit nobler than charity (*caritas*). Therefore, too, nothing follows charity (*caritas*), but the very same one that exists on the journey is perfected in the kingdom. Or, better, one may say that dowries are not assumed to accord with habits, to the extent that they are nobler or less noble, but rather to the extent that they join the soul more or less directly to God, because a dowry attends to the soul's union with God. And for this reason, since the three theological [virtues] correspond to this most directly, dowries agree with these habits (*habitus*) more than with others.

90. The cardinal virtues are prudence, temperance, fortitude, and justice.

§3. What is the difference between the dowry of love (*dilectio*) and the virtue of love (*dilectio*)?

Third, one asks, what is the difference between the dowry of love (*dilectio*) and the virtue of love (*dilectio*)?

And it seems there is none, because if there were a difference, either it would stem from a habit (*habitus*) or the act or the object. It follows that it does not stem from the act, because to love (*diligere*) pertains to both. Likewise, it does not stem from the object, because God is the object of both. Moreover, it seems, too, that it does not stem from a habit (*habitus*), because the Philosopher says that whatever the activities are, such are the habits (*habitus*), and conversely.[91] Since, then, there is no difference in the acts, neither will there be a difference in the habits (*habitus*).

Moreover, just as "by definition acts exist prior to potencies,"[92] so too [acts exist prior] to habits, because just as we know potencies through acts, so too for habits.

Solution: We say that a difference exists with respect to definition (*ratio*) according to the habit and according to the object. In fact, a virtue is specifically that which crosses from a state of grace to a state of blessedness, but a dowry is that which is given at the bride's induction to the marriage bed of the bridegroom over and above what is deserved. And although God is the object, nonetheless [God is the object] not insofar as he is God, but he will be the object of virtue insofar as he is the highest Goodness, and [he will be] the object of the dowry insofar as there exists a capacity for union into one spirit.[93]

From these, a solution to the objections is apparent.

Art. 11. On the dowry that is comprehension (*comprehensio*)

Next, one asks about the third dowry, which is comprehension. And first, one asks whether this is a dowry; second, what it is insofar as it is a dowry; and third, how it differs from the comprehension that is said to follow hope.

91. Ar., *Eth. Nic.* 2.1 (1103b21–22). Cf. Alb., *De bono* tr. 1 q. 4 a. 2 (ed. Colon. 28, p. 47, 18–20).

92. Ar., *De anima* 2.4 (415a18–20). Alb., *De anima* 2.2.1. Cf. Ar., *Metaph.* 9.8 (1049b10–11). *Supra* p. 207, 69.

93. For almost identical language, see Hugh of Ripelin, *Compend. theol. veritatis* 7.26, ed. Borgnet 34, pp. 686–87.

§1. Whether comprehension is a dowry

To the first, one proceeds in this way:

1. Every power (*potentia*) of the soul in the kingdom will comprehend the final end for which it exists, that is, God. But not every power of the soul will have the dowry, insofar as the dowry is divided into three dowries for the soul. Therefore, comprehension is not a dowry.

2. In addition, to see by sight (*per speciem*) establishes a union of the intellect to the First Truth, and in this way the intellect comprehends truth. Likewise, to love (*diligere*) establishes the will's union to the highest Goodness, and in this way the will comprehends goodness. Since only the comprehension of truth and goodness will exist, therefore it seems that there is no third comprehension stemming from vision and from love.

Solution: We say that comprehension is the soul's third dowry. Just as there exists a specific power (*potestas*) in the soul for retaining the character of images (*habitum similitudinum*) that are in the soul, and that power is called memory, to which the intellect and the will also turn owing to the double image retained there (namely, of the true and the good), just as there is a specific power for retaining the appearance (*species*) or the reality (*res*) of the First Truth itself and of the First Goodness, which the intellect will examine or gaze upon ceaselessly, so too the will loves.

1. To the first, therefore, one must reply: If comprehension means to attain something, then every power will attain its end. If it means, however, to embrace something, such that it holds the whole within itself, then no power will comprehend God. But comprehension is not said to be a dowry in either way, but rather comprehension is called a dowry insofar as it takes hold of (*tentio*) the truth and the First Good by sight (*per speciem*).

2. To the next, one must reply that the intellect does not have a reward with respect to the end that is taken hold of (*tenti*), insofar as it has been taken hold of, but rather with respect to the end of the intellect or of truth, insofar as it is such. It is the same for the will, which exists with respect to the good or to the loved, insofar as it is such. Therefore, since the acts of the

soul differ in accord with ends, there will be three acts with respect to three ends: namely, [one] with respect to the truth insofar as it is truth; and [another] with respect to the beloved insofar as it is beloved, or with respect to the good insofar as it is good; and [another] with respect to what is taken hold of or possessed, insofar as it is such.

§2. What it is, insofar as it is a dowry

To the second, one proceeds in this way:

Comprehension is the intellect's encounter with the attributes (*termini*) of an object. But God does not have attributes (*termini*), for he is infinite. Therefore, he is not comprehended.

If one should say that comprehension is not understood here in this way, but rather according to its usual meaning, by which we say that someone comprehends an object that he has pursued when he holds it or seizes it, it seems that in this sense comprehension is not a dowry, because in this way the earlier objection returns, that every power and also every virtue pursues its end in this way.[94]

To this, one must reply that comprehension is understood here in the sense that it denotes the perfection of the union of the bride to the bridegroom. Later, to see and to love is to possess the completion of the union; and to possess that completion is nothing but comprehension. And it can be defined in this way: comprehension is the possession or the taking hold of (*tentio*) what is seen and loved having been united in one spirit.

And in this way a solution to the question is apparent, because comprehension is not understood in the way in which the objection proceeds.

§3. How does what is said to follow hope differ from comprehension?

To the third, one proceeds in this way:

1. There is a certain comprehension that follows hope, and this is a part of beatitude and not part of the dowry. Therefore, one asks what the difference is.

2. Moreover, the true and the good exist in God, and they

94. See Alb., *De res.* tr. 4, q. 1, art. 11, §1 (ed. Colon. 26, p. 333, 21–22).

are the objects of beatitude, and there are two dowries in relation to them. Therefore, since a third also exists there, namely majesty or omnipotence, it seems that there ought to be a third dowry in relation to the third.

One must reply to this that the comprehension that follows hope, as the masters say,[95] exists in relation to the continuing hardship of waiting. But comprehension, to the extent that it is a dowry, does not take into account the hardship, for the bride does not attend to the majesty of the bridegroom, but rather to the kiss and embrace. And for this reason, a dowry does not exist in relation to the majesty but only in relation to what is seen and loved and possessed in joyfulness of the spirit.

And in this way a solution is evident to both.

Art. 12. On the number of the dowries of the soul

Next, one asks about the number of the soul's dowries.

1. And it seems that there ought to be very many, because every power of the soul will be joined to God. Therefore, since there are many powers, there will be many dowries.

2. Again, one asks about the statement of those who say that the number of dowries is understood in accord with the rational, irascible, and concupiscible [parts of the soul].[96] And it seems this [statement] cannot stand, because the concupiscible and irascible are parts of the sensible soul, as Damascene[97] and Avicenna[98] say. The rational, however, although it is a part of the rational soul, nonetheless receives nothing without combination and composition. This is clear from the definition that Isaac provides for it in the *Book of Definitions:* Reason is a power of the soul "making it pass from the cause to the caused."[99]

95. "Masters": Wm. of Auxerre, *Summa aurea* IV tr. 18 cap. 3 q. 3 a. 1 (ed. Ribaillier, vol. 4, pp. 496–502); Alex. Hales, *Glossa* 1 d. 1, 6 (p. 9, 20f.).

96. Cf. Alex. Hales, *Quaestio de dotibus animae* (Cod. Toulouse Bibliothèque de la ville 737, fol. 162ra). Bonaventure, *IV Sent.* d. 49 a. 1 q. 5, *Opera* 4: 1009.

97. John Damascene, *De fide orth.* 2.12 (PG 94: 925CD; cf. 928C; ed. Buytaert p. 117, 87–89; cf. p. 118, 108ff.).

98. Avic., *Liber VI Nat.* pars 1, c. 5 (fol. 4b in *Opera*).

99. That is, it is a discursive power leading the soul from the known to the unknown. Cf. Isaac, *De diff.* (ed. Muckle, p. 321, 18–19; cf. p. 338, 9–10). Cf. Alb., *De homine* q. 60 sol. (ed. Colon. 27/2, p. 459); *De bono* tr. 4 q. 2 a. 5 (ed. Colon. 28, p. 254, 30); *Super Porphyrium de universalibus* 1.1, in *Albertus Magnus*

Therefore, since the acts of the dowries are the simplest acts, it is clear that they are not determined in accord with powers of this sort.

In addition, the Apostle says that woman is the image and glory of man.[100] Therefore, it seems that the union of bride and bridegroom ought to be understood in accord with the image, and in such a way it will be understood in accord with the intellective [power], memory, and will.[101]

But opposed to this seems to be the fact that comprehension, which is the last dowry, ought to belong to the last power among the powers of the image, and thus belongs to the will. This is false.

Solution: We say that the number of dowries can be understood in three ways: namely in accord with powers, and in accord with acts, and in accord with the objects of the acts.

In accord with powers in this way: There are three powers of the image that are simplest, according to Augustine,[102] because in them the soul imitates God. Therefore, to see will belong to intelligence, to love will belong to the will, and to hold onto will belong to memory. And then the last objection should be resolved by saying that memory is first according to one order, but memory is last according to another order. Memory is first according to the change to natural habits, but it is last according to the change of acquired habits. And Augustine makes both of these statements—one in *On Genesis* and the other in *On Ecclesiasticus* 18.[103] That, however, which will exist in the kingdom, namely the soul's union to God, will exist in the manner of an acquired [habit], since it will not possess it from nature.

It is understood in this way with respect to acts: the acts that

---

Über Logik und Universalienlehre, ed. Manuel Santos Noya and Uwe Petersen, Philosophische Bibliothek 635 (Hamburg: Felix Meiner Verlag GmbH, 2012), 4.

100. Cf. 1 Cor 11.7.

101. Cf. Aug., *De trin.* 14.8.11 (PL 42: 1044); Peter Lombard, *I Sent.* d. 3 c. 2 (p. 33). Alb., *I Sent.* d. 3 a. 20 ad qla 1.

102. Aug., *De trin.* 10.12.19 (PL 42: 984).

103. Aug., *De trin.* 10.11.17 (PL 42: 982). Cf. Alb., *De homine* q. 73, the gloss on Sir 17.1 (ed. Colon. 27/2, p. 550). The deuterocanonical book, the Wisdom of Jesus Ben Sira, usually called Sirach, began to be named Ecclesiasticus in the Latin West in the third century of the Common Era. Cf. Alb., *I Sent.* d. 3 a. 38 sol.

are able to perfect the union of the bride to the bridegroom either draw toward or perfect the union. I say, however, they draw closely (*propinque*). If they are drawing toward, then they are vision and love, and one of them, namely love, draws toward more closely, but comprehension perfects the union.

In regard to the object [of the acts] there are three that move the bride to the bridegroom, namely, honor and goodness and [their] social union. Vision exists in relation to honor, love exists in relation to goodness, and comprehension in relation to the union. And although there are many others, the bride does not consider these, insofar as she is a bride.

1. To the first, one must reply that every power of the soul will be rewarded, but the reward cannot be called a dowry. In fact, a dowry denotes that which unites the soul to God in one spirit without a medium. And this only befits the soul with respect to its simplest part.

2. We believe the next opinion to be false, as has been demonstrated.

On the Dowries of the Body

Next, one asks about the dowries of the body, and first about the individual ones and then about their number.

Concerning individual ones, one asks first about luminosity. And first one asks whether luminosity is a dowry. Second, how much luminosity there will be.

Art. 13. On luminosity[104]

§1. Whether luminosity is a dowry[105]

To the first, one proceeds in this way:

1. In 1 Cor 15 the Apostle seems to enumerate the dowries when he says: "It is sown an animal body, it will rise a spiritual body. It is sown in corruption, it will rise in incorruption. It is sown in dishonor, it will rise in glory. It is sown in weakness, it will rise in power."[106] And luminosity is not among those enumerated here. Therefore, it does not seem to be a dowry.

104. *luminositas:* "luminosity" or "splendor."

105. Cf. Alb., *IV Sent.* d. 44 a. 27–28.

106. 1 Cor 15.44, 42–43.

2. Moreover, we will not be transformed into another nature. Since, therefore, the principles of nature are the principles of properties, and the property of light is caused by the nature of heaven, it will not be caused by the principles of human nature. And so our bodies will not be luminous.

But the opposite is in the Gospel of Matthew: "Then the just will shine as the sun, in the kingdom of their Father."[107] And also in Wisdom 3: "The just will shine, and will run to and fro like sparks among the reeds."[108]

Solution: We say that luminosity is a dowry and is included under glory. Indeed, what the Apostle enumerates is not a dowry, but a property of the glorious body. And this is clear because glory, power (*virtus*), incorruption, and the spiritual state are general names and indicate general properties. Dowries, however, are specific properties, and for this reason they have to be denoted by specific names. And one sees this from the explanation of the names, because they are explained in one way by Damascene in his last chapter[109] and in another way in the Gloss,[110] and this in many ways because each one receives some specific content under the general [property].[111] Nonetheless, we say this without offense (*sine praeiudicio*), because some say that they are dowries that the Apostle enumerates.[112]

2. To the next we say that the property of light is not caused by the parts of our nature, namely matter and form, on account of the fact that they are united to elemental qualities according to act, but on account of the fact that all dishonor is removed [from them] by glorification.

§2. How much luminosity there will be[113]

To the second, one proceeds in this way:

1. In 1 Cor 15 the Apostle says, "One is the radiance of the

107. Mt 13.43.

108. Wis 3.7.

109. John Damascene, *De fide orth.* 4.27 (PG 1225A; ed. Buytaert, p. 383, 112–15).

110. Peter Lombard, *In epist. Pauli* 1 Cor 15.44 (PL 191: 1687B).

111. John Damascene, *De fide orth.* 4.27 (PG 94: 1225A; ed. Buytaert, p. 383, 112–15).

112. "Some say": Hugh of St. Cher, *De dotibus resurgentium* (fol. 303rb).

113. Cf. Alb., *IV Sent.* d. 44 a. 29–31.

sun (*claritas solis*), another the radiance of the moon, and another the radiance of the stars. For star differs from star in radiance. So also will be the resurrection of the dead."[114] Thus it seems that one will not possess radiance from oneself, but from another, namely the one who is like the moon.

2. Also Daniel says in chapter 12 that "those who are learned will shine like the brightness of the firmament, and those who instruct many according to justice, [will shine] like stars for all eternity."[115] But the firmament has no brightness, as is apparent. Therefore, some will shine not at all.

Solution: We say that the magnitude of radiance (*quantitas claritatis*) has to be inferred from three things: the first is the proportion of nature's capacity, the second is the abundance of merit, and the third is the supererogation of divine generosity. Now, the fact that nature has a proportionate capacity for light is clear in the principles of nature, which are the elements and the heaven, which at that time will shine. Therefore, there would be equal [brightness] in the first and the last, if there were no middle. And for this reason, in accord with the middle one especially, one admits a difference in radiance among the blessed.

1. To the objection concerning the moon, one must reply that the only analogy is that it shines less than the sun. Or, better, one could say that Christ's resurrection is compared to the sun, and the resurrection of baptized infants is compared to the moon, since the latter only shine with another's light, because they did not have their own merit. The resurrection of those others who did have their own merit, however, is compared to the light of the stars.

2. To the next, one must reply that light exists in heaven, but it is not so dense (*calcatum*) that it emits rays as the stars do.[116] Therefore, the learned who possess justice in themselves, but do not instruct others, are compared to heaven. Those who send forth the rays of their teaching to shine upon others are compared to the stars, however. Moreover, it is commonly said by

114. 1 Cor 15.41–42.

115. Dn 12.3.

116. Cf. Alb., *De IV coaequ.* q. 15 a. 2; *De caelo et mundo* 2.3.6; *Summa* II q. 57 m. 2 sol.

the saints[117] that the light of the moon will exist then, just as the light of the sun existed when the sun was created.[118] Moreover, the light of the sun was greater when it was created than it is now, as was determined in the "Question on Renewal."[119] The light of the sun will be seven times greater in the future than it was at the beginning, however, and at that time the human body will shine seven times more brightly than the sun.[120]

Art. 14. On impassibility

Next, one asks about impassibility. And two questions are asked, namely what it is and how much [there is].

§1. What impassibility is

To the first, one proceeds in this way:

1. "Im-"[121] either operates privatively or negatively. If privatively, then it posits a potency while removing the act, and in this way glorious bodies do not suffer although they could suffer, which is false. If negatively, then it posits nothing; and in this way it will not be the name of a dowry.

2. In addition, one raises a question about what some people say,[122] that impassibility is the power to resist external injury. With respect to this, it is necessary that we have another dowry to resist internal injury. And if one says that that is a spiritual nature or power (*virtus*), it is clear that neither one of these contains in its definition "resistant to internal injury." In fact, "power (*virtus*) is the end of a thing's potency (*potentia*)," as the Philosopher says in book two of *On Heaven and Earth*.[123] This agrees especially well with a passive [power], as is clear from the example in the same place. Moreover, a spiritual nature does not imply "resistant to injury," which is clear in demons and in the souls of the damned.

Also, a negation removes more than an affirmation posits.

117. Cf. Peter Lombard, *IV Sent.* d. 48 c. 5 (p. 1025f.).

118. Cf. Is 30.26.

119. See Alb., *De res.* tr. 2, q. 10 (ed. Colon. 26, p. 292, 32ff.).

120. Cf. Alb.'s treatment of this in his *Problemata determinata* q. 37 (ed. Colon. 17/2, p. 62).

121. That is, the "im-" of impassibility.

122. "Some": Hugh of St. Cher, *De dotibus resurgentium* (fol. 303rb).

123. See Ar., *De caelo et mundo* 1, c. 11 (281a11–17).

This is clear [from this]: When one says, "A man runs," it is true for some individual man, but when one says, "A man does not run," it is negated for all. Therefore, analogously, although passibility may be said equally in terms of an internal or external injury, impassibility, on account of the privative negation, indicates a power to resist both.

3. After this, one asks why impassibility is mentioned rather than immortality.

4. And again, why impassibility should be a dowry of the body rather than of the soul, since the soul also can suffer and will possess through glorification the capacity not to suffer.

Solution: We say that impassibility is the body's dowry, with which the body resists every injury, whether internal or external.

1. And what is asked concerning the preposition, I say that it operates privatively. But privation is twofold. For one privation posits a subject, or matter, with a disposition toward a form that deprives [it of an attribute], such as "blind," "nude," "unjust," "silent," and "dark." The other, however, posits a subject without a disposition toward a form that deprives [it of an attribute], as is a privation in infinite terms, like non-man. And in this sense I say that privation exists in the second way in this term, not that it is an infinite term, but that it is analogous to an infinite term because the power and act of suffering (*actus passibilitatis*) is removed and the subject remains.

2. We concede the next point, just as the objections proceed.

3. To the next, we say that immortality does not remove the power to be weakened, and for this reason it does not denote a power to resist every injury. Therefore, the bodies of the damned will be immortal, yet they are not impassible, just as the Apostle says in 1 Cor 15:[124] "and the dead will rise again, but we" that is, the saints, "will be changed" at the glory of the resurrection.

4. To the last, one must reply that by its very nature the soul, released from the body, is impassible and suffers only in an accidental fashion (*per accidens*), namely, when subject to sin, and for this reason impassibility belongs to its nature and is not a dowry for it.

From this, a solution is clear to another question that could

124. 1 Cor 15.52.

arise, namely, how the impassibility of those who are risen differs from Adam's impassibility in the state of innocence. To be sure, Adam did not possess it [impassibility] as a dowry but from the grace of innocence, on the condition that he not sin.

Again, it is clear that it is not the same impassibility for him, except perhaps in the first root of principles, but not in a disposition and habit (*habitus*). This has to be discussed, however, in the "Question on the State of Innocence."[125]

§2. How much impassibility there is[126]

To the second, one proceeds in this way:

The least in the kingdom will have impassibility sufficient to resist every injury. The greatest, therefore, cannot have any more. And so impassibility will be equal for all.

If one should say that the quantity is thought to be in accord with the number of things it resists, opposed to this is the fact that, no matter how many injuries may be received, the least of the saints resists them. And so it seems that a quantity of impassibility cannot be imagined, either according to a discrete quantity or according to a continuous quantity.

Solution: We say that it is thought in accord with the degree (*quantitas*) of merit, which is the cause of impassibility. And we readily concede that it cannot be thought in terms of an effect, [that is] of resisting injury, just as was objected.

Art. 15. On subtlety

Next, one asks about subtlety. And two questions are raised: what it is, and how much there is.

§1. What subtlety is[127]

Concerning the first, one objects in this way:

1. Something subtle, says the Philosopher, easily enters into mixture, and the cause of this is that it is easily divisible into what is smallest.[128] From that, this follows: No glorious body is divisible. Therefore, none is subtle.

125. Perhaps *De bono* tr. 3 q. 5 a. 6 (ed. Colon. 28, p. 214, 29–30, and ibid., p. Xia).

126. Cf. Alb., *IV Sent.* d. 44 a. 15.

127. Cf. Alb., *IV Sent.* d. 44 a. 23–24.

128. Ar., *De gen. et corr.* 2.2 (330a1–3).

2. If one says that in that context "subtle" means "spiritual," then to the contrary: a spiritual substance is not extended in size, but glorious bodies will have size. Therefore, they will not be spiritual [substances].

Solution: We say that subtlety is a dowry that removes the body's coarseness (*grossities*), which is caused by the composition of elemental parts in a body.

1. To the first objection we say that "subtle" is said in two ways, namely from the loose texture of parts that are not situated close by one another, and the Philosopher says of this [way] that it is easily divisible and able to enter into mixture. Something is called "subtle" in a second way from the perfect victory of form over matter, and the perfect victory of the properties of form over the properties of matter. Therefore, since it pertains to form to unify, that [second type] will be in no way divisible. And in this way heaven is said to be subtle, and in this way our bodies will be subtle.

2. To the next, one must reply that spiritual and corporeal are intermediates between spirit and body. To be sure, a body is what exists from a corporeal nature, and a spirit is what exists from the nature of spirit. But there is a spiritual spirit, and there is a corporeal spirit. The spiritual spirit has a property of spirits, whereas the corporeal spirit agrees in some property with a body, such as to be defined by place. And in this way Gregory[129] and Damascene[130] say that angels and souls are corporeal spirits, in comparison to the uncircumscribed Spirit, namely to God. And analogously one says that the sensible and vegetable [souls] in brute animals are corporeal spirits, because they are destroyed by death, as is the body. Similarly, there is a spiritual body and a corporeal body: a corporeal body, which does not share in the properties of spirit, [and] a spiritual body, which possesses the properties of spirit, such as not occupying a place and being impassible. And thus our bodies are said to be spiritual.

129. Greg., *Moral.* 2.3.3 (PL 75: 557A).

130. John Damascene, *De fide orth.* 2.3 (PG 94: 868A; ed. Buytaert, p. 69, 14–17).

§2. How much subtlety there is[131]

There is an objection of this sort concerning the second:

The body of the Lord entered through closed doors,[132] although the doors had not been opened or the walls divided. Since our bodies will be just like his, there will be so much subtlety that it will penetrate any body whatsoever without any division. Therefore, by the same argument it will exist in any body locating itself in a place, without causing its division and without filling it up.

If perhaps one should say that this is true of dense bodies, such as wood, a stone, and a wall, but it is not true of air and heaven and the like, this seems absurd, because far less will that which offers no resistance to the dense offer resistance to the subtle and the rarified.

In accord with this, it seems that our bodies will cross over from the place of resurrection into the empyreum without dividing the medium through which they have crossed.

To the contrary: our bodies will have the requisite size of a thirty-year-old, a size that will necessarily exist in a space appropriate to that size.[133] If it is moved, therefore, through the appropriately sized space, either it will exist partly at the starting point (*terminus a quo*) and partly at the end point (*terminus ad quem*), in such a way that it will make itself commensurate [in size] to the parts of the place, or not. If so, then necessarily it divides the place. If not, then it is necessary that it be moved through points, and then two unsuitable outcomes follow: One is that as much will exist at a point as in a place, and the other is that it will never reach the end of the smallest space, because there are an infinite number of points in the smallest space.

In addition, one asks how various saints understood subtlety's difference.[134] It does not seem to be understood in accord with an effect, because one who is least in glory will not divide [a space], no matter how dense it is.

131. Cf. Alb., *IV Sent.* d. 44 a. 25 sol.

132. Cf. Jn 20.19.

133. Cf. Alb., *De res.* tr. 2, q. 6 (ed. Colon. 26, p. 264, 33ff.).

134. Cf. Alb., *IV Sent.* d. 44 a. 26.

Solution: One must reply to this that the nature of light is divisible without an admixture with another nature, and without its destruction. And when light issues from a lantern, it passes through every "pore" of the glass according to its whole nature, but not according to its entire quantity. Since the light that belongs to the bodies of the blessed is simpler, however, than that [light], from two causes—namely, because it is derived from the soul's merit and because it descends from the First Light, which is God—its subtlety will be greater than the subtlety of corporeal light, and thus it will be better able to penetrate any body whatsoever, both according to its whole nature and according to its quantity. And the proof for this is taken from the Lord's body, which entered closed doors, just as was objected first.

To the objection to the contrary, one must reply that there are two things in a body, namely quantity and the principles that compose a body, namely matter and form. Subtlety is, however, a property of the principles and not of quantity, because the quantity is one and the same in both a coarse body and a subtle body. To what was asked concerning motion through a place, or concerning existence in a place, one must reply that quantity is readily made commensurate with quantity, but the substance of what locates (*substantia locantis*) does not resist the substance of what is already located there. The manner in which it is moved will become clear in the "Question on Eternal Life," where progressive motion will be debated.[135]

Art. 16. On agility[136]

Next, one asks about agility. And two questions are raised: what it is, and how much there is.

§1. What agility is

Concerning the first it is objected thus:

1. There are many powers of the soul in addition to the power of moving with respect to place. Therefore, it seems that we ought also to have, likewise, a dowry that perfects the other acts just as there is for motion with respect to place.

2. Also, since there are many types (*species*) of motion in ad-

135. See Alb., *De res.* tr. 4, q. 2, art. 4 (ed. Colon. 26, p. 342, 90–91).

136. Cf. Thomas Aquinas, *ST* Suppl. q. 84 a. 1.

dition to local motion, why do we not have a dowry for some other type of motion?

Solution: We say that agility is the dowry that causes a body to be moved easily by the soul according to every motion by which the soul moves the body. And this dowry rightly removes the defect that exists in a mortal body stemming from the solidity and heaviness of the members. Because of these two, a body is not easily rendered movable by the soul according to the motion of quickening (*vegetatio*) and sensation and progressive motion.

1. And in this way a solution to the first is apparent, because a false premise is assumed in that objection, namely that this dowry exists only for progressive motion.

2. To the next we say that the other types of motion posit some change in the movable, and for this reason they are appropriate only for a passible body, although bodies that rise again will not be such as this. But local motion changes nothing in the movable, and for that reason in some manner it can be appropriate for a body that rises again.

§2. How much agility there is[137]

To the second, one proceeds in this way:

1. The saints[138] say that agility will exist at the command of the will and the command of intelligence; that is to say that they exist where they will and where they understand. But it seems that this is impossible, for the intellect is not confined by a place's extension, and on account of this [it will move] with equal velocity to a distant place and to one nearby. But a body is measured by size with respect to a place. Thus it seems that it is impossible for it to move with equal velocity to a distant place and to one nearby.

Also, it exists either at one and the same time in different places, or not. If it exists at one and the same time in different places, then what is the same in number is reckoned to be in different places at one and the same time, which contradicts

137. Cf. Alb., *IV Sent.* d. 44 a. 20–22.

138. "Saints": cf. Aug., *De civ. Dei* 22.30.1 (PL 41: 801; CSEL 40/2, p. 665, 10–11).

the Philosopher, who says that whatever are numbered by place are numbered by subject.[139]

If one should say that this is not unsuitable, because God exists in many places, this is the same as saying nothing at all, since God is not defined by place nor circumscribed in the way that a glorious body is.

If it does not exist in different places at the same time, however, then when it exists in the middle, it will not exist at the end (*terminus*), and in this way it does not move with equal velocity to a distant place and to one nearby. And so it follows (*redit*) that the saints' statement is not true.

2. In addition one asks how differences in agility among the saints are understood, since they cannot be grasped according to the effect, which is motion.

Solution:

1. We say without offense (*sine praeiudicio*) that if glorious bodies are moved, they are moved quickly, that is, in an imperceptible time period.[140] And the saints' statement is understood in this way, namely that the time [required] for the motion of the body and the will and the intelligence does not differ by a known quantity.

If someone should object, however, that by the same argument an angel will be moved in time, because it does not exist in many places at the same time, we say that this is not the same thing. Actually, the angel's substance that is moved is not divisible in motion, so as to exist partly at the starting point (*terminus a quo*) and partly at the end point (*terminus ad quem*). But we readily concede that in the same "now," when it exists in the middle, it does not exist at the end. But a "now" plus a "now" do not produce anything larger, because the Philosopher says that if you add a point to a point, you will not make it any larger.[141] But a body possesses a size that is commensurate with the size of the place through which it is moved. And for this reason it is necessarily moved in time. This is notwithstanding what Aristo-

139. Ar., *Metaph.* 5.6 (1016b3ff.); *Metaph. nova text.* 11. Alb., *Metaph.* 5.1.7.

140. Cf. Alb., *De res.* tr. 2, q. 8, art. 2 (ed. Colon. 26, p. 274, 3ff.).

141. Ar., *De gen. et corr.* 1.2 (316a29–31). Cf. Alb., *De gen. et corr.* 1.1.13. Ar., *Metaph.* 3.4 (1001b11–13).

tle says at the end of the eighth book of the *Physics*,[142] that if the heaven is moved by an infinite power of a mover, it is moved in the "now," because this is said with regard to the one moving and not with regard to the one that is movable.

2. To the last, one must reply that the differences, just as with impassibility, are understood according to a cause having to do with merit, because one who has deserved more will have nobler dowries.

Art. 17. On the number of the dowries of the body[143]

Next, one asks about the number of the dowries of the body, how they are understood.

1. And it seems that there are many. In fact, it is granted to the body at the resurrection that one member be connected to another member, and that it not require food, and many other things of this sort. And so it seems that they are dowries.

2. In addition, some acts are linked together, like to see and to live, to sense and to speak and to quicken. And again things of this sort will be granted to the body or to what has been united at the resurrection. And so it seems that they are dowries.

Solution: The dowries of the body can be understood in three ways. Some understand them according to the nature of heaven,[144] which will then rule in us, over and above the elements. Indeed, that nature is luminous, subtle and penetrative, swift, and impassible. In accord with these four [properties] they understand that there are four dowries.

They can be understood in another way according to the four compositions of the human body that have been restored to a perfect condition.[145] The first composition is a mixture of contraries, and this will be perfect when the contraries are in equal balance, so that no one can contend against another, neither externally nor internally. And this dowry is impassibility.

142. Ar., *Phys.* 8.10 (266a24–31); cf. Alb., *Phys.* 8.4.2; Alb., *De res.* tr. 2, q. 8, art. 1 (ed. Colon. 26, p. 271, 85).

143. Cf. Alb., *IV Sent.* d. 44 a. 32; *Quaestio de dotibus sanctorum in patria,* art. 6: *De numero dotium* (ed. Colon. 25/2, pp. 109–10).

144. "Some": cf. Rich. Fishacre (fol. 339va). Bonaventure, *IV Sent.* d. 49 a. 2 q. 1, *Opera* 4: 1016a.

145. The compositions are the four complexions: choleric, sanguine, melancholic, and phlegmatic.

Similarly, there exists a composition of matter with form there, and that is perfect when form prevails over the entire matter. And subtlety exists in accord with that perfection, as was made known above in the "Disputation on Subtlety."[146] Third is the composition of an organic body with the soul, and its perfection is that all the organs will be able to be moved by the soul without impediment. And agility is understood in accord with this, as was made known in the "Disputation on Agility."[147] The fourth composition is of the body with the lucid spirits by which the body is moved by the soul. And luminosity corresponds to that [composition] according to a perfect condition.

In the third manner, it is understood better in accord with this: that the dowry of the body is caused by the dowry of the soul, for the body is referred to the soul's glory in accord with the soul's perfection in nature or in accord with its perfection in the operation of glory. If [understood in accord with the soul's perfection] in nature, this can be in two ways, namely so far as the principles of nature and so far as a property consequent upon those principles. If in the first way, then it receives impassibility, and if in the second way, then it receives subtlety. If, however, it is referred to the work of glory, then it will imitate, to the extent that it can, its work according to intellect and according to affect. If in the first way, then there is luminosity, because Augustine says that in the first instance it denotes the spiritual light of truth, and in the second instance it denotes a corporeal light.[148] If in the second way, then there will be agility in which it follows the motive powers of the soul.

1. To the objection concerning the connection of parts and a lack of need for food, one must reply that these cannot be dowries, because such things will also exist among the damned.

2. To the next, one must reply that the acts that are linked together are not dowries, but they are acts of eternal life, of which there has already been a discussion.[149]

146. Alb., *De res.* tr. 4, q. 1, art. 15, §1 (ed. Colon. 26, p. 337, 44ff.).

147. Alb., *De res.* tr. 4, q. 1, art. 16, §1 (ed. Colon. 26, p. 338, 64ff.).

148. Aug., *Contra Faustum Manich.* 22.9 (PL 42: 405; CSEL 25, p. 598, 4–6).

149. Cf. Alb., *II Sent.* d. 24 a. 7 ad 2. Cf. *IV Sent.* d. 48 a. 4; *De bono* tr. 3 q. 3 a. 14 (ed. Colon. 28, p. 178, 16–21).

Question 2. On eternal life

Next, one asks about eternal life. And two questions are asked: first about life in itself, and then about the acts of life.

On Eternal Life in Itself

Concerning the first, two questions are raised, namely whether there is eternal life, and what it is.

Art. 1. Whether there is eternal life[150]

To the first, one proceeds in this way:

1. What is always connected to one side of a contradiction is never connected to the other. But all created life is connected to having a beginning. Therefore, it will never be connected to not-having [a beginning]. But the eternal is what does not have a beginning. Therefore, it seems that no angel and no soul can have eternal life.

2. If it is said, in accord with Augustine,[151] that true eternity is true immutability, this is understood either with respect to nature or with respect to the will and the intellect. If in the first way, then the soul always has eternal life, whether it exists in hell or in heaven, because its nature is not changed. And this is evident from Dionysius's remark in *On the Divine Names:* "We say that the natural gifts (*dona*) given to them are never changed."[152] If [understood] in the second way, it again seems to be false, because Damascene says that everything that can be created is subject to change, that is, is mutable, either with respect to nature or with respect to choice (*electio*).[153] Since, therefore, angels and souls are not mutable with respect to nature, they will be mutable with respect to choice.

3. If perhaps one should say that some are mutable before

150. Cf. Alb., *IV Sent.* d. 46 a. 4.

151. Aug., *De trin.* 1.1.2 (PL 42: 821).

152. Dion., *De div. nom.* c. 4 §23 (PG 3: 725C; Dionysiaca I, 281–82); transl. Sarr. Cf. Alb., *Super Dion. De div. nom.* 4, 193 (ed. Colon. 37/1, pp. 275–76); Alb., *De res.* tr. 3, q. 7, art. 1 (ed. Colon. 26, p. 319, 21).

153. John Damascene, *De fide orth.* 1.3 (PL 94: 796AB; ed. Buytaert, p. 16, 24–p. 17, 32).

[their] confirmation in beatitude, but that they receive immutability from confirmation, as Augustine appears to say in the twelfth book of the *Confessions,*[154] this seems to contradict Dionysius, who proposes that among the confirmed angels there are those who illuminate and those who purge and those who perfect and those who are illuminated and purged and perfected.[155] Which cannot occur, it seems, without change.

4. In addition, when one thing falls within the definition of another, that which falls within the definition cannot be named by that within whose definition it falls.[156] But life falls within the definition of eternity, as Boethius says: "Eternity is the complete simultaneous possession of unending life."[157] Then nothing seems to be called eternal life, because the one is named for the other.

5. Moreover, one asks next whether the demons and the damned have eternal life.[158] And it seems so, because they live without end.

Solution: We say that eternal life exists in saintly souls and in the blessed angels and also in God. But it exists in God essentially, whereas it exists in the others by participation.

1. To the first, then, one must reply that life can be called eternal from both its immutability and its interminability. And if it is called eternal from its interminability, then it will be called eternal with respect to that which is the cause of life. In fact, this is God. If, however, it is called eternal from its immutability, then it will be called eternal in both ways, namely with respect to the cause of life and with respect to participating in life, because the blessed are rendered immutable by participation in the divine life.

2. To the objection from Damascene, one must reply that it is understood before confirmation in beatitude.

154. Aug., *Conf.* 12.15.21 (PL 32: 833; CSEL 33, p. 323, 15–21).

155. Dion., *De cael. hier.* 3 §2 (PG 3: 165BC; Dionysiaca II, 791–92); transl. Scotus. Cf. Alb., *Super Dion. De cael. hier.* 3 (ed. Colon. 36/1, pp. 56–58).

156. See Ar., *Top.* 6, c. 4 (142a34); Boethius, transl. ant. PL 64: 974C; cf. Alb., *Top.* 6, tr. 2, cap. 2.

157. Boethius, *De cons. phil.* 5, prosa 6 (PL 63: 858A; CSEL 67, p. 122, 12–13); cf. Alb., *De res.* tr. 3, q. 5, art. 4 (ed. Colon. 26, p. 314, 50).

158. Cf. Alb., *IV Sent.* d. 46 a. 7.

3. To the objection from Dionysius, one must reply that they are not said to be changed by perceiving illuminations, but rather [they are said] to approach the immutable one. Now, mutability (*mutabilitas*) is directed toward what is worse or away from what is worse.[159] For that reason, something is cast aside there and something else is introduced, which does not occur among the blessed, but there is exaltation there in the divine light.

5. To the last, one must reply that the demons do not live with eternal life, because eternal life is not said to be the life of nature, but rather the life toward which the principle that is God moves. The life of nature, however, is that toward which the principle that is the soul or created spirit moves.

4. To the objection concerning a definition, one must reply that life does not fall within the definition of eternity as a genus or *differentia,* but rather as the subject or matter regarding which eternity exists, just as nose falls within the definition of snub-nosed, or leg within the definition of lame.[160] And for that reason it can be readily denominated by it.

Art. 2. What eternal life is[161]

To the second, one proceeds in this way:

The Lord says in the Gospel of John 17: "This is eternal life, that they may know you, the only true God, and Jesus Christ, whom you have sent."[162]

Similarly, the Philosopher says, "Life is a movement following upon the nature of a genus that is capable of nourishment."[163]

Moreover, it has customarily been defined in this manner: "Life is the continuous act of the soul upon the body."[164]

159. In other words, change always must be either a change for the worse or a change for the better.

160. Cf. Ar., *Phys.* 1.3 (186b22–23). Alb., *Phys.* 1.2.8, 2.1.8.

161. Cf. Alb., *IV Sent.* d. 46 a. 5.

162. Jn 17.3.

163. Ar., *Top.* 6.10 (148a26–28); Boethius, transl. ant. PL 64: 982D. Cf. Alb., *De homine* q. 4 a. 7 (ed. Colon. 27/2, p. 52); *Super Dion. De div. nom.* 4.23–24 and 2.13 (ed. Colon. 37/1, pp. 130–31; p. 52); *De anima* 2.1.6; *Top.* 6.5.1.

164. Alfred of Sareshel, *De motu cordis* c. 8 (ed. Cl. Baeumker, *Beiträge* 23/1–2, p. 30, 19). Cf. Alb., *IV Sent.* d. 46 a. 5.

Also, in the commentary on the *Book of Causes* on this proposition, "All things have essence," etc., [it says] "Life is a procession proceeding out from the first being which is at rest, always [existent], eternal, and [is] the first movement."[165]

1. One objects in this way to the first definition: To know God is the act of life, and there is nothing whose act it is. Therefore, it seems that to know God is not essentially eternal life.

2. Moreover, life is established prior to the powers in a spiritual nature. This is well known: for let us posit that an angel or a soul does not understand. Nonetheless, there will still be life in them. And in this manner it seems that life is established poorly by knowledge.

3. Against the second, one objects: A genus there is understood on behalf of the nature of the vegetative soul, and life is found in the sensible and intelligible [soul] and also in an angel. How then is it said to be "a movement of a genus capable of nourishment"?

It is not necessary to object to the third [definition], because this is the life of nature.

4. Against the last, which seems to be [relevant] to the case in question, it seems that nothing set down in the definition restricts [it] to a type of life. In fact, "procession" applies generally to all that proceed from the First Being.

5. Likewise, this is what he says: "from the First Being." It seems rather that he ought to have said "from the First Life," just as is presented, moreover, in the proposition that "all things have essence on account of the First Being, and living things are moved by their essence on account of the First Life, and intelligible things have intelligence on account of the First Intelligence,"[166] so that in this way life would be from life, being from being, knowledge from knowledge, etc.

6. Moreover, why is it said, "at rest, always [existent], eternal," when one is understood to imply the other? For whatever is eternal is at rest, and is always [existent], but the reverse is not the case.

7. Moreover, what is that which he calls the "first movement"?

165. Alb., *De causis et proc.* lib. 2 tr. 3 cap. 14 (ed. Colon. 17/2, p. 151).

166. Alb., *De causis et proc.* lib. 2 tr. 3 cap. 14–15 (ed. Colon. 17/2, pp. 151–52).

For local motion is first in the genus of motion, as is demonstrated many times in nature.[167]

Solution: Just as the principle of natural life is intrinsic to and united to that which has life, and this is soul or spirit—according to which we say that angels and demons have the life of nature—so too there is a principle that is the cause of eternal life, indeed that is intrinsic but distinct by essence, because the whole [principle] is inside and the whole is outside; and that is God. Therefore, eternal life is nothing but the immediate participation in the first movement by a principle united [to it] in the mode of glory, which [principle] is God. And I say "immediate" on account of the life of nature that God creates in the soul or spirit, as in an angel. And I say "of the first movement" in the order of life's motions, because just as there is a first cause in the order of causes, which all those [causes] that follow later presuppose in causing and it [the first cause] presupposes no other—therefore, owing to its simplicity it is only definable through one posterior to it, such as being is—so too in the order of life's motions the first is that which all the others presuppose, and it does not presuppose any motion from them. And for this reason it is the most simple and can only be defined by those that are posterior to it, as is clear in these examples: to live, to nourish, to grow, to generate, to understand, to sense, to be moved progressively; all these that follow after life presuppose it, and it does not presuppose any of those that follow it. And I say, "united [to it] in the mode of glory," because, although all life comes from God, nonetheless they do not possess this motion from him alone, but also from another principle that is created by him, such as spirit or soul, because in such as these he exists only by means of essence, presence, and power, and not in the mode of the one glorifying.

1, 2. To the first definition, then, one must reply that that is given for the later and noblest act of life itself and not for the first and essential [act]. And from this a solution is clear to the following.

3. To the objection from the second definition, one must reply that Dionysius is speaking of the life of nature in relation

167. Cf. Ar., *Phys.* 8.7 (260a26–29). Cf. Alb., *Phys.* 8.3.1.

to the first principle of life; this is the vegetative [principle].[168] And for this reason he also says, "following upon the nature," because the vegetative is the first principle above nature.

Nonetheless, some say that he says "following upon the nature" for this reason, because it exists in the manner of nature.[169] "Life is the being (*esse*) for living things,"[170] just as the act of the natural form is the being of a thing.

4, 7. To the objection concerning the last one, one must reply that it was given in relation to the cause of life, which is "[the first] being at rest, always [existent], eternal," and "procession" is the genus for every effusion of goodness, whether it [goodness] flows out in the manner of creation, like being (*ens*), which presupposes nothing in whatever is created, or whether it flows out in the manner of informing, which presupposes something in whatever is created, like life, which presupposes being (*ens*). That which is called the "first movement" is posited, however, just as a completing difference,[171] as is clear from the aforesaid.[172] And in this way a solution is apparent to the first and the last, which is opposed to that definition.

5. To the next, one must reply that when he says "from a being at rest" as in the first [being], namely in God, it implies no distinction among being, life, and intelligence. But Aristotle's premise attends to the proper definition of attributes in the cause and the caused.

6. To the next, one must reply that the three, "at rest, always [existent], eternal," follow each other in such a way that the "always" that follows adds to the one preceding it, just as customarily occurs in definitions. And for this reason there is no objection, because although the one that follows presupposes the one that precedes it, nonetheless it only does so implicitly. But those things which are in a definition have to be explicit.

168. See Ar., *Top.* 6.10 (148a26–28), Boethius, transl. ant. PL 64: 982D; Alb., *De homine* q. 4 a. 7 (ed. Colon. 27/2, p. 54); *Super Dion. De div. nom.* 4, 23–24; *De anima* 2.1.6; *Top.* 6.5.c. unic; Boethius, transl. ant. PL 64: 982D; *Super Dion. De div. nom.* 2.13; *De res.* tr. 4, q. 2, art. 2 (ed. Colon. 26, p. 341, 34).

169. Cf. Alb., *De homine* q. 4 a. 7 (ed. Colon. 27/2, p. 52).

170. Ar., *De anima* 2.4 (415b13); cf. Alb., *De anima* 2.2.2.

171. "Completing difference": cf. Boethius, *In Isag. Porph.* Ed. II, 4.7 (CSEL 48, p. 258, 9ff.). Alb., *De V univ.* 5.3.

172. See *De res.* tr. 4, q. 2, art. 2 (ed. Colon. 26, p. 342, 5ff.).

On the Acts of Eternal Life

Next, one asks about the acts of eternal life. And first, one asks about the acts of the vegetative soul, and second the acts of the sensible soul, and third the acts of the intelligible soul.

Art. 3. On the acts of the vegetative soul

To the first, one proceeds in this way:

Potency is determined by act. But in the kingdom nourishment will not be employed, nor will growth and generation occur. Therefore, it seems that the acts of such potencies will not exist for the acts of eternal life.

If perhaps one should say that these potencies will persist in their ends, just as was said above in the "Question on the Truth of Human Nature," still it seems that this is not the case for eternal life, because it was demonstrated in the preceding article that life is an immediate procession from God.[173] But these states will proceed from the vegetative soul.

In addition, one asks, what are the ends in which these potencies will persist?

Solution: One must reply that these potencies will persist in their ends. And these ends are existence (*esse*) and having a requisite size and abiding forever.

To what contradicts this, one must reply that God will fill the entire soul and the entire body with glory. And for this reason such a union of these potencies to their ends is beyond the powers of the soul, and God produces it in the potencies themselves.

Art. 4. On the acts of the sensible soul

Two questions are raised concerning the second:[174] first, concerning the potencies of the sensible soul in itself, and second concerning the motive [power] with respect to place.

173. See *De res.* tr. 4, q. 2, art. 2 (ed. Colon. 26, p. 341, 33f.).
174. See *De res.* tr. 2, q. 8, art. 2 (ed. Colon. 26, p. 271, 25ff.).

On the Potencies of the Sensible Soul in Itself[175]

Concerning the potencies of the sensible soul in itself, first one asks about the sensible powers that are outside, and second about the sensible [powers] inside.

§1. On the sensible powers that are outside

For the sensitive [powers] that are outside, one asks about the five senses, whose acts will remain in eternal life.

And one asks first about sight, whether it exists there through a medium and through a change in the pupil, just as it does here, and through the act of what is light-bearing.

It seems not. For all such things originate from creatures, because divinity is not a sensible object. The acts of eternal life and glory originate from God, however. Therefore, it seems that they do not exist by means of something outside.

In addition, now sense perceptions arise from what is outside, either for the sake of [finding] food or for the sake of instruction, just as it is said that sight and hearing are senses subject to instruction.[176] But in the future we will receive neither food nor instruction from outside, when "we all shall be taught by God."[177] Therefore, it seems that the senses will not remain in this manner in the kingdom, namely for receiving [sense perceptions] inwardly.

In addition, although for certain [people] this may not seem absurd with respect to vision,[178] nonetheless clearly an absurdity follows for hearing and for the other senses, for hearing does not exist without sound. Sound does not occur, however, without the vocal element, which is air, and in the future we will not exist in such an element. In fact, heaven is not an element that may be breathed in, nor is it one capable of being formed into

175. Cf. Alb., *Quaestio de sens. corp. glor.*, art. 2: *De singulis sensibus* (ed. Colon. 25/2, pp. 115–25).

176. Cf. Ar., *De sensu et sens.* 1 (437a1f.). Alb., *De sensu et sens.* 1.2 (ed. Colon. 7/2, p. 22); *De anima* 21.1.3.16.

177. Jn 6.45.

178. Cf. Alb., *Quaestio de sens. corp. glor.* l.c. Thomas Aquinas, *IV Sent.* d. 44 q. 2 a. 1 qla 4.5.

speech. It is even more absurd for smell; and look for a discussion in "On the Punishments of the Damned."[179]

Solution: Without offense (*sine praeiudicio*) we say that the senses will not exist there in the way they do here, but that God will fill up the senses by means of glory. And the sensible object, which differentiates the senses, will descend from the intellect. For just as now the universal, which differentiates the intellect, ascends to the intellect by the extraction of sensible forms, so in the future conversely the sensible object will descend from the intelligible object, distinguishing the senses by clothing them and surrounding them with sensible forms. But whether the intelligible is universal or particular will become clear later.[180] And so it also is clear how the acts of the senses will originate from God, and in this way they will pertain to life eternal. And it is also clear that the question that asks whether we will see in a straight line or a circular one or one that is curved is meaningless (*nulla*).

If, however, one should ask about differentiation among the senses, one must reply that it is understood in terms of the intelligibles, and the perception of sweetness for the understanding of sweetness results from being surrounded by sensible forms. And it is the same for the rest.

§2. On the interior senses

Next, one asks about the interior senses, namely common sense, phantasy, and estimation, the concupiscible and irascible [faculties], [and] memory. And one asks in which acts they will remain.

1. Now, if phantasy is a "motion produced from sense" according to the preceding determination,[181] it does not seem that it remains that way, but rather it seems to be a motion from the intellect to sense. If this is conceded, then to the contrary: Every phantasm is a particular, and every intelligible is a universal; therefore, the universal moves by act to the particular. This is false, because the particular is in the universal only po-

179. *De res.* tr. 3, q. 4 (ed. Colon. 26, p. 310, 46–49; p. 311, 72–73).
180. See *De res.* tr. 4, q. 2, art. 4 (ed. Colon. 26, p. 345, 20ff.).
181. See *De res.* tr. 3, q. 4 (ed. Colon. 26, p. 311, 11).

tentially, but the universal is in the particular in act. And for this reason phantasy can readily move the intellect in act, but not the reverse.

2. Similarly, one asks about estimation. Actually, estimation exists beyond divided or composite phantasms, and establishes in them the intention of something agreeable or injurious.[182] But in the future everything will be agreeable, and so it seems that estimation will not be necessary.

3. It seems to be the same for the concupiscible and irascible [faculties]. Now the concupiscible[183] seeks what is pleasing to life, and the irascible[184] powerfully repels what is injurious. And these are necessary only for animal life.

4. It is the same for memory, which is the storehouse of sensible species that cannot be preserved in sense according to act.[185] Since in the future knowledge will descend from a superior [faculty], then memory will appear to be empty.

Solution: We say that all knowledge that will exist in the kingdom will be without error, and for that reason it cannot take its origin from sense.[186] To be sure, the proper object of sensation is represented without error. But in the sensible powers of the soul, as in common sense and phantasy, etc., frequently there arises an undue mixture and division of their forms owing to ignorance of the subject, in such a way as when gold's redness is mixed up with copper's subject, and for this reason error enters. But in the future, knowledge begins with an intellect sure of its object, and for this reason the sensible forms that are positioned around it are positioned around what is certain. And for this reason error does not occur in such a mixture. Therefore, it is clear that it is necessary for it to begin from the interior [faculty]. And I believe that this is Augustine's understanding in the book *On Spirit and Soul,* when he says, "Sense will be turned into reason, reason into intellect, and intellect

182. Cf. Alb., *De homine* q. 39 a. 1 sol. (ed. Colon. 27/2, p. 294).

183. Cf. Alb., *De homine* q. 66 a. 1 sol. (ed. Colon. 27/2, p. 494).

184. Cf. Alb., *De homine* q. 67 a. 1 sol. (ed. Colon. 27/2, p. 497).

185. Cf. Alb., *De bono* tr. 4 q. 2 a. 1 (ed. Colon. 28, p. 246, 28–31); *De homine* q. 40 a. 1 sol. (ed. Colon. 27/2, p. 297).

186. See *De res.* tr. 3, q. 4 (ed. Colon. 26, p. 311, 74ff.).

into intelligence."[187] For sense to be turned into reason means nothing other than that sense is changed into reason, so that, just as now sense is the foundation (*principium*) for rational understanding, so too in the future rational understanding will be made the foundation for sense.

1. To the objection concerning phantasy, one must reply that it [phantasy] will be moved by the intellect, as was demonstrated. And the objection concerning the universal ought to be solved by dispensing with this [statement]: "Every intelligible is a universal." In fact, this is true only for the intelligible received from a phantasm, which will not be the sort of intelligible that exists in the kingdom, but rather one that is godlike (*deiforme*) and divine, as will be shown later.[188]

2. To the next, which asks about the estimative faculty, one must reply that the act of estimation is twofold, namely to estimate what is injurious and what is agreeable, and to judge (*sententiare*) concerning the end of estimation, or concerning the [object] estimated. And it [estimation] will remain with respect to this last act, but not with respect to the first.

3. To the next, which asks about the concupiscible and irascible [faculties], one must reply that these are turned toward the will, which they obey, and they are shaped in their ends by the overflowing of the will into them.

4. To the objection concerning memory, one must reply that the entire mode of knowing and understanding that exists here will cease [then]. Hence, Augustine says, on the Apostle to the Corinthians, that knowledge, in the way that it exists now, will be destroyed.[189] But nonetheless memory can be a storehouse of sensible species that are positioned around the divine intelligibles, about which we will speak later.[190]

187. Ps. Aug., *De spir. et anima* 12 (PL 40: 788).

188. See *De res.* tr. 4, q. 2, art. 4 (ed. Colon. 26, p. 345, 20ff.).

189. Aug.: Peter Lombard, *In epist. Pauli* 1 Cor 13.10 (PL 191: 1662B). That text refers to Aug., *De doc. Christ.* 1.38.42 (PL 34: 35). Cf. Peter Lombard, ibid. 1161D.

190. See *De res.* tr. 4, q. 2, art. 4 (ed. Colon. 26, p. 345, 20ff.).

On the Acts of Eternal Life with respect to the Intelligible Soul

Next, one asks about the acts of eternal life with respect to the intelligible soul. And first, one asks about the acts of the apprehensive powers,[191] and second about the acts of the motive [powers].

Art. 5. On the acts of the apprehensive powers

Since, then, there is a double intellect, namely the agent intellect and the possible intellect, one asks about the acts of eternal life with respect to each of them.

1. And it seems that no act of life exists with respect to the agent [intellect]. It pertains to the agent [intellect] to abstract form and not to receive any form, because to receive is to undergo change (*pati*).[192] So in this way the agent [intellect] would be the possible [intellect] if it received [form]. Since, then, the act of eternal life exists by the unmediated contemplation of God, it is necessary for the contemplating intellect itself to be distinguished from the intelligible, which is God. But it [the agent intellect] receives nothing, as is thought. Therefore, it is not distinguished from this intelligible, and so too it does not live according to the act of eternal life.

2. Similarly, it seems that it is not the possible [intellect]. In fact, that one [the possible intellect] needs the light of the agent [intellect], just as the eye needs the light of the sun. But the light of the agent [intellect] cannot illuminate the intelligible that is God, because a lesser light cannot illuminate a greater, but rather the other way around. And so the possible [intellect] will not exist in act with respect to this intelligible, as is seen. And so in this way it does not live by the act of eternal life.

Solution: We say that each intellect is immediately united to God. For just as sight exists in two lights, both of which remain distinct with respect to substance and are united in illuminating, so too the agent intellect that is distinct from the divine

191. "Apprehensive powers": i.e., the powers for apprehending.

192. Cf. Alb., *De homine* q. 55 art. 3 ad 3–7 (ed. Colon. 27/2, p. 413). Cf. ibid., ad 17 (ed. Colon. 27/2, p. 414).

intellect with respect to essence is united to it in illuminating the possible [intellect] in glory.[193] Whether the agent intellect is capable of being united to an angelic intellect, however, has to be discussed in the "Question on the Difference and the Agreement between a Soul and an Angel."[194] Regarding how the possible [intellect] will understand God in an unmediated fashion, however, it has been stated above in the "Question on the Dowry of the Soul, which is Vision."[195] And so it appears that God is united to the agent [intellect] as the one that illuminates in an unmediated fashion, and God is united to the possible [intellect] as the object that is understood in an unmediated fashion. In these two unions, the act of eternal life exists with respect to the intellect.

1. To the first, then, one must reply that it is unnecessary for the agent intellect to be distinguished [from the intelligible], since it itself receives nothing. But it is united to God in another way, as has been said.

2. To the next, one must reply that, just as in sight one thing is visible through itself, like light, and something else is visible through another, like color, so it is the same in the intellect, that one thing is intelligible through itself, like God, and something else is intelligible through another, such as creatures. And for this reason we readily concede that the illumination of the agent [intellect] does not exist in relation to the intelligible, which is God, but nonetheless it does exist in relation to the possible intellect, for which illumination is necessary, just as the external sun illuminates not only color but also the eye.

Note, nonetheless, that with respect to creatures the possible intellect will possess forms that are likenesses of the divine ideas, and they are not abstracted from things, but they are imprinted on the [possible] intellect by the creating wisdom. And through these forms it arrives at objects (*in res*) by a natural cognition, and these forms are neither universals nor particulars. In fact, a universal form only exists in potency (*in potentia*) as this or as that, whereas a particular form exists as this

193. See *De res.* tr. 4, q. 1, art. 9, §3 (ed. Colon. 26, p. 330, 59ff.).
194. Cf. Alb., *De IV coaequ.* q. 30; *II Sent.* d. 1 a. 13.
195. See *De res.* tr. 4, q. 1, art. 9, §1 (ed. Colon. 26, p. 328, 48).

one but not as another. But ideal forms exist for the object, as those from which objects go forth in creation, and they have one relationship to the universal and to the particular, just as forms also are established in angels. And these are the forms by which the sensible objects that surround them perfect sensible cognition.

On the Acts of the Motive Powers

Next, one asks about the motive [powers]. And because previously we discussed the powers of the image among the dowries of the soul,[196] one must speak of synderesis[197] and free will, and of the superior and inferior part of reason, and of the will. Now, since all these powers (*potentiae*) are ordered toward acts of merit or demerit, one first asks how they are united to God with respect to [their] proper and simple acts, and then how [they are united to God] with respect to composite acts, just as enjoyment is.

Art. 6. How the motive powers are united to God with respect to [their] proper and simple acts

To the first, one proceeds in this way:

In the Gloss on Ezekiel, chapter 1, it is said that synderesis is to mutter against evil and to incite toward the good.[198] But it will not remain there [in heaven] in this sense, because works (*opera*) which are for merit or demerit will not exist there.

In addition, this would not be an act of eternal life, since that act is not the basis for glory, but rather for merit or demerit.

The same objection exists for free will and for the superior and inferior part of reason.

Also, one asks how the will will be united to God, since nothing will be willed by it except what preceded it in the inferior or superior part of reason, as Augustine says in Book 12 of *On the Trinity*.[199]

196. See *De res.* tr. 4, q. 1, art. 11, §2 (ed. Colon. 26, p. 334, 43ff.).

197. "Synderesis": an innate moral principle found in humans.

198. *Glossa ord. super Ez.* 1.9. Jerome, *In Ez.* 1.9 (PL 25: 22B). Cf. Philip the Chancellor (O. Lottin, *Psychologie et morale,* vol. 2/1, p. 140).

199. Aug., *De trin.* 12.3.3 (PL 42: 999); cf. ibid., 11.3.6 (PL 42: 988).

Solution: The basis for all merits is the beauty of eternal justice, toward which the motive powers are turned according to the right order, in such a way that the superior ones, like synderesis and the will, immediately participate in that [justice] which pertains to the ultimate end. Others, such as free will and both parts of reason, participate, however, by overflowing.

And from this a solution to all of the objections is clear, because, although the works will not exist there, nonetheless the eternal basis and the end of the works will exist there.

On Enjoyment and Use

Next, one asks about enjoyment (*frui*), and, for the sake of contrast, one ought to ask too about use (*uti*), although it is not an act of eternal life. Four [questions] are asked about enjoyment. First, one asks about enjoyment in itself; second, about enjoyment in relation to the one enjoying; third, about enjoyment in relation to what is enjoyable; and fourth, in relation to the disposition or habit (*habitus*) by which we enjoy.

Question 3. On enjoyment in itself

Two questions are asked concerning enjoyment in itself, namely, concerning its definition and concerning division with respect to that definition.

Art. 1. On the definition of enjoyment[200]

To the first, one proceeds in this way:

In his book *On Christian Doctrine* Augustine says, "Enjoyment is to cling with love to some object for its own sake."[201]

Also he states in his book *On the Trinity:* "We enjoy things known, in which the will that has taken delight reposes."[202]

Also, in the same place, "To enjoy is to use with joy, no longer the joy of hope but of the thing already present."[203]

1. To the first, one objects in this way: Enjoyment is an act of

200. Cf. Alb., *I Sent.* d. 1 a. 12, 17; *Summa* I q. 7 m. 3.

201. Aug., *De doc. Christ.* 1.4.4 (PL 34: 20).

202. Aug., *De trin.* 10.10.13 (PL 42: 981).

203. Aug., *De trin.* 10.11.17 (PL 42: 982).

eternal life. Since, therefore, all the virtues exist in eternal life, it should not be defined by love more than by another virtue.

2. Moreover, friendship clings to something, namely to friends for their own sake, as the Philosopher says in the third [book] of the *Topics*.[204] Therefore, friendship is enjoyment.

3. Also, charity (*caritas*) clings to something with love, namely to what is beloved for its own sake. Therefore, charity is enjoyment.

4. In addition, one is accustomed to ask why it is said to "cling to" rather than to "adhere to" or "be joined to."

5. Moreover, "for its own sake" (*propter se*) denotes either a material cause or a formal or efficient or final cause, or all of them or several of them. But it seems that it is not the efficient cause, because matter and the efficient cause are never identical in a thing, but instead the "itself" (*li 'se'*) denotes the matter of enjoyment. When the "on account of" (*li 'propter'*) is posited, therefore, about the same thing, it cannot denote the condition (*habitudo*) of an efficient cause.

Actually, the same objection proves that it cannot denote the form and the end either, because they are not identical with matter. If perhaps one should say that they can readily be identical in an object, but not identical on the basis of causality, this is meaningless, because no cause is identical to another on the basis of causality, and in the same way the Philosopher says nothing meaningful in the second book of the *Physics* [when he says] that the three sometimes coincide in one.[205] But matter never coincides with any of the others.

6. In opposition to the second, one objects that it seems to be opposed to the first. In fact, the first supposes that we enjoy the things that are beloved, because we only cling with love to those that are loved for their own sake, but the second states that we enjoy things that are known.

7. In addition, the good is divided into the pleasurable, the useful, and the fitting.[206] Neither the pleasurable nor the useful

204. Ar., *Top.* 3.1 (117a1–3); Boethius, transl. ant. PL 64: 935D.

205. Ar., *Phys.* 2.7 (198a24–25). Cf. Alb., *Phys.* 2.2.22; *De bono* tr. 1 q. 4 a. 8 (ed. Colon. 28, p. 64, 56).

206. Cf. Ar., *Eth. Nic.* 2.2 (1104b30–31).

is desired for its own sake, but only the fitting is.[207] Therefore, he [Augustine] ought not to have said, "in which the will that has taken delight," but he ought to have proposed something that is appropriate to the fitting.

8. In addition, one asks why he says "in which it reposes" (*conquiescit*), for if it is the will alone that takes delight, as he seems to suppose in the definition, then the prefix *con,* which denotes a plurality, is meaningless.

9. One objects to the third in this way: Use is contrasted with enjoyment just as what exists for its own sake is contrasted with what exists for the sake of another. Therefore, it should not be included in the definition of what enjoyment is.

10. Moreover, why is it that he says, "no longer [the joy] of hope," because "to cling with love," etc., readily occurs in hope?

11. In addition, one asks how the three definitions should be understood.[208]

Solution:

1. To the first it was customarily said that "with love" does not suppose there an act of a designated virtue, which is charity (*caritas*), but an act that exists in every virtue.[209] In fact, every virtue has love, in accord with which Augustine says that virtue is nothing but the order of love.[210] And that love is the ordered disposition of the appetite. And in this respect the objection fails.

In another way it could be said that love (*amor*) implies there the act of charity (*caritas*), with respect to which that act follows upon the sight of what is loved and possessed. To be sure, when the object that is loved is seen and possessed, then its enjoyment is perfected in love, as was said above in the "Question on the Dowries of the Soul."[211]

And in this way a solution to the first is apparent, because the definition (*ratio*) is not the same for the other virtues. For this reason, it is not defined by acts of the other virtues.

207. Cicero, *De invent.* 2.53.159.

208. Cf. Alb., *I Sent.* d. 1 a. 17 qla. 3.

209. Cf. Alb., *De bono* (ed. Colon. 28, p. 177, 6–8).

210. Aug., *De civ. dei* 15.22 (PL 41: 467; CSEL 40.2, p. 109, 5–6); cf. Alb., *De res.* tr. 2, q. 10, art. 12 (ed. Colon. 26, p. 301, 79).

211. See *De res.* tr. 4, q. 1, art. 11, §1 (ed. Colon. 26, p. 333, 19ff.).

2. To the next, one must reply that in friendship we cling in one way, and in enjoyment we cling in another way, just as that which is possessed in itself differs from that which is possessed in another. To be sure, one friend loves another friend on account of the state of virtue in him, but enjoyment (*fructus*), which is a habit (*habitus*), clings to what is enjoyable owing to the sweet taste found in it. And some are wont to say that one denotes the pleasure (*dilectio*) of friendship and the other the pleasure of concupiscence.[212]

3. To the next we say that charity (*caritas*) does not designate an act that exists toward an end in some respect, that is, with respect to the condition of beatitude. And on account of this it does not pertain to charity (*caritas*) to cling with love (*amore*) in such a way that this is the whole being of charity (*caritas*), because charity also desires, as long as it is on the journey. Or it may be said better that charity clings in one way, and enjoyment (*fructus*), namely the habit (*habitus*), in another, because enjoyment [clings] by means of tasting, whereas charity [clings] by means of the bands binding the lover to the beloved.[213]

4. To the next: [we say] that to "cling to" indicates a greater union than to "adhere to" or to "join to." Therefore, since enjoyment consists in the taste of innermost sweetness, it is more fitting for it to cling to than to adhere to or to join to.

5. To the last, one must reply that the "on account of" (*li 'propter'*) refers to every cause. The fact that it indicates the efficient and final cause is clear *per se*. But the form is identical with the end. And the objection concerning matter according to the statement of the Philosopher has to be understood concerning the matter from which a thing exists, not for which an operation exists. In fact, the matter concerning which[214] the operation especially of the soul exists is also always the end of the soul itself that is operating, just as what has been willed is the

212. Cf. Wm. of Auxerre, *Summa aurea* II tr. 2 cap. 4 (ed. Ribaillier, vol. 2/1, pp. 40–44).

213. See *De res.* tr. 4, q. 1, art. 10, §1 (ed. Colon. 26, p. 332, 1).

214. *Materia circa quam:* perhaps the material context for the operation. See Stanley B. Cunningham, *Reclaiming Moral Agency: The Moral Philosophy of Albert the Great* (Washington, DC: The Catholic University of America Press, 2008), 83.

end of the will, and what is understood is the end of the intellective power.

6. To the objection based on the other definition, one must reply that the known and the loved are not opposites, but they indicate two acts that follow one another according to nature in enjoyment itself. For every thing that is loved is known. And this is acknowledged from the fact that Augustine adds "in which [things]," namely in things known, "the will that has taken delight reposes" through love.

7. To the next, one must reply that the good that is divided into the pleasurable, the useful, and the fitting is not divided by means of co-equals (*coaequaeva*) but [by means of] things ordered. This is clear because the good itself exists in them according to prior and posterior. And for this reason the pleasurable exists in the useful, and the pleasurable and the useful exist in the fitting, but not conversely, and for this reason pleasure also can exist in the fitting.

8. To the last, one must reply that, although the will enjoys, nonetheless it is ordered to intellectual understanding. And thus there exists there a certain plurality of ordered things. And this is made known through the preposition.

9. To the objection concerning the third, one must reply that there is a certain use that exists in relation to what exists only as an end, and that is not included in the definition of enjoyment, and there is a certain use that exists in relation to what exists for an end and for obtaining an end, and this endures with the end. And this can exist in the definition of enjoyment. Or one can say in a smoother way (*levius*) that use is understood there according to the definition of Victorinus, who says that use is a continuation of an act elicited from potency.[215]

10. To the next, one must reply that Augustine is speaking there of complete enjoyment. Or one can say in accord with the Master in the *Sentences*[216] that even when we live in hope, we attain something of the thing hoped for through a foretaste

215. M. Victor., *Explan. In Reth. M.T. Ciceronis* 1.2 (ed. Halm, p. 160, 9–10). Cf. Bonaventure, *I Sent.* d. 1 a. 1 q. 1, *Opera* 1: 31,2. Alb., *De bono* tr. 1 q. 5 a. 1 (ed. Colon. 28, p. 73, 2); *Super Dion. De eccl. hier.* 2 §2.

216. Peter Lombard, *I Sent.* d. 1 c. 3 (p. 17).

of things eternal, and thus necessarily joy is produced. And in accord with this, too, we live outside the world and beyond the world, as Augustine says.[217]

11. To the last one must say that the first is given by means of the act in relation to the end; the second by means of the matter that is proper to enjoyment; and the third by means of the effect.

Art. 2. On the division of enjoyment

Next, one asks about the division. And it seems that enjoyment should be divided according to the division of the appetite that is joined to knowledge and taste. Therefore, enjoyment is found in the sensible soul apart from the rational [soul], such that Augustine says that herd animals enjoy food.[218] And sometimes it is found in a sensible soul with reason, and this occurs in two ways: namely, in accord with the state of the journey and in accord with the state of the kingdom. And in accord with the state of the journey it is found in two ways: namely, in accord with a correct order in regard to reason and in accord with an incorrect [order]. In accord with an incorrect [order] Augustine says, "All human perversity consists in the enjoyment of things to be used and the use of things to be enjoyed."[219] According to the correct order, it [enjoyment] occurs in two ways, namely in accord with the correct [order] by the rectitude of political virtue or according to the correct [order] by the rectitude of theological virtue, which exists with grace. And in the first way the Stoics and certain other philosophers enjoyed the sweetness of virtue, [and] in the second way the saints [do]. If [this is considered] in accord with the state of the kingdom, however, then there exists the unmediated enjoyment (*gustus*) of divine goods. And this is said by the Master in the *Sentences* to be true, proper, and perfect:[220] true owing to the order of reason, proper owing to the consummation of grace and glory, but perfect owing to the immediate attainment of the object of enjoyment.

217. Aug., *Enarr. in Ps.* 114.8 (PL 37: 1490).

218. Aug., *De div. quaest.*, q. 30 (PL 40: 19).

219. Ibid.

220. Peter Lombard, *I Sent.* d. 1 c. 3 (p. 17). This is based on Aug., *De doc. Christ.* 1.33.37 (PL 34: 33).

Concerning Enjoyment on the Part of the One Enjoying it

Next, one asks about enjoyment on the part of the one enjoying it. And first, one asks: according to what power will enjoyment exist? And next, according to which virtue [will enjoyment exist]?

Art. 3. According to what power enjoyment will exist[221]

To the first, one proceeds in this way:

1. The acts of the soul's powers are designated by the powers themselves, just as to understand is designated by the understanding, [and] to will is designated by the will. But to enjoy is not designated by any power. Therefore, it seems that it is not the act of any power.

2. Conversely, it seems that [it is the act] of all the powers, because enjoyment is the act of eternal life, and all the powers (*vires*) of the soul will be rewarded in the act of eternal life. Therefore, enjoyment will exist according to every power of the soul.

3. Again, it seems that it exists only according to the understanding, because enjoyment is to adhere to God, and God is the simplest object. Therefore, [it exists] according to the simplest act and the simplest power; but this is understanding. Therefore, enjoyment will exist only according to the understanding.

4. Again, it seems that [it exists] according to the will alone, because enjoyment indicates a certain taste of sweetness. This is clear from the definition that states "to cling with love," etc., and from another definition that states, "[in] things known, in which the will that has taken delight reposes."[222] Therefore, it seems that enjoyment exists only according to the will.

Solution: We say that enjoyment is a movement of the will ordered toward the intellect that recognizes and determines what is itself enjoyable. And this should be understood concerning enjoyment in the sense in which it exists in the kingdom, which is said to be enjoyment truly and properly and perfectly.

221. Cf. Alb., *I Sent.* d. 1 a. 12 sol a. 23; *Summa* I q. 7 m. 2 q. incidens.

222. See *De res.* tr. 4, q. 3, art. 1 (ed. Colon. 26, p. 346, 3–5).

1, 3, 4. And from this a solution is apparent to the first, the penultimate, and the last, because the acts that are designated by the powers [of the soul] are simple acts of powers that are not ordered to one another.

2. To the next, one must reply that the whole soul will be rewarded with respect to every one of its powers. But nonetheless, immediate enjoyment exists in the superior [powers], and in the inferior [powers] through overflowing.

Art. 4. According to which virtue enjoyment will exist[223]

To the second, one proceeds in this way:

1. Every virtue will remain in beatitude. Therefore, it seems that every virtue will dispose [the soul] toward enjoyment, and in this way we will enjoy every virtue as it disposes.

2. But it seems that by faith alone, because Augustine says that "vision is the entire reward," and vision follows faith.[224] Since, then, enjoyment indicates the whole reward, it seems that we enjoy only by faith as it disposes, or because it follows faith.

3. Again, it seems by definition that by charity (*caritas*) alone, because "to enjoy is to cling with love," etc.[225]

4. Again, it seems we enjoy by the three theological [virtues] alone,[226] because perfect beatitude is what follows the three theological [virtues], namely to see, to love, to comprehend or to possess. Since, then, enjoyment indicates the act of beatitude, it seems that we will enjoy only by these three [theological virtues] as they dispose.

To this, one must reply that every virtue, insofar as "virtue is the order of love," as Augustine says, disposes to enjoyment, but not with equal immediacy.[227] And how this is so is clear above in the "Question on the Definition of Enjoyment."[228]

1. And from this a solution to the first is clear.

223. Cf. Alb., *I Sent.* d. 1 a. 21; *Summa* I q. 7 m. 2 q. incidens.

224. Aug., *Enarr. in Ps.* 90.16 (PL 37: 1170). Cf. Peter Lombard, *In Ps.* 90.16 (PL 191: 854C).

225. Aug., *De doc. Christ.* 1.4.4 (PL 34: 20); cf. Alb., *De res.* tr. 4, q. 3, art. 1 (ed. Colon. 26, p. 346, 3).

226. Faith, hope, and charity.

227. Aug., *De civ. dei* 15.22 (PL 41: 467; CSEL 40.s, p. 109, 5–6); cf. Alb., *De res.* tr. 2, q. 10, art. 12 (ed. Colon. 26, p. 301, 79).

228. See Alb., *De res.* tr. 4, q. 3, art. 1 (ed. Colon. 26, p. 346, 57ff.).

2. To the second, one must reply that the vision that is the entire reward is a satisfying vision, and this is the vision of the one loved and possessed (*habiti*).[229] And for this reason it indicates more than what follows faith.

3. To the next, a solution is clear from the things said in the "Question on the Definition of Enjoyment."[230]

4. To the next, one must reply that those that follow the three theological [virtues] are more immediate dispositions to enjoyment than are those that follow the cardinal [virtues].[231] Nevertheless, all dispose [to enjoyment].

Concerning Enjoyment on the Part of What is Enjoyable

Next, one asks about enjoyment on the part of what is enjoyable. And three questions are raised: first, whether a rational creature ought to be enjoyed; second, whether the virtues ought to be enjoyed; third, how God ought to be enjoyed.

Art. 5. Whether a rational creature ought to be enjoyed[232]

To the first, one proceeds in this way:

The Apostle says to Philemon:[233] "Yes, brother, may I enjoy you in the Lord." Therefore, it seems that a rational creature ought to be enjoyed.

Likewise, we will rejoice over the blessed, as Augustine says, and this joy will be the joy of beatitude.[234] And in this way it seems that it will belong to enjoyment; and so we will enjoy the blessed.

To this some say,[235] with Augustine, that it is one thing to enjoy a human in the Lord, and another to enjoy a human. One who enjoys a human in the Lord has the Lord as the end of enjoyment, and when he considers the end of enjoyment, he enjoys the Lord rather than the human.

229. *Visio pascens:* "satisfying vision"; cf. Alb., *IV Sent.* d. 1 a. 19 sol, a. 23; *Summa* I q. 7 m. 2. q. incidens. Alex. Hales, *Glossa* 1.1.30 (ed. Quar. p. 21, 1).

230. See Alb., *De res.* tr. 4, q. 3, art. 1 (ed. Colon. 26, p. 346, 57ff.).

231. Prudence, temperance, fortitude, and justice.

232. Cf. Alb., *I Sent.* d. 1 a. 18; *Summa* I q. 12 m. 1.

233. Phlm 20.

234. Ps. Aug., *De spir. et anima* 57 (PL 40: 822).

235. Cf. Wm. of Auxerre, *Summa aurea* III tr. 14 cap. 4–5 (ed. Ribaillier, vol. 3/1, pp. 258–64); Aug., *De doc. Christ.* 1.33.37 (PL 34: 33).

But then one asks why we enjoy a rational creature in the Lord rather than an irrational one, for the irrational possesses a trace likeness (*vestigium*) through which one comes to the Lord, just as the rational possesses an image (*imaginem*). If it is said that this is because a trace likeness is not as explicit a likeness as the image, this does not seem to be an impediment, because an explicit trace likeness is sufficient to lead the intellect to God. And to the extent that the intellect that determines what is enjoyable goes first, the will that enjoys can follow. So too, in this sense, we can enjoy such an [irrational] creature in the Lord.

Moreover, according to this [argument] we could enjoy in the Lord a sinner or one who has been damned, because the image remains in them, which is not customarily said.

Therefore, we say that one should not enjoy either a rational or an irrational creature.

And we reply to the authority of the Apostle, with Augustine,[236] that the Lord is the end of his enjoyment, not owing to an image or trace likeness, but owing to the representation of the highest good in those in whom it shines forth by grace or glory, such as in Philemon and in the blessed; for enjoyment achieves satisfaction in goodness. And for this reason, if we enjoy some object in the Lord, it is necessary that the Lord be made manifest in that object as the highest goodness.

And through this a solution to the whole is evident.

Art. 6. Whether one should enjoy the virtues[237]

To the second, one proceeds in this way:

Tully[238] says that what is honorable draws us by its power and attracts us by its dignity, and under the honorable he distinguishes the virtues.[239] Therefore, the virtues draw affection (*affectus*) by their power. And whatever draw by their own power (*virtus*) ought to be loved for themselves (*per se*). Therefore, the virtues ought to be loved for themselves, and those ought to

236. Aug., *De doc. Christ.* 1.33.37 (PL 34: 33).

237. Cf. Alb., *I Sent.* d. 1 a. 21; *Summa* I q. 9 ad 6.

238. I.e., the Roman philosopher and rhetor, Marcus Tullius Cicero (d. 43 BCE).

239. Cicero, *De invent.* 2.52.157; 159f.

be enjoyed that should be loved for themselves. Therefore, one ought to enjoy the virtues.

Again, Ambrose says, and the authority is established in the first book of the *Sentences*,[240] and Augustine says in the book of *83 Questions*,[241] that just as the useful and the honorable differ, so too do use and enjoyment. But the useful exists for use; therefore the honorable will exist for enjoyment. But it is assumed by all that the virtues belong to the genus of the honorable. Therefore, the virtues ought to be enjoyed.

For the contrary conclusion, Augustine's authority is invoked in a distinction in book 1 of the *Sentences*,[242] which says that the virtues should not be desired for themselves (*per se*) and that only the God who makes us blessed should be enjoyed.

Solution: One must reply that one should not enjoy virtues in the sense that enjoyment expresses the act of the kingdom. But if enjoyment is understood in the ordinary sense, then it can be conceded in some manner.

To the objection stemming from Tully and Augustine and Ambrose, one must reply that "for themselves (*per se*)" is contrasted in two ways: namely, [it is contrasted] to "in an accidental fashion (*per accidens*)" and to "through something else (*per aliud*)." And when these authorities say that the virtues ought to be desired *per se,* one must understand that that is not *per accidens.* But in another sense, in the sense that *per se* is contrasted to *per aliud,* one must distinguish when something is desired *per se* absolutely as the ultimate end of intention and desire, and when something is desired *per se* but not absolutely, but rather as a goal (*terminus*) for intention and desire in a limited sense. For example, God is desired as the ultimate end; but this or that virtue is desired as the goal of this or that work. Similarly, felicity is desired *per se* in the state of the virtues as the goal of that state. Similarly, the beatitude intrinsic to the kingdom, which exists formally in the blessed, is desired as the goal of felicity *per se.* But then the "*per se*" does not exclude "*per aliud*"

240. Peter Lombard, *I Sent.* d. 1 c. 3 (p. 19).

241. Aug., *De div. quaest.,* q. 30 (PL 40: 19).

242. Peter Lombard, *I Sent.* d. 1 c. 3 (pp. 18–19). Aug., *De trin.* 13.8.11 (PL 42: 1022ff.).

absolutely, but it excludes the "*per aliud*" which is the proximate goal of intention and desire.

Art. 7. How one should enjoy God

Third, one asks how one should enjoy God. And first one asks whether he will be the object of enjoyment on the basis (*ratio*) of [the] person or of some essential attribute. Second, one asks whether God enjoys himself; third, whether any creature enjoys [him].

§1. Whether God is an object of enjoyment on the basis (*ratio*) of [the] person or of some essential attribute[243]

To the first, one proceeds in this way:

1. Augustine says, "Those which one ought to enjoy are the Father and the Son and the Holy Spirit."[244] Therefore, one ought to enjoy God on the basis (*ratio*) of [the] person.

2. If this is conceded, however, then one asks whether the primary basis of enjoyment is in the Father, just as he is himself the source of the whole divinity. And it seems that this is the case, according to the chapter "If there is one that is unoriginate" (*Si quis innascibilem*)[245] in the first book of the *Sentences*, where Hilary says that through the Son all are restored to the unoriginate Father.[246] And in this way it seems that since he is himself the ultimate end of that restoration, he ought to be enjoyed in the first instance (*in prima ratione*).

3. Likewise, among essences it is the case that one ought to enjoy the essence that is the source and end of all essences. Therefore, it will be the same among persons, that one ought to enjoy the person who will be the source of the [other divine] persons.

But if this is conceded, then one asks whether one ought to enjoy him on an absolute basis (*ratio*) or on a relative basis. Not

243. Cf. Alb., *In Sent.* d. 1 a. 14 qla 1; *Summa* I q. 9, 10.

244. Aug., *De doc. Christ.* 1.5.5 (PL 34: 21). Cf. Peter Lombard, *I Sent.* d. 1 c. 2 (p. 15).

245. "Si quis innascibilem ...": that is, "If someone [says] that [the Son is] unoriginated ..."

246. Peter Lombard, *I Sent.* d. 31 c. 2 (p. 194f.). For Hilary, see *De synod.* 59.26 (PL 10: 521AB). See also Alb., *De res.* tr. 2, q. 10, art. 12 (ed. Colon. 26, p. 302, 31).

on an absolute basis, because he is neither Father nor a person in this way [that is, absolutely], because Augustine says that what is said of him (*ad se*) is said essentially and generally for all.[247] If, however, we enjoy him on a relative basis, then enjoyment will apply to the Son, since one is said to be a father in relation to a son. Likewise, enjoyment of the Father and the Son will apply to the Holy Spirit, and so in this way a certain circularity will exist, which is unsuitable, because the enjoyment does not differentiate [Father from Son, etc.].

Moreover, we enjoy what is known and loved, and there is one knowledge of the three of them, because it is truth which is known [and] which is one. Likewise, there is one love of the three, because the goodness that is loved is one. And so in the same way there will be one enjoyment of the three. Therefore, we do not enjoy on the basis of the person, but on the basis of an essential attribute.

Solution: We say that we enjoy God insofar as he is the highest truth and the highest goodness, and not on the basis of the person.

1. To the objection taken from Augustine, we say that Augustine names the Father and the Son and the Holy Spirit because they are understood to be undivided in truth and goodness, and not because he wants to say that we enjoy them on the basis of the person.

2. To the next objection, stemming from Hilary, one must reply that Hilary is thinking of the relationship of the originated (*principati*), insofar as it is originated, to the origin (*principium*), insofar as it is the origin. In fact, to have an origin is found in creatures and in divine persons, just as Basil says that to receive is common to the Son and the Holy Spirit and to every creature, but they possess by their own nature.[248] Therefore, the originating principle (*principiatio*) of the persons precedes the originating principle of creatures as a cause, and the latter is directed back to the former just as effect to cause. The originating principle (*principiatio*) of the persons, however, is direct-

247. Aug., *De trin.* 5.8.9 (PL 42: 916f.).

248. Basil, *Hom. 6 De fide* 2; transl. Rufinus (PG 31: 1783B). Cf. Bonaventure, *I Sent.* d. 29 a. 1 q. 2, *Opera* 1: 510a.

ed back further to the origin (*principium*) of the whole divinity, and this is the unoriginate Father. But enjoyment does not proceed in this way, because it does not refer to the source insofar as it is the source, but to the ultimate end, which is the true and the good, in which there is highest refreshment and rest.

3. To the objection based on the order of essences, one must reply that there is no analogy because essences are divided [one from another] and each possesses its own goodness and truth. But the divine persons are undivided, and [their] goodness and truth is undivided. And for this reason we enjoy them by means of one enjoyment, insofar as they are the highest truth and the highest good.

If one asks next, however, whether we enjoy the persons *per accidens* or *per consequens* or *per se,* one must reply that it is not *per accidens,* because persons are not accidental to the nature, nor even *per consequens* in the sense in which we say that the universal is posterior to the particular and, *per consequens,* is understood from it. But we enjoy them according to reality (*secundum rem*) as undifferentiated from the true and the highest good.

§2. Whether God enjoys himself[249]

To the second, one proceeds in this way:

Gregory, commenting on Job 40,[250] says that God, provided that he enjoys himself, needs no external good.[251] Therefore, God enjoys himself.

To the contrary: Enjoyment is rest and refreshment in the ultimate end. And according to this it seems that one who enjoys and what is enjoyed are not one and the same.[252]

Here again one can ask whether the Father enjoys the Son insofar as he is the Son, and conversely, and also whether the Father and the Son [enjoy] the Holy Spirit on a personal basis, and conversely.

Solution: We say that God enjoys himself insofar as he is the highest truth and the highest good. This is not something perverse in him, because his goodness is the true goodness, which

249. Cf. Alb., *I Sent.* d. 1 a. 19.

250. Jb 40.5.

251. *Glossa ord. super Iob* 40.5; cf. Greg., *Moral.* 32.6.8 (PL 76: 639D).

252. See Alb., *De res.* tr. 4, q. 3, art. 7, §1 (ed. Colon. 26, p. 350, 73–77).

is not received from another source and does not exist in any creature. Therefore, he enjoys himself, and he is the end of his own enjoyment, because nothing is better than he is.

To the question concerning whether he enjoys himself on the basis of the person, etc., it should be solved as it was earlier.[253]

§3. Whether God enjoys any creature

To the third, one proceeds in this way:

Use is a means (*via*) to an end; therefore, it is not the same as the end. But God is the ultimate end. Therefore, use is not the same as he is. Since he loves us, therefore, it seems that he loves us with the love of enjoyment.

But to the contrary: Whatever enjoys something else needs its good. But God does not need the good of any creature. Therefore, God does not enjoy any creature.

We concede this, saying to the first that use is related to two things, namely to the one using and to what is useful. And in the sense that it is related to the useful, in this way it is not the same as the end, as is objected. But in the sense that it is related without distinction to the one using, it is the same for that which is an end and for that which is not an end. Therefore, he uses us by referring this to his own goodness, as Augustine says.[254]

Question 4. On use

Next, one asks about use. First, one asks what it is. Then, what it concerns.

Art. 1. What use is[255]

To the first, one proceeds in this way:

Augustine says that to use is to refer to another whatever has come into use.[256]

Also, Augustine says that "to use is to take up something into the faculty of the will" by referring it to obtaining what ought to be enjoyed.[257]

253. See Alb., *De res.* tr. 4, q. 3, art. 7, §1 (ed. Colon. 26, p. 350, 54–56).
254. Aug., *De doc. Christ.* 1.32.35 (PL 34: 32).
255. Cf. Alb., *I Sent.* d. 1 a. 13, 16; *Summa* I q. 8 m. 1; *Ethica* 4, tr. 1 c. 2.
256. Aug., *De doc. Christ.* 1.4.4 (PL 34: 20).
257. Aug., *De trin.* 10.11.17 (PL 42: 982).

Also, Victorinus [says] that use is a continuation of an act elicited from potency.[258]

1. Contrary to the first definition, one objects in this way: One and the same [thing] is posited in its own definition.

2. Contrary to the second, [one objects] in this way: the faculty of will is posited there as the source (*principium*) of "the use," although the faculty of the will is produced from use, because the will becomes easy only through the practice of acts.

3. Contrary to the third, one objects in this way: Because this pertains to enjoyment as well as to use, namely to continue an act from potency.

Solution: One must reply that use has two meanings, one of which includes the other. The first meaning is the one that Victorinus proposes, and according to this, use exists in a kind of practice (*in genere exercitii*), according to which it is said that practice is the cause of power, and according to which it is said that use and art have taught what every man knows. The second meaning is the sense in which use exists for one act for the purpose of obtaining some end beyond what is useful. And in this way it is set over against enjoyment, and Augustine speaks about use in this way.

1. One can say to the first, then, that use in the first meaning is posited in the definition of use in the second meaning. Or better, one could say that an act related to an end—whence it has to be known, since the end is the basis of the act, because according to reason objects are prior to acts—is better known than act in an absolute sense (*simpliciter*).[259] And in this way one and the same thing can readily be proposed in its own definition, but not in the same way.

2. To the next, one must reply that use, in the sense in which it is defined by Victorinus, is the origin of the faculty of the will, but not in the sense in which it is defined by Augustine; rather, in this way use is produced from a will [acting] easily.

258. M. Victor., *Explan. in Rhet. M.T. Ciceronis* 1.2 (ed. Halm, p. 160, 9–10); cf. Bonaventure, *I Sent.* d. 1 a. 1 q. 1, *Opera* 1: 31, 2; Alb., *De bono* 1.5.1 (ed. Colon. 28, p. 73, 2); *Super Dion. De eccl. hier.* c. 2 §2; Alb., *De res.* tr. 4, q. 3, art. 1 (ed. Colon. 26, p. 347, 43).

259. Ar., *De anima* 2.4 (415a18–20); Alb., *De anima* 2.3.1; cf. Ar., *Metaph.* 9.8 (1049b10–11); cf. Alb., *De res.* tr. 4, q. 1, art. 10, §3 (ed. Colon. 26, p. 333, 1–2).

3. To the last, now a solution is clear, because Victorinus does not define use in the sense in which it is opposed to enjoyment, but according to a general meaning.

Art. 2. What use concerns[260]

To the second, one proceeds in this way:

1. Augustine divides things, [saying] that some are the highest good,[261] "which one ought to enjoy, like the Father, the Son, and the Holy Spirit,"[262] and there are others, "which one ought to use, like the world and the things created in it,"[263] and there are still others that lie in between, which are used and enjoyed, like angels and humans.

It seems that this division is empty. For if this division is granted concerning the object of these acts of enjoyment and use, then it will only have two members (*bimembris*), because everything that exists is either useful or enjoyable. If, however, it is granted in accord with the sources of those acts, namely the one using and the one enjoying, then again it is empty, because God uses and enjoys. But if it is given partly in one way and partly in the other, then it is utterly empty, because there is nothing that is shared in common.

2. Moreover, elsewhere he [Augustine] seems to distinguish goods in a different way, because he says that "the virtues, by which one lives rightly, are great goods, and the powers of the soul without which one cannot live rightly and with which one lives rightly not from any necessity, are intermediate goods,"[264] whereas health, or "the appearance of any bodies whatsoever, are the lowest goods." And here he says that humans and angels are intermediate goods.

Solution:

1. We say that a first division is granted on what is shared in

260. Cf. Alb., *I Sent.* d. 1 a. 11; *Summa* I q. 12 m. 1.

261. Alb. derives this from Peter Lombard, *I Sent.* d. 1 c. 2 (p. 15).

262. Aug., *De doc. Christ.* 1.5.5 (PL 34: 21).

263. Peter Lombard, *I Sent.* d. 1 c. 2 (p. 15). Cf. Aug., *De doc. Christ.* 1.3.3 (PL 34: 20).

264. Aug., *De lib. arb.*, 2.19.50 (PL 32: 1268; CSEL 74, p. 85, 7–10). Cf. Peter Lombard, *II Sent.* d. 27 c. 2 (p. 444f.), which attributes this to Aug., *Retract.* 1.9.4 (PL 32: 597; CSEL 36, c.8, p. 42, 12–15).

common, which is the object related to desire. And the members [of the division] are gathered together in this way, that there is a certain object (*res*) that is the goal of desire with respect to itself and to others, and that object is the last and the best and is one that enjoys and is enjoyable, and Augustine calls it the highest good in that division. Other [objects] are referred to desire as things useful only for something else, and he calls these the lowest goods. And other [objects] that are intermediate goods are grouped together on this basis: that they are a source (*principium*) of use and enjoyment.

2. To the objection concerning the next division, one must reply that that is granted for the good in the sense that it is required for a correct life, which is clear in the degrees of that division. Therefore, what is called the lowest good there is only a support, like the health of the body. What is called an intermediate good, however, is a cause whereby, once it has been destroyed, the good life is destroyed, but when it is not posited, [the good life] is posited.[265] What is called the highest good, however, is the cause whereby, once it has been destroyed, the good life is destroyed, and when it is posited, [the good life] is posited. And so it is clear that the objection is empty, since the one division and the other are granted on a different basis.

Question 5. On the spiritual senses[266]

Next, one ask about the spiritual senses, which Augustine sets forth. And first, one asks whether there are spiritual senses, and, second, about their distinction.

Art. 1. Whether there are spiritual senses

To the first, one proceeds in this way:

1. Augustine says, and it is set forth in the third book of the *Sentences,* that externally, seeing is not the same as hearing, but

265. Cf. Alb., *I Sent.* d. 1 a. 11 ad 3.

266. Cf. Alb., *Super Dion. De cael. hier.* c. 15 §5–6. For historical investigation of the five spiritual senses, see *The Spiritual Senses: Perceiving God in Western Christianity,* ed. Paul L. Gavrilyuk and Sarah Coakley (Cambridge: Cambridge University Press, 2014).

internally, seeing is the same as hearing.[267] Therefore, spiritual senses do not exist, or they are nothing other than the intellect.

2. Likewise, a pure universal is extracted by the senses through abstraction from the five sensibles.[268] Therefore, it seems that such a distinction[269] does not exist in the intellect. In the same way, nothing is said concerning spiritual senses.

3. Moreover, we do not perceive the five sensibles with one sense because the sensible power is a power attached to an organ, whose formation is proportionate to only one or two sensibles. But the intellect is not a power attached to an organ. Therefore, in this respect it is not proportioned to one or two sensibles. And so there is no distinction among the senses in the intellect.

Solution: We say with the saints that there are five spiritual senses in accord with a spiritual object, which is God.[270]

1. To the first [objection] that is to the contrary, one must reply that if these senses are understood to be in the sentient power considered in itself, then they are one and the same, as Augustine says. But if the power is considered as related to act and to an object, then they are not one and the same, but rather they differ essentially.

2. To the next, one must reply that these senses are not distinguished according to sensible qualities, but according to the essential elements (*rationes*) found in a spiritual object, which bear an analogy to sensible bodies. Therefore, they are also called senses by way of a metaphor (*per translationem*).

3. To the next, one must reply that there is one power (*virtus*) in these senses, but there is not just one relationship of it to an act and to an object, as is clear from the things already said.[271]

267. Peter Lombard, *III Sent.* d. 13 (p. 603). Aug., *Epist.* 187, 13.40 (PL 33: 847; CSEL 57, p. 117, 3–7). Cf. Aug., *In Joh.* 18.10 (PL 35: 1542). Alb., *III Sent.* d. 13 a. 4; *Super Is.,* prol. (ed. Colon. 19, p. 3, 65).

268. I.e., the proper objects of the five senses.

269. I.e., between internal and external senses.

270. "With the saints": cf. Origen, *Hom. super Lev.* 3.7 (PG 12: 432AB). Bern., *Sermo* 10 *de diversis,* 1ff. (PL 183: 567Bff.). Cf. Alb., *III Sent.* d. 13 a. 4.

271. See *De res.* tr. 4, q. 5, art. 1 (ed. Colon. 26, p. 353, 9–11).

Art. 2. On their distinction

To the second, one proceeds in this way:

Touch is a sense that perceives a sensible object only when matter is present, and by contact with it. But there is no touching God. And thus it does not seem that a metaphor can apply in this case. If one should say that the metaphor does apply in relation to the sensible itself, and not in relation to the mode of perceiving: but [reply that] the hot is a sensible, and the cold, the moist, the dry, the soft, the hard, etc., and these or those like them do not exist in spiritual [objects], as it seems.

Similarly, one may raise an objection concerning taste, because taste only occurs when there is a flavorless salivary humor as intermediary. Therefore, in spiritual [objects] it is necessary for one thing to have an appetizing flavor and another to be flavorless, by which what is flavorful may be diffused in the gustative power. And it follows that there is nothing that is flavorless in spiritual [objects], especially in God.

Likewise, what would be sweet and bitter there, for which there may be a metaphor?

Similarly, one objects concerning odor and smell, because smell only occurs when there is a mediating evaporative dryness. In spiritual [objects], however, there is nothing like this.

Likewise, among humans odor is drawn in through inhalation, and thus it is necessary that there exist something like inhalation there, by which the divine odor may be drawn in.

Similarly, one asks about hearing. Now, hearing occurs from a striking of air. There is nothing like this in God, for which there may be a metaphor.

Again, one raises an objection concerning sight, because sight only occurs at a distance, and in the appearance (*species*) that will be seen in the kingdom, there will be no distance from our intellect, as was said above in the "Question concerning the Dowry, which is Vision."[272]

Solution: We say that there are five spiritual senses, but, as Dionysius says in *On the Celestial Hierarchy,* chapter 1, "Sensible

272. See *De res.* tr. 4, q. 1, art. 9, §2 (ed. Colon. 26, p. 329, 77).

sweets are symbols of an invisible diffusion,"[273] and at the end of the same book, "We say indeed that the powers of sight signify the clearest gaze upon the divine lights, and also the reception—impassibly and gently and clearly and without resistance, but flexibly and purely and openly—of divine illuminations. The powers to discern smells indicate the reception, so far as possible, of a diffused sweet fragrance that is beyond understanding and of those that are not discernible by knowledge and those that ought to be avoided altogether. The powers of hearing signify the participant and knower who is receptive to divine inspiration. The [powers of] taste have to do with the fullness of invisible nourishment and a receptiveness to divine and nourishing streams. The [powers of] touch have to do with distinguishing the beneficial from the harmful through knowledge."[274]

Therefore, we say that the senses are considered in two ways, namely in relation to the sensible—and in this way they belong to brute animals and to human animals—and in relation to the intellect, and in this way they pertain to instruction (*disciplinales*) and belong to spiritual humans. And with respect to this, they possess certain likenesses (*similitudines*) by which they are adapted to the spiritual senses. Therefore, it is the case that sight makes clear the form of an object by means of a proper likeness, whereas hearing does so by a sign of its likeness. The sense of smell produces some knowledge of an object's complexion, moreover, by means of evaporation. Taste discovers suitable food, however, by the extraction of a humor, whereas touch discovers the first natural qualities of an object by touching it.

Based on these assumptions, we say that the perception of God exists by means of truth and goodness, and by means of a union of the true and the good. If there is a perception of truth,

273. Dion., *De cael. hier.* c. 1 §3 (PG 3: 121C; Dionysiaca II, 736), transl. Scotus. What are these "sensible sweets"? For the Carolingian commentator John Scotus Eriugena, they are corporeal and include chrism and incense. See his *Expositiones in hierarchiam caelestem,* ed. Jeanne Barbet, CCCM 31 (Turnhout: Brepols, 1975), 15. Cf. Alb., *Super Dion. De cael. hier.* 1 (ed. Colon. 36/1, pp. 13–14).

274. Dion., *De cael. hier.* c. 15 §3 (PG 3: 332A; Dionysiaca II, 1003–1005), transl. Scotus. Cf. Alb., *Super Dion. De cael. hier.* 15 (ed. Colon. 36/1, pp. 233–38).

either it is perceived in itself just as in a likeness (*similitudo*) and proper form, or in its sign or image (*iconia*).[275] If [it is perceived] in the first way, then there is the spiritual sense called sight; if in the second way, then there is that sense which is called hearing. And if one asks what these signs may be, I say that they are revelations and infusions of spirit, just as is understood from Dionysius's authoritative statement. If, however, there is only the perception of goodness, it exists either in itself or in its proximate effect. If it exists in itself, then there is spiritual touch; if [it exists] in its proximate effect, then there is taste, because spiritual taste is nothing but the perception of the sweetness of God's goodness in his gifts. If, however, there is a perception of the true and the good at the same time, then this occurs by means of a kind of evaporation: for the good is extracted from the true. And then there is smell. And on account of this, Dionysius calls the diffused power (*virtus*) one that imitates the good and recoils from evil.

A solution is apparent from these, because they are not transferred to the spiritual senses in accord with those properties that the senses have in relation to their sensibles, but rather in accord with those that pertain to instruction, and they produce knowledge of the object in the intellect.

275. *Iconia:* cf. Alb., *De sacram.* tr. 1 q. 3 (ed. Colon. 26, p. 7, 6ff.).

INDICES

GENERAL INDEX

INDEX OF HOLY SCRIPTURE

Old Testament

New Testament

RECENT VOLUMES IN THE FATHERS OF THE CHURCH, MEDIAEVAL CONTINUATION

ST. ALBERT THE GREAT, *On Job, Volume 1,* translated by Franklin T. Harkins, Volume 19 (2019)

ST. HILDEGARD OF BINGEN, *The Book of Divine Works,* translated by Nathaniel M. Campbell, Volume 18 (2018)

ALBERT THE GREAT, *On the Body of the Lord,* translated by Sr. Albert Marie Surmanski, OP, Volume 17 (2017)

PETER THE VENERABLE, *Writings Against the Saracens,* translated by Irven M. Resnick, Volume 16 (2016)

JOHN DUNS SCOTUS, *Questions on Aristotle's* Categories, translated by Lloyd A. Newton, Volume 15 (2014)

PETER THE VENERABLE, *Against the Inveterate Obduracy of the Jews,* translated by Irven M. Resnick, Volume 14 (2013)

ROBERT GROSSETESTE, *On the Cessation of the Laws,* translated by Stephen M. Hildebrand, Volume 13 (2012)

PETER ABELARD, *Commentary on the Epistle to the Romans,* translated by Steven R. Cartwright, Volume 12 (2011)

THOMAS AQUINAS, *The Academic Sermons,* translated by Mark-Robin Hoogland, CP, Volume 11 (2010)

WORKS OF ST. ALBERT THE GREAT IN THIS SERIES

Questions Concerning Aristotle's On Animals, translated by Irven M. Resnick and Kenneth F. Kitchell, Jr., Fathers of the Church, Mediaeval Continuation 9 (2008)

On the Body of the Lord, translated by Sr. Albert Marie Surmanski, OP, Fathers of the Church, Mediaeval Continuation 17 (2017)

On Job, Volume 1, translated by Franklin T. Harkins, Fathers of the Church, Mediaeval Continuation 19 (2019)

On Resurrection, translated by Irven M. Resnick and Franklin T. Harkins, Fathers of the Church, Mediaeval Continuation 20 (2020)